The Contrary Experience

HERBERT READ

The Contrary Experience

Autobiographies

Personal Foreword

by

GRAHAM GREENE

. . . fostered alike by beauty and by fear
WORDSWORTH

HORIZON PRESS

New York

Printed in Great Britain

Contents

CONTENTS

A Personal Foreword

He was the most gentle man I have ever known, but it was a gentleness which had been tested in the worst experience of our lifetime. The young officer, who gained the Military Cross and a DSO in action on the Western Front, had carried with him to all that mud and death Robert Bridges' anthology *The Spirit of Man*, Plato's *Republic* and *Don Quixote*. Nothing changed in him. It was the same man twenty years later who could come into a room full of people and you wouldn't notice his coming – you noticed only that the whole atmosphere of a discussion had quietly changed, that even the relations of one guest with another had changed. No one any longer would be talking for effect, and when you looked round for an explanation there he was – complete honesty born of complete experience had entered the room and unobtrusively taken a chair.

It is typical of Herbert Read's character that I cannot remember where or how we first met. I think it must have been in 1935, the year when his only novel, *The Green Child*, was published, a novel which I would put among the great poems of this century along with David Jones's *In Parenthesis*. I was already an ardent admirer of *English Prose Style*, which should be compulsory reading for any would-be writer, of his *Wordsworth* – no one had ever written so revealingly of Wordsworth, or so self-revealingly – and of *The Innocent Eye* which forms part of this volume, the account of his childhood on a Yorkshire farm, perhaps the best autobiography in our language.

T. S. Eliot and Herbert Read were the two great figures of my young manhood (they meant more to me than Joyce, and as for Pound he was somehow always a very long way off – an explorer of whose survival at that moment one was never quite certain). I would never have had the courage to approach Eliot or Read myself. What interest could they feel for a young and rather unsuccessful novelist? So it must have been chance which led to my first encounter with Read that I cannot even remember today, and I was proud, surprised and a little daunted when I received a letter from him inviting me to dinner. 'Eliot is coming, but no one else, and everything very informal.' To me it was a little like receiving an invitation from Coleridge – 'Wordsworth is coming, but no one else.' He gave me very clear directions with a small map that looked like the sketch of a trench system on the Western Front torn from that young officer's pad, and then for a moment the countryman, the author of *The Innocent Eye*, peeped out. 'The Mall is what I call a "ginnel", a narrow passage through a double gate,' and I felt nearer to Yorkshire than to Belsize Park.

Two years later when I became part-editor of a weekly magazine *Night and Day* I had the temerity, perhaps because I had gained more confidence in myself, to ask the author of *Art Now* to write for me regular reviews of detective stories and he promptly accepted. (At that dinner with Eliot we had talked of Arsène Lupin – a subject which always helped Eliot to unbutton – perhaps for a moment it made him feel safe from ladies going to and fro talking of Michael Angelo.) Our new relationship was celebrated by a verse in red ink which accompanied the first review.

> Shall it be Graham or be Greene?
> There's nothing betwixt or between.
> Shall it be Graham or be Greene?
> Neither is Christian or intime,
> But one is milk the other cream.
> So Graham let it be, not Greene.

I would like one day to see those reviews republished, so different are they from the stock image of Herbert Read the intellectual. Perhaps they could appear as an appendix to his bibliography. The first, on 8 July 1937, contained a devastating and deserved criticism of Dorothy Sayers' *Busman's Holiday*. Later he was unfriendly to Peter Cheyney, but had a charitable word for Agatha Christie. I really believe he enjoyed writing these reviews more than that long series of art books which hid from so many eyes his real genius as a poet, critic and autobiographer. He knew I didn't care very much for them and he never resented it; even when I put my feelings into print he only wrote, 'You

did make my bread and butter look pretty stale, but then it is . . .'
His reviews in *Night and Day*, I like to think, were a holiday to
him, and his humour streamed suddenly and volcanically out. He
quoted hilariously from second-rate authors who had certainly
not learnt the lessons of *English Prose Style*.

> ' "Maynard poured some more coffee and broke the narcissistic shell of
> another egg." We have always found our eggs distinctly indifferent to
> their own appearance.'

Alas that *Night and Day* died at the end of 1937, for on 4
November of that year in an essay called 'Life without a Shoe-
horn', Herbert Read made his *début* as a comic writer under the
name of James Murgatroyd. I seem to have objected to the
pseudonym which was at first simply Murgatroyd, a name I
thought more suitable to a character of Wodehouse. He wrote
firmly back: 'In Defence of Murgatroyd. It is a perfectly real
name, and if I had been born in the West instead of the North
Riding it might easily have been my own name. Would it do if
I gave him a Christian name as well, say James? In any case, I
refuse to be called Bertram Meade. I once knew a man in the
Ministry of Labour called that, and that is what it sounds like. I
want something funny, and something vaguely evocative of
something square and squat with protruding amphibian eyes;
something weary and patient, like a frog in a drought. If it can
wait until Tuesday, I will try and think of an alternative. But if I
am to go on with the creature, he must have an inspiring name –
like Murgatroyd.'

So Murgatroyd it was. He was planning a series. If he had
completed it, we might have had a worthy successor to *The Diary
of a Nobody*. Is it possible that a few of these essays remain among
his papers?

I write of trivial matters, but when one loves a man, as I loved
him, it is the small things which others may have forgotten or not
known which first come to mind before the great enduring
achievements, *The Green Child*, *Wordsworth*, *The End of a War*,
The Contrary Experience, and that essay on Vauvenargues, in
which he suddenly speaks of the ruling passion that links these
Autobiographies with a steel thread: the search for glory. 'Glory
is now a discredited word, and it will be difficult to re-establish it.
It has been spoilt by a too close association with military grandeur;

9

it has been confused with fame and ambition. But true glory is a private and discreet virtue, and is only fully realised in solitariness.' He had known military glory: from the danger and squalor of the front line he was able to write in a private letter: 'If I were free today, I'm almost sure I should be compelled by every impulse within me to join this adventure,' but when, on 11 November 1918, as a Canterbury bell pealed for victory and with heart numb and mind dismayed, he turned to the fields 'and walked away from all human contacts', it was towards glory that he walked, glory 'realised in solitariness' and finally achieved in his last years among the hills and moors, within hearing of the mill-stream of his childhood, the setting of *The Innocent Eye*.

Nothing became him better than his terribly painful end – the young man in France would have suffered less from gas or shell-burst, but courage in facing agony and death had not diminished in the fifty years that had passed, and the deep sense of glory which he had first felt as a lonely boy in the streets of Leeds was maintained through the savage suffering at the end. He looked at death with the same clear, shrewd, gentle eye he turned on a friend. In the last months of his life he had been planning, after yet one more operation, to go and stay awhile in a small cottage I possess in Anacapri, and he wrote to me more frequently and intimately during that last period than ever before. 'I am haunted by the thought of Freud and did you read Jones's life of him? I have exactly the same condition in the same place . . . I don't think I worry about my own remaining years – it is only the thought of leaving Ludo alone, though there again I could comfort myself with the thought that we have such devoted children.' Then suddenly the last letter came, the last he ever wrote, to say that he must abandon the idea of Anacapri – 'I had built up the Lourdes' spirit and there was going to be a miraculous cure.'

The reference to Lourdes from this most Christian of un-believers came as no surprise. Hadn't he written in the Auto-biographies of another essential aspect of his idea of glory? 'At certain moments the individual is carried beyond his rational self, on to another ethical plane, where his actions are judged by new standards. The impulse which moves him to irrational action I have called the sense of glory.'

Graham Greene

JR TBR STR
PPR BWR

filiis meis sodalibusque

Preface to the 1962 Edition

In this volume are assembled four autobiographies written at different times and under very different circumstances. The first, an account of the author's childhood, was first published in 1933. The second is in the form of a diary extracted from letters addressed to a single correspondent between 1915 and 1918 and now published for the first time. It is followed by some further chapters of autobiography first published in 1940 as the substantial part of a volume entitled *Annals of Innocence and Experience*. Finally, I have added some chapters written within the last year or two.

I do not pretend that these fragments constitute an artistic unity. The volume is nevertheless offered as the story of the growth of a poet's mind in a confusing period of history. It is my hope (to repeat some words from the preface to the *Annals*) that these pages will make sufficiently clear that I consider the no-man's-years between the wars as largely futile, spent unprofitably by me and my kind. I do not pretend to know how we could have made them more positive: the forces against us were not human, but satanic—blind forces of economic drift and political ineptitude with the walls of faith and reason turning to air behind us.

I also said in the same preface that in spite of a disillusion at once personal and universal, I persisted in a simple faith in the natural goodness of man. A faith of that kind was perhaps never simple and is certainly no longer tenable. The death wish that was once an intellectual fiction has now become a hideous reality and mankind drifts indifferently to self-destruction. To arrest that drift is beyond our individual capacities: to establish one's individuality is perhaps the only possible protest.

1962   H.R.

PART ONE

The Innocent Eye

I

The Vale

When I went to school I learned that the Vale in which we lived had once been a lake, but long ago the sea had eaten through the hills in the east and so released the fresh waters, leaving a fertile plain. But such an idea would have seemed strange to my innocent mind, so remote was this menacing sea. Our farm was towards the western end of the Vale, and because all our land was as flat as once the surface of the lake had been, we could see around us the misty hills, the Moors to the north, the Wolds to the south, meeting dimly in the east where they were more distant. This rim of hills was nearest in the south, at least in effect; for as the sun sank in the west the windows of Stamper's farm in the south caught the blazing rays and cast them back at us, continually drawing our eyes in that direction. But we never travelled so far south as those hills; for the Church and the Market, the only outer places of pilgrimage, lay to the north, five or six miles away. By habit we faced north: the south was 'behind'.

I seemed to live, therefore, in a basin, wide and shallow like the milkpans in the dairy; but the even bed of it was checkered with pastures and cornfields, and the rims were the soft blues and purples of the moorlands. This basin was my world, and I had no inkling of any larger world, for no strangers came to us out of it, and we never went into it. Very rarely my father went to York or Northallerton, to buy a piece of machinery for the farm or to serve on a jury at the Assizes; but only our vague wonder accompanied him, and the toys he brought back with him might have come, like sailors' curios, from Arabia or Cathay. The basin at times was very wide, especially in the clearness of a summer's day; but as dusk fell it would suddenly contract, the misty hills would draw near, and with night they had clasped us close: the centre of the world had become a candle shining from the kitchen window. Inside, in the sitting-room where we spent most of our life, a lamp was lit, with a round glass shade like a full yellow moon. There we were bathed before the fire, said our prayers kneeling on the hearthrug, and then disappeared up the steep stairs lighted by a candle to bed; and once there, the world was finally blotted out. I think it returned with the same suddenness, at least in summer; but the waking world was a new world, a hollow cube with light streaming in from one window across to a large bed holding, as the years went by, first one, then two, and finally three boys, overseen by two Apostles from one wall and adjured from another, above a chest of drawers, by a white pottery plaque within a pink-lustre frame, printed with a vignette of an angel blowing a trumpet and the words:

PRAISE YE THE LORD

Sometimes the child's mind went on living even during the darkness of night, listening to the velvet stillness of the fields. The stillness of a sleeping town, of a village, is nothing to the stillness of a remote farm; for the peace of day in such a place is so kindly that the ear is attuned to the subtlest sounds, and time is slow. If by chance a cow should low in the night it is like the abysmal cry of some hellish beast, bringing woe to the world. And who knows what hellish beasts might roam by night, for in the cave by the Church five miles away they once found the bones of many strange animals, wolves and hyaenas, and even the tusks of mammoths. The night-sound that still echoes in my mind, however, is not of this kind: it is gentler and more musical—the distant sound of horse-hooves on the highroad, at first dim and uncertain, but growing louder until they more suddenly cease. To that distant sound, I realized later, I must have come into the world, for the doctor arrived on horseback at four o'clock one December morning to find me uttering my first shriek.

I think I heard those hooves again the night my father died, but of this I am not certain; perhaps I shall remember when I come to relate that event, for now the memory of those years, which end shortly after my tenth birthday, comes fitfully, when the proper associations are aroused. If only I can recover the sense and uncertainty of those innocent years, years in which we seemed not so much to live as to be lived by forces outside us, by the wind and trees and moving clouds and all the mobile engines of our expanding world—then I am convinced I shall possess a key to much that has happened to me in this other world of conscious living. The echoes of my life which I find in my early childhood are too many to be dismissed as vain coincidences; but it is perhaps my conscious life which is the echo, the only real experiences in life being those lived with a virgin sensibility—so that we only hear a tone once, only see a colour once, see, hear, touch, taste and smell everything but once, the first time. All life is an echo of our first sensations, and we build up our consciousness, our whole mental life, by variations and combinations of these elementary sensations. But it is more complicated than that, for the senses apprehend not only colours and tones and shapes, but also patterns and atmospheres, and our first discovery of these determines the larger patterns and subtler atmospheres of all our subsequent existence.

2

The Farm

I have given the impression that the Farm was remote, but this is not strictly true. Not half a mile on each side of us was another farmhouse, and clustering near the one to the east were three or four cottages. We formed, therefore, a little community, remote as such; in 'Doomsday Book' we had been described as a hamlet. The nearest village was two or three miles away, but to the south, so that it did not count for much until we began to go to school, which was not until towards the end of the period of which I write. Northwards our farm road ran through two fields and then joined the highroad running east and west; but eastward this road soon turned into a road running north and south, down which we turned northwards again, to the Church five miles away, and to Kirby, our real metropolis, six miles away.

The farmhouse was a square stone box with a roof of vivid red tiles; its front was to the south, and warm enough to shelter some apricot trees against the wall. But there was no traffic that way: all our exits and entrances were made on the north side, through the kitchen; and I think even our grandest visitors did not disdain that approach. Why should they? On the left as they entered direct into the kitchen was an old oak dresser; on the right a large open fireplace, with a great iron kettle hanging from the reckan, and an oven to the near side of it. A long deal table, glistening with a honey gold sheen from much scrubbing, filled the far side of the room; long benches ran down each side of it. The floor was flagged with stone, each stone neatly outlined with a border of some softer yellow stone, rubbed on after every washing. Sides of bacon and plum-dusky hams hung from the beams of the wooden ceiling.

By day it was the scene of intense bustle. The kitchenmaid was down by five o'clock to light the fire; the labourers crept down in stockinged feet and drew on their heavy boots; they lit candles in their horn lanthorns and went out to the cattle. Breakfast was at seven, dinner at twelve, tea at five. Each morning of the week had its appropriate activity: Monday was washing day, Tuesday ironing, Wednesday and Saturday baking, Thursday 'turning out' upstairs and churning, Friday 'turning out' downstairs. Every day there was the milk to skim in the dairy—the dairy was to the left of the kitchen, and as big as any other room in the house. The milk was poured into large flat pans and allowed to settle; it was skimmed with horn scoops, like toothless combs.

At dinner, according to the time of the year, there would be from five to seven farm labourers, the two servant girls, and the family, with whom, for most of the time, there was a governess— a total of from ten to fifteen mouths to feed every day. The bustle reached its height about midday; the men would come in and sit on the dresser, swinging their legs impatiently; when the food was served, they sprang to the benches and ate in solid gusto, like animals. They disappeared as soon as the pudding had been served, some to smoke a pipe in the saddle room, others to do work which could not wait. Then all the clatter of washing up rose and subsided. More peaceful occupations filled the afternoon. The crickets began to sing in the hearth. The kettle boiled for tea. At nightfall a candle was lit, the foreman or the shepherd sat smoking in the armchair at the fireside end of the table. The latch clicked as the others came in one by one and went early to bed.

The kitchen was the scene of many events which afterwards flowed into my mind from the pages of books. Whenever in a tale a belated traveller saw a light and came through the darkness to ask for shelter, it was to this kitchen door. I can no longer identify the particular stories, but they do not belong to this period of childhood so much as to my later boyhood and youth, long after I had left the Farm; and even today my first memories easily usurp the function of the imagination, and clothe in familiar dimensions and patterns, exact and objective, the scenes which the romancer has purposely left vague. Perhaps the effect of all romance depends on this faculty we have of giving our own definition to the fancies of others. A mind without memories means a body without sensibility; our memories make our imaginative life, and it is only as we increase our memories, widening the imbricated shutters which divide our mind from the light, that we find with quick recognition those images of truth which the world is pleased to attribute to our creative gift.

3

The Green

The Green, a space of about an acre, lay in front of the
kitchen door. It was square; one side, that to the left as we
came out of the house, was fully taken up by a range of
sheds. A shorter range of buildings continued in line with the
house on the right—first the saddle-room, one of my favourite
haunts, then the shed where the dog-cart and buggy were kept,
and finally the blacksmith's shop. Beyond this were the grind-
stones and the ash-heap (in just such a heap, I imagined, Madame
Curie discovered radium) and then a high hedge led to the corner
of the Green, where three enormous elm-trees, the only landmark
near our farm, overhung the duck-pond. On the other two sides
the Green was bounded by hedges. The farm-road led past the
sheds and then to the left through the stackyard; to the right there
was a cart-track leading across the fields to the next farm with its
cluster of cottages.

Our dominion was really four-fold: the Green I have just
described, and then three other almost equal squares, the one to
the left of the Green being the farm outhouses, a rectangular
court of low buildings enclosing the Fodgarth, or fold-garth, and
two others to the south of the house, the orchard to the east, the
garden to the west. Each province was perfectly distinct, divided
off by high walls or hedges; and each had its individual powers or
mysteries. The Green was the province of water and of fowl, of
traffic and trade, the only province familiar to strangers—to the
postman and the pedlar, and the scarlet huntsmen. In winter we
made the snowman there; in summer avoided its shelterless waste.
On Mondays the washed clothes flapped in the wind, but for the
rest of the week it was willingly resigned to hens, ducks, geese,

guinea fowls, and turkeys—whose discursive habits, incidentally, made it no fit playground for children. The pond was more attractive, but because of its stagnation it could not compete with the becks not far away. I remember it best in a hot summer, when the water dried up and left a surface of shining mud, as smooth as moleskin, from which projected the rusty wrecks of old cans and discarded implements. Perhaps it was a forbidden area; it serves no purpose in my memory.

The pump was built over a deep well, in the corner of the Green near the kitchen; it was too difficult for a boy to work. One day, underneath the stones which took the drip, we discovered bright green lizards. Behind the pump, handy to the water, was the copper-house—the 'copper' being a large cauldron built in over a furnace. Here the clothes were boiled on a Monday; here, too, potatoes for the pigs were boiled in their earthy skins, and the pigs were not the only little animals who enjoyed them, for they are delicious when cooked in this way. Outside the same copper-house the pigs were killed, to be near the cauldron of boiling water with which they were scalded. The animal was drawn from its sty by a rope through the ring in its nose: its squealing filled the whole farm till it reached the copper-house, and there by the side of a trestle its throat was cut with a sharp knife and the hot blood gushed on to the ground. The carcass was then stretched on the trestle, and the whole household joined in the work of scraping the scalded hide: it was done with metal candlesticks, the hollow foot making a sharp and effective instrument for removing the bristles and outer skin. The carcass was then disembowelled and dismembered. The copper was once more requisitioned to render down the superfluous fat, which was first cut into dice. The remnants of this process, crisp shreds known as scraps, formed our favourite food for days afterwards. In fact, pig-killing was followed by a whole orgy of good things to eat— pork-pies, sausages and pigs'-feet filling the bill for a season. But the scenes I have described, and many others of the same nature, such as the searing of horses' tails, the killing of poultry, the birth of cattle, even the lewdness of a half-witted labourer, were witnessed by us children with complete passivity—just as I have seen children of the same age watching a bull-fight in Spain quite unmoved by its horrors. Pity, and even terror, are emotions which develop when we are no longer innocent, and the sentimental

adult who induces such emotions in the child is probably breaking through defences which nature has wisely put round the
tender mind. The child even has a natural craving for horrors.
He survives just because he is without sentiment, for only in this
way can his green heart harden sufficiently to withstand the
wounds that wait for it.

On the south side of the Green were two familiar shrines,
each with its sacred fire. The first was the saddle-room, with
its pungent clean smell of saddle-soap. It was a small whitewashed room, hung with bright bits and stirrups and long loops
of leather reins; the saddles were in a loft above, reached by a
ladder and trap-door. In the middle was a small cylindrical stove,
kept burning through the winter, and making a warm friendly
shelter where we could play undisturbed. Our chief joy was to
make lead shot, or bullets as we called them; and for this purpose
there existed a long-handled crucible and a mould. At what now
seems to me an incredibly early age we melted down the strips of
lead we found in the window-sill, and poured the sullen liquid
into the small aperture of the mould, which was in the form of a
pair of pincers—closed whilst the pouring was in progress. When
opened, the gleaming silver bullets, about the size of a pea, fell
out of the matrix and rolled away to cool on the stone floor.
We used the bullets in our catapults, but the joy was in the making
of them, and in the sight of their shining beauty.

The blacksmith's shop was a still more magical shrine. The
blacksmith came for a day periodically, to shoe or re-shoe the
horses, to repair wagons and make simple implements. In his
dusky cave the bellows roared, the fire was blown to a white
intensity, and then suddenly the bellows-shaft was released and
the soft glowing iron drawn from the heart of the fire. Then
clang clang clang on the anvil, the heavenly shower of ruby and
golden sparks, and our precipitate flight to a place of safety.
All around us, in dark cobwebbed corners, were heaps of old
iron, discarded horseshoes, hoops and pipes. Under the window
was a tank of water for slaking and tempering the hot iron,
and this water possessed the miraculous property of curing
warts.

In these two shrines I first experienced the joy of making
things. Everywhere around me the earth was stirring with growth
and the beasts were propagating their kind. But these wonders

passed unobserved by my childish mind, unrecorded in memory. They depended on forces beyond our control, beyond my conception. But fire was real, and so was the skill with which we shaped hard metals to our design and desire.

4

The Orchard

The front garden was formal, like the drawing-room; it was not part of our customary world. If we went there during the day, it was to see if the forbidden apricots were ripening, or to play for a short time round the monkey-puzzle-tree which grew in the middle of a small lawn. But a monkey-puzzle-tree is not a friendly shelter; its boughs are too near the ground, it is hirsute and prickly. The lawn was enclosed by hedges of box, through which narrow arches led to the flower garden in front, to the vegetable garden on the right, and to the orchard on the left. Again, all these provinces were rectangular, without any picturesque charm, but riotous with natural detail, with great variety of shrubs, fruit-bushes and vegetables. The Garden, too, had its shrine. The northern end, in line with the back of the house, was bounded by a high stone wall, sheltering pear-trees. Between this wall and a line of plum-trees, a path, bordered by flowering-currants and honesty, led to the ivy-clad privy. This green retreat, always in memory a place spangled in leaf-flecked sunlight, with ivy-fruit tapping against the small window-pane, has no grosser associations. Its friendliness, its invitation to sociability, was further emphasized by its furniture of two seats, and there we could sit side by side, the needs of our bodies relieved in no furtive secrecy, but in unabashed naturalness.

On the other side, through the wicket that led into the Orchard, there came first the water-trough, an immense stone tank fed from the eaves; this rain water was very precious for washing purposes, so we were forbidden to play with it. It is one of the few memories I have of the sternness of my father, that on one occasion finding me transgressing this law, he immediately picked me up by the seat and immersed me bodily in the water.

Above the trough, high up on the gable of the house, was another forbidden object: the bell which was pealed at midday to announce dinner to the scattered labourers, none of whom was likely to wear a watch.

Behind the saddle-room, in this region of the trough, was the Sand-heap, in a corner formed by a lime house and a low cow-shed. The hours we spent in this corner were too habitual to linger much in the memory. It was a generous heap, allowing an extensive system of trenches and castles; near-by was the shade of the apple-trees and the elms; our days there were timeless. Once, playing there, I slipped into the cow-shed to stroke a young calf housed there, closing the door behind me. The calf was lying in fresh clean straw, and did not stir at my approach. Hours later I was missed, and after long searching and much shouting in the farm and the fields, I was discovered sleeping with my head against the calf's warm flank.

The Orchard, like the Green, must have been about an acre in extent. I have no memory of it, except in spring and summer, when the branches, with their succession of blossom, leaf and fruit, met to form an overgrowth supported by aisles of trunks, green with moss or misty grey-blue when the lichen was dry and crusted. One old russet tree sloped up from the ground at a low angle, easy to climb; and in its boughs we shook the blossom till it fell in flakes like snow, or helped ourselves unchecked to the sweet rough-skinned apples. I think the Orchard only held two treasures besides the trees: an old disused roller about which we clambered, and in a far corner, by a bush whose hollow twigs made excellent stems for improvised pipes (in which we smoked a cunning mixture of dried clover and pear leaves), a small trough which usually held rock salt, brown and glassy. In the orchard, and in the paddock beyond, we dug up sweet pig-nuts, and ate them without much regard for the soil engrained in them.

When we emerged from the Paddock, where our pony and the mare for the dog-cart used to graze, there was a sudden sense of space. The ground sloped down gently towards our main stream, the Riccall, which formed the southern boundary of the farm. Beyond the Riccall, which flowed rather deeply in the soft earth and was quite impassable to us, lay a mysterious land we never explored: the south, with the hills rising in the distance, the farm with the fiery windows hidden in their folds.

5

The Foldgarth

The fourth kingdom, the Foldgarth, was the animal kingdom. We usually entered it from the north corner of the Green, and here on the right were the main cow-sheds, the most familiar part of this complex of buildings. Morning and night, and most often by lanthorn light (perhaps it is only the winter scene which is impressed on my memory) the cows were milked in a glow and atmosphere which is for me the glow and atmosphere of the Nativity. The patient beasts stood in their stalls, exuding the soft slightly sickly smell of cow breath; a girl or a man sat on a three-legged stool, cheek against a glossy flank, and the warm needle stream of milk hissed into the gleaming pails. At first it sang against the hollow tin drum of the base, but as the pail filled it murmured with a frothy surr-surr. Here I learnt my first bitter lesson of self-limitation; for try as I would I could not learn how to milk. To manipulate the teats so as to secure a swift and easy flow of milk demands a particular skill; I never acquired it, though my brothers, younger than I, seemed to find no difficulty. This was my first humiliation in the practical affairs of life; another which I might mention here was an inability to make the kuk-kuk noise between the tongue and palate which is the proper sound to urge a horse on gently. These failures in trivial things loom much larger in childhood and affect us much more deeply than any backwardness in learning manners or facts, for they reflect on our physical capacity, and that is much more real to us than any mental power.

Then, along the northern side of the Foldgarth, ran the stable for the carthorses. We were a little scared of these immense noble beasts, for some of them were known to be savage, and ready to bite anyone but the man whose duty it was to look after them.

At the end of the stables a gateway led into the stackyard, and so out on to the road and the fields beyond. At this gateway I once witnessed a terrible scene; an ignorant labourer had taken a pregnant mare out to plough, and by overstraining her, caused a miscarriage. My father and I met him bringing in the horse, with her ghastly trail, and so terrible was my father's passion that he quite forgot my presence as he heaped his curses on the offending man.

My memories of my father are too intermittent to form a coherent image. His sensitive face, his soft brown eyes, and his close curly black hair were not the features of a normal farmer. He loved his farm and was well known for his fervour and enterprise, a tradition he had inherited from my grandfather: he brought some visionary quality to his life and labour. He was a man of austere habits and general uprightness, whose friendship was sought by men of a more recognized intellectual standing. I do not remember that he read much or was in any sense bookish (as I shall relate later, books were scarce in the house). The life of a farmer is hardly consistent with a life of even elementary scholarship, but a sensitive and intelligent mind, in daily contact with all the problems and processes of farming, acquires more than a weather wisdom—an intuitive sense of reality and right values which are not acquired by the mere process of reading.

Along the western side of the Foldgarth ran a line of higher, double-storied buildings. The first was a big hay-barn, open to the rafters, with the pigeon-house built in at the gable end. It was a favourite playing-ground in wet weather: we could make giddy leaps from one level of hay to another; we could burrow into caves and hide completely in its scented warmth. A door at the other side of this barn led to a circular building, with a grinding mill in the middle and a circular track round which a horse could drag the mill-beam.

Then came various sheds for fodder and implements, and over these, approached by stone steps at the end of the building, and outside the Foldgarth, was the granary—a long dry sweet-smelling loft, with bins of golden wheat and stacks of oil-cake, and a store of locust-beans which we ate when we were hungry. A machine for crushing oil-cake stood against one wall, and in this one day I managed to crush my little finger. I fainted with the pain, and the horror of that dim milk-white panic is as ineffaceable as the scar which my flesh still bears.

THE FOLDGARTH

The other two sides of the Foldgarth were occupied by pig-sties and cow-sheds; the middle by a steadily steaming morass of urine-sodden straw known as the Mig Heap, the infinitely precious store of manure from which the land recovered some of the strength given forth in corn and pasture. The acrid stench of this heap, never unpleasant to any one brought up with it, pervaded the whole of the Foldgarth. The pigeons flocked from roof to roof. An inquisitive calf would lift its head over the low door of its stall. A scurry of hens, an occasional grunt or squeal of pigs, the running of a rope through a ring in the stables: these were the only sounds that disturbed the day's peace, until the men returned from the fields with the weary horses, and the Foldgarth was filled with the clatter of hooves on the stone sets, with the whistling and hissing of the men over their grooming.

On the southern side of the Foldgarth, some of the stables opened outwards, into a lane whose other side was the high wall on the north of the vegetable garden. Here lived the hunters, beautiful pedigree horses which were the pride of the farm—lived in a cleanliness and comfort which put them in a class apart, half-way between humans and animals. I fancy that the fortunes of the farm depended far more on these splendid pampered darlings than on the normal crops and cattle. It was a great day when they were paraded in all their glossy splendour before some horse dealer, and a bargain struck. But sorrow must have been mingled with satisfaction when they left us, and a farm is, indeed, the scene of many sad farewells: pet lambs and ducks stolen away to go to the market with the rest, leaving a broken-hearted child to weep the day away until some consolation is found.

6

The Stackyard

Beyond the Foldgarth lay the Stackyard, looking like an African village, especially after the harvest when it was stored to its limits. The stacks were of two shapes—circular and rectangular—with swelling sides and neatly thatched roofs. The ridges of the rectangular ones were braided with osiers; the round ones were finished off with a fanciful panache of straw. Birds sheltered under the narrow eaves, and would dart out at our strident approach. One summer evening something not bird nor bat fluttered among the stacks; the farm was roused to excitement and the winged creature finally netted. It was a rare Death's Head moth, for which some collector paid the fabulous sum of five shillings. That such riches could lurk in a stackyard was a new portent. We learned that the Death's Head moth was fond of the potato-flower, and the season never afterwards passed without a vain hunt among these despised blooms.

The great festival in the Stackyard was threshing time. Late one afternoon we would hear the chuff and rattle of the engine and threshing machine far away on the high-road, and away we would race to meet it. The owner of the engine, Jabez by name, was a great hero in the eyes of children. He was a small man with a little twinkling face and a fuzzy black beard. He would stop his rattling train and take us up into the engine cabin. I love to this day that particular smell of hot steam and oil which was then wafted to us. With amazement we watched Jabez push over his levers and set the monster in motion. With more chuffing and much complicated shunting the machines were steered into position for work, and then left shrouded for the night.

Very early the next morning we would hear a high-pitched musical hum coming from the Stackyard, and it was with diffi-

30

culty that we could be made to eat any breakfast. Then we would run across the Green and find round the corner the most exciting scene of the year. The engine stood before us, merry with smoke and steam; the big fly-wheel winked in the sunlight; the bright balls of the revolving 'governor' (Jabez had taught me the technical names) twinkled in a minor radiance. Jabez was in the cabin stoking the glowing furnace. The big leather belt swung rhythmically between the fly-wheel and the threshing-machine. Two men on the top of a stack threw down the sheaves; two others cut them open and guided them into the monster's belly; the monster groaned and gobbled, and out of its yammering mouth came the distracted straw; elsewhere emerged the prickly chaff and below, into sacks that reached the ground, trickled the precious corn. A cloud of dust and chaff swirled round everything. As the stack disappeared, and approached ground-level, we were armed with sticks and the dogs became attentive and expectant. The last layer of sheaves was reached; out raced the rats which had made a home in the bedding of thorns on which the stack rested, and then for a few minutes the Stackyard was an abode of demons: dogs barked, men and children shouted in a lust of killing, and the unfortunate rats squealed in panic and death agonies. Sometimes we found a nest of newly-born rats, and then we were suddenly sad.

I think this festival used to last two or three days; it was our only contact with the Machine God. I suppose we were dimly aware of the railway six miles away, and must have travelled on it, for I know that once or twice we went to Scarborough; but for some reason I have no vivid memory of these excursions, nor of anything associated with them. They were not lived, but pushed without roots into the soil of our daily existence. One curious experience, however, remains with me, and it may well be mentioned here; it is the first of several instances in my life of which I remain incapable of asserting that the experience was of the dream-world. My reason tells me, in this case at least, that it must have been a dream, but the mind does not necessarily assent to its reasoning. I 'appeared' (as we say) to walk down the cart-track that led along the top side of two or three fields towards Peacock's farm; I climbed on to the gate that separated the last field from the high-road, and as I rested there I was terrified by the sudden onrush of a large steam-roller, travelling northwards.

It was distinguished from ordinary steam-rollers (which I had no doubt seen at work on the roads) by the fact that the boiler rested on an enormous bellows, and as the engine roared onwards, these bellows worked up and down and so seemed to throw up through the chimney a fiery column of smoke, steam and sparks. This apparition, which came to me perhaps in my seventh year, remains in my mind today distinct in every detail.

I do not think I was more than usually subject to nightmares (if such this was), but one, which I fancy belongs to a common form, is also remembered by me with peculiar vividness, though it is difficult to describe. I am laid as in bed on a bank of clouds. The sky darkens, grows bluish-black. Then the darkness seems to take visible shape, to separate into long bolsters, or objects which I should now compare with airships. These then point themselves towards me, and approach me, magnifying themselves enormously as they get nearer. I awake with a shriek, quivering with terror. My mother hears me and comes quickly to comfort me, perhaps to take me back with her to sleep away the sudden terror.

7

The Cow Pasture

There was a sandy rankness about the fields stretching towards the river, but these were the main pasture-lands. The Cow Pasture, by far the largest field on the farm, lay on the west of the farm-buildings and its boundary was the western boundary of our land. A path led across the middle of it, and across the neighbouring fields to Riccall House, distinguished from the rest of us by its whitewashed walls and thatched roof. This pasture was rather a godless waste: it was pock-marked with erupted rabbit-warrens, countless mole-hills, and dark fairy-rings in the grass. We implicitly believed in the mysterious origin of these rings, and felt that we might any misty morning find the fairies dancing. Periodically the rabbits had to be decimated, and then fierce dark men with waxed moustaches appeared, bringing ferrets in canvas bags. We would go out in a party, carrying guns and spades, to attack the warrens. The ferrets were loosened from their bags and disappeared down the holes. We listened for sub-terranean squeals, watched for the sudden dart of terrified rabbits, and for the eager inquisitive emergence of the baffled ferrets. The spades, digging easily in the sandy earth, discovered the labyrinths and occasionally a nest of newly-born rabbits.

There was a wide watery ditch on the south side of the Cow Pasture, inhabited by frogs, which spawned among the cress and king-cups. Beyond were narrow fields, running parallel with the river, lush and marshy. The river itself ran between banks, for it was liable to flood over. Eastward it ran for about half a mile, till it disappeared under a bridge which carried the road near Pea-cock's farm—the road of the dream engine. By the bridge was a pool with a projecting pier; this was the sheep-dip, where annu-ally the sheep were given some kind of antiseptic bath.

c

I remember the oily smell of sheep, sheep-shearing, their ludicrous nakedness when first shorn. Most years there was a pet lamb, a weakling that had to be wrapped in blankets before the kitchen fire, fed from a bottle, and gradually nursed into life. His field would be the Green, and we were his playmates until the inevitable day of parting came. We used to think that the long tails of lambs were bitten off by the shepherd, but actually the animals were gelded by this reputedly safe means. The tails of young colts were cut off with special clippers, and then seared with a red-hot iron. The feet of full grown sheep rot and have to be scraped; maggots burrow into their flesh and pullulate, are gouged out and the sheep anointed. Their wool is infested with nauseous black ticks. Only on the moors, where the sheep are black-faced and agile, with curled horns and quivering nostrils, does this animal acquire any dignity.

The greater part of the Farm was given over to various crops—wheat, oats, barley and rye—and the fields devoted to these spread northwards. Some of them seemed very remote to us. One was sinister, for a large oak-tree grew in the middle of it, and here a man sheltering under it had been struck by lightning and killed. Another field, at the extreme north of our land, had high hedges full of may-blossom; there was a sparse wood on one side; and here, years afterwards when the Farm was only a memory, I staged incidents from the Morte d'Arthur.

In the nearer fields we watched the labours of the months. We were aware of the ploughing, the harrowing, the rolling, the sowing, and finally of the harvest. We followed the plough-man, and sometimes ran between the shafts of the plough, pre-tending to guide it to a truer furrow. At the harvest, as soon as we could walk we became labourers; because then the whole house-hold would turn into the fields, the women to bind the sheaves and pile them into stooks. At lunch-time my mother would drive out with the buggy laden with sandwiches, cheese and bread, and great stone jars of draught beer. We played at hide-and-seek among the stooks, gathered the shorn poppies and cornflowers, watched the field-mice scurry in fright among the stubble and scarlet pimpernel. At the end of the harvest, the last wagon was escorted back in triumph, often late at night in the moonlight, and a great harvest supper was spread in the kitchen, at which my father and mother presided.

THE COW PASTURE

In November the hedges were trimmed and layered; the thorns were raked up into great heaps and fired. When we were old enough, my father would have a cart-load of thorns pitched on the Green, and there one night we would dance round the bonfire.

Almost in the middle of the Farm was the fox-covert—a piece of land of perhaps four acres, thickly covered with gorse and scrub, hedged with hazel trees. Twice in a season the Hunt met at our house. They assembled on the Green—the master, the kennel-man and several others in their scarlet coats and peaked caps, the farmers and their ladies in hard billycock hats. The hounds moved in a compact mass, their upcurved tails swaying rhythmically. When the meet was present, they moved off to the fox-covert, and always without much difficulty started a fox. My father rode one of his beautiful hunters; my mother had her pony. At first we children went on foot as far as the Covert and saw them take off, and piped our tally-ho's if we caught sight of the fox. We heard the huntsman's horn as they sped across the fields, waited until we could hear it no more, then went home to wait until the weary hunters returned. But when I was about seven I was given my first pony, and then rode away with the hounds—my first hunt ending in the middle of a hedge which my impetuous pony had taken too rashly.

At the first kill at which I was present I had to be 'blooded'. The severed head of the fox was wiped across my face till it was completely smeared in blood, and I was told what a fine huntsman I should make. I do not remember the blood, nor the joking huntsmen; only the plumed breath of the horses, the jingle of their harness, the beads of dew and the white gossamer on the tangled hedge beside us.

8

The Abbey

Occasionally we made excursions to regions beyond the Farm. Once a year, perhaps in early autumn, we went with wagons to some woods eight or nine miles away, on the edge of the Moors. There we had the right to fell a certain amount of timber, and to bring it away on our wagons. It was a long day's expedition, and an immense adventure when we were allowed to go. We took our food with us and picnicked among the resinous chips and stripped bark.

This is the only expedition I remember taking from the farm. My wider explorations were done from other bases. Three or four times, in times of illness or when, I now suppose, a brother or sister was expected, I went to stay with relations for a few weeks. My mother was the youngest daughter in a family of nine, so we were richly provided with aunts. One of these, a widow, lived with her two sons and our grandfather in a cottage at Helmsley, and there I stayed on at least two occasions.

Helmsley was six miles to the west. The road passed through Harome, a hamlet of white thatched cottages, in one of which lived a woman, my mother used to tell us impressively, with twenty-three children. A mile outside Helmsley the road crossed the railway, and then ran in a straight slope into the town. My aunt's cottage was on the right as we entered, by the side of a saw-mill. When a saw was working a high melancholy whine rose above the houses and filled me with a vague dread. This first treet, Bondgate, opened into a wide market-place, with a market-cross and a monument in the middle. On one side the houses were still half timbered, with overhanging gables; the tower of the church rose above them, scattering a merry peal from its numerous bells. Once a week, on Saturdays, the market-place was filled with booths, dense with farmers and their wives. At other times it was a wide deserted space, with perhaps a child or two and a dog at the foot of the cross. Sometimes a cart drawn by bullocks passed slowly across, as if to emphasize an air of almost Eastern sleepiness—such carts being an affectation of the Earl whose park gates were at the end of one of the streets leading out of the market-place.

Beyond the market-place stood the castle with its ivied keep, still massive and imposing in spite of deliberate destruction by the Parliamentarians. Here again was a stage-setting for my later romantic notions, but my authentic memory of this time only associates it with a tennis tournament in which my father took part, and I still see the white figures of the players set against the vivid green of the lawn. Sheep grazed in the empty moats and jackdaws nested in the ragged turrets. The castle might have been more impressive but for still more romantic monuments within my reach. Duncombe Park was an amazing wonderland, which we entered but rarely, and always with an awe communicated by our deferential elders. My eyes searched the wide vistas for some limiting hedge, but in vain. We stopped to stroke a newly-born deer. Vanbrugh's mansion was something beyond my comprehension, of which I only preserve, as fragments from a strange feast, the white ghosts of marble statues incongruous in this greenery, an orange-tree in fruit in the conservatory, and a thatched ice-house. Overhanging a steep valley at the end of the park is a famous terrace, with a lawn as smooth as a carpet and a Grecian temple at each end. Down in this valley is the abbey of Rievaulx.

Rievaulx played an important part in the growth of my imagination, but I cannot tell how much of its beauty and romance was absorbed in these years of childhood, how much built on to these memories in later years. It was the farthest western limit of my wanderings, and so lovely then in its solitude and desolation, that I think my childish mind, in spite of its overweening objectivity, must have surrendered to its subtle atmosphere. One day, years later, I happened to be there when a new church, built under the shadow of the ruins, was consecrated. A choir had come from York Minster, and sang a *Te Deum* between the ruined arches; their sweet voices echoing strangely under the roof of the sky, their white surplices fluttering in the wind. The tomb of Sir Walter l'Espec, the knight who had founded the abbey and had afterwards died as a monk in these cloisters, stood at the end of the chancel. It was not dedicated to any known God, but in a moment of solitude it would serve as an altar to a sense of glory denoted by these ruins and this tomb, and their existence in this solitary place.

Around Rievaulx, and especially through the narrow wooded dales which strike like green rays into the purple darkness of the Moors, I wandered with my cousin, a boy five or six years older than myself. He was a keen collector of birds' eggs, butterflies and flowers, and had great cunning in the pursuit of these objects. From him I learnt how to handle birds' eggs, to empty them through one blow-hole, to pack them in match-boxes. We carried catapults and I was taught the honour of the chase: which birds it was legitimate to shoot, how many eggs one could take from a nest, how to rob a nest without spoiling it or discouraging the mother-bird. One day in mistake I shot a robin, a crime my cousin made more terrible by promising to keep it a secret from the world.

Sometimes we would be out all day, regardless of meals. We gathered wild gooseberries and stewed them in a tin over a fire of twigs. We ate the tender shoots of sweet-briar, sorrel and pignuts. I imagine we were severely scolded on our return, but such unpleasantnesses do not endure in the memory. I remember instead the upright figure of my grandfather, white-haired and gentle in his armchair by the kitchen fire, the singing kettle and the cheeping cry of the crickets. We had only candles to light the cottage in the evening. There was a long window full of geraniums, a steep wooden staircase with a latched door that clicked loudly. In this house I have always pictured the story of the Three Bears.

Behind it was a long straggling yard, with outhouses belonging to a builder, and at the end a walled garden where my grandfather grew vegetables and kept bees in straw hives. The privy was here too, and a shed containing, among other junk, some old gas pipes from which I used to try and construct a fountain. I have never met again their pungent metallic smell. Beyond the garden was a lane leading to the cemetery, which with its orderliness and symbolic cypresses was a place very different from the graveyard at Kirkdale. It was usually bright

THE ABBEY

with flowers, and the Sisters of Mercy passed along the gravelled paths with their billowing black robes and white-winged caps. I see now that there was something a little foreign in the whole aspect of this town, with its highly ritualistic church, cloudy with sweet incense, where men and women sat in opposite aisles, its tyrannical vicar, its musical bells, its cart-oxen and its air of seeming to live intently on the four sides of a wide open square.

9

The Church

Every Sunday the dog-cart was yoked up and the whole family climbed into the high seats, my father and mother in front with the youngest of us between them, the rest of us clinging to the precarious back-seat. When it rained an immense gingham umbrella, like the roof of a pagoda, sheltered us all. The big wheels crunched on the gritty roads. The Farm retreated from us as we trotted down the northern road to our parish Church, five miles away. The road had three points of interest: the Little Beck, the Big Beck, and the peacocks. The becks excited us because they had no bridges: they widened out into shallow fords through which the horse splashed as if born to this watery element. In spring the becks were often flooded, and sometimes the water stretched for hundreds of feet in a lake of incalculable depth. Then the excitement was intense, but my father must have known the safe limits of the flood. I remember the water coming up to the horse's belly, and our anxiety for the rug, which had a way of hanging below the footboard.

About a mile before we reached the Church we passed a small village in the middle of which was a country-house known as 'The Hall', and here, on a high wall, we sometimes saw the peacocks which inhabited the garden beyond. For us they were fabulous birds, and the glory of their plumage the most exotic sight of those days. A mile farther on, the road descended steeply into a narrow valley, and there, in complete isolation, stood our Church. First came a row of sheds and stables, where the horse was unyoked and the trap put under shelter. Then the path led a little lower down to the gate of the churchyard, where in summer a few men would be standing, enjoying the air until the last moment. The bell, or rather the clapper, clanged in the squat tower. The Church is of grey stone with a slated roof, and stands out clearly as you approach it against a dark wood of firs. Ancient tombstones lean out of the grassy mounds at all angles. We were taught that it was wicked to walk over a grave, but this grave-yard is so ancient and so thickly populated, that we had to wander as if in a maze. Either before or after the service we made our way to the family graves, at the east end of the Church; but it was not until Mariana died that this duty became a melancholy one, the sight of my mother's tears communicating a wondering sense of woe.

In summer we brought flowers to this grave, and sometimes I was sent to throw away the withered remains of last week's wreath. At the end of the churchyard there was a low wall, and below this a deep ravine in which the river ran, quite over-shadowed by trees. Into this gloomy cavern I threw my handfuls of wisps, glad to hide my uneasiness in this gesture.

Over the porch of the Church is a famous Saxon sundial with an inscription carved on the stone panels at each side which tells us that Orm the son of Gamal bought Saint Gregory's minster when it was all broken down and fallen, and he caused it to be made new from the ground, to Christ and Saint Gregory, in the reign of Edward the King, in the days of Tosti the Earl. Round the dial itself are the words:

THIS IS DÆGES SOL MERCA ÆT ILCVMTIDE

—this is the day's sun mark at every tide; and below the dial is written: Hawarth made me and Brand the priest.

Inside, the walls are whitewashed, and an aqueous light filters through the foliage-bound windows. The nave was then filled with square box-pews, very high, so that we retired into a little private world, to pray as a family safe from the distractions of less familiar human beings. But the family included our Howkeld relations, of whom I shall soon speak; and my uncle, so patriarchal in his crisp white beard, officiated within our box. He was too stout to kneel on the hassocks which saved our knees from the cold stone floor, but the rest of us, sometimes eight or nine in number, knelt rigidly with hands pressed palm to palm.

The service was of extreme simplicity and dispatch. The sermon never lasted more than ten minutes, sometimes only five.

The music came from a small harmonium, and there was a sur-
pliced choir of perhaps two men and three boys. The congregation numbered in all not more than forty—many less when the
weather was wild. In winter the Church was very cold, so we
kept our overcoats on, and our breath issued in plumes as we sang
the hymns. Once a month there was a Communion Service, and
then for a few minutes, when our elders went to receive the Sacra-
ment, we were left in possession of the box, at liberty to fidget
and to let our eyes wander to the heraldic monsters displayed on
the painted wooden hatchments, to the gallery where the servants
sat, and to the trees waving across the leaded trellis of the windows.

After the service (which alternated each week between morning
and afternoon, for the vicar served two parishes) the congregation
gathered in groups and chatted peacefully as they walked up the
path to the gate, and waited for the traps to be yoked up. The
inhuman stillness of the situation aided our friendliness; our
Church was still where the monks who first built it twelve
centuries ago had wanted it to be, in a wild valley, near a running
beck, grey like a wild hawk nesting in a shelter of dark trees.

10

The Mill

About half a mile above the Church the beck suddenly slackens; part of its waters (in summer all) disappear down a fissure in the rocky bed. They keep to a subterranean channel for a mile and a half and suddenly reappear, bubbling up from a great depth, at the head of a field which belonged to my uncle, whose small estate was on that account called Howkeld, which means 'springhead'. Here we came often and always with great joy, as to an enchanted kingdom. My uncle was a miller, and the mysterious water, which left its proper course and dived underground as if on very purpose to come up again in this particular spot to offer him its services, ran deep and strong in a willow-fringed bend round the large field separating the mill from the road. At the end of the field it became a walled dam, and to the right overflowed through a sluice into a round lake, which acted as a reservoir for times of drought. The private road to the mill followed the course of the stream and the dam, and then crossed by a bridge under which the water disappeared, combed by an iron grill. It emerged in a swift channel at the other side, and then sluiced in a roaring torrent over the water-wheel. The churned water fell in a dazzling white foaming cascade to a whirling pool below the wheel, and then flowed away with diminishing contortions in a stream which ran round the large gardens and through the fields until it rejoined the mother stream a mile and a half farther south.

There was so much here for childish wonder! The mill itself, with its swinging straps and flickering wheels, the bright chains that hoisted the grain to the top storey, the dusty machines in which we could see, through little windows, the grain trickling, and the general earth-shaking hum and whirr. The foreman's

43

bright eyes twinkled from a face all powdered with flour, his clothes were like white mouse-skin, his beard hoary. His voice was piping high, from having to make himself heard in the din. On Sundays, when the mill was still, flour-dust deadened the sound of our feet on the worn wooden floors; our hands ran sweetly along smooth step-ladders and horny ropes.

Perhaps because there was always a plentiful supply of grain, my aunt kept all kinds of poultry, and in the yard round the mill the most motley assembly of fowls strutted and pecked—not only various breeds of hens, but guinea-fowl, turkeys, ducks and geese. The house was at the end of the yard, T-shaped, its leg in line with the mill. A side door led into the leg, which was a low extension of the original building and here was the Little Room where the family always lived, except on festive occasions. It was a very low room with a varnished wooden beam running across the ceiling. Most of the space was taken up by a sideboard and a large dining-table, and it is hard to think of this room without its comple-ment of food. This was always spread in the most lavish way, with great hams and sirloins of beef, pies, pastries and puddings, and, at tea-time, cakes and tarts of the most alluring kind. My aunt was a famous cook: the mill and the gardens and the farm poured forth their plenty at the doorstep; by barter, in exchange for flour, most of the other essentials and luxuries of life were forthcoming. A deep spring of purest water flowed in the nearest field. War and famine could pass over the land and leave such bounty unaffected.

It was always peaceful here, a peace of guelder-roses and peonies, of laden fruit-trees and patient waters. Perhaps this im-pression means that our visits were mainly confined to the summer; in winter I only remember the frozen lake, on which we learned to skate. People came from far and near on such occasions, and the ice rang with the swift metallic strokes of the skaters' feet. In summer the lake, round which a path led among the reeds and rushes, was given over to the water-hens and wild ducks. Sometimes a flight of wild geese would come sweeping out of the sky on their way north.

I have already described my uncle as patriarchal, and this was true of him in more than appearance. My aunt was the eldest (and my mother the youngest) of the large family I have already mentioned. Some of these had married and migrated to other parts of the world, but such as remained, a goodly number, looked up to my uncle as the head of the clan into which he had married. His stout figure, his crisp white beard and twinkling eyes, his little linen bags of sample grain, his chuckle and his soft rich dialect, were familiar to the whole countryside; and at the time I speak of he was blessed with much happiness and prosperity. But during the next thirty years (he lived to be nearly ninety) he was to suffer many afflictions: the death of his favourite son, the bankruptcy of another, followed by the mortgaging of his own estate and finally a moratorium—and during all these tribulations he remained, a Lear of these Steppes, magnificent in courage and faith.

His children were contemporaries of my father and mother, and this introduced complications into our childish minds, for we called our cousins simply by their Christian names, whilst others who seemed their equals were aunts and uncles. The youngest of these cousins was not too old to despise the part of guide and initiator. One day he organized an expedition to explore the cave at Kirkdale. This famous cave extends for three hundred feet underground, and has more than one branch inside. The expedition, therefore, had to be undertaken with proper precautions. These consisted of candles, a large ball of binder-band, and the retriever, Jet. At the entry of the cave we made the end of the band secure, lit our candles, and crept forward unrolling the ball as we went. The sides of the cave glistened in the candle-light; drops of moisture fell from the stalactites above us; the air we breathed was cold and dank. I cannot remember how far we penetrated, but at one point we were terrified by the sudden appearance of two fiery eyes in the darkness confronting us. Could it be one of the ancient hyaenas, not yet a remnant of bones? But it was only Jet, who had run round some loop in the cave and come to meet us.

Once or twice we made expeditions up the dale beyond the cave and the Church. It is one of the wildest and most beautiful places in the whole country; and I still remember my father driving some fine lady from the outer world along the track that went along the ridge of the dale, and how she swore that it was more beautiful than Switzerland, a country of which we had no conception, but which we thought must be wonderful because people travelled far just to look at its hills and dales. This track up the dale ended at a house about two miles from the Church; here the dale became narrower and was filled with thick woods where lilies grew. No road led through these woods, not even a path; but an adventurous spirit could make his way along the bed of the stream, and after a mile or two he would discover that the dale opened out again, to give space to a mill and a few farms and cottages. This is Bransdale, an oasis on the Moors, which in our time only had a poor moorland track to link it with the outer world. The people who lived here were strange and dark and beautiful even to my childish eyes. For sometimes, when staying at Howkeld, I would go out for the day with the wagoners. Our load of grain and flour was drawn by great shaggy-footed cart-horses, their harness bright with brass ornaments, their manes and tails plaited with coloured ribbons—drawn over the wide purple Moors, where God seems to have left the earth clear of feature to reveal the beauty of its naked form, till we dipped down into the green dales and lifted our burden.

11

The Attic

The successive governesses who helped my mother with our upbringing remain utterly vague to me. They must have occupied a large place in our lives, but except for one insubstantial ghost of dark hair and spectacles, none of them can I recall. I know that they taught us to read, but I doubt if I had acquired that accomplishment before the age of seven. Then books immediately became my element. There was nothing to encourage me in this taste: there were no books in the living-rooms, and my father read little except the *Yorkshire Post* and various agricultural papers. On Sunday he would read to us the lessons of the day (perhaps this was only when it was impossible to go to Kirkdale) and he made us learn the Collect by heart. The only book of his I still possess is *The Poetical Works of Sir Walter Scott*. My mother read to us often, especially *Little Arthur's History of England, Evenings at Home, Forget-me-not*, and a tendentious story published by the Religious Tract Society called *Little Meg's Children* (by the author of *Jessica's First Prayer, the Children of Cloverley*, etc.). I still possess *Little Meg's Children*, and I see now that its grim pathos, too simple to be wholly sentimental, may have worked into the texture of my unfolding imagination, above all to prepare me for the shock of death which waited for me so near; for the first chapter describes the death of Little Meg's mother, and the plight of the orphaned children.

'She turned her face round to the wall with a deep sigh, and closed her eyelids, but her lips kept moving silently from time to time. Meg cried softly to herself in her chair before the fire, but presently she dozed a little for very heaviness of heart, and dreamed that her father's ship was come into dock, and she, and her mother, and the children, were going down the dingy streets

47

to meet him. She awoke with a start; and creeping gently to her mother's side, laid her warm little hand upon hers. It was deadly cold with a chill such as little Meg had never before felt; and when her mother neither moved nor spoke in answer to her repeated cries, she knew that she was dead.

'For the next day, and the night following, the corpse of the mother lay silent and motionless in the room where her three children were living. Meg cried bitterly at first; but there was Robin to be comforted, and the baby to be played with when it laughed and crowed in her face. Robin was nearly six years old, and had gained a vague dim knowledge of death, by having followed, with a troop of other curious children, many a funeral that had gone out from the dense and dirty dwellings to the distant cemetery, where he had crept forward to the edge of the grave, and peeped down into what seemed to him a very dark and dreadful depth. When little Meg told him Mother was dead, and lifted him up to kneel on the bedside, and kiss her icy lips for the last time, his childish heart was filled with an awe which almost made him shrink from the sight of that familiar face, scarcely whiter or more sunken now than it had been for many a day past. . . .'

We must have wept often over the tribulations of Little Meg, and may have been duly impressed by her Christian constancy. Were we held by anything but the pathos of the story? This strange country of dingy streets and attics (an attic perhaps I could visualize), of lack of bread and clothes, of evil and misery— it was as fairy-like as any story that I had heard—as hard to realize, but just as easy to believe. The emotions were involved, and the imagination, but nothing like reflection or reasoning. We were moved in exactly the same way, and perhaps even to a greater degree, by the adventures of Little Red Riding-hood. Both she and Meg were 'Little', and both survived the perils they encountered. When even the perils we ourselves encounter as children leave so little impression on our sensibility (just because we have no reasoning power to trace their consequences) why should the fictitious pathos of a story have more effect? The perturbations of the intellect are a danger to the instinctive basis of life; no wonder, then, that nature is wise enough to wrap us in a cocoon of insensibility, until such time as we have the power to counter intelligence with deeper intuitions.

Little Meg's attic could be visualized because we had our own attic at the top of the house. It was approached by a steep staircase just outside the nursery door. On the left, when you reached the top, were two bedrooms, partitioned off and occupied by the maids. But the rest of the space under the roof was free. One side was used for storing apples, and their musty sweetness pervaded the whole room. There were several chests and wardrobes, full of old wedding-dresses, and many other things which I do not distinctly remember. But here also was the only considerable store of books in the house, a miscellaneous collection of foxed volumes of sermons and devotional works which can have had little appeal to me, but which I pored over with an instinctive love. But two larger tomes were an inexhaustible mine of delight. They were bound volumes of the *Illustrated London News* for the year of the Great Exhibition (presumably 1850), full of the steel engravings of the period.

My lust for books was not satisfied in the attic; I soon craved for novelty. But I must have realized thus early that such a longing was a personal affair, to be fulfilled only by a personal effort. Looking round for a means to this end, I seized on the postman as the only link with the printed world. He came daily on his long pedestrian round, for if there were no letters to bring, there was always the *Yorkshire Post*. I made friends with him, and confided to him my secret desires. He was sympathetic, but his acquaintance with literature was limited. It was limited, in fact, to a lurid pink periodical called, I think, *The Police Gazette*, and this he passed on to me; but though I remember the act of reading it, it left no particular impression on me. Evidently its contents had nothing of the reality of a fairy world.

I return again and again, in retrospection, to this early untutored interest in books, for how could it have developed, in such isolation and such neglect, but for the presence of some inborn disposition. And faith in such a disposition becomes, with the growth of the personality, a controlling factor. We are only happy so long as our life expands in ever widening circles from the upward gush of our early impulses; and even love, of which the child is ignorant, is only real in so far as it is a transformation, in adolescence, of our first instinctive attachments.

12

The Musical Box

One day my father brought a delightful toy back from Northallerton: it was a small musical box which played 'For there's nae luck about the house'. But my mother, perhaps then, or perhaps shortly afterwards, when there was sufficient cause, thought the tune was ominous. My only sister was a baby then, between two and three years old. Our farm was called the Grange, and though it had no moat, this daughter was christened Mariana. Perhaps that too was ominous, for a sad song goes by her name. Mariana was fair as sunlight, and smiled to the tinkle of the musical box. And that is all I remember of her, for that spring I was suddenly sent away. A few days later my aunt told me that Mariana had become an angel, and the next time we went to Kirkdale I was taken to see the unmeaning mound that covered her body.

Apart from this fatal musical box, the only other music I ever heard in my childhood was Fiddler Dick's. Every year the young horses bred on the Farm had to be 'broken in', and this was work for a specialist, who, like the blacksmith, paid us periodical visits. Fiddler Dick was a natty little man, with a hot swarthy complexion and waxed moustaches—probably he was of gipsy blood. He would stay a few days at the Farm, sleeping in the loft above the saddle-room. He always brought his fiddle with him, and after dinner, or in the evening, used to play to a wondering audience. I was fascinated by this man—fascinated when he stood in the Cow Pasture, his neat leggings winking in the sunshine, a wild young colt galloping, trotting, walking in a circle at the end of a long rope, controlled by Fiddler Dick's flicking whip—still more fascinated when the brown fiddle came out of its box and a sound, never imagined before, was conjured out of the air. Now,

I had seen, in a chest in the attic, just such a brown fiddle, and one day when Fiddler Dick was at the Farm, I brought it down and asked him to teach me to make such music. But some of the strings were broken, and the bow had no horse-hair. Some untwisted binder-band served to repair the bow, and we got some cat-gut from the nearest cobbler for the strings. Fiddler Dick rejoiced in the word cat-gut, and cats took on a new significance for me. I cannot now believe that the sounds which issued from this improvised instrument bore any resemblance to the plaintive voice of a violin, but I retained my longing to play. Later, when I went away to school, I persuaded my mother to let me take music as an extra subject, and she consented. But I was put to the piano, which had no charm for me, no urgency of aspiration. I could not rival Fiddler Dick on such an instrument! Besides, instead of Fiddler Dick, I had for a teacher a fierce Dutchman, bristling with long hair and a silk bow-tie, flashing with rings. At the end of the year my enthusiasm had so waned that I could not urge my mother to pay the extra fees for music. But I still clung to the old violin, with the vague hope that I might one day learn to play it. It was still in my possession at the beginning of the war, but my mother died at this time, and in the subsequent confusion the violin disappeared. I had expected to find it among the few possessions I had stored in a cellar against my return, but it was not there. I should perhaps never have given it another thought but for an experience of several years later. I came late one evening, after a walk along a forest road in Bavaria, the moon staring at me through the cage bars of the trees, to a large castle where many guests were being entertained. Supper was finished and there was not a soul to be seen, except a porter who took my bag, and told me that everyone was in the music-room—even the servants— and that I had better make my way there and wait for the end. I was directed to a small balcony, which I could enter without disturbing the audience. The room was in darkness, except for an electric lamp at the far end of the room, above the dais where the music was being played. It was a violin sonata, and I was immediately held, not so much by the music as by the image which came into my mind as I gazed at the woman playing the violin. Her slender body was like a stem on which nodded, to the rhythm of the music, a strange exotic flower. The corolla of this flower was a human face, very white beneath an arch of raven black hair, and it seemed to brood over the coiled tawny petals of the instrument, preserving an essential stillness in the midst of the force that agitated them. The notes of the piano, to whose rise and fall it seemed bound in some inevitable way, might have been the voice of a stream urging its way past the resisting stem of the flower that swayed above its swift current.

All my early fascination for this instrument, awakened long before by Fiddler Dick and long dormant, awoke again at this moment with a glow in which there was no longer any sense of aspiration or self-directed interest, a fire of renunciation and surrender. Once more an early impulse had found its fulfilment, its transformation, to become a conscious interest in my life.

13

Death

These scenes of childhood end abruptly with the death of my father. In the winter of my ninth year, he was taken ill with a fever; and the house became muted and silent. Mrs. Walker, the nurse from one of the cottages by Peacock's farm, whom I have not mentioned before, but who had attended my mother in all her confinements, was called in; and our cousin the doctor came from Kirby daily. He and my father were fast friends, and when the illness became critical, all his energies were devoted to the saving of this precious life. But in vain. Rheumatic fever developed. The air of anguish in every one, my mother's tearful eyes—these were obvious even to us children. One day leeches were brought, and stood in a glass jar on a shelf in the dairy. They were black, blind and sinister. But then we were taken away. I went to Howkeld, and one night I suffered intolerable earache, so that I cried aloud, and was poulticed with onions. The pain had gone in the morning, but by my aunt's tears I knew that my father was dead. The next day I was driven back to the Farm. The blinds were drawn, everywhere it was very still, and dark. We were taken upstairs to say good-bye to my dead father. The cold wintry light came evenly through the open slats of the venetian blind. My father lay on the bed, sleeping, as he always did, with his arms on the coverlet, straight down each side of his body. His beautiful face was very white, except for the red marks on his temples, where the leeches had clung. I was told to kiss that face; it was deadly cold, like the face of Little Meg's mother.

I felt stunned, but could not comprehend my loss, nor the grief of those about me. I moved away in the unnatural stillness, walking in a living sleep. Downstairs candles were burning on a table laden with cold meat and cakes. Then we all drove to Kirkdale,

slowly over the frozen flint roads, and there a grave was ready
dug at the east end of the Church, by the side of Mariana's. The
dark cirque of fir-trees rose in the background, sighing in the
frosty wind. The bell in the grey tower clanged its toneless note.
The horses were not unyoked. Six friends of my father carried his
coffin into the ancient church, and then to the grave. The earth fell
with a hollow sound on to the lowered coffin. My mother sobbed
against my uncle's shoulder. The last amen was murmured in
that immemorial stillness, and when we had taken a last look at
the forlorn coffin, we drove back swiftly over the frozen flint
roads, horse-hooves beating clearly in the metallic air.

A few weeks later the sheep were driven into pens, the cattle
labelled, and a crowd of farmers from far and near assembled at
the Farm. A wagon was drawn out on the Green, to serve as a
platform for the auctioneer. Everything was sold, except a few
pieces of old furniture which my mother was fond of—even the
books from the attic, the sermons tied in bundles, and the two
volumes of the *Illustrated London News*. *Little Meg*, *Little Arthur*,
Evenings at Home, and *Forget-me-not* alone were left for me.

We went to stay with a cousin at the other end of the Vale, but
only for a few months. Then the elder of my two brothers and I
left for a boarding-school, far away from these scenes; my childhood, the first phase of my life, was isolated: it grew detached in
my memory and floated away like a leaf on a stream. But it
never finally disappeared, as these pages witness. Instead, as this
body of mine passes through the rays of experience, it meets
bright points of ecstasy which come from the heart of this lost
realm. But the realm is never wholly lost: it is reconstructed stage
by stage whenever the sensibility recovers its first innocence,
whenever eye and ear and touch and tongue and quivering nostril
revive sensation in all its child-godly passivity.

To-day I found a withered stem of honesty, and shelled the
pods between my thumb and finger; silver pennies, which grew
between the fragrant currant-bushes. Their glistening surfaces,
seeded, the very faint rustle they make in the wind—these sensations come direct to me from a moment thirty years ago. As they
expand in my mind, they carry everything in their widening
circle—the low crisp box-hedge which would be at my feet, the
pear-trees on the wall behind me, the potato-flowers on the patch
beyond the bushes, the ivy-clad privy at the end of the path, the

cow pasture, the fairy rings—everything shimmers for a second on the expanding rim of my memory. The farthest tremor of this perturbation is lost only at the finest edge where sensation passes beyond the confines of experience; for memory is a flower which only opens fully in the kingdom of Heaven, where the eye is eternally innocent.

PART TWO

A War Diary 1915–18

I

Introduction to the War Diary

One lives with a few familiar ideas. Two or three. By the chance of worlds and men who are encountered, one polishes them and transforms them. It takes ten years to have an idea fully one's own—about which one can talk. Naturally this is a little discouraging. But in this way man gains a certain familiarity with the beautiful face of the world. Up to that point he looked at it face to face. But then he has to step to the side to gaze at its profile. A young man looks at the world face to face. He hasn't had the time to polish the idea of death and nothingness, the horror of which, however, he has tasted.

ALBERT CAMUS. *Noces* (1950)

A young man looks at the world face to face, as Camus says, but he hasn't had the time to polish the idea of death and nothingness, the horror of which, however, he has tasted. The young man whose diary of the First World War is now resuscitated many years after the event had not had the time to polish any of his ideas. He had already encountered more than a few and one finds him turning them over in all their crudity, testing them in the turmoil of an experience that had overwhelmed him with its violence and despair. The contrariness of that experience can be imagined by anyone who has read *The Innocent Eye*, the story of a child face to face with the beautiful world. Some years later he made an attempt to contrast this age of innocence with a world that had known war and revolution, but the letters from which this diary has been abstracted were not then available to him. They are now offered as additional evidence of an experience that was to have effects fatal to any confident revival of faith in God or Man. It is all too easy to dramatize the tragedy of the generation that came of age between 1914 and

59

1918, but the events have now become cool history, too cool and impersonal to have much relevance to the heat of battle. Here the process of getting familiar with the idea of death and nothingness can be observed in all its unconscious fatality. The mind in action was unformed, which meant it was all the more pitilessly exposed to those still unfamiliar ideas, like a snail that had not yet had time to grow a shell. It is curious to observe how difficult it was for such an exposed organ of sensibility to accommodate itself to the horror of a world for the first time committed to universal destruction. In their innocence the young men of that time thought that a monstrous mistake had been made—that by accident foul gases had been released which would drift away with the dawn of peace. They were impatient to make a new world once the old world had disappeared, but they were to be deceived. The war ended, they found themselves powerless. Exhausted by their sufferings, they submitted to the fiercer energies of the old men who had watched and waited from a safe distance. It was only ten years later with the publication of a German narrative that unexpectedly caught the attention of the whole world, that we could begin to speak again of our experiences. For most of us it was then too late.

The young man we meet at the opening· of the Diary, in January 1915, had recently attained the age of twenty-one, and more recently still had been commissioned as a second-lieutenant in the infantry. He had just joined his battalion, then under canvas in a hastily improvised camp in the South of England (a country strange to him, for hitherto he had not left his native county in the North of England). He had lost both his parents and was now homeless. For two years he had been a shy and isolated student at a provincial university. He had made no friends there, but just before the outbreak of the war, or perhaps during its first weeks, he had one day plunged into a debate at the University Union on some question of public morality. He expressed an unconventional view and had found an unexpected supporter in a young student of biology, a woman of approximately his own age. It was with this almost casual acquaintance that he began to exchange letters as a relief to the otherwise intolerable loneliness of his new surroundings. As there was at first no possibility of pursuing the friendship 'face to face', the letters were given the impersonal form of a diary, and it is as such that they are presented in the following pages. No attempt has been made to soften their occasional crudity: whatever value they have is due to their authenticity. They are scrolls from a tomb and bear witness to the preoccupations of a lost generation; they may help a later generation to understand how the world they now confront with such distrust came into being.

In the years after the First World War the phrase 'a lost generation' was often on our lips. It was used emotively, of course, but it had a justification in awesome statistics. These, no doubt, are recorded in some official document, and can be looked up if the reader is curious. The diarist does not need them because he was, in a literal sense, a living witness of the slaughter, one of the few survivors. In the course of those four years he must have known, as sentient human beings, instinct with affections, aspirations and constructive purpose, several hundred young infantry men between the ages of eighteen and twenty-eight (older men, too, but this was the bracket that enclosed the great majority). Of those hundreds, at the end of the war, only a score or so were still alive. Of those that were killed, a fair proportion would have distinguished themselves in a peaceable world, as poets, painters, architects, scientists, philosophers and statesmen, or as good and simple men contributing to the health and happiness of their kind. The few that came through carried with them the knowledge of this loss; they stumbled into the post-war world like stragglers from a fallen outpost. It is to their credit that they rarely indulged in self-pity.

Such observations have been made before, and there is now no point in raking over those particular ashes. A new generation had filled the vacant places before the old had had time to count its losses. The point of this publication is rather to try and reconstruct the state of mind that could in such circumstances attempt to build a Heaven in Hell's despair. The world now seems intent on building a Hell in Heaven's despite, and, to continue with Blake's metaphor, seeketh only Self to please. The attrition of hope; the idea of death and nothingness; cruel, jealous, selfish fear; innocence and experience; shame and pride—we see how all that Blake called 'the Human Abstract' took root in the mind of the diarist.

Sympathy is needed for such an Innocent, cast into the frenzy of war with no better covering than the philosophy of Nietzsche.

He had lost his traditional faith some three years earlier—under no particular pressure other than the rampant rationalism of those days—and all the paths that opened up in the darkness of his soul (signposts that were painted with such names as Ibsen, Strindberg, Shaw, Orage) converged on this tragic German philosopher, whom he pictured (as the philosopher had intended his disciples should) as a lonely mountain spirit, a wanderer, a star-gazer, with an eagle and a serpent for his only companions. Zarathustra entered deep into his soul, so deeply that he has never wholly departed. The name of Nietzsche will be found on the first page of this diary, and the reader may wonder how it was possible, at a time when he was being proclaimed as the representative philosopher of the enemy we were fighting, for one of his disciples to enlist in the war against his nation.

This is only the first of many contradictions that will be found in the mind of this young soldier. The explanation is that it is perfectly possible, even normal, to live a life of contradictions. Was it any more absurd that a Nietzschean should fight against Germans (in any case, a race Nietzsche despised) than that a Christian should fight against his fellow-Christians? No: that is not the worst anomaly to be found in these pages. Consider rather the strange fact that this Nietzschean in arms was also a pacifist! And yet even in that matter there was no real sense of confusion in his mind. Pacificism, before 1914, was an idealistic doctrine: it had not yet been tempered by universal war, and war had not yet reached the dimensions of universal horror. Pacifism, an expendable ideal in 1914, could become a rooted conviction before the end of the war—a conviction rooted in blood-soaked soil. In 1914 it could be argued that even Nietzsche had distinguished between the saints of wisdom and her warriors. Better, of course, to aspire to sainthood; meanwhile prepare yourself by the discipline of war.

It would be wrong to give the impression that such philosophical considerations determined the youth's actions in 1914. At the outbreak of a war a man should be thankful if he can retain any kind of identity—if he can act like an individual rather than be swept down the stream of national hysteria. There was no hysteria in this case, but some excitement. There was a challenge—even Rupert Brooke's expression of it was not to be despised at the time, and there was the desire to test oneself. It could be said, to adopt a mountaineer's metaphor, that one went to war because war was there, like some unscaled peak of experience. But at the outbreak of that war no one realized the climb would be so long, so arduous, or so wasteful of the human spirit. These pages show how the disillusionment grows as the hopeless carnage prolongs itself into a third and fourth year.

His response to the challenge was so reassuring that, incredible as it came to be in later years, the young Nietzschean did for a time contemplate staying on in the Army after the war. But there was an element of desperation in this thought, as in the actual attempt to transfer to the Royal Flying Corps. The more hideous trench warfare became, the more one's gaze was lifted to those free spirits floating in the sky above the trenches. The danger of it was not in our thoughts, for that was the element we breathed every day. The swift fall of an Icarus might have seemed a romantic exit compared with ignoble death in a ditch.

The greater part of the diary is not about the ardours and endurances of the campaign (an echo of Vigny that is not intended to deceive the reader) but about the urgent blossoming of a mind still innocent and unformed (the French word *éclosion*, presumably because it is so near to the English word explosion, seems more apt). This mind, like Wordsworth's, had had a fair seed-time, and had been 'fostered alike by beauty and by fear'. There is no need to question the fearsomeness of Wordsworth's early experiences—he had witnessed certain episodes of the French Revolution; but those of an infantryman in the First World War were far more acute, and perhaps more harmful. Wordsworth had in mind some dialectic of beauty and fear, a process leading to a higher synthesis; he believed that the process was 'extrinsic', not to be deliberately planned. His intercourse with beauty 'old as creation' was unconscious; pain and fear a discipline to be calmly accepted. The beauty experienced by this young soldier in his formative years could hardly be a pure organic pleasure; nature had been blasted by gunfire, and it was only rarely, and ominously, that its influence worked on him unconsciously. The hunger for beauty was there, but it had to be satisfied by books, with difficulty acquired and precariously retained. His most extrinsic experience at this time was, oddly enough, his discovery of Henry James, an unanticipated but complete surrender to the spiritual enchantment of that writer. In a sense Henry James preserved his sanity in the worst days of the war, and it seems poetically just in retrospect that the first day of peace was spent in reading *The Sacred Fount*.

The comparison may have been made before, but it can be made again without loss of point. In 1849 Dostoevsky was arrested for complicity in a plot, and after eight months in the Peter and Paul Fortress in St. Petersburg, he was led out early one December morning to be shot. He was already on the platform awaiting execution (it is said that the rifles of the shooting squad had already been lifted) when a counter-command arrived from the Tsar. Dostoevsky was then twenty-eight, and not so innocent, but he was, in the vivid sense of the old cliché, snatched from the jaws of death, and then for four years (note the exact period) lived a life of 'complete uselessness and absurdity' in a prison in Siberia. A fair comparison with the diarist? Perhaps not. Dostoevsky had to face the certainty of death only once. In the trenches death at any time was not an immediate certainty, but a probability a hundred times enacted, and the effect was the same: a mingling of horror and gratitude. A scar was burnt into the mind that was to endure to the end of life, and with it, as in Dostoevsky's case, a new faith in humanity. After he had returned to his cell on that day of execution Dostoevsky wrote a letter to his brother which has survived. It was a joyful letter.

'My brother, I am not dejected, I have not lost courage. Life is life everywhere, life is in ourselves, not in the world that surrounds us. There will be people around me, and to be a *man* among men, and to remain a man forever, under whatever circumstances, not to weaken, not to fall, that is what life is, that is the real meaning of life. I understand all this at last. The idea has entered into my flesh and my blood! Yes, it is true, that head which created and lived in the high realm of art, which came to know the gravest demands of the spirit and was familiar with them, that head has already fallen from my shoulders. There remain only my memories and the characters I have created which have not yet assumed flesh! It is true, of course, that they will tear me apart! But I still have my heart, and this flesh and blood which will always be capable of loving and suffering and lamenting and remembering, and, after all, I shall be alive. *On voit le soleil.* . . .'

Dostoevsky had reserves of spiritual energy which the diarist was never to possess, but his reaction explains this paradox of hope in the midst of despair. It also explains his turning to the people around him, his desire to be a man among men. His revolutionary zeal had received a severe shock when, in August 1914, the workers of the world failed to act with unity and prevent a war that could bring them only misery and physical suffering. It was to receive a still severer shock when, at the end of the war, there was no universal desire to shake off the politicians and capitalists who had been the instigators and promoters of war. Obviously, as a self-confessed syndicalist, he could not have had much faith in the trade unions of his own country, but the syndicalist movement in France and Italy might have survived the war and might have led Europe towards a new social order. But in that, as in many other matters, he was to be deceived.

It would be to claim too much prescience for the diarist to suggest that the disillusionment produced by the failure of inter-national socialism in 1914, or the lack of any revolutionary intention among the decimated battalions demobilized in 1919, were immediately seen as pointers to a political future in which he could find no place. But as Camus (the only contemporary political writer apart from Silone with whom, in the years to come, he was to feel any deep sympathy) as Camus was to say, 'the great event of the twentieth century was the forsaking of the values of freedom by the revolutionary movement, the progres-sive retreat of socialism based on freedom before the attacks of Caesarism and military socialism. Since that moment a certain hope has disappeared from the world and a solitude has begun for each and every man'. A solitude without hope is to be preferred to a politics without freedom.

The reader will consequently find, in the pages of this Diary, an evolving philosophy of individualism, and alongside it, a growing sense of comradeship, of sympathy for and identity with the men with whom the individualist was sharing the experience of war. It would be a great mistake to think of that comradeship as in any sense sentimental. It was a feeling of unanimity aroused by common stresses, by common dangers. A certain amount of sifting goes on in such circumstances—the weak and the cowardly do not so much fall by the wayside: they tend to be discarded as perilous elements in a structure whose strength is measured by its weakest element. In a fighting battalion there are ways of getting rid of the undesirable elements—they can be relegated to duties at the base, they can even be sent home, and above all they are prone to sickness and even wounds (one might say, even death). At any rate, until the last months of the war, when the rate of attrition became too great, the sense of unity and of unanimity were wonderfully maintained; and this 'reality' was to have a great influence on the subsequent social attitudes of the diarist—it might explain his instinctive beliefs in small independent units of production, in guild socialism, in anarchism, in a complete rejection of any ideal that compromised human freedom.

But the sense of unity was fatefully dependent on the surrounding stress, which was womb-like in its exclusiveness, its self-sufficiency. Surprisingly, perhaps, there is little mention in the Diary of external events—politics, home affairs, the general course of the war. The Russian Revolution itself passes without a mention. It will be difficult for anyone born into a world of 'mass-communications' to realize how isolated a soldier could be, out there in Belgium or France. There were, of course, no broadcasts in those days, and no newspapers. Even a company officer would hardly know what was happening in the brigades to the right or left of him. Again the mountaineering simile is apt—each little group was isolated on some ridge of a high mountain. All it shared with the people on the other ridges of the mountain was the same storm.

When he left his isolated outpost and went back to England wounded or on leave the soldier found himself in an alien world. Siegfried Sassoon was to give perfect expression to the feelings of anger and disgust which were then experienced. Even if, as in the case of Sassoon, the committed soldier was given the opportunity to stay in this 'bitter safety', he was finally driven back by feelings of remorse and by memories of those he had left 'in the mud':

> 'Why are you here with all your watches ended?
> From Ypres to Frise we sought you in the Line.'
> In bitter safety I awake, unfriended;
> And while the dawn begins with slashing rain
> I think of the Battalion in the mud.
> 'When are you going out to them again?
> Are they not still your brothers through our blood?'

But all that comradeship was to vanish once the storm was over and the expeditionary forces (as they were significantly called) had returned to the platitudes of life—old soldiers might continue to meet at regimental reunions, battalion dinners; but they were now so many particularities, repelling each other by their different interests, different occupations, different places in the civilian hierarchy:

> *The world was not renewed.*
>
> *There was hope in the homestead and anger in the streets*
> *But the old world was restored and we returned*
> *To the dreary field and workshop, and the immemorial feud*
> *Of rich and poor. Our victory was our defeat,*
> *Power was retained where power had been misused*
> *And youth was left to sweep away*
> *The ashes that the fires had strewn beneath our feet.*

A few may for a moment have thought of forming a militant League of Ex-Combatants, of making this a political and revolutionary unit in the post-war scene. But they were quickly disillusioned. Some went back to the mines, some to the factories; a few tried to build a new life in countries not fouled by war. The majority—the diarist himself!—sought security and marriage and *bourgeois* comforts. In their new habitats they met, if ever they met again, as released animals who had returned to the jungle to take on the colours of a familiar environment. In spite of all those days of danger and of joy shared together, they were now strangers to each other, and would suddenly feel embarrassed and dismayed.

It was perhaps always an illusion to think that the sense of unity and comradeship that had been forged in the heat of battle (the rhetorical metaphor has some relevance) could survive in days of peace. Losing this illusion these demobilized particles lost the basis for their political ideals. They may have thought of the unity and comradeship of a battalion at the Front as a paradigm for the factory and the workshop. But except possibly in the coal-mines, or on board a ship, the same external pressures did not exist: the womb had no walls. Instead just an aimless centrifugal search for more space, for more comfort, for a 'standard of living'. The Trade Unions that, transformed into Guilds, were to be the revolutionary agents of a new world, returned to a profitable strife with employers and the State. The State itself increased its power, and the free individual, the Nietzchean Superman, disappeared like a chimera in the darkness. This naked warrior, the diarist, became a civil servant.

More than forty years later young intellectuals are still discussing the problems that were for the first time found urgent in 1919. They are worried by the failure of a democratic way of life to raise the general level of culture. 'Mass culture', they begin to realize, is an illusion. Culture cannot be imposed on 'the people'; culture remains obstinately of the 'minority', if not of the individual. Society remains a patchwork of divided minds however desperately we try to hide the seams. All social and political developments since the First World War, not excluding the revolutions in Russia and China and elsewhere, have done nothing to deprive the intellectual of his intellectuality—by which we mean his private sensibility, his uniqueness, his exclusivity. Comradeship, alas, does not create culture—it is a sense of mutuality in alien circumstances. It is incompatible with comfort.

The last pages show the diarist making contact with those fellow-intellectuals with whom he was to be associated for the next ten or fifteen years. Not many of them had experienced the war in all its immediacy—for those who had, such as Richard Aldington and Wyndham Lewis, he was to feel a sympathy which for a time disguised a lack of any common ground. No intellectual movement emerged which had any basis in the experience of war. The cultural achievement of those years, which was real enough, by-passed the war. Its founders—Joyce, Pound, Eliot—were men who had taken no direct part in the fighting. The two experiences —to live in action and to live in meditation—are forever incompatible.

From the point of view of later generations, our submission was to seem like a retreat into futility. But what were the practical alternatives? Political faith and action could not be evoked in England, for reasons which the Diary makes clear. In a general way the achievements of communism might be admired but the cost in human freedom could not be condoned. The ends could never justify the means. What was left? The return to capitalist enterprise, and the welfare state as an antidote to revolution? These, it is true, have been less costly than communism, have offered less affront to the moral sensibility; but another world war with all its casualties had to be waged in their defence, and all our ideals of social security now rest precariously on the edge of nihilism. There are no values in our present welfare world to justify the surrender of ideals that had been proved in the stress of warfare—leadership, comradeship, unanimity, poverty, austerity, endurance, gaiety, fearlessness and fatalism. And where, and where only, do we find *all* these virtues celebrated? The diarist could only whisper: *in Nietzsche!* but that name was now taboo.

The great task of humanity, now that 'God is dead', is, as Nietzsche was the first to realize, the conquest of nihilism. The world has not made much progress in that direction since his famous announcement. God has not risen again from the dead, and the ideal of the Superman that was to replace him has been vulgarized by barbarians like Mussolini and Hitler. Nihilism—nothingness, despair, and the nervous hilarity that goes with them—remains the universal state of mind. From such an abyss the soul of man does not rise in a decade or two. If a human world survives the atomic holocaust—and it is now difficult to see how such a holocaust is to be avoided—it will only be because man has first overcome his Nihilism. A few prophets have already pointed the way—Gandhi, Buber, Simone Weil, C. G. Jung—but the people are also few who pay heed to them. Spiritually the world is now one desert, and prophets are not honoured in it. But physically it still has a beautiful face, and if we could once more learn to live with nature, if we could return like prodigal children to the contemplation of its beauty, there might be an end to our alienation and fear, a return to those virtues of delight which Blake called Mercy, Pity, Peace and Love.

1962

2

Extracts from a Diary

28.i.15   Wareham, Dorset
I am in very uncongenial surroundings here.

I thought perhaps Karl Marx's Materialistic Interpretation of History developed in *Das Kapital* would also support the theory,* but I have not had time to read Marx yet. The book I am most indebted to is Professor Loria's *Economic Foundations of Society* which is in the University Library.

I am beginning to suspect that Nietzsche's appeal to me is largely poetical. Nevertheless I think he is a fine stimulus. Just before I came away I was trying to reconcile his idea of the Superman with Democracy. Democracy always seems to me to be lacking in ideals. If we could graft on to it the idea of a Super-*race*.

As to his attack on Democracy, it must be remembered that it is the sentimental Christian Socialism that he chiefly attacks—though his position is untenable. It is a divine rage rather than a reasoned argument.

Here Nietzsche and all divine heretics seem like a dream. The only compensation this life offers is that it brings me into direct contact with a class of men I wanted to know. They are a rough lot—mostly miners from Durham and Middlesbro'. And how different they are from the newspaper fiction. I don't think one per cent. are here for spiritual motives. They are always grumbling about their food and pay and I must say I sympathize with them. Their food is disgusting. Most of them make allowances to their wives or mothers and so only get 3*s*. a week pay. And these are men who have earned as much as 10*s*. a day. The huts they live

* I had written an essay entitled 'An Economic Interpretation of Morality.'

in are filthy. If we get away before an epidemic breaks out I shall be surprised. The attitude of the average officer to them is overbearing and supercilious. My position as one of these little, homage-receiving gods is very quixotic . . .

Yesterday I had to take the names of men in my platoon who had weak eyes. There were several. It appears that the weakness is caused by staring at molten steel. One man had been blind for a week. Our civilization again!

6.iii.15

I don't think I am satisfied with the tendency of modern Democracy. Though it is a fine ideal in that it strives for the Utilitarian principle of the greatest happiness of the greatest number, yet it offers no encouragement to the development of the personality of the individual. It will ensure happiness, but scarcely nobility. It will be fatal to even a spiritual superman. Surely its essential affirmation should be *man's right to choose*. And surely the results of Democracy which we already see are the negation of this right (the Insurance Act, for example). Perhaps my dissatisfaction arises from the fact that, though in economics I am a communist, in ethics I think I am an individualist. Are these two creeds incompatible?

What would be the virtue of the super-race to which I wish democracy to aspire? I am afraid I cannot give a very satisfactory answer. I can't even decide what Virtue is. We Atheists must get away from the salvation-or-damnation test of Christianity. We must find a new test—a religion of human perfectibility. My own ideal is aesthetic rather than ethical. I don't desire a world of saints. Nor do I worship a Nietzschean tyrant. More I cannot say, except that the highest expression of virtue that I know of is found in the last lines of Shelley's 'Prometheus'—emphasis being laid on Hope and Defiance.

24.vi.16*   Rugeley Camp, Staffordshire
I came to this dreadful place a week ago. The Medical Board gave me 'light duty'—but they don't understand the term here. We get up at 5.30 a.m. and are at it till tea time and sometimes

---

* In the interval of fifteen months I had been to the Front. I was accidentally wounded in March, 1916, and returned to England for twelve months. For a reference to this intervening experience see pages 213–4.

later. And all the time the same monotonous work—shouting oneself hoarse, trying to initiate remarkably dense recruits into the mysteries of 'forming fours', etc. I think I shall flee to the Front for a little peace at the earliest opportunity.

I've got something you *must* read—Bernard Shaw's preface to *Androcles and the Lion*, just published. It is, I think, the last word on Christianity, and one of the best things Shaw has ever written.

Sorel I must tell you all about sometime. He is very fine—certainly the most important Socialist writer since Marx. He is really the philosopher of Syndicalism and his theories are positively exciting.

I get the *New Age* every week. It is the exponent of Guild Socialism—of which more later.

17.vii.16   Rugeley Camp, Staffordshire

I don't know whether you would be interested in this life of mine here. I don't think I am a sympathetic enough critic to give it the faintest tinge of glamour. I have hated the Army as such ever since the first day I knew it. And my hate grows rather than diminishes. Not that I am bitter about it. There is so much to amuse one in a quiet way. But to be the dumb pawn of any fool who happens to be your senior, is a position that anyone with any decent will of his own must needs find irksome. But of course there are compensations—above all that delightful camaraderie which, I suppose, is peculiar to a fighting Army, and which is something finer and manlier than anything I experienced either at School or College.

This place is made more hateful by the fact that we have for a Colonel one of the most unpleasant and objectionable men I ever met, or hope to meet. On the other hand I have made one or two good friends (of the transient kind).

I have a jolly little cubicle which I share with one of these friends. Naturally we make it cosy (as only *men* can). Carpets, curtains, easy chairs—everything complete. Our walls are adorned with the most select pictures (including some of my own futurist efforts, which cause no little sensation, and, I must confess, a good deal of scorn and amusement). And of course I have my book-shelf: I had one in the trenches.

I'm afraid the *New Age* is rather poor just now—several of its best writers are busy in the Army. But it is the only paper I know that is full of fresh ideas; and it is absolutely fearless and independent in its criticisms.

One great joy we have at this place. That is a really decent Band. And what is more, a first class string orchestra. Don't be afraid that I'm one of those terrible people who scorn everyone save Bach and the 'scientific' musicians. I think my musical appreciation is purely emotional. Beethoven, Mozart, Chopin—such are my favourites. Wagner I do *not* like, generally speaking.

By the way, I've been to France and back since I last wrote. I took a draft out to the Base and had a most enjoyable trip. We went via Folkestone and Boulogne. Then on to Etaples, which is the Base. Coming back I spent a day in Boulogne which I think is quite a decent place. It has old walls, like York, but prettier.

31.vii.16   Rugeley Camp, Staffordshire

I think a pessimistic attitude is essential to all clear thinking. By a pessimistic attitude I mean a realization of the imperfections and limitations of Man. The belief in the 'divinity' of mankind has resulted in all that false idealism and romanticism which is the curse of literature, philosophy and art.

And now I want to know what on earth you mean by 'the essence of XXth Century'. It is evidently something terrible, and I should have taken you to mean all the false idealism and romanticism I mentioned above had you not called it the 'essence' (which surely means the refined and rare), and had you not given G.B.S. as a representative of the monster. You must reconsider 'the essence of XXth Century'.

In philosophy you will find Bergson and Croce; a new school of Anti-Humanists; a new individualism. In political science you will find Sorel and his theories; also a new objective conception of the State (represented in England by that *negative* journal—the *New Age*). In Art you will find the Post-Impressionists and Futurists (on whom I am tremendously keen). In Literature Henry James and the Imagist Poets. All this, believe me, is the essence of XXth century and something not to be lightly dismissed.

And now for your attack (or rather agreement with an attack) on Hardy and Meredith. I don't give either of them wholesale admiration, but I refuse to have them condemned on the flimsy grounds of morbidity. In the case of each writer there is one book which you can take as representative of the good in them. Hardy's

Jude the Obscure. Here you have an absolutely faultless presentation of the animal in mankind (and remember the animal is latent in us all); and also, in the character of Jude, a presentation of the finer aspirations of mankind. And in the heroine you have, it seems to me as a mere man, one of the finest female characters ever conceived.

And besides, in all of Hardy's novels, there is a fine pagan spirit which you must admire—a revelation of the essential cruelty of nature, and of the damning blight of religious creeds.

As to Meredith, the book I take as representative is *The Egoist.* Here you have, I think, the finest synthesis and analysis of character yet achieved in fiction. The figure of Willoughby is a superb satire: and this we can say in spite of the fact that we know Willoughby to be one's self (that is, the essence of man). Perhaps his women are rather artificial, but I think Clara, Diana and Rhoda Fleming are assured of as much immortality as any women, fictitious or otherwise.

But if you really want the best of modern fiction, you must read Henry James. Here I do give my unqualified admiration. I 'discovered' him only about a year ago, but since then I have read him almost continuously and have never tired and have a feeling that I never shall. His is a blending of the finest style with the subtlest psychology. One feels that not one of his characters is false: and the only possible criticism I can make is that he is far too indifferent to the 'problems' of life: he is purely an observer. But this, from an aesthetic point of view, is an advantage.

I don't know if all this is boring you. I will another time, if you like, pull the Wells-Bennett school to pieces. Also give you my own ideas on the novel. For I am going to attempt one as soon as this beastly war is over.

15.viii.16   Rugeley Camp, Staffordshire

I believe our difference about Pessimism is merely terminological. My pessimism does not deny all effort or defeat all hope—there never was such a hopeful and ambitious soul as this (of course ambitious in the spiritual sense—I don't care a damn for worldly regard). This pessimism sees life at its real worth *and accepts it as such.* It does not look on the world with the rose-coloured spectacles of optimism—for some day the fierce light of the sun will crack the glasses and your mind will be full of misery and disappointment. And it does realize the possibilities of man—but in realizing the possibilities of man don't we at the same time admit present imperfections? My old friend Nietzsche was a pupil of Schopenhauer and a pessimist of the first water; but there never lived such a prophet of the noble and enthralling possibilities of man.

'Why on earth' I call my attitude 'pessimism' is because, I suppose, that is the philosophical term for it. We call the Greek philosophers pessimists—but not because they were gloomy (they were anything but that) but simply because they considered man 'worse' than the gods—and not, like the modern Utilitarian or Christian, essentially divine.

This leads me naturally on to the next subject upon which I desire to 'hold forth'—Romanticism. Romanticism is—in literature—the confusion of the human with the divine. Now you can regard the divine as merely an abstract idea, or as 'an atmosphere, ubiquitous yet intangible', or as something very real and omnipresent; but whatever you do you must not imagine for a moment that man is a constituent of it. The divine is something objective and absolute, and we poor mortals should strive to serve it. Once you regard the divine as something subjective, something within one as a matter of course, then you get all the absurd sentimentality and romanticism that vitiates all literature since the Renaissance. Anything scientifically analytic or artistically synthetic is practically non-existent in Literature.

The same, and for the same reasons, applied to Painting and Sculpture, till we got the Neo-Realists.

And of course you see the same false spirit in Idealism in Philosophy, and in Christianity.

Someone described a Romantic as a person who didn't believe in the Fall of Man and Original Sin.

By the way, neutrality is the worst and most cowardly of attitudes. Hasn't every question a right and a wrong? If you are neutral you are never right, even if sometimes you avoid being wrong. Remember Nietzsche: A yea, a nay, a straight line, and a goal.

I must tell you about Sorel and the New Socialism, and, if you have the slightest interest in the matter, the *raison d'être* of Post-Impressionism and Futurism in Art: but just now I want to deal with a most heinous offence you have committed against all the canons of intellectual decency. You suggest you are possessed of a 'Puritan'. I suspect a Philistine. You seem to imagine that it is the aim or object of Literature to give moral instruction to its generation! Do, for heaven's sake, assure me you don't mean this. The 'purely literary standpoint' is all that matters not only in Literature, but in Life. Or to put it more generally, Art is the redemption of Life. Only through esthetic emotions can we experience that which is exquisite in Life. Only thus can we cultivate our souls (and not our minds). Only thus can we approach the Divine—only thus become immortal. There you have my creed! I stand or fall by it.

27.viii.16   Rugeley Camp, Stafford

I find our differences crystallized in one sentence of your last letter—'And though one must agree that man is not a constituent of the divine (who has said he is?) surely you agree that the divine is one of the constituents of man?' I don't agree anything of the sort. *Man is a constituent of the divine. The divine is not a constituent of man.* There you have my creed plain enough. Read, mark, and learn: and call yourself a pessimist.

Apart from names I believe I have as much zest for life as you. I regard it as a great heroic fight—a challenge to be accepted with laughter and song. Besides which there is all the intense joy in the beauty of things and in the love of persons. And I can live untroubled by the thoughts of an 'After'—gloomy thoughts at the best. The only immortality that troubles me is the immortality to be created in 'things of beauty, joys for ever'. That immortality achieved, I shall be happy when 'the stars are setting, and the Caravan, Starts for the Dawn of Nothing'.

I am a happy exultant Pessimist!

I quite agree with you that only they who stand alone, stand firm. I think you rather mistake my meaning in venturing to put faith in an individual. I don't mean to pin my faith in life upon any person. But in the social relations of individuals I know that there can be bonds which strengthen one's mental fibre. And I have a craving for such a bond. That's all. What you say on this subject makes me think you might agree with my Individualism. L. calls it rank Egoism. But I have a conviction that it is the only true faith. I believe that it is much more important to cultivate the individual than the mass. That individual development is of more supreme urgency than social development. And this belief I base on the fact that you must recognize that, in the past, individuals have been the determinant influences in all save transient events. Great philosophies and great works of art are not the products of an age or of a civilization. They are rather the individual revolt against an age or a civilization. This being the fact we must look for enlightenment and progress in the creation of a higher individual. That means that our own personal efforts should be in the direction of self-realization and self-development. One must love one's self. Of course, this is Egoism. But I'm not ashamed of it. For I am convinced that only in this way can mankind be brought to any kind of a realization of the divine.

Did you read that letter of Huntly Carter's in this week's *New Age*? The Regionalism he talks about seems to me to be the political expression of my Individualism. It certainly appeals to me strongly—especially when it deals with the association of character and natural environment. Besides, it fits in with my anarchical *tendencies*.

I will start again—or rather finish. I've just returned from the Colonel's farewell tea party. You said some time ago, when I told you how everyone detested the man, that probably he had a nice side to his character. You were quite right. He has a charming wife, a nice house and garden and—a baby! And in these surroundings even he seemed charming.

I've got a wonderful little book—*The Freudian Wish**—the pathology of thought, etc. Also a fine volume of poems by D. H. Lawrence.

2.X.16   Rugeley Camp, Staffordshire

Amusement seems to be the only emotion my 'art' inspires in others—excepting, of course, in the initiates. So may I explain the enclosed Manifesto.†

Firstly, the Designs. I see no reason why decorative art should not be as abstract as music. (But I don't imply that *all* decorative art should be abstract.) In any picture there are two elements of supreme value: design and colour. Design may or may not be suggested by nature. It should never be a slavish copy of nature—

---

* By Edwin B. Holt (London, 1915).

† A manuscript brochure of poems, with abstract decorations.

photography is good enough for that. If design is suggested by nature, it should aim at expressing some unity or vitality observed by the artist in nature. This is most expressively done by symbols invented by the artist. Symbols are generally a simplification of the natural object: e.g. hair is represented by flat brushes of paint, instead of each separate hair being painted.

If design is not suggested by nature, it may be just an aesthetic fantasy of the artist, as, for example, a Persian carpet. Or it may be an aesthetic representation of an idea. The design on the front of this little book is a pattern representing the emotional contest of my soul. *Perhaps* you will be able to divine suggestive form in it.

Colour, the second element in a picture, is more personal than design. It is harmony as interpreted by the artist's temperament. Now, colour in nature is not always harmonious. Red roofs would clash with bright green grass and a blue sky. It is the artist's duty to harmonize the colours of nature. A shadow in nature may be turgid and interfere with the colour scheme: so the artist is at perfect liberty to paint the shadow a cool lilac. Everywhere the artist must *interpret* and not copy.

Colour in abstract pictures is a pure harmony thought out by the artist.

The decoration on the back of the booklet is not abstract, being suggested by the play of sunlight on a flower. It is not particularly good, I'm afraid.

And now for the 'poems', if I may call them such. Here my aim is to express an emotion felt by me with the object of inducing that emotion in the sympathetic reader. Now that is an extremely difficult thing to do with words, which are not definite enough to express exactly our ideas. It is much simpler to do in music. But music needs an interpreter; so the poem is, if a more difficult, a more direct medium. To express an emotion one must be *exact*: one must use the exact word and not the merely decorative word ('man' is more expressive than 'wight') or the word that may happen to rhyme but does not exactly express the idea. Hence rhyme and mere prettiness disappear from the essentials of Poetry.

There is another element of Poetry—Rhythm. Here again the rhythm must express the emotion. The emotion may vary in quantity (intensity) as the poem proceeds—in a long poem the emotion may completely change. Hence a hard and fast rule or law of rhythm is impossible. The rhythm must harmonize with the idea expressed: even as the melody is varied in a musical symphony.

There are two degrees of success in Poetry. One may express emotion artistically: and in so doing, one may cause an emotion in the reader. The latter, of course, is the greater success. And if a poem does that it is as immortal as the emotion aroused. But that is seldom done, and for that reason, Poetry may be regarded as the severest and therefore the highest form of art. It is relatively easy to induce emotion by a picture or a melody.

The nobler the emotion induced the greater the work of art.

> *The noblest emotion is the joy in abstract beauty.*
> *And, of course, beauty is truth.*

There I think you have my artistic creed.

The *New Age* has accepted another article of mine—a diary of a soldier at the Front. Here's a confession—I have started my first Novel—very passionately psychological.

Farnley Park, Otley

Let me begin my discourse with a parable. Once upon a time when I was a little, little boy (so long ago!) I lived in an old and lonely farmhouse. Up some narrow and creaking stairs there was a big dark garret. I would creep up those stairs with a thumping heart and enter that garret with fearful eyes, ready at any moment to spring back with a cry of fear. How that garret to me was full of mystery and unimaginable things! But sometimes my mother or one of the servants would be there and I would enter more boldly. And soon I discovered that the garret was full of wonderful things—old books and old pictures, the Dolly Vardens and crinolines of a past generation, and a big heap of green apples. These treasures tempted me and I began to know them and their home, the garret. The garret became my refuge and no longer a place of mystery and an object of fear. *For I knew it.* And so life— 'the mystery which surrounds us on all sides—the millions of possibilities which may exist outside the range of our consciousness . . . it still frightens me at intervals'—isn't life like that garret and isn't its mystery to be dissipated by knowledge? And if there still (after all our researches) remains the Inexplicable, must we not put it down to our ignorance, to the limited range of our perception, and not make of it a fear-inspiring God.

21.xii.16   Rugeley
   I have been told to expect orders for France very soon.

29.xii.16   Rugeley Camp
   I am in a condition such as demands amusement as a cure: that is, I am an invalid—though not a despondent one. I have been struggling with the demon of bronchitis for more than a week (he was with me last Sunday and must have made me rather a dull fellow). The demon conquered in the end and we're now good bedfellows. Don't imagine that I desire or deserve a scrap of condolence—I rather look for envy: An excellent little servant to attend to my every need: a Scotch cook who, despite her scorn of my vegetarian proclivities—which I thought sickness might excuse—is otherwise ideal: a stove which, although it sometimes smokes out of the wrong end, is nevertheless nice and warm: an easy chair—a dressing-gown and Meredith at his best (in *One of our Conquerors*)—and all this in my fashionably furnished 'studio'. Did I ever describe the latter? 15′ × 12′. Floored with antique matting—Greek couch (some people call it a camp-bed)—my walls decorated with a series of Japanese prints, three charcoal sketches of Watteau's, two of Whistler's, three or four of my own productions (note the conceited company I keep), a shelf of books, an oak table, a writing table and a few photographs of friends. Add to this a tapestried dado of discarded coats (etc.) drooping in languorous attitudes around the room and you get a *tout ensemble* that makes an illness Elysium!

23.i.17   Brocton Camp, Stafford
   I've a theory that all the evil things in the world are static, passive and possessive; and that all the good things are dynamic, creative. Life is dynamic: death is static. And as life is dynamic, passive remedies of society are false. Hence the folly of having cut and dried Utopias as ultimate aims; by the time you get to them life has left them behind. Hence the folly of basing society on possessive institutions (such as property and marriage, as a rule). Our institutions should appeal to our creative impulses: what a man *does* and not what he *has*.

Of course all these arguments might be used as a defence of war. But war is a tragic paradox: it destroys that which it should preserve. To any right-minded person life is sacred: so that the question of war becomes a question of values: is such an ideal *which can only be attained by war*, of more value than life? Modern war is largely actuated by economic aggression. And that 'ideal' can hardly be compared with life. But a war for justice, for liberty, he who loses his life in such a war shall find it.

I am glad you liked 'The Altar of the Dead'. I had a letter yesterday from my uncle, who is between 50 and 60, and to whom I introduced Henry James. In it he said: 'I am glad to know you think of James as your "Master". You could follow no nobler. When I feel sad I read a little of his Altar of the Dead, and the quiet beauty of it floods my soul like a benediction.'

Don't think that James is uniformly so sad. He isn't: some of his books are the most amusing comedy ever written. Last week I added two more volumes to my collection of his Tales. I must have nearly twenty now.

What is the soul—if any? Is it mortal or immortal? If the latter, why so? I've been reading Plato's 'Phaedo' lately and so I'm rather full of the subject: though I must confess I find it hard to formulate a definite opinion. I don't agree with all Plato's arguments. They altogether neglect our modern theories of evolution. I'm inclined to give a high moral value to the soul; but I cannot see any probability of immortality. And intuition doesn't help me in the matter, either. It would be rather a joke if I have to confess myself a materialist!

14.ii.17   Brocton Camp, Stafford

Thank you for the criticisms of my 'yarn'. I've adopted nearly all your suggestions—and, I think, improved not a little. I've rechristened it as 'A Glimpse of the Garden' ('for adventure, you know, is the garden of life'). The old title was rather violent.

As to the opening balance and your charge of inconsistency— If I had left out the suggestion of energy—the hopping leaves and the glistening dew—I think I should have had too much of a monotone. Besides, I always want to convey a sense of life in the most somnolent of nature's scenes. I also wanted an autumnal atmosphere right thro' the tale—one must have an atmosphere of some sort, and autumn seemed to harmonize best.

You say you would like to see a similar thing written from the inside—and that such a method would be more convincing. Of course, it is the old controversy as to whether the subjective or the objective method is the better. You will find that the one you want—the subjective method—is little used by good writers today. I think that is because it has been found too limited—both for analysis and synthesis. In the objective method you get a much better chance of focusing a character into its right relation to environment—you can correlate. In the subjective method you look at everyone and everything through the same particularly coloured glasses. But I wouldn't say that the subjective method is played out by any means. I doubt if it would be more difficult—assuming both done well.

Enclosed you will find my criticisms of two articles and I think from them you will manage to get at my ideas about ART. I'm afraid I take these ideas pretty seriously—at any rate I've none to which I'm more anxious to convert you. You say that conversion is a bad thing between us—because it puts an end to discussion. But I don't think this objection applies here. You see Art is, to my mind, a thing of such fundamental value that it should colour one's whole outlook on life. It gives the World a fuller richness, a greater spiritual value; and to the individual it gives a sense of joy in things. Allied to love, it is a complete philosophy of Life. Love gives us the fellowship of our species: Art unites us with something vaster—with the whole cosmic process. Love teaches us the beauty of Man: Art reveals the beauty of Life. This I believe deeply, and I should count myself happy if through me you came to believe it too. Then I think we should find a finer affinity in many things.

I rather think your difficulty has something to do with your democratic idealism. You think of Art in terms of Democracy. But you can't do that. No one is a more convinced *social* democrat than I am. But it seems to me Art and Thought are essentially aristocratic things. They are the product of the finest senses and the finest brains. G. K. Chesterton defends Christianity on the grounds that that Religion which is the Religion of the majority and the average is on that account the true religion. But this argument 'with one fell swoop' destroys every incentive to progress, whether in Religion or Philosophy. Why aspire to a nearer truth, a nobler thought, a finer Art if all such progress is to be condemned if it be unacceptable to mediocrity. No: great art and true religion are for us if we can lift ourselves up to their plane. They never descend to the level of ordinary men.

This may sound priggish, but it isn't if you believe—as I do—that every man has in him, given freedom and a clean environment, the capacity to travel a long way into these aristocratic realms of Thought and Art.

Did you notice in the *New Age* mention of a paper called *The Guildsman*. I sent them an article on 'The World and the Guild Idea' and they have accepted it for the April number. It is rather ambitious, dealing with World Peace and the future (or rather absence of future) of the State.

My delightful military picnic here passes like lightning. Only another three weeks! And then France—I expect, and I think I hope.

28.ii.17   Brocton

I've finished *The History of the Fabian Society* and I now return it to you with many thanks for the pleasure it has given me.

One can't criticize the *History* as such—it is all that an history should be. But I have a few remarks to make about the Fabian Society.

Of course, in its inception it was ideal. One couldn't exaggerate the magnificence of its pioneer work. It's like the inspired beginning of a religion. But it wasn't to last for ever. I don't know when the change crept in—with the advancing age of the founders, I suspect. But the change did creep in and was quite evident in the Wells episode, if not before. Wells really wanted them to *lead* the coming Socialist régime. They preferred the critical position of interested spectators. And after that they ever remained critical spectators—still, I admit, of tremendous value. But the inspiration, which always is found in the van of any movement, had left them.

And once bereft of inspiration, they rapidly became a society of intellectual fogies. They became, to use one of your words, 'stodgy'. Their imagination no longer flowed with the life-stream of the Socialist movement. This has become acutely apparent within these last few years. A new spirit came from France with the propaganda of Syndicalism. Now Syndicalism has many faults, but one thing it does possess in no negligible quality—that is intellectual vitality. Then was the Fabian's chance—to drink in this new vitality. They absolutely denied it as a Society. And in doing so signed their death warrant.

But not all of them, thank God. Orage, Cole, S. G. Hobson and others broke away and through the medium of the *New Age* developed the theory of Syndicalism—i.e. assimilated it to *their* Fabianism. Result—Guild Socialism.

G.B.S., in his appendix on Guild Socialism, says that so long as the emphasis is on the Socialism and not on the Guild, then Guild Socialism is, for all practical purposes, identical with Fabian Socialism. But the emphasis is most distinctly on the Guild. Then, says the dear old gentleman, all bosh! And that is precisely because his imagination is decadent—his inspiration gone. Pease rather pathetically admits, in the last chapter, the coming of a new generation with which the old generation is out of sympathy. And so the old generation must go—it is the law of progress. Fabianism is dead—long live Guild Socialism!

But in our youthful confidence we don't forget that it is the Fabian Society that has made us possible: so let us still honour them, so long as we don't get priggish about it. And so long as we don't take them too seriously.

16.iii.17   Brocton

Before we break up, I *must* describe to you Our Society—à la mode de Richard Steele.

Understand then that we are twelve in number and live in a wooden hut situated upon a high waste land. We are all of an amiable disposition and have dwelt in harmonious fellowship for a period of two months—and this despite the fact that one half of us belong to that argumentative race of Scotland. But so diverse are our individual characteristics that any general description would be inadequate. So you must bear with me whilst I parade my gallery of portraits.

I would place first in our Society a member who is the proud possessor of two names, given him by us in our corporate capacity of Godparent. His name used to be Bill Snowden, but that was given him by a world we've forgotten. So we call him 'Philip'. This he understands, knowing but not admiring the politician of that name. But his other name is a mystery to him—I believe he thinks it Greek or Japanese. (One of our Society, who in his spare time reads a Greek 'Thucydides', successfully deluded 'Gunga Din' —for that is his other name—into a belief that he is reading Japanese.) Well, Gunga is one of those old soldiers of the song, who never die. He is the proud possessor of 23 years service (in the ranks) and the Order of St. George of Russia. He is a pragmatic philosopher—on occasions. These occasions are induced— by liberal libations of 'Scotch', of which he can *safely* absorb amazing quantities. When 'induced' he is excessively polite and solicitous. He will come in from the Mess at a late hour and from his pocket produce two flasks and two soda-water bottles full of 'neat'. One of these he will reverently hand round—'just a wee deoc an doris'—the remainder he stows away in his gumboots— for use in the night watches. Then he begins to philosophize— making use of an immoderate experience. In the writer he takes a truly paternal interest and often comes and sits on his bed to give him 'the benefit'. His philosophy consists of two principles— variously enunciated. The first is: 'Keep your right fist there!'— 'there' being in front of your own nose. That one can promise to do to the best of one's ability. But the second principle is rather more complex: 'Get the right girl and stick to her through thick and thin!' And then a long disquisition on the happiness his 'wee wifey' has brought him—and all the rosy side of matrimony . . . I promise—my head is patted, and my bed, perilously creaking, is saved once more.

Next in our Society is the Philosopher proper—a Scotch metaphysician. He has studied Philosophy and Divinity for many years at the University of Edinbro' and, having exhausted their curriculum, did cross the seas to Germany, and became profound in the University of Jena. To his knowledge add a truly native capacity for argument and you can imagine the rest. He delights to spend an hour or so defining a definition. But he is modern in spirit and wonders if his prospective Church (Presbyterian) offers him enough latitude. His ideas on immortality are immodest. But this description conveys little of his charm. A truly noble generosity distinguishes him, as does a clean mind and a deep perception.

Yet another Heelander is our Bonny Purple Hetherington. Though youthful, a year of campaigning in France has left him with a gouty physique and a consequent choleric disposition— employed, however, in defence of our mutual geniality.

Vanity is personified in another of the same clan. His kilt and

85

his sporran, his M.C. and the 'fine figure of a man' he is, are all so disposed as to delight the fair frail ones—and not unsuccessfully, I believe.

Then there's The Hen—another Scotsman! The poise of his head—with a bonnet on the top of it for a comb, his very henny eyes, his henny legs, his hennier walk—they make us scream. But he comes fra Aberrrdin 'Varsity and has 'opinions' and has been known to vote in our Debates for a very debatable Socialist we have in our Society.

Another member is The Elephant—so named for his immense stature, and his throwing about of the same. He is gifted with uncommon sarcasm, but good-natured withal.

There's a 'Keptin' who is married to a Belgian refugee and 'lives out'. But he puzzles our unsophisticated views of matrimony by a wife-denying love of our Society—especially when Bridge is on the programme. And he has a curious habit of coming every Sunday to dine with us—'for a walk'. But where does the wifey walk? . . .

There are three 'mutes'—Rabbit, Uncle and Karl Marx. But Uncle is not altogether inglorious. Sometimes he abuses that most excellent thing—wine. And then he is transformed, and finds it very funny to hurl chairs at unoffending members of our Society. We let him amuse himself awhile, and then quietly, but very forcibly, put him to bed. He has some most original curses.

Karl Marx is the most unsociable member of our community. 'Tis he who finds joy in a Greek Thucydides.

Another 'mute' is Sir Henry Irving—original in that he is the recipient of innumerable letters. He must be one of those 'lonely subalterns'.

25.iii.17   Brocton

When I was asked to open a debate on 'The Personality of God'—not believing in a God, I was in a difficulty, for I did not wish to miss the fun. So I managed to express opinions on an Impersonal God, which, if accepted, virtually denied the idea of God in any accepted sense.

I have lost the basic belief of my old pessimism—a belief in the doctrine of original sin. And for these reasons. Firstly, as Edward Moore* has shown, because it is inconsistent with any faith in the

*Edwin Muir, who wrote under this name in the *New Age*.

future of Man, and the latter I possess strongly. Secondly because it really implies a denial of mental evolution. Original sin postulates a permanent static spiritual condition of the human mind: which in its turn postulates a permanent static condition of the physical constitution of the brain: which in its turn does not agree with experience. At any rate, away with Original Sin and all the heresies it involves.

As for Ethics, it seems to me that the only test of a moral rule is: Does it work? Virtue is, as Plato would say, Knowledge— i.e. knowledge of the attendant consequences of our actions and the resulting discrimination. Innocence was the primitive virtue, and so far as it exists, is still a virtue. But alas! our species has become rather sophisticated.

We agree on Immortality. That which is a creation of environment (internal and external) must dissolve when its material foundation becomes extinct. What we rather vaguely call the soul seems to me to be merely mind plus the will to live differentiated into personalities by physical formation and experience. Something highly complex and spiritual—the fount of all our capacity for beauty and goodness, but human in its continuity as in its capacity.

It is splendid of you to rally to the *New Age*. I know it is not uniformly interesting, but it keeps up a high level of ideals and is never lacking in originality. I was beginning to wonder how I'd manage to send it you when I get to France—if I ever do get there before the end of the war. There's no news yet. But I'm not exactly impatient. I've got several nice books to read, and they're more important than fighting.

Here's a big lump of amusing swank. I am exhibiting half a dozen of my weird drawings at the Grafton Galleries, London, in June. The occasion is the annual exhibition of the Allied Artists Association, which is a sort of Artists Trade Union. It will be amusing to hear what people say about them—highly amusing if they sell!

9.iv.17   The Base

I've been wondering whether to write to you now or to wait until I had more to tell you. And then it struck me as rather a good idea to write when I could and what I could, more or less in the form of a diary, and then to send you the results when they had accumulated so as to make a decent sized budget. Having thus determined, and my tent being cool i' the sun, and secluded withal, *alors*—I kick off!

We did not depart for France until Saturday—the 7th—lucky number! The day was calm, etc., and so was the sea, and there was a terrific squash on board. And I announce with triumph. I WAS *NOT* SICK!!! The chemist said I shouldn't be. Nothing happened at Boulogne—I had a good feed and bought a book, and then we came on here. I've nothing but praise for the French railways: we did 15 miles in 4 hours, thus enabling us, when the mood took us, to get out and stretch our legs. We arrived at this Base about midnight. We saw brown tents extending for miles across the sand-dunes, and looking mighty romantic in the moonlight. But I didn't feel romantic: our valises could not be transported to our camp until the following morning: so we had to make the best of two 'doubtful' blankets and the bare boards. I tried to forget a year of luxurious ease (relative), but my hipbone kept reminding me of it.

When we awoke we found it was Easter Sunday. We spent the morning completing our equipment, getting such things as 'tin' helmets and gas-bags. We were told we might disappear between the hours of 3 p.m. and 9 p.m. So disappear we did. Went down into the town—a place much favoured by artists before the war. I had been to the place twice before, and knew it fairly well, so I delegated unto myself the rôle of guide to my companions. I pointed out to them the curious absence of a sewerage system—they thought it was evident. We fled from it . . . and arrived by a beautiful walk through a wood at Paris Plage—an ultra-fashionable sea-side resort, much favoured by Americans in the days when they could get there. At present given over to the entertainment of officers—British, French and Portuguese—and Nurses. We had tea there. And so, back by tram, supper and to bed.

This morning we started training and we keep it up until we get posted to our units and then more travelling.

I might have known you were reading Wells—by the dots . . . It's at least three years since I read *The New Machiavelli*, and my memory is not of the best. But I've always thought it the best novel Wells has written, but that isn't saying much. A lot of the

characters in it are drawn from life, as you perhaps know. Mr. and
Mrs. Sidney Webb are obvious with their blue-books.

Of Wells in general, I agreed with Edward Moore the other
week in the *New Age*. I don't like his treatment of sex. Besides,
the man is damned artistically. His style isn't simply negative—it
is positively rotten. And the architecture of his books is poor and
he seems to have no sense of aesthetic selection. But it is also easy
to criticize.

12.iv.17

Three weary days have passed, waiting rather impatiently for
orders to proceed up to the line. I was inoculated this morning—
and now umteen million germs are disporting themselves in my
blood, making me somewhat stiff—and cross.

But I really feel extraordinarily calm and happy—very different
sensations from those that accompanied my former 'coming out'.
Then I felt reckless with the rest—and rather bacchanalian. Didn't
care a hang what happened. And, in a way, I don't care a hang this
time, but it's a different way, a glad way. And it rather troubles
my soul to know why? Because, as you may know, I'm not
exactly a warrior by instinct—I don't glory in fighting for fighting's sake. Nor can I say that I'm wildly enthusiastic for 'the
Cause'. Its ideals are a bit too commercial and imperialistic for
my liking. And I don't really hate the Hun—the commonest
inspiration among my comrades. I know there are a lot of nasty
Huns—but what a lot of nasty Englishmen there are too. But I
think my gladness may be akin to that Rupert Brooke expressed
in one of his sonnets:

> 'Now God be thanked who has match'd us with His hour,
>   And caught our youth, and wakened us from sleeping,
> With hand made sure, clear eye, and sharpen'd power,
>   To turn, as swimmers into cleanness leaping,
> Glad from a world grown old and cold and weary,
>   Leave the sick hearts that honour could not move,
> And half-men, and their dirty songs and dreary,
>   And all the little emptiness of love.'

Though I must say I'm not yet so 'fed up' with the world as
the sonnet implies. I haven't yet proved 'the little emptiness of
love'. The half-men I still have with me in goodly numbers. And

I've still faith that there are hearts that can be moved by honour
and ideals. But England of these last few years has been rather
cold and weary, and one finds little left standing amid the wreck-
age of one's hopes. So one is glad to leap into the clean sea of
danger and self sacrifice. But don't think that I am laying claim
to a halo. I don't want to die for my king and country. If I do die,
it's for the salvation of my own soul, cleansing it of all its little
egotisms by one last supreme egotistic act.

All this is rather melodramatic; and forgive me if it is morbid.
It is only a mood and has more to do with inoculation than
anything else. I simply must not write any more until I'm properly
'sterilized'.

16.iv.17

Le diable est mort—long ago. In fact, God's in his heaven, all's
right with the world, and I'm feeling quite Browningesque. I
haven't got my movement orders yet, but I've been posted to the
10th Battn., so my address will be: 10th Yorkshire Regt., B.E.F.,
France.

I would rather have gone to my old battn.—the 7th—but I
have two or three friends in the 10th, so I mustn't grumble.

I've just finished *Esther Waters* by George Moore. Did you
ever read it? I've always had an instinctive prejudice against
Moore, but I must admit power and beauty here. It's a study of a
simple soul, and illustrates one of those purely feminine beauties
that fill decent men with wonderment. It is similar in theme to
Hardy's *Tess*, but of course, has not the same tragic significance.
And then it is 'realistic' in its method, and realism, to the minds
of the neo-romantics (who don't exist yet, but I'm one of them)
is 'played out'. I've now got hold of *Evelyn Innes*, by the same
author.

28.iv.17

I arrived at my battalion last night, after wandering over the
face of France for three days. The first day we trained: the next
two we had to march: and 'march' doesn't mean a pleasant
country stroll—it means stumbling along rocky roads, getting
pushed into the gutters by passing lorries, one's back breaking
with a heavy pack.

On the second day's march, the scenery began to be interesting, but not exactly inspiring. Before long we came to the old line of trenches, occupied about a month ago. Thereafter the country we passed thro' had, until recently, been in the hands of the Boche. I'm not going to attempt to describe the desolation of it: Philip Gibbs & Co. do that well enough: it is enough to say that it is simply flattened, every feature (trees, houses, everything) just pulverised.

From this you will guess that I am in the thick of the new fighting. We are not in the trenches, but expect to go up sooner or later. But it is intensely interesting: no fear of getting bored here. The guns are going all day and night. This morning, very early, we were wakened by a furious strafe. You know what ordinary thunder is like: imagine that continuous for a couple of hours and yourself not listening to it, but inside the heart of it: that's something like it. And then the air is one continuous quiver of gun-flashes: and there's a battery just behind us which just gives the final touch to the entertainment: every few minutes it goes off with such a bang!-bang! that one fairly jumps out of one's skin.

I like my new battalion very well on first impressions: there are three other officers in my company, and they are all very decent fellows: the Captain exceptionally so. So I expect I shall be quite happy. We are all optimists out here. We've got the Boche absolutely cowed, and our men are splendid. There are big events pending—and if they go as we expect the war will be over in no time. With a bit of ordinary luck I'll see you sometime these summer holidays.

8.v.17

I think it's about ten days since I wrote to you last. Then I had just joined my battalion and we were basking indolent in the sun. But they didn't leave us basking long. On the Sunday we moved nearer the line and bivouacked for two nights. Then we moved up into the front line. Things have changed a lot in the last twelve months. Trenches as I knew them then are a thing of the past. This time I found myself with my platoon in an isolated outpost in front of the Hindenburg line. We were 'dug in' in a narrow trench, with no dug-outs or any of the conveniences of a permanent trench. During the day we had nothing to do save endure with what patience we could muster the continuous bombardment.

But at night I had to go out on patrol with an N.C.O. to examine the enemy's wire to see what damage our artillery had done to it during the day. Of all the ghastly jobs! It was bright moonlight every night. The enemy is at least 500 yards away. We walk the first 300 yards or so. Then we crawl, from shell-hole to shell-hole, until we dare go no further. It is difficult to say where prudence ends and fear begins. We stay there for about half an hour listening and peering into the dark, occasionally lit up by the enemy's rockets. Everywhere around us are indefinite shadows which every now and then our imagination endows with evil life.

We were in that outpost five days, with never a wash, living on tinned food, biscuits, and drinking tea that tasted like a mixture of ink and petrol. Then we came out into the reserve trench, a mile behind. And, thank God, a wash. But still I haven't had my clothes off for 9 days and see no immediate prospect of getting them off. And never a BATH since 20 days ago, I, to whom a bath is a daily shrine, in which I do not merely tepidly glow, but ecstatically exult. I feel the dirtiest of sinners.

Here we are in the midst of an immense battle, accounts of which you will see in the papers. Any day we may have to go up and make an attack: otherwise our existence is lazy, and consists of eating, sleeping and enduring shellfire. Two officers who came out with me, have already been wounded, so I guess I shan't be long.

I think I should agree word for word with your criticism of The New Machiavelli. It is curious that you should mention Aylwin. A friend I made at Brocton once said to me, 'Judging by what I know of you, I should say that Aylwin was your favourite book.' I asked him why, but he didn't give me any definite answer. I had to confess that I had never read it. So he made me promise to do so at the earliest opportunity. This opportunity I have neglected, and so I still remain in ignorance of its beauty. But I'll promise you to send for it and read it out here. The Open Road is an old friend of mine too, but I chose Bridges' Spirit of Man to bring with me out here, because it was more portable. I've also got with me Plato's Republic and Don Quixote.

9.v.17

One thing troubles me: that you don't understand why I am

out here: I thought I had made that clear. I've no doubt about my position. If I were free today, I'm almost sure I should be compelled by every impulse within me to join this adventure. For I regard it as an adventure and it is as an adventure that it appeals to me. I'll fight for Socialism when the day comes, and fight all the better for being an 'old soldier'. It is my desire to disassociate myself from the red, white and blue patriot that makes me 'growl'. Why a person like myself *can* fight with a good heart in a war like this, I have tried to express in the enclosed unfinished article. I have one or two good friends who are active conscientious objectors (one of them in prison) and they fail to see why I should be so militant in what they regard as an extraneous cause. I've always *felt* that I was in the right and now I am trying to express my feelings.

Your criticism of Hardy and James is *shallow* (I hope I don't offend). It fails to realize the nobility of suffering—the greatness of man in tragedy. 'Untrue to the facts of life'—look around you! When will we aspire to nobility of character, instead of maudlin happiness?

10.v.17

You make the following assertions:

1. 'Beliefs' depend on the character of the believer for their importance and power.

I don't like this *personal* valuation of things. 'Beliefs' are good or bad in themselves independently, or, as the philosophers would say, values are absolute. Therefore they do not depend for their *importance* on the character of the believer and only indirectly for their *power*: great ideas will appeal to the best characters. *Put the idea first*, judge men in the light of it. I grant you that for great ideas to influence society, they must depend on men of character to translate them: but the idea comes first.

2. It's impossible to have any satisfactory philosophy of life at any very tender age.

I've heard this before, but not from the lips of a 'tender age'.

3. Lives governed largely by emotions . . . nobility of soul content . . . impulses.

I take these sentences to imply a doctrine that personality is the sole criterion of character and I agree. But you must admit that in all people who possess a personality at all, the character of

93

the ideas are part and parcel of the character of the personality. I assume sincerity, for the absence of it is the absence of personality.

4. The form of the religion you adopt influences the use you make of the nobility of your soul, but the nobility or lack of it is there independent of the religion.

Here we come across our old friend—the different use of the same term. To me religion, pagan, Christian or atheist, is just an expression of the 'conditions of soul'. You seem to use it in a narrower sense—Catholic, Quaker, P.S.A.'s and whatnot.

5. After all the lives of most men and women are governed largely by emotions . . . the rest do not even know themselves and act in obedience to conflicting impulses.

I smell a Puritan Rat here. Obviously 'emotions' and 'impulses' are spoken of in rather a derogatory sense. 'Do not even know themselves'—the wisest commandment ever laid down by any religion the world has known, was that saying of the Greek (Delphic?) oracle: 'Know thyself.' Observe that it does not say: 'Deny the *self*'—nor even: 'Contort thy *self*.' Just *know* thy *self* and knowing, discriminate by the grace of what knowledge you possess. One of the books I would like to make you read, is Bertrand Russell's *Principles of Social Reconstruction*. It expounds a philosophy of impulse. Man is a creature of impulse: and his impulses are either *creative* or *possessive*. Out of the former proceeds all good: out of the latter all evil. It should be the aim of all philosophy, ethics, government, art and religion to foster creative impulses and to restrain possessive impulses. It is fatal to deny our impulsive nature: thus we destroy that element of vitality which is the salvation of all. But you must read the book: it is full of good meat.

My *past* belief in Original Sin took much the same form as that long screed of Maupassant's that I sent you: a fear that brute nature would *ever* be liable to break through the mask of civilization: that we were at the mercy—inevitably—of our flesh. Of course, Evolution (and its implication) has killed that belief. That is why Evolution breaks up irrevocably that corner-stone of Christianity—the doctrine of Redemption. Since I lost this stupid belief things have 'straightened out' wonderfully in all my ideas on philosophy and religion.

11.vi.17

There's a pleasant rumour today that we are going back a mile or two nearer civilization. But we know that it is only the calm before the storm. Nevertheless there's the alluring prospect of a primitive bath.

Picture us, with the help of the enclosed smudge, in our hovel— a place you wouldn't put a hen into in England. We are dirty but cheerful. Our Captain plays the flute, like any pagan from Arcady. The other fellow who completes our little company, and I, grovel on our only couch—Mother Earth. We are clothed in strange array—Tommy's clothes—'gladrags', a gas respirator like a small chemical laboratory, and steel helmets—the only poetic thing in the British Army, for they are primeval in design and effect, like iron mushrooms. We do growl occasionally—at the guns that keep us awake, at the petrol that flavours everything we drink, but generally we are always merry and bright. C. ascribes this fact to the absence of women within a radius of at least 10 miles, and I do not vigorously dispute his cynicism.

22.v.17

Your letter arrived yesterday and did indeed manage to convey to me the very spirit of spring in England, so that I was away in Yorkshire, with the daffodils in Farndale and the brown moors reviving with green—away until my eyes were dim and my breath was still . . . and then I began to curse the chance that makes of me an exile, and then to curse myself for a sentimental fool.

Spring we do have here, but in an abortive sort of way. The felled trees bloom, but for the last time, and forget-me-nots spring up among the ruins. But everything is sad, and our few flowers are like wreaths among so much desolation.

The lull I told you of is lasting longer than we expected and we have now been in rest ten days. It is significant that during this time I have never been tempted to write to you—our present existence is rather passive and unimpressive. We spent most of the first week cleaning—skins and clothes. We are up early, drilling, etc., until noon, and then the rest of the day is left to our own devices, which mostly take the form of football, riding, eating, reading and various shooting competitions. Last night we had a pierrot party to entertain us—*al fresco*. But any day—any hour—

we expect sudden orders to go back into the thick of it. And none of us really cares how soon these orders come, for the sooner our fate is settled the better, we argue.

I don't know what to say about your opinion of *Songs of Chaos*★: in a way it's so unexpected. I'm glad, very glad, that you like them: you make me ashamed of my sophistication, and do reassure me. I grant you Crystallized Fifty will never do better: but the Spirit of the Twenties soars to dizzy heights.

Thank you for the 'fragments', but I don't see how Kipling fits in. He is one of my *bêtes noires*—a landmark in Philistia, though that is rather a rash judgment of the author of *Kim* and *Puck of Pook's Hill*. It's the man's Idealism that is wrong—not his pure imagination. I'll second your favour of Richard Jeffries and Morris, and Ruskin is good as art but not as opinion. Matthew Arnold no *bon*—encrusted—neither native nor inspired. The Rossettis are fine—I carry a copy of 'The Blessed Damozel' and Christina Rossetti is the sweetest of all women poets. Your mention of *The Light of Asia* reminds me that that book is a chapter in my own life. At the time of the incubation and birth of the *Songs of Chaos* I became acquainted with my brother's employer, who had, at one period of his highly romantic life, poetic aspirations. I ventured, very shyly, and after many heart-searchings, to show him some of my efforts. I think he saw in me himself reincarnated: at any rate, he encouraged and to some extent directed my muse. He lent me *The Light of Asia* telling me that all his life it had been his favourite poem. And I think the common joy we found in it completed the bond between us. On the death of my mother he insisted on me (as well as my brothers, who were both employed with him) making his home my home. The weird coincidence is that his name is exactly the same as ours. It is his kindness that has balanced the sadness of our early life, and, I believe, saved me from a bitter heart, and so earthly damnation.

19.vi.17

I hope you will be able to spare a little of your busy life and devote it to *Lollingdon Downs*. I have never had a great opinion of Masefield as a poet, because hitherto I have never found enough

★ The author's first volume of poems, published by Elkin Mathews, London, 1915. *See* pages 162–4.

beauty of thought to excuse his lack of esthetic delight. (If you look at that sentence hard enough you will find my definition of Poetry.) But in his latest volume I find a philosophy, and a philosophy so much to my liking that (at the present moment) I wouldn't mind leaving it as my last testament. It isn't 'in the air', like most poetic philosophies, but has a sound foundation of scientific fact.

15.vi.17

My present location is not too bad. We are now in the third week of our period in the line. (We went in shortly after my last letter to you.) We had seven days in the trenches and rather terrible days they were. But you can have no desire for me to 'paint the horrors'. I could do so but let the one word 'fetid' express the very essence of our experiences. It would be nightmare to any individual. But we create among ourselves a wonderful comradeship which I think would overcome any horror or hardship. It is this comradeship which alone makes the Army tolerable to me. To create a bond between yourself and a body of men and a bond that will hold at the critical moment, that is work worthy of any man and when done an achievement to be proud of.

Incidentally my 'world-view' changes some of its horizons. I begin to appreciate, to an undreamt of extent, the 'simple soul'. He is the only man you can put your money on in a tight corner. Bombast and swank carry a man nowhere out here. In England they are everything. Nor is the intellect not a few of us used to be so proud of of much avail. It's a pallid thing in the presence of a stout heart. Which reminds me of one psychological 'case' which interests me here: to what extent does a decent philosophy of life help you in facing death? In other words: Is fear a mental or a physical phenomenon? There are cases of physical fear—'nerves' 'shell-shock', etc. There are also certainly cases of physical courage —men who don't care a damn for anything—and there are men who have never thought a single moment on life and death or any 'problem'. And there are, I think, men who funk because they haven't the strength of will or decency of thought to do otherwise. These are fairly simple cases and to me obvious in daily experience. But I would like to think there was still another class (and I one of them) whose capacity for not caring a damn arose not merely from a physical incapacity for feeling fear, but rather from a *mental* outlook on life and death sanely balanced and fearlessly followed. But perhaps I idealize. At any rate, I moralize.

After seven days in the line we were a few days in Brigade reserve, which is fairly 'cushy'. Now we are up again, not actually in the trenches but in a sunken road, from which we daily or nightly sally forth to *dig* in or about the front line. But we do get a decent sleep fairly regularly and don't grumble. And there is the prospect of another 'rest' not far away.

This morning three prisoners were brought into the Cage which is just a few yards away. I was present at the examination by the Intelligence Officer and an interesting hour or two I spent. They were caught by a patrol last night. The most remarkable thing about these (and all the Boche we see) is their comparative cleanliness. And they always have greatcoats on whenever they are caught. And the weather is simply 'sweltering'. One of the prisoners was a very intelligent specimen and gave us a lot of valuable information. Another was a mere kid—said he was twenty but looked seventeen—and was so tremulous that he too, unwittingly, but perhaps not unwillingly, told us many things we wanted to know. I think we rather envied them: no doubt they have a rough time before them: but their 'fate' has arrived.

17.vi.17

One item of news I must not forget to tell you. *Aylwin* came. I read it (in the trenches, of all incongruous places) and it conquered me. I've nothing at all to say against it and much to praise it for. First of all its tang of mountain air, and then for not a little beauty of style. In the latter respect it reminds me of Hawthorne, especially *The House of the Seven Gables*. I don't think he has quite the beautiful simplicity of Hawthorne: on the other hand he lacks Hawthorne's suspicion of puritanical smugness. For the passionate intensity of some of its scenes I would rank it with *Wuthering Heights*. But then I think the plot is rather strained—I mean more particularly the reappearance of Winifred. Life may contain so many facts more wonderful than fiction: but Art must not have anything to do with them. Then I agree with you that the opening love scenes between Hal and Winifred make Meredith's Richard and Lucy seem rather shallow and artificial. And I was very interested in D'Arcy: I didn't know the book contained a study of Rossetti: else I might have sought it earlier. I must thank you for finally driving me to such delight.

After surmounting many difficulties (the Board of Trade even) *Art and Letters*★ has bloomed before the public. Of course, it isn't so 'sumptuous' as it might be, or as it *will* be after the war. But still I think I might be permitted to say it is modern without being cranky. I think Ginner's article sums up the present position of modern art to perfection. Marriott on Dancing is good too. Shall I ever make a reviewer (*vide Portrait of the Artist*)? This is my first shot at a review.

I was a little doubtful about the second poem—it is abrupt—even if it is read as it should be—crescendo to 'pond'—long pause—even tone to 'water'—pause—diminuendo last line. But Rutter was so keen on it that I let it go. 'Curfew' I think is one of my true 'inspirations'. It too depends a lot on rendering. It is one of my aims—to restore poetry to its true rôle of a *spoken* art. The music of words—the linking of sounds—the cadence of phrase—unity of action. Each poem should be *exact*, expressing in the *only* appropriate words the emotion experienced. The fact of emotion unites the art to life. Any 'idea', i.e. ethical or critical, or philosophy should only be basic—ground from which the beauty springs. Or perhaps the unifying principle of a man's art viewed as a whole.

I've been chosen for a death or glory job soon to come off. I am very glad—glad in the first place because it gives me the first chance I've had of doing something—glad in the second place because it means that others recognize that I'm of the clan that don't care a damn for anything.

All the same I intend to 'come through' as full of life as anything.

1.viii.17

Well, the 'stunt' is over, so now I can tell you something about it.† I, along with another officer, was detailed to get as many volunteers as we could from our company and, on a certain dark and dirty night, to raid the enemy's trenches, kill as many as

★ See page 257.
† I leave this immediate account of the incident, although I relate it again with more analytical detail in the next Part of this volume (pages 220–7).

possible and bring back at least one prisoner for identification purposes. Out of a possible 60 we got 47 volunteers . . . That was a jolly good start. We had about a fortnight to make our plans and rehearse. This we set about with enthusiasm—everybody was keen. Our plans were made with all the low villainous cunning we were capable of. When the battalion went into the front line we were left behind to train and take things easy. We two officers had to do a good amount of patrolling and observation. We had to discover the weak points in the enemy's wire, the best routes thither and as much of the enemy's habits as we could . . . This went on until the fateful night arrived. Picture us about midnight: our faces were blackened with burnt cork, everything that might rattle was taken off or tied up. We armed ourselves with daggers and bombs and various murderous devices to blow up the enemy's wire and dugouts—and, of course, our rifles or revolvers. The raid was to be a stealth raid and depended for its success on surprise effect. So out thro' our own wire we crept— our hearts thumping but our wills determined. We had 540 yards to traverse to the objective. The first half were simple enough. Then we began to crouch and then to crawl—about a yard a minute. Suddenly, about 150 yards from the German trenches, we saw and heard men approaching us. We were following one another in Indian file. They seemed scattered to the right and left as far as we could see. In a moment all our carefully prepared plans were thrown to the winds. New plans had to be made on the spur of the moment. Our position was tactically very weak. My fellow-officer began to crawl carefully back to reorganize the men into a defensive position, leaving me in front to deal with the situation if necessary. I could now see what was happening. The Huns were coming out to wire (had already started as a matter of fact) and were sending out a strong covering party to protect the wirers from surprise. This party halted and took up a line in shell-holes about twenty yards from us. Then some of them began to come forward to reconnoitre. We lay still, looking as much like clods of earth as we possibly could. Two Boche were getting very near me. I thought we had better surprise them before they saw us. So up I get and run to them pointing my revolver and shouting 'Haende hoch' (hands up), followed by my trusty sergeant and others. Perhaps the Boche didn't understand my newly acquired German. At any rate they fired on me—and missed. I replied with my revolver and my sergeant with his gun. One was hit and shrieked out. Then I was on the other fellow who was now properly scared and fell flat in a shell-hole. 'Je suis officier!' he cried in French. By this time there was a general fight going on, fire being opened on all sides. In a minute or two the guns were on and for five minutes it was inferno. The real object of the raid was achieved—a prisoner and a valuable one at that had been captured. So I began to make my way back with him whilst the other officer organized covering fire. In another five minutes we were back in our own trenches, and, all things considered, very glad to get there. Our casualties were only one missing and two slightly wounded. We must have inflicted twenty on the enemy, for, besides our rifle fire and bombs, we drove him back into a barrage put up by our trench mortars.

I took the prisoner along to Headquarters. He spoke a little French, so on the way we carried on a broken conversation. He told me his name, age, that he was married and where he came from. When we got to H.Q. there was an officer who spoke German and then the prisoner began to talk twenty to the dozen. We gave him a drink, cigarette, etc. He turned out to be an ex-schoolmaster of some sort and a very intelligent fellow. We got any amount of useful information from him. He was very interesting on things in general. Does not think we shall ever win this war, but neither will they. Says the new man, Michaelis, is a people's man and will gradually democratize the German government. But the Kaiser is still the people's hero and we must not expect the German nation to consent to his dethronement in the terms of peace. He says there is no chance of a revolution in Germany. Did not think much of the French, but was almost enthusiastic in his praise of the English. Said it was a mistaken idea to think the Germans hated the English. That was only an idea propagated by the German militarists and our own Press. We were of the same racial stock—should be allies—not enemies—etc., etc.

He himself won the Iron Cross at Verdun where he took 85 French prisoners.

We had to take him down to Brigade—an hour's walk. It was a beautiful early morning and everything was peaceful and the larks were singing. In our broken French we talked of music. He played both the violin and the piano and we found common

enthusiasms in Beethoven and Chopin. He even admired Nietzsche
and thenceforth we were sworn friends. He wrote his name and
address in my pocket-book and I promised to visit him after the
war if I ever came to Germany. By the time I handed him over
to the authorities at the Brigade we were sorry to part with each
other. And a few hours previously we had done our best to kill
each other. *C'est la guerre*—and what a damnable irony of existence . . . at any rate a curious revelation of our common humanity.

I've got a beautiful automatic revolver as a souvenir.

In my next letter I'll answer the futile attack on *Art and Letters*
in this week's *New Age*.

14.viii.17

I intended answering R.H.C.'s criticism of *Art and Letters* in
detail. But I will only add this to Rutter's reply in this week's
New Age. In the first place, a counter criticism: The *New Age* is
too fond of assuming the rôle of despot among the moderns and
of course, despotism in matters of the spirit, like art and literature,
is disastrous. Besides in some matters the *New Age* is getting too
reactionary. Have you noticed those sonnets of J.A.M.A.'s—full
of 'reminiscence' and the clichés of the Victorians. In the second
place it is not fair to judge *Art and Letters* by a first number appear-
ing in war-time. It (the first number) is but a pale edition of what
we do intend it finally to be. Against the *New Age* we intend to
insist upon the primacy of beauty—even in economics. And hence
a return to the socialism of Morris in preference to that of Karl
Marx. Qualitative rather than quantitative ideas. And then can
the *New Age* in any sense be said to represent decorative or
pictorial art or even the theory of it? And even if it did, *Art and
Letters* represents a certain group or school, who as such, have a
right to gather together and record their distinctive ideas. They
represent, in *Art and Letters*, the interpretation of Life in terms of
beauty. They oppose the Realists who only show us life in a
section: the Romanticists and Abstracts (poor me!) who do not
relate their art to life at all: and so I think *Art and Letters* has a
distinct right to exist. Moreover I think we are on the way to
perform both the miracles of culture suggested by R.H.C.—to
pay our way and to satisfy all our contributors. When this is
done I hope R.H.C. (=Orage of course) will climb down.

Now to satisfy your curiosity *di histrionis*—if I can. Frank Rutter is the one I know best and he is a very sincere friend of mine. Age 42: married (to a wife whom men like and women hate); no children: the most charming conversationalist I ever met. Something like this in looks—(picture)—very like R.L.S. as a matter of fact. Has the most wonderful memory I ever met. Can remember every character of every novel he has read—and that is every novel that is worth reading. It is my delight to get him into a quiet corner in some café and over coffee and cigarettes to listen to him whilst he talks Meredith and Henry James by the hour. I think it was our common enthusiasm over H.J. that first brought us together.

He once—before I really knew him—gave some lectures at the University on the Post-Impressionists. But he had a beard then.

We correspond fairly regularly and his letters are as delightful as his conversation. He is a charming (that's the only word for him) man and a perfect critic. Has written books on Whistler and Rossetti, *The Way to Paris, Revolution in Art*, etc. He went to Cambridge in his youth and since then, though married, has somehow or other, managed to live on art criticism. Until six months ago he was Curator at the Leeds Art Gallery, but he was always quarrelling with the Council on matters of aesthetic judgement: so now he has a temporary job at the Admiralty—in his beloved London. And, I believe, a charming little house in Putney.

Ginner is a funny stick. All you realize of his person is a pair of glasses, a straggly moustache, and a smile and a very still small voice. The most untidy clothes imaginable. And I believe, general untidy surroundings, of which he is absolutely unconscious. Sort of man who never knows if he has had dinner or not. But he is a beautiful artist. A wonderful sense of design and perfect colour schemes. I know nothing of his life—one never does of such people.

Gilman is similar but neater. They are all charming. Kauffer I haven't met yet. He came from America about eighteen months ago.

22.vii.17

Yesterday I had a day in Amiens. The Army is becoming quite a benevolent old gentleman, arranging little joy-rides for us when we are in reserve. This time it was too far for a bus and we had to put up with a French train. It meant getting up at 5 a.m.

and walking 2½ miles to the station, but that was done willingly enough. Then rather a weary journey lasting 2½ hours. We passed through the valley of the Somme—past Albert, with its leaning Virgin—(when it falls, according to the superstition of Tommy, the war ends.—I would like to have charge of a German battery for a few hours)—finally arriving in Amiens, about 9.30 in time for breakfast—so we thought. Then we made a discovery: In civilized France they have food regulations. You may not eat in a public restaurant before 11 a.m. Not even a cup of coffee could we get. So we raided a *pâtisserie* and ate cream cakes over the counter. Thus refreshed, we wandered round the city. Naturally we made for the Cathedral and spent an hour or so there. I can't go into ecstasies about it. It is fine, of course, especially the exterior. The front is really great—delicate and finely wrought without any sacrifice of massive nobility. But the body of the cathedral tails off miserably and has a mean slender spire out of harmony with the frontage. There are some fine flying bastions, or whatever they call them, which would make a finer 'vorticist' design. The interior is disappointing—neither austere nor beautiful. A service was in progress and a priest was delivering a remarkably dramatic sermon—all about poor little Belgium and the horrible Hun. Vergers walked up and down dressed in the gaudiest uniforms I've ever had the pleasure of seeing—and all alike as two peas—with mutton-chop whiskers like English butlers.

After the cathedral we did our shopping. I had to buy crockery for the Mess (being Mess President) and I did this in great style. Other 'necessaries' soon made our money go and we ourselves were soon aware of our stomachs. So then lunch—nothing unusual except peaches. After lunch more sightseeing. Amiens itself is like any other cathedral town except that it has more fine modern buildings—one of the best of the latter is the Musée de Picardie where we saw the famous mural decoration of Puvis de Chavannes and a bust by Rodin.

23.vii.17

I've just finished Wells's *God the Invisible King*. I have to write a criticism of it for the friend who sent it me—the Scotch philosopher I met at Brocton. I began it with the firm conviction that I was going to disagree with it: I finish it in almost complete agreement. Nevertheless, I don't like it. It strikes me as the work of a *hard* nature glossed over with sentiment. His general position is as follows: Firstly, 'complete agnosticism in the matter of God the Creator, and second, entire faith in the matter of God the Redeemer'. He uses the word God for the God in our hearts only, and he uses the term the Veiled Being for the Ultimate Mysteries of the Universe. Briefly he deifies 'the moral law within'. I'm not sure of this point and want your opinion: Is such a deification of the Moral law within a sentimental affectation, or can we in any measure call it a reality. His deification is no vague process. He declares that God is a Person 'who can be known as one knows a friend, who can be served and who receives service, who partakes of our nature . . . God is no abstraction nor trick of words, no Infinite. He is as real as a bayonet thrust or an embrace'. At the same time he says that his nature is of thought and will. He is not of matter nor of space. He comes into them . . . He is a Being of the minds and in the minds of men. He is in immediate contact with all who apprehend him. But he exists in time . . . He is the undying human memory, the increasing human will.

Then he says God is Courage, and Youth, and Love . . . and with all these we can agree.

And God is *finite*—an idea I have not previously given any thought to, but which now rather fascinates me.

His criticisms are, as usual with Wells, the better part of his book. One lot deals with Heresies or things that God is not—none of them very original but all well stated. Another chapter deals with 'the Religion of Atheists' and it is here that Wells irritates me most. He takes the theories of scientists like Mechnikoff, Chalmers Mitchell and writers like Joseph McCabe, Gilbert Murray, etc., and merely sentimentalizes over their sanity. He admits all their facts, and insists that they imply his God, despite their several repudiations.

He then writes rather well on a world theocracy and the Will of God, which is the realization of the Kingdom of Heaven on earth, and points out the social obligations of such a religion. He speculates on the growth of the new religion and is brilliant in his repudiation of the need of a Church. 'We want our faith spread, but for that there is no need for orthodoxies and controlling organizations of statement. It is for each man to follow his own impulse and to speak to his like in his own fashion.'

The State is God's Instrument and the Kingdom of God is at hand—Fabius volens.

So you see, a book worth reading.

27.vii.17

We are in the line again now. It promises to be rather an interesting trip for me, but of this more later.

Art and Letters I am pleased to tell you is a good success. Already the expenses of the first number have been covered by subscriptions and they still roll in. Rutter is very enthusiastic and full of after-war plans for the development of the magazine.

Did I tell you that Rutter and I are scheming for a joint enterprise after the war? It was Rutter who started and still runs the Allied Artists Association. This Association has been such a success that he thinks of carrying the principle further. You may know that it is practically an artists' trade union, run on trade union principles. Any person with any claim to be an artist can join and by his membership becomes entitled to exhibit three pictures at the yearly show. Now if instead of a yearly show of three or four weeks' duration we could have a permanent Gallery, the thing ought to buzz. So imagine a small gallery somewhere in the West to which the buyer in search of something 'modern' and original will of necessity come. But why, say I, confine the idea to pictures? Why not apply it to books? Why not an Allied Authors Association to be run on something like the following lines: the Association to be open to anyone who has the cheek to claim that he is an author. From these members a Committee to be formed. This committee to select a certain amount of work by members for publication. Such works to be published (and printed and bound) by the Association. The Association to establish a shop where books by its members may be bought. So the Art Gallery is to have a bookshop in front of it and the show as a whole to be the centre of all modernist activity. The idea is the democracy of Art. All the aesthetic principles of Ruskin and Morris as to book production we hold strongly. But we make the idea accessible to talent and not to wealth. The havoc wrought by Capitalism in industry and the life of the workers is obvious. The havoc wrought by capitalism in Art is less obvious but no less vital. It is not too much to say that for the last two hundred years or so, Art has been strangled to death in Europe. No work of art, however great a masterpiece it may be, has a chance today unless it can be guaranteed 'to pay'. We shall alter this. . . .

Here is rather a come-down from the intellectual arrogance of 'autrefois'. You know that it is a journalistic commonplace that 'out here' the man who has never thought before in his life bursts forth into pregnant utterances upon his destiny. In some respects this is true. The contrast of Life and Death is too obvious to be neglected. So also we who had ideas before the war begin to revise them. I don't think our ultimate ideals change much. I know mine haven't. But the road thither becomes different. We begin to see the best way there. And so the old high-sounding phrases—'the moral law', 'the will to this, that and the other' and a hundred like them—begin to sound a bit hollow, and I begin to realize that quite the most important thing in life is to possess the vague qualities of, and be upon every occasion, a 'gentleman'. If you ask: what is a gentleman? you have asked the hardest question of life. It is a question you can only answer by the intuition of your own mind. Personally I 'get at' the ideal somewhat if I separate the word—a gentle man. But that is only vague.

But if one cannot define a gentleman, much of the difficulty disappears by the ease with which we can distinguish his opposite. God, how many we must brand: how few we can elect!

Must one's standards of judgement be necessarily personal and egotistic? or are there universals in the matter? I haven't thought it out yet. This I know: The gentle man, unconsciously as often as consciously, fulfils our finest ideals.

2.ix.17

We are now 'enjoying' a rest! That blessed word 'rest'. It has terrors for us almost equal to any the line can produce. It means a constant scrubbing and polishing and an almost Bond Street atmosphere in the midst of some dirty old broken down village. And then a continual state of *qui vive*, for safety releases all kinds of horrors upon us: fellows with red hats and monocles who seldom molest us in our natural haunt. Then that figure familiar to all in England through Bairnsfather's sketches—Old Bill—has to be renovated, drilled and cursed until he somehow resembles his pre-war edition. No mean task this—only to be accomplished by the expense of much raucous voice and more patience. Then we've got in our Company forty odd recruits raw from England without the foggiest notion of war. *Then* Tommy takes it into his head to write letters to all his old pals and sweethearts long neglected, and so two or three weary sub-alterns have to wade through two or three hundred uninteresting letters every day. *Comme ci:* 'Dear old pal—Just a line hoping as how you are in the pink of condition as this leaves me at present. Well, old pal, we are out of the line just now in a ruined village. The beer is rotten. With good luck we shall be over the top in a week or two, which means a gold stripe in Blighty or a land-owner in France. Well, they say it's all for little Belgium, so cheer up, says I: but wait till I gets hold of little Belgium.

From your old pal,

Bill.

And so on until they become anything but funny.

But there are compensations. After tea we are generally left to our own devices. Sometimes Col and I will get horses and away for a ride. Sometimes I think a ride together beats a walk. There is more exhilaration. A sense of communion, not only between yourselves, but also between you and your horse. Here and there a cross-country track gives us the chance of a gallop and away we go! We get back just before dark, glowing with the exercise and hearts as happy as can be. Again, the nights this last week have been divine—cold moonlight. Washed in this silver light this land loses all its look of desolation. The whitewashed houses make the village streets look almost painfully English. The fields are all misty and the shadowy trees mysterious. In many places we have just reaped a harvest sown by the Germans in spring. And what scene can compare to a harvest-field by moonlight? Yellow stooks pitched like the tents of an army: perhaps a dark wood flanking one side of the picture: and the clumsiest farm-stead you could possibly desire somewhere in the misty perspective. Such joys as these make us forget entirely the horrors none of us desires to remember. Things even seem 'worthwhile'.

5.ix.17—very p.m.

Life is 'intense' nowadays—never a minute to one's self, as they say. On the 3rd Col and I went to Amiens together for the day. Up at 5 a.m. and a glorious ride to the nearest station, with the day scarce dawned. We had a happy school-boy sort of day, buying things and eating enormous meals. You would laugh at the tremendous importance 'food' assumes out here. We romped all day till we were wearied out—and then a four hours' journey in a crowded train! And we didn't get corner seats, and it was a third-class carriage, which, in this benighted land, isn't much better than a cattle-truck. We tried to prop each other up and go to sleep like Babes in the Wood, but not with much success. But joy revived in the ride back in the moonlight, and finally we agreed that it was 'the end of a perfect day'.

Just now in from another moonlight ramble—and as happy as a lark.

9.ix.17

We move soon to another part for a big show.

I was 'dished out' with a ribbon this a.m. by the Major-General. Terrible ordeal in front of the Brigade. But it's over now.

A new number of *Art and Letters* is to appear in October: I'm afraid there won't be much me in it—I haven't had the time. The 'rest' as strenuous as ever. Would you like to see me race a bare-backed mule?

[I went to England on leave in this interval.]

7.x.17

When I arrived behind the line I found that the Battalion were in the thick of the fight. I had to stay behind until they came out, along with two others who had straggled in. All such stragglers for all the Brigade are billeted together—about 15 of us. We have a large mess-hut wherein some passing genius has built a wide open old-English fireplace of bricks. Fuel in plenty appears miraculously, so, as the weather is vile and tempestuous we build the fire high and sit round in a circle. We are rather quiet, not knowing what has happened to our friends. Vague rumours come down to us every now and then. So-and-so is killed, so-and-so is wounded. The —— have only two officers left out of the twenty that went in to action. I hear that Col is wounded, but still 'carrying on'. That sounds like him. Later someone comes down with shell-shock. He seems distracted and does not know anything definite. Some he has seen killed, others wounded. A few

grim details he can give us. The attack was a great success—all
objectives taken and so on. But for all we want to know we shall
have to wait until they come out. The latest rumour says that is
tomorrow and that we are going back to reorganize. We can
only hope so.

I feel a little ashamed of having escaped it all. There is always a
regret in not having shared dangers with friends. Perhaps one is
jealous of their experiences. Only I have some consolation.

9.X.17

Yesterday I was detailed to go to a village about 30 miles
behind and find billets for the battalion who were coming out
of the line for a rest. I took four NCOs with me and boarded a
bus for the benighted little place I am now in. Consists of one
church, about twenty estaminets, and, of all things on earth, a
corset factory! I have spent part of yesterday and all today doing
my Sunday best in French with people who talk a weird half-
Flemish lingo that is to French about what Cockney is to good
broad Yorkshire. The majority of them are rather suspicious and
hostile and I've had a terrible time with them. But the result is
fairly satisfactory and now I am waiting for the battalion to come
in—sometime in the 'small hours'.

Last night I found a jolly old dame, who provided me with
a truly magnificent 'chambre', all curtains and crucifixes. She was
an admirer of 'les braves anglais' and treated me to innumerable
cups of coffee and talked away far into the night. As she grew
tired she became sentimental, finally weeping over *tous les morts,
français, anglais et boches*. Then she went to sleep in her chair and
I retired to the magnificent 'chambre'. Today I met the priest, a
big man in long flowing black robes and a horribly dirty face. He
plays weird music on a cracked piano and is awfully proud of a
w.c. he has—'the only one in the village'. Another kind old man
insisted on cutting me several bunches of grapes that were growing along the roof of his house. I went to see the 'maire' expecting
to find a very important personage, especially as I was directed to
the 'château'. I found the dirtiest man I've ever seen picking
potatoes in a field! He didn't seem to know very much about
anything and referred me to his secrétaire, who turned out to be
the publican of 'The Cyclists' Rest'. He rummaged amongst a
heap of 'sugar tickets' and grubby children and produced a list of

householders and a plan of the village. After that we were fast friends and I got along swimmingly. But I still hae ma doots whether they'll all 'get in' or not. *Mais c'est la guerre*, as they all say.

10.X.17

They came in shortly after midnight, very weary and ready to drop down and sleep anywhere. It isn't three weeks since I left them, but it was like greeting long lost friends. Col is all right, only a scratch or two: but it will take time for him to throw off the gloom of their terrible experiences. It isn't only fancy that makes them seem to have aged five years and more. They have gone through what was probably the most intense shell fire since the war began. As a battalion we have been remarkably lucky—only one officer killed and not so many men as one would expect. A lot wounded, but most of them can be considered lucky. One or two of my special pals among the men have disappeared, especially a jolly little Irish boy who was worth a thousand for his cheerfulness. I don't know how long we shall be out at rest. I am afraid not long.

I shall be sending you a book in a day or two which I got in England and am now reading. Not *too* stodgy and really important: *Old Worlds for New* by A. J. Penty. Really a criticism of the Fabians and the *New Age* and a very suggestive one too. He has given me a lot to think about and I've not yet decided how far I go with him. The Fabians he criticizes wholesale and with good reason. 'Collectivism is dead. It never presumed to be an artistic ideal. It has ended in not even daring to be a human one' . . . and so on. A revival of craftsmanship and craft guilds is his universal panacea. He falls foul of the *New Age* on the question of large organizations. He doesn't believe in them. Decentralization is his cry for every industry. He is passionate in his attack on machinery and scientific production, division of labour, middlemen, etc., and writes some good stuff on these subjects. He pleads for revolution and not for the evolution advocated by the *New Age*.

His, of course, is the aesthetic attitude (he is a disciple of William Morris): and I am convinced that ideally he is right. But the change he advocates is a change of heart and you can't effect that by a revolution. It is something co-existent with the economic basis of society. Therefore you must first alter that economic basis and then educate. Only by that roundabout means is it possible to establish craftsmanship in industry. And so the methods advocated by the *New Age*—the extension of Trade Unionism, the assumption by these Unions (National Guilds) of national industrial functions, and *then* a putting in order of one's own house. That seems to me to be the only practical means to what after all is the aim of all true socialists: more decency and beauty of life.

26.x.17

Your letter was waiting for me when we came out of the line ... nothing better could have greeted me. We have had a terrible time—the worst I have ever experienced (and I'm getting quite an old soldier now). Life has never seemed quite so cheap nor nature so mutilated. I won't paint the horrors to you. Some day I think I will, generally and for the public benefit. I was thoroughly 'fed up' with the attitude of most of the people I met on leave—especially the Londoners. They simply have no conception whatever of what war really is like and don't seem concerned about it at all. They are much more troubled about a few paltry air raids. They raise a sentimental scream about one or two babies killed when every day out here hundreds of the very finest manhood 'go west'. Of course, everyday events are apt to become rather monotonous ... but if the daily horror might accumulate we should have such a fund of revulsion as would make the world cry 'enough!' So sometimes I wonder if it is a sacred duty after all 'to paint the horrors'. This reminds me of a poem I'll quote— by one of our moderns and a woman at that.

> *Another life holds what this lacks,*
> *a sea unmoving, quiet,—*
> *not forcing our strength*
> *to rise to it, beat on beat—*
> *a stretch of sand,*
> *no garden beyond, strangling*
> *with its myrrhlilies—*
> *a hill not set with black violets,*
> *but stones, stones, bare rocks,*
> *dwarf trees, twisted, no beauty*
> *to distract—to crowd*
> *madness upon madness.*

EXTRACTS FROM A DIARY

Only a still place
and perhaps some outer horror,
some hideousness to stamp beauty
a mark
on our hearts.

H.D.

My military progress continues—strange to say. I am now commanding a company and may soon be a captain. I believe I have been rather conscientious since I came to this battalion—I don't know why—perhaps life is so much more enjoyable if one works hard. At any rate, I am satisfied. I thoroughly enjoy my despotism and a company commander is a terrible despot. He tries all his criminals and dispenses what he may consider justice, or sends them to a higher court (the Colonel): he gives promotion to all who serve him well; exacts obedience: directs his government—redresses all grievances. So imagine me, if you can, in the rôle. I am democratic so far as the Higher Powers permit. For example, I put it to the vote whether RUM should be issued last night or this morning—a question that interests our community intensely—i.e. the rum: they don't care very much about the 'when' so long as it is reasonably often. I have got a fine lot of lads though they are fastly decreasing in numbers. 'Always merry and bright'—it's my aim to keep them so. And they are a gallant crew: we have more decorations in our company than in any other in the battalion. I got four Military Medals today out of seven for the battalion. And damn proud of it we all are.

My subalterns (notice the 'my'—sort of possessive pride) are quite a good lot and mostly my seniors in age—Gipsy Lee is almost old enough to be my father. Bevan is the youngest and a good friend. He is Devon born, lives in Wales and has sojourned a good while in Canada. Hence he is sturdy, frank and sensible. His nice eyes, hazel and liquid perhaps betray his inner nature. Sentimental, of course. He was, and still is, madly in love, but alas! the fickle maid has jilted him. But his heart is not broken nor his cheery outlook much affected.

Hart is a famous runner and like all competitive sportsmen, rather boastful. But he is a good fellow and runs our Mess in an ideal manner. He would make an excellent hotel manager. He, too, is very sentimental, and plays patience with a pack of photos of the fair one.

113

Gipsy Lee has just joined us and is still a mystery.

Martin is a young rake of the Cockney variety with a wonderful variety of oaths, yarns of a doubtful nature, and a stutter that does not prevent him talking all day long.

There you have a scandalous account of our society and I'm not really ashamed of being the author of it, for I know they do the same by me, and I don't mind.

14.xi.17

Today the post arrived just as Col and I were off for a ride. We read our letters—he had one of the right kind too—as we ambled along in the winter sunlight. Then we both laughed gladly and vowed we had never known such a perfect moment.

We are out of the line again, after another terrible week. We hope never to see this sector again. Expect to go back for a few weeks rest any day now. Then I will write to you. I feel too unsettled now—my present home a tent in an ocean of mud. I fear I was rather a dull fellow in my last letter. I'm going to give economics a rest.

I think I too have 'the glad consciousness' of returning to England soon. At any rate, some fine day.

19.xi.17

We are on the trek: for three days we have marched away from the northern horrors and still we march—for another two days. I am enjoying it all immensely—I suppose it is the reaction—and the weather is quite passable—ideal for our purpose—misty November days, with an occasional gleam. So contented are we that we don't mind much the fact that our long promised rest has been postponed a while—but only a short while.

This is where we touch the romantic fringe of war—for it is only a fringe, the romance. Now we have all the thrills of a sentimental journey—all the excitement of changing environment and of strange meetings. Our experiences vary: the first journey's end was rather disconcerting. Our billet was the almost inevitable farm-house: our men were safely and snugly packed into a hay loft; and we ourselves entered the house; and the dourest (I think that is the exact word) face imaginable greeted us. Our 'rooms' were good enough, though rather bare. But we were tired and hungry and would partake of the usual café and omelettes. But no: she would not make us anything. Would she let our cook use her stove? No. There was a stove in our rooms, so would she let us have some coal to cook with? Again a gruff refusal. 'Madame no bon,' is the frank opinion of Towers (my servant). So we are left to our own devices. I forgot to mention that we had bought some fish as we passed through a town. 'You *must* cook that fish, or go and drown yourselves' were our final orders to the domestic staff. Thus having delivered ourselves we went and sat, glum as moulting hens, in our bleak bedroom. After a while we heard the chopping and cracking of wood, then the frizzling of a frying-pan and finally the fish appeared and jolly good it was.

The epilogue was a little account delivered to me in the early morning before we set out:

5 hen perches . . . 1 fr. 50.

I blinked amazedly for a few moments and then I remembered the cracking and chopping of wood!

The next journey's end was very different. The N.C.O. who had gone in advance, on our arrival, pointed out to me an innocent enough looking house and said, 'That's your mess.' I entered boldly enough, only to gasp and fall back on to the toes of whoever was behind me. Seated round a table, enjoying a meal of some sort, were at least six beaming maidens. They all shouted out 'Entrez!' So I thought I had better take my hat off and make another advance. 'Mess?' I weakly inquired. 'Là!' they pointed. And somehow I circumnavigated them and entered the next room, followed by my flabbergasted friends. Again we were tired and hungry, so again we asked (this time more humbly) for café and omelettes. Nothing could have pleased the old lady better (there was *one* old lady) and we had a delightful meal on the table in no time. This finished, and our morale recovered, we ventured back into the kitchen, where a gramophone was playing selections of English music, and, perhaps more inviting still, a French stove was roaring away and dispelling the chill of the November twilight. Chairs were pushed forward and we *had* to accept: and so a very pleasant hour or so . . . Col came in then and we decided to go forth in quest of adventures to the fairly big town that was only a mile or so away. I was loath to leave that friendly kitchen, but Col was keen, so off we went, with another fellow (Hart—the runner.) We arrived there 5.30 p.m. Went to order dinner at an hotel: saw an advertisement of *the* Pierrots: dashed off there and heard the best concert you can imagine. It was a Sunday, so the programme was perhaps more select than usual. At any rate, a violin soloist who seemed perfection. (Fancy, one week in the horrors I can't describe and the next listening to Chopin perfectly rendered). There were other things on the programme, all delightful, even if sentimental . . . Then dinner, rather ordinary and back to bed by 10 p.m. . . . . Up again at 6 a.m. and the trek is resumed. And here I am in another hospitable billet, but no chorus of fair maidens, but an equally jolly old man, who has lit a stove in the room for us, and provided us with all he can— *even clean white sheets*—and that is heaven, or will be in an hour or so.

21.xi.17

I'm reading just now *God and Mr. Wells* by William Archer —an R.P.A. publication. It is rather delicious and I'll send it on when finished with. I've recently read two posthumous books by Henry James—*The Sense of the Past* and *The Middle Years*. They are both fine and I must let you have them some time. But I want, if you will be kind and humble enough, to initiate you into the cult of H.J. in quite a religious manner. I know you will then treasure him even as I do. I am going to get you *The Princess Casamassima* soon—she is much nicer than her name and Hyacinth is a dear. It is the best of the early period and was written under the influence of your Dickens.

10.i.18

We are midway through a long weary tour of trench duty. We do four days in the line and then four in support and four in reserve—and this sometimes for more than a month. The four in reserve are the only ones during which it is possible to be civilized—to wash and change and write letters. As a Company commander I get a much easier time in the line—no long dreadful night-watches. I manage to get a little reading done. I've just finished one of Conrad's novels—*Under Western Eyes*. Like all Conrad's it is extraordinarily vivid and a fine appreciation of life. You must read Conrad: he is the finest of our subjective psychologists, regarding Henry James as an objective psychologist. Get hold of *Lord Jim* if you haven't already read it. There's a human hero for you: your own theory of character as the supreme value made evident.

I also managed to write a short article and send it on to the *New Age*. I don't really expect them to accept it, as it is very much against their point of view. I called it 'Our Point of View' and my chief points were:

(a) That the means of war had become more portentous than the aim—i.e. that the game is not worth the candle.
(b) That this had been realized by the fighting soldier and on that account there has been, out here, an immense growth of pacifist opinion.

Of course, it might offend the Censor. But it is the truth. I know my men and the sincerity of their opinions. They know the impossibility of a knock-out blow and don't quite see the use of another long year of agony. We could make terms now that would clear the way for the future. If, after all that Europe has endured, her people can't realize their most intense ideal (Goodwill)—then Humanity should be despaired of—should regard self-extinction as their only salvation. But I for one have faith, and faith born in the experience of war.

26.ii.18

I've just been reading the Report of the Inter-Allied Labour and Socialist Conference and it has wonderfully revived my rather flagging socialist heart. I'm inclined to think it is really great—the best statesmanship the problem of the war has yet produced . . . It is so sane that we can now really hope for some good from the Movement. I wonder if Henderson is our best man, or if he is too much of a T.U. Official to be revolutionary. Camille Huysmans I believe has done more for Inter-nation Socialism in a quiet way than any other man living. And Vandervelde is rather fine. Do you remember hearing him speak at Leeds? I think we met coming down the Hall stairs and discussed him: and you asked if I thought we had so good a man in England: or I asked you. At any rate we were both rather pessimistic. I've long been of the opinion that we shall never come to a military decision in this war. So, I think, at the bottom of them, have the (writers in the) *New Age*. But their idea is that you discredit German militarism the longer you fight—i.e. fight without a German victory. And that in time this will so disgust the German people that they will kick. My idea is that the war unites the German people against what they believe, with some grounds, to be an aggressive English Imperialism: that as soon as peace is declared they will kick: therefore the sooner peace is declared the better. An inconclusive peace would in many ways be a blessing: it would for ever discredit war. As soon as peace is declared the one and only hope is in International Socialism. If it does not *recreate* the world, then International Capitalism will *restore* it. The recent conference shows that Internationalism has some life in it. So *nil desperandum*.

27.ii.18

I've got a new enthusiasm in my literary world. Unfortunately he's a Frenchman—Jules Romains by name. I'm getting hold of as many of his books as I can. He became fairly well known about 1911, when he published *Mort de Quelqu'un*. He has a theory, of course: I love people with theories. I think he calls himself a Unanimist, but I'm not yet quite sure what all that implies. But roughly I think this is his idea: The world has so progressed and society become so complex, that the individual has been transcended: that is, transcended as a subject for artistic treatment. Romains takes as his subject any collection of things animate or of things animate and inanimate which possesses a 'soul'—i.e. things of one soul (unanimus) and that unanimity is his 'hero'. Thus in *Puissances de Paris* he describes the streets, boulevards, squares, opera-house, picture houses and in really marvellous imagery unfolds their personalities and reveals their souls. In *L'Armée dans la Ville*—a play in five acts—he takes as antagonists (heroes) two groups of people possessing a common 'soul'—the army—the army of occupation and the people of the occupied town. These two souls are antipathetic and the people plot against the army: the idea being for each family to take into its family circle a soldier and on a given night every family is to murder the soldier they are fêteing. All does not go well: The soul of the men of the town becomes distinct and falters in the common purpose. Against this weakness the soul of the women rises to the highest pitch of heroic sacrifice. The women remember their past sufferings and are determined on revenge. The last act is on the appointed night at the Mayor's House, to which the General of the Army of Occupation has been invited. Midnight, the appointed hour approaches: the Mayor refuses to kill the General: the town is now aroused with cries and calls to arms. In desperation the Mayor's wife makes violent love to the General: which does the required trick, for the Mayor then shoots the General in a jealous rage. The plot as a whole is failing and the dying General realizes this and his last words are a kind of triumphal song of the Army's soul: and as the General slowly dies, the Mayor's wife realizes that she really does love him. So the two virile and heroic souls are united. And that weak faltering soul of the men of the town is deservingly defeated.

The whole play is perhaps much finer than this hasty description makes it appear. There is a real tragic element in it and a fine dramatic unity. And you see the idea (of the 'souls') has possibilities.

Now for *Mort de Quelqu'un*, which is slightly different. Here the author just takes an ordinary retired railway engine driver, living in Paris, and lets him die. The man is lonely and lives in a lodging house with apparently neither friend nor foe. On the surface it looks as though such an event could have no possible artistic significance. But Romains shows that it is just as though you had dropped a pebble into a still pond and the concentric rings ripple outwards and outwards until they die. He traces the ripples caused by the man's death. The experiences of the lodging house keeper who finds the dead body. The telegram to the man's aged parents, living in the country. The effect of the telegram there. The journey of the old father to Paris. The burial of the engine driver. The reflection, many years afterwards, of a man who suddenly remembers this particular funeral, and how he then thought of death and how he now thinks of it. There is one fine scene: The simple funeral cortège is proceeding along the streets and in front is perceived a mob and a tumult. It is a conflict between the police and a demonstration of strikers and things are getting hot. The funeral approaches slowly and unobserved. It enters the outskirts of the mob. Then they see it and as though moved by the wand of a magician, break away, move to a side and reverently uncover their heads as the coffin passes. Such power had the death of 'a nobody'. But the book is full of wonderful pictures like that, and a clear definite appreciation of character and scenes. But that is not the greatest thing in the book. It is such a magnificent piece of architecture. It has that unity of idea I talked about in my article on Poetry.★ The book is built on one idea (I don't mean *idea* in the ethical sense: I mean something that has an artistic whole). The only metaphor that is exact is rather a cheap one—there is a string upon which all the pearls of the book are strung. There is more—it is like a cathedral built with perfect harmony and balance.

9.iii.18

It is June here. For three days there hasn't been a cloud in the sky and the larks have been singing all day long. And though we are actually in the line, we find it hard to realize that there is a war on. Things are unearthly quiet. I am writing this out in the sun, and the scene round me is a wide amphitheatre about 600 yards in diameter, an old sand quarry. It looks great in the early sun—a rich golden brown, but as the sun gets higher it turns yellower. Our dugouts are deep down in the sides of the quarry and quite comfortable with beds and tables. We keep a cat—a beautiful brown and white one, very clean and full of play and a foot-warmer by night. Yesterday I was down in the dugout all by myself and a big setter dog flopped in from heaven only knows where. The floor of the dugout is partly boarded and partly bare sand. Without taking the slightest notice of me he flopped down on the boards and proceeded to go to sleep. About ten minutes later, he got up and went over to the unboarded part of the dugout and there he clawed the sand until he had made a round basin. This he found more comfortable and I thought he had finally settled. But soon after, his conscience must have pricked him, for he got up and came to me and was most affectionate, trying to lick my face and rubbing his snout against me. And all this without a word of invitation! So I concluded that it was another case of the Wonders of Instinct. When we had sweethearted long enough he went under the table—and there he got a shock for Pussy had taken up a position under there. So many growls on the part of Pussy and whines and whimpers on the part of the dog. Eventually he disappeared and I've never seen him since. Pussy is much happier though.

★ "Definitions towards a Modern Theory of Poetry". *Art and Letters*, vol. I, pp. 73–8.

EXTRACTS FROM A DIARY

I've just finished Hardy's *The Return of the Native* and I've been rather disappointed with it. I think better people, James in particular, have spoilt Hardy for me. His plot creaks like an antiquated machine and his characters are put together to suit Hardy's ideas and are not revelations of any human value. I don't think he digs very deeply down into the individual. He has a philosophy of no little value which is a world-view, a generalization, and his art is constructed according to it. But that, of course, is not art. Art should construct *out of* a philosophy if you like: it must do so because a writer's character and temperament are his philosophy. But the final things should have a value of its own, a beauty, an individual human value. But I'm not dismissing Hardy with these words: he has a fine sense of tragedy, and he can make the puppets of his mind act with some significance.

14.iii.18

Summer is still with us and spring yet hardly due! I don't know how long this sunny miracle will last. The interpreter came up to me yesterday and in his quaint English said: 'You Eenglish used to say "Zunny France" and to shrug your shoulders; but now *I* can smile and say, "Voilà—Zunny France."'

Meanwhile everything is beautifully quiet and life a day-long laze. But I don't waste a minute. I'm making excursions into modern French Poetry, reading an account of the Philosophy of Benedetto Croce, and even a novel at the tag-end of the day.

The more I read of French poetry, the more I realize how un-English it is. It is too metaphysical, too questioning and not lyrical enough. Even when it is most lyrical, its lyricism is of the quiet, contemplative sort. Here is a translation of one by Georges Duhamel, and perhaps the most appealing one I've found so far:

EDUCATION

I find on your hands gloves
Covering them like a shell
And weighing them down.

They are like hawks
Blindfolded and tame
As we take them to the chase,

121

They are afraid and seem shy;
It is time to let them take the air,
To rid them, quickly and completely
Of their strange covering.

Strip them as of a rind;
Bare their miraculous flesh,
And in the wind as in a stream
Plunge them with sudden strength

Free from their thick film
Move in the wind your sensitive fingers,
Move and gather and take the things that crowd there,
And then, as you would run with a little water in your palm,
Come back with eager haste, bringing me those riches.

I've finished the final proof of 'Kneeshaw'—the realistic war poem I told you of, and sent it off to Rutter for No. 4 *Art and Letters*. It is to form the nucleus of a small volume of its kind, which I hope to get published in autumn—if I can overcome the paper scarcity. I've already got nearly as many poems as I want—about twenty. I want to write a preface and design a frontispiece and then I shall be ready. It isn't exactly a joyful book: it is a protest against all the glory camouflage that is written about the war: It means I have to be brutal and even ugly. But the truth should be told, and though I'm not quite conceited enough to imagine that I can do it finally, I think my voice might get a hearing. But I'd rather write one 'pastoral' than a book of this realism. My heart is not in it: it is too objective.

17.iii.18

The great days are still with us. I went a walk this evening with Col to the top of a small hill that commands most of this flat country. The sun was just in his last glory and there was a slight mist on the ground. Westward this mist fused with the mellow sunlight and the land seemed to be covered with a thick golden dust. It hung about the distant trees like golden snow, and like snow, soon melted away, but not without a last transient flare of colour. I sat on the hill and watched it till it was all cold and colourless, and Col asking me if I had finished 'dreaming'.

I have started *Walden* and find it full of wisdom, especially as to the use to be made of life.

1.iv.18

'It's lovely by the seaside' and that is where I am.

I always feared that the beautiful peace I was telling you about was rather ominous. Suddenly one morning early (the 21st) it turned to a raging hell. What has happened since then I shall never get you told about until I have written a book about it. At present you must be satisfied with very bare facts.

We were rushed up to the line in the early hours of morning and from then and for six days and nights we were fighting as I never dreamt I should fight—without sleep—often without food and all the time besieged by hordes of the Boche. The Colonel was wounded during the second day and I had to take command of the battalion. We were surrounded in our original position and had to fight our way through. We took up position after position, always to be surrounded. On the whole the men were splendid and there were many fine cases of heroism. But our casualties were very heavy and we who have come through may thank our lucky stars eternally.

I couldn't let you have word before. Things like the post 'go to pot' in an affair like this. But I am all right now. I was a bit of a scarecrow at the end of it, but now we have been withdrawn to a beautiful quiet place near the sea, with nothing much else to do save sleep and eat.

Colin missed the first four days and I was glad of it (though he wasn't). We are sharing a billet here and are happier than ever. It is wonderful how happy you do feel when you find peace once more and yourself alive to enjoy it. I think the experiences of the last ten days have had rather a deep effect on me. I'll talk to you more about it when I'm more collected. I saw humanity very naked and life both precious and pitiful. By chance as I went out that morning of the 21st I slipped a book into my pocket. It was *Walden*. I didn't get a chance of looking at it the first six days, but in my wandering since I have read it and found much comfort there. In a very different way—the very opposite way—old Thoreau got to the naked reality of life and came to the same conclusions. It all drives me to an individualism, an anarchy which

it is for each of us to realize. But more of this when I've thought
more.*

6.iv.18

Moore's (Edwin Muir) 'theories' are about to be republished
in book form. I will get them, re-read them and then we will
discuss them.

You must read *Walden*—though he seems to have been rather
a loveless old stick. But his 'nearness' to Nature is wonderful and
his general opinions very sensible. Will you read him in my copy?
It is only an 'Everyman' but it lived in my pocket all those terrible
days and has acquired a 'soul'.

I don't think I'm ready to discuss the change that is taking place
in my 'political' sentiments. It is a revolt of the individual against
the association which involves him in activities which do not
interest him: a jumping to the ultimate anarchy which I have
always seen as the ideal of all who value beauty and intensity of
life. 'A beautiful anarchy'—that is my cry. I hate mobs—they
fight and kill, build filthy cities and make horrid dins. And I begin
to think that their salvation and re-creation is none of my concern, but the concern of each individual. Only so can these associations be broken—cell by cell, segment by segment.

Your criticism of 'Education' leads me to think that here we
may at present find an intellectual gap between us. You value the
'cosmic' generalizations of Wordsworth more than the 'intensity'
or 'individuality' of the poem I quoted. It is because individual
experience is so intense that 'we moderns' value it more than
Wordsworth's cosmic utterances. The individual *experiences* himself: he only guesses beyond his own soul.

15.iv.18

There was a tempting question in one of your recent letters.
In what manner does an Evolutionary Theory affect our attitude
to Life? Perhaps you guessed it would tempt me. So like a fish I
rise—I hope not to be eaten. I think my general trend of thought
on this matter will agree with yours. I see so much philosophy and
ethics absolutely made null and void by the want of a little evolutionary knowledge, that perhaps I am driven to exaggeration of
its importance. To me evolution seems the essential *fact* of Life:

* See "In Retreat", pp. 228-54.

and so it should colour *every theory* of Life. But it doesn't. Most philosophers and moralists are blissfully ignorant of its very hypothesis. They have vaguely heard the name: but hearing it have labelled it 'science' and dismissed it from the abstract holiness of their minds. Especially do the religious kidney exasperate me: they hastily assume that Evolution has to do with the material side of life: that their concern is with the spiritual: and so Evolution is no concern of theirs. They never realize that Evolution contradicts the dualism of mind and matter which makes the distinction possible. For I reckon nothing much to the theories which start with organic life and merely show the origin of species. I reckon with the wider and bolder theories which evolve matter from ether, organic life from matter, and mind from organic life. I am prepared to swallow the whole lot as the only reasonable (and spiritually satisfying) explanation of the universe.

The 'proof' does not concern me just now: there is a useful summary of the latter process in McCabe's *Evolution of Mind* which I have at home and which is yours whenever you are ready for it. The first process—matter from ether—needs imagination and scientific faith. I give it any amount of both. But even if 'proof' did concern me, I would argue that the only proof necessary was pragmatic proof. Pragmatism says that if a philosophy, a theory of life, or a moral law *works*, then it is true. The theory in action is the test. My theory of Evolution works; I can prove that to my own satisfaction: therefore for me it is true.

Now for a philosophy of Evolution. This is where I think Nietzsche comes in. He had a philosophy of Evolution and for that reason I think we must hesitate before we reject him as a mere prophet of brutality and force. We have touched on Nietzsche many a time before, and I can't go very deeply into him with you until I have tackled him again. But some idea of the Superman I believe to be the essential Idea of any evolutionary attitude towards Life. I mean the theory makes possible a higher race: and what is possible and desirable should be aimed for.

That is our concern for the future. And I think it implies as to method certain measures towards ensuring a progressive physical evolution of the human race, such as Eugenics or Birth Control. The details of these measures I haven't given much thought to: I'm not yet sure that there should be any public or state action in the matter. It is useless developing the physique unless you can be sure of a decent mind to grace it. And the development of the mind is such an individual thing. And once you have developed the mind, and decided what measures of birth control, etc., are necessary, the individuals with the requisite mentality would adopt these measures independent of any state action. Adapt your Civilization to your Culture and not vice versa: that's a truth I've gleaned from the Dostoevsky articles. And culture is never state-made or state-controlled without disaster to civilization. That's the lesson Germany is learning. And be sure that the cultured individual will look after the future of the race. He cannot, in the true sense of being cultured, do otherwise. You see what an individualist I am becoming! This attitude towards the future is not the only implication of an Evolutionary theory of life. That is, as it were, the religion of Evolution. There are also the Ethics of Evolution: the effect of this religion on our relations with the present. I find this well expressed in a 'Home University' book by Thompson & Geddes which is very fine and expresses well the attitude evolution implies. I make one exception: There is too much emphasis on the *strenuous* life: the end of the strenuous life is success and civilization rather than culture. I would substitute the *vivid* life: the end of that is character, which includes culture. People whose sole aim in life is 'to get on' are quite beyond the pale. They usually get so far on that they leave all decent people by the wayside: and they never find them again.

Old Thoreau knew the truth of this: he, of all men I have ever met or read, is the best witness in defence of 'the vivid life':

'I went to the woods because I wished to live deliberately, to front only the essential facts of life, and see if I could not learn what it had to teach, and not, when I came to die, discover that I had not lived. I did not wish to live what was not life, living is so dear: nor did I wish to practise resignation, unless it was quite necessary. I wanted to live deep and suck out all the marrow of life, to live so sturdily and Spartan-like as to put to rout all that was not life, to cut a broad swath and shave close, to drive life into a corner, and reduce it to its lowest terms, and, if it proved to be mean, why then to get the whole and genuine meanness of it, and publish its meanness to the world; or if it were sublime, to know it by experience, and be able to give a true account of it in my next excursion. For most men, it appears to me, are in a strange uncertainty about it, whether it is of the devil or of God, and have somewhat hastily concluded that it is the chief end of man here to "glorify God and enjoy him forever".'

That, I think, is the gospel of Evolution, according to Thoreau and me.

18.iv.18

Meanwhile—talking of the adventurous and strenuous life—I lead it. We have had a ten days' trip in our new sector, which isn't much of a change from the last, except in scenery. But it is a life that has little spiritual beauty in it, so hardly comes up to the demand of Thoreau & Co.

28.iv.18

I'm afraid the days of long letters are over for a while. Of course we have become involved in the fighting again and our life is terribly strenuous. We are all weary and almost broken-hearted. But we manage to keep up an appearance of unconcern. But it needs a strong will. I'm afraid Colin is affected: he is no longer the gay heart he used to be and even I have to infuse some spirit into him—a circumstance I should never have thought would come about—rather the other way round from my own idea of our respective temperaments.

Forgive me for writing in this gloomy mood. But nowadays to be false to the reality would choke me. I don't want you to think we are unhappy—we have comradeship in our troubles and that makes all the difference.

9.v.18

Our precious Colin is missing. We have been through hell for the second time in seven weeks and once again been cruelly smashed. Col was in the front line with his company. They were gassed and barraged with heavies for about four hours and then surrounded from all sides by the Boche. All day we had no news of them but in the evening we counter-attacked and took several prisoners—among them an officer who spoke very good English and was a fairly intelligent specimen. I questioned him about the morning's happenings and he said that a good few prisoners had been taken, among them a captain. Now Col was the only captain in the front line, so I feel pretty confident that it was he. Besides, the prisoner said that he had gold stars on his shoulder-straps, was

very young and fair—all of which points to Colin. So I feel fairly
happy about him. He, at any rate, is out of it and with ordinary
luck should come through all right. I am the unfortunate one: I am
robbed of my best friend in circumstances which make such a
friend as Col half one's life. But for his sake I am glad.

How sick I am of the whole business. Most of the prisoners
we took were boys under twenty. Our own recent reinforcements were all boys. Apart from uniforms, German and English
are as like as two peas: beautiful fresh children. And they are
massacred in inconceivable torment. This is the irony of this war:
individually we are the one as good as the other: you can't hate
these innocent children simply because they dress in grey uniforms. And they are all magnificently brave, English and German
alike. But simply because we are united into a callous inhuman
association called a State, and because a State is ruled by politicians
whose aim (and under the circumstances their duty) is to support
and maintain the life and sovereignty of this monster, life and
hope are denied and sacrificed. And look at their values. On the
one hand national well-being and vanity, commercial expansion,
power: on the other love, joy, hope—all that makes life worth
living—all that persuades one to consent to live among so much
that is barbarous and negative. So perhaps you will begin to see
the connection between 'the German push, Thoreau and anarchy'.
And perhaps you will get 'a glimpse of how, in my heart of hearts,
I regard my whole connection with the Army and its work'. I
could make my connection with it something of a success *if I had
the will. Without* the will I have not done so badly. I like its man-
liness, the courage it demands, the fellowship it gives. These are
infinitely precious things. But I hate the machine—the thing as a
whole and its duty (to kill), its very existence. My will is to
destroy it and my energies must be devoted to that end. Is this the
glimpse you wanted?

Colin's fate rather alters my outlook. Now I don't think I
should hesitate to take the Staff job—it is no use making a martyr
of one's self and clinging to this worst of existences in the Army.
The Army does not take account of martyrdom and besides, I've
been a martyr long enough to satisfy even my vanity. On the
other hand the Staff job is a very uncertain one. In the meanwhile
the certainty of flying may come.* What then? I don't funk it by

* I had applied for a transfer to the Royal Flying Corps.

any means—I rather hanker after its 'romance'. On the other hand (the 'hands' are getting rather confusing, but never mind), to start flying now is to revolutionize my Army life to an unknown extent. That would have been all right with Col. But alone? And besides, the others in the battalion—old 'Pick' especially, ridicule the idea of me 'leaving them in the lurch'. To go to the Staff is a natural step—they would be 'proud' of me there. But to go to the Flying Corps is to desert them, to take an unnatural step. But in a family where 'desertions' are so often forced, a voluntary 'desertion' does not matter so much. I rather think I shall settle this muddle of 'to be or not to be' by accepting the first fate that comes my way: and if it is flying I shall fly.

17.v.18

I don't quite know where I left off in my last letter. So much has happened since then. We have wandered down to a new sector and have become practically a new battalion in all but name and I've been rather overwhelmed with work. But suffice it to say that I am now trying to do the almost impossible, which in this case is to lie my full length on the grass and write a letter. It is so hot that it is cruelty to move. But the grass is the lawn of a deserted garden, green and shady, with a few restful narcissi (almost my favourite flower, I think) to delight my eyes, birds 'cheeping' and only the drone of an aeroplane to remind one that war is our existence. Perhaps the quiet is a little too reminiscent of those happy days before St. Quentin to be altogether a joy. But still it is a blessed balm to our weary souls.

19.v.18

The days remain sweetly uneventful and never before has Nature been so 'motherly' to me. In my rather dazed mood I look around me to find summer on me with a rush. Winter seems only yesterday and spring a disturbed dream. There are all sorts of flowers, known and unknown in the deserted gardens—tulips, forget-me-nots, snowballs, stocks and the lilac just dying. The trees are great (we are in a part that war has dealt kindly with) and as I write I watch them shiver against the twilight sky. There is an odd gun or two going off, but they seem to accentuate the stillness. You can tell how keenly I am plunging into this natural peace, for when I recall yesterday's events nothing seems to have possessed any significance at all save the sudden discovery, in the morning, of five wonderful dragonflies all on one shrub. Four of them were beautiful golden things whose wings you could only see by moving your head until you got the angle of reflection. Their golden bodies were pulsing and throbbing with life and their antennae were busy exploring the leaves. The fifth one was different—a long slender body, like a greyhound of his species and all marked out in a wonderful colour scheme of grey, bright blue and green. His wings were like an infinitely delicate and fragile piece of lace. Nothing else mattered in the whole day but those dragonflies, and the joy they gave me.

I have finished the Hazlitt and I think it is worth sending on. It only contains ten essays, rather too copiously annotated; but they are all beauties and I think you will like them—perhaps you know some of them already. Of all literary forms I think the essay most demands peace and leisure, and in this case they have rather suffered from the lack of such accompaniments. So I look forward to re-reading them some day. There is a delightful one 'On making a Journey' which would be fuel for much discussion. But they are good for their style and general qualities of tone and content.

The loss of Colin drives me more than ever to the companionship of books. So you must not grumble if they overwhelm my letters. Apart from just a slight uneasiness, which will disappear when I hear definitely that he is safe, I cannot but feel quietly satisfied with his fate. The strain was killing his spirit, and in the comparative calm of a prisoner's life he would recover his buoyancy and will.

By now it is night outside—beautifully starlit. But there is a German aeroplane somewhere in the sky with evil intent and I have had to close the shutters to hide my light and to divide me from the beauties outside. You see how fugitive our peacefulness is!

30.v.18.

I have just finished devouring Kenneth Richmond's latest book: *Education for Liberty*. It is more technical than anything else of his I have yet read, and for that reason might have more interest for you than for me. But I defy you to enjoy it more than I have done. Of course, it is not quite so exciting as *W. E. Ford*—it is much sedater. I almost thought, at times, too sedate. I suppose he wants to reach as wide an audience as possible among your benighted colleagues, and so takes care not to appear too cranky. To me he makes your profession quite a romantic affair: I feel like a prince cheated of his kingdom. I suppose really I am a dreamer well away from the tyrannic reality of a bureaucracy.

The anarchy question can wait. There are points one can't very well discuss in a censorable letter. And, at any rate, I'm not settled yet. I'm wondering if Tolstoy would help me. His ideas on Art have always prejudiced me against him, but his social philosophy is perhaps very fine. Rutter is a great admirer of *War and Peace* which I have never read. I must tackle it soon, but it is no light task—it runs to 3 volumes Everyman. Three other rather big things I have resolved to read. 1. Florio's Montaigne. 2. Bagehot's Literary Studies. 3. Lamb's Letters. O for a month among the Lakes with these!

2.6.18

I have now finished the Coleridge and I will send it and Richmond's book off to you today. I don't advise you to read every word of the *Biographia*. There is a lot of out-of-date metaphysics in it. But luckily the metaphysics are confined to certain chapters and I have marked those worth reading in the 'Contents'. The others remind me of a piece of advice Rutter gave me not long ago: To the effect that I should be careful to distinguish between Philosophy and Metaphysics and avoid the latter as the Devil. It only leads to involutions and mental gymnastics of no permanent value, and though showing you to be a mighty clever fellow, damning the artistic interest of your work. A piece of advice which, as I look back to those who have survived as great artists and those whose reputation died with their era, I recognize as very true.

You will find, as I did, that the most interesting part of the book is concerned with Wordsworth. It is a magnificent criticism, so exhaustive and final that one wonders how a contemporary could have done it, especially when the critic makes mistakes in other cases (as in the laudation of one Bowles, whose poetry is as dead as Queen Anne as far as I know). One criticism of Wordsworth he makes is exactly my feeling (predominant in my case more than in Coleridge's—who only thought it a minor fault) and that is the 'matter-of-factness' of Wordsworth's poetry. I quite realize the immense task Wordsworth set himself in ridding poetry of its flamboyancy and bombast. He did incalculable good there. But he went to the other extreme—his simplicity *did* become simpleness.

My other feeling about Wordsworth is one that Coleridge couldn't very well detect as he himself is tarred with the same brush: that is the *unreality* of his moral sentiments. They are magnificent, noble, sublime. I can see how beautiful and ideal was the philosophy of Wordsworth—he thought in terms of immaculate virtue. But he would not have recognized it when he met it in the street—if ever he frequented such a low place. His whole life was so sheltered from reality that the only way he had of creating a philosophy and a world-view was by looking into the imaginative purity of his own mind.

Now as you know (did you not once teach this to me before I had realized how every fact of life demonstrated it?) the value of any man is not in the doctrine he professes but in the character he reveals and the life he leads. But I have a sure feeling that Wordsworth would have put his money on the man full of virtuous sentiments. And even Coleridge. But not Hazlitt or Lamb.

But Coleridge has shown me the beauties of Wordsworth's poetry and I am ready to admit my past blindness. The two examples on pages 254 and 255 are conclusive. The 'Ode with the long title', as I call it for short, I have always admired, though I think the 'idea' of the poem too fanciful and unreal. And there are blotches of pompous sentiment—like:

'The thought of our past years in me doth breed Perpetual benedictions':
'Clouds of glory'—'Nature's Priest'—'blank misgivings of a Creature'—'cherish', etc.

We have had eight days in the line—beautifully peaceful. We are not, I am glad to say, involved in the latest débâcle. During the eight days I managed with much sweat to finish the essay I started months ago on Jules Romains and now it is ready for any who will receive it. But I'm blessed if I know where to send it. I'm not quite satisfied with it—it shows traces of its disjointed creation and is rather too expository. But the subject is almost untouched in English and is really great and full of suggestion. But more of it when you have seen the essay.*

8.vi.18

Colin is all right. His Elsie wrote to tell me that they had had a cable to say he was a prisoner and well. That's a great relief—to know for certain. I had persuaded myself to be very sure—but—war is war.

I'm very busy nowadays—but all very dull. I should say that being an Adjutant out here is worse than being the Managing Director and Secretary (rolled into one) of a firm of 1,000 employees in business. And I don't profess to be anything like a business man.

I've done scarcely any reading lately—'no time'. But I have got and started to re-read *We Moderns.*† It gains from being gathered together in a volume and I don't remember a book that I have found so full of acceptable suggestions. Of course, it is a series of texts rather than a sermon—but that is part of its value.

We are 'out' just now. Yesterday we had battalion sports which went off in great style. I never enjoyed sports so much before. Plenty of fun in the fair besides the usual events. Today was rather interesting. We marched a few miles (I on four legs, as usual) and after lunch in the open—to the strains of our mighty brass band—we did a practice stunt with Tanks. Coming back (across the battle-field) all the men (including me) were allowed to 'mount' the tanks and have a ride. I got nearly baked—choked with petrol smoke and my clothes greased (much to the annoyance of the faithful Towers)—but enjoyed it all immensely. But it *has* made me sleepy.

14.vi.18

The transfer has come through.‡ I ought to be in England by the 19th. I have to report there (London)—endure a medical board and then I hope get leave.

9.vii.18

On Friday I got a wire ordering me to report to the 3rd Battn. at West Hartlepool *for duty*. Arrived here on Saturday: they have

---

* It was published in *Art and Letters*, Vol. II, pp. 44-52 (Winter, 1918-19).
† By Edwin Muir.
‡ To the Royal Flying Corps. I was rejected by the medical board.

not heard anything about me from the War Office. I got 48 hours'
leave and went to London for my kit and to Leeds for some more
and back here last night. Still no orders about me. But the
adjutant here thinks it means at least a long stay in England.

20.vii.18

This you can regard as good news or otherwise: The doctor
here examined me and says there's nothing much the matter with
me except general 'run-down'. So France may not be a too distant
prospect.

This is rather good: Grant Richards, the publisher, having seen
'Kneeshaw'*, has asked to see more with a view to publication.

Also the Editress of *The Egoist* writes to me that the Italian
professor of English in the University of Turin greatly admired
'The Orchard' which appeared in her paper. So you see my fame
is cosmopolitan already.

1.ix.18

Yesterday I had a very interesting if not even a very momentous
day. Did I tell you that there was a writer called Hueffer stationed
at Redcar? I met him last Monday at dinner and told him I
wanted a talk with him so he invited me over on the Saturday.
What a day I had! He talked to me for a solid eight hours. Just
imagine the joy of walking along the cliffs from Redcar to Saltburn with a man who knew Henry James *intimately*. I did 'pump'
him, as you can guess. He is, I should say, about 45, a man of
charming manners and immense knowledge. Quite a sportsman
too, for he has been to the front and been wounded. I can't quite
see *why* he is in the Army because he could so easily be out of it if
he wanted. It must be some ideal within him. He is married and his
wife (Violet Hunt, the novelist) is taking a house (or rooms) at
Runswick of all places. But he has stayed there before and loves it
and Whitby dearly. He told me an immense lot about James, his
delightful personality, his methods of work and so on. Remind
me some day to tell you a delicious story about James and Kipling.
Also one about Arnold Bennett. It will interest you to know that
when Wells was young and unknown and penniless, dying of
consumption, James came to the rescue. In this way: Wells had
scraped enough money together to pay his and his wife's (Jane)

* A poem published in *Art and Letters*, Vol. I, No. 4.

fare to Romney, where a certain doctor in whom Wells had a strong belief practised. When they got there they found this doctor had suddenly gone abroad. They hadn't enough money to pay their railway fare back to London and H.G. was terribly ill. So Jane, remembering that Henry James lived at Rye, a few miles away, went there and told James that her husband, a young genius, was dying of starvation. So James immediately went down to Romney, took a furnished house for Wells and his wife, provided food and attendance and acted the good fairy in every way. About a week afterwards *The Wonderful Visit* was published and was an immediate success and since then, of course, Wells has ever prospered. Hueffer discovered Wells, before those Romney days. He came into the *Saturday Review* office and asked for reviewing work (scientific) and Hueffer, rather attracted by him, walked home with him and Wells confided to him that he was penniless and must have that reviewing work, so Hueffer went back to the office and arranged for some, but advised Wells to write scientific short stories, which Wells didn't want to do but was persuaded to try and with such success.

There were others he told me about—Galsworthy, Ezra Pound (!), Rebecca West (great fun she, he says, but promising).

I had read one or two of Hueffer's books—the one on James and his latest volume of poems particularly and these two, together with one called *The Good Soldier* which I am going to get, are the only ones that he considers really matter. But he rather prides himself on being one of the few stylists in the English language. I guess—I don't know *yet*—that he is little but a stylist. But we shall see.

14.ix.18   Middlesbrough
This last week I've been in a queer dazed sort of mood. The week before I really did work, doing a solid two or three hours every day at the novel in the evenings and was rewarded by getting my first Part off to Toby last Sunday. Since then I've done nothing—theatre and that sort of waste of time.

I've been reading Hueffer's novel *The Good Soldier*. It is very grim and tragic but I rather think a great book. The style might be neater but it is a good narrative style.

170 Chinese Poems, translated by A. Waley, are great. These also you must read. I've just got *Green Mansions* by W. H. Hudson.

Didn't I lend you his *Crystal Age*? Hueffer thinks the latter not up to his standard, but that the standard of *Green Mansions* and *Purple Land* is *the finest in modern literature*. It looks beautiful.

I've now got an unread James—*The Ambassadors*.

29.ix.18   Middlesbrough

I sent you *Tarr*—you must digest it. Don't pay too much respect to the *New Age* criticism. Wyndham Lewis belongs to a clique which the *New Age* opposes—rather stupidly sometimes—though the clique rather suffers from an obsession as to their own exclusive omniscience. But *Tarr* is very important: but for reasons that it is still more important to bear in mind. It is *not* good writing. The style is vivid but that is about all. But it is the expression of an extraordinarily acute mind. His theories are good and true: about art, about the conduct of life and—within its abnormal limits— about sex. On life and sex it misses so much value because the protagonists or exemplars—Tarr and Kreisler—are so useless or rather valueless—though the value of art, you know, is not neces- sarily utilitarian. Lewis, of course, is an admirer of Dostoevsky— and that is D's fault too: to treat of abnormals rather than of human beings.

I don't mean that you mustn't write about nasty people. The artist who makes a nasty man *live* in the pages of his book has as much right to our admiration as the creator of the purest and loveliest heroine you like to imagine. But your nasty man must have a place in life. Kreisler hasn't: he wanders about Paris like a devil in Paradise: or worse than that—like a bird's wing on a woman's hat, that should be part of a living flying thing, but is a disjointed, dead thing, yet still wandering amongst living things.

Tarr is also rather disjointed—Bertha I think is all right: she is alive, at any rate. So is Anastasya: but she is rather too good to be true.

The Part called 'holocausts' *is* good style: the best form of adventure narrative that I can imagine. It is as vivid, swift and relentless as the action itself.

But Wyndham Lewis is the ringleader of 'les jeunes' and has a personality *and* a BRAIN: that is why he must be read.

24.x.18   28 Half Moon Street, Piccadilly

Arrived about 10.30 p.m. Toby met me with the news that

everybody at 148 down with 'flu. So he had taken rooms for us at the above address—which really is much better—no time wasted travelling to and fro. A quaint house—scores of little rooms. Mine has a bathroom attached and is quite jolly—and they only charge me a guinea for the week—not at all bad. Meals we get at all sorts of weird places.

The only thing that really impressed me this night was the beautiful quiet of London. Here I am in the very heart of it and it is silent as a mountain top.

25.x.18

I'm a new man in this atmosphere. My eyes gleam and I relish every sight and sound.

Remember as I go on describing what we do that Toby and I are most of the time planning and plotting the future. Lord, we do talk!

This morning we did not rise very early. Went to the bank and found my state of affairs remarkably prosperous. Nothing is going to spoil this wonderful week.

Then we went to see Beaumont, who is publishing my poems and who I thought might possibly offer some opportunity for the future. But previously Toby had cast doubt on this project.

Visit settled it. He won't do. A very self-opinionated young fellow with whom it would be difficult to agree. Besides his business does not offer much scope for development. He hand-prints and colours all his editions, and his things have their peculiar value precisely because they are craft work and limited. But he is quite keen to publish me but can't promise any very early date. But I think I shall leave them with him, as I don't think I shall ever be popular enough to sell well (I mean in thousands) and if I'm going to be select I might as well do the thing well. Besides, I believe that a book should be a beautiful thing in itself, apart from its content.

In the afternoon we went to the Russian Ballet—Schumann's 'Carneval'. The dancing is beautiful, sheer poetry of movement and pose. 'Carneval' is rather dainty but vivacious, mostly depending on the old Pierrot, Pierrette and Harlequin motif. Music quite good. You remember I heard it on the piano (Moiseiwitch) at Harrogate. You would like the Russian Ballet. I promise myself at least two more visits this week.

We went to Ginner's to tea. Three women and a Hungarian musician there. He has two bare rooms off Tottenham Court Road, but things to sit on and a cheery fire. Women rather the usual Bohemian type, but it struck me that you would rather like them. They are silly in some ways but beautifully frank.

Two soon disappeared. Then the Hungarian played Chopin to us—he is a wonderful player but I suppose a more wonderful composer, but his own things are too difficult for himself to play!

Then the five of us went out to dinner—not very exciting. Afterwards the Hungarian went home—he is an alien and has to be in by 9 p.m.—and soon after the remaining lady disappeared. We three men then went round to look up Wyndham Lewis, but he was out. So we went back to Ginner's room and discussed the future in detail. But I'm writing this in bed and my shoulders are cold and my arm aches and I'm getting sleepy so the future can wait until morning. But it is very exciting, you know.

26.x.18

But the future will have to wait a bit longer. It's already midnight but the day has been crammed and I must keep up with the present. Besides, the future is still in a state of flux, except that I have definitely decided that I must get out of the Army at the earliest opportunity.

Today I have met the veritable lions.

In the morning we 'did' the British Water Colour Society—nothing very exciting.

Lunch at Eustace Miles'—vegetarian!

After lunch (it had been arranged over the 'phone) we went down to Kensington to see Wyndham Lewis's big war picture which he is painting for the Canadian Government. Found a characteristic note pinned on the door to say he would be back 2.30–3. So Pound's place being very near we went round and saw the real live Ezra in his den. Ezra is very nice after all. As you would *not* expect he speaks in a quiet soft voice and though affected in appearance is delightfully normal in manner. We were only there about 20 minutes and then we had to rush off to Lewis again—But I go to Pound's again Monday morning.

Lewis was late again. But he came at last, and of course he is not half so ferocious as you might imagine. But I do not think I shall ever really love Lewis as I could love the Pounds—but that is probably because he is more entitled to a different feeling. He is rather brusque, very energetic, quite normal in appearance, and a good talker. His big picture is quite interesting but not so fine as some drawings he showed us later.

We left him after about ten minutes arranging to go to his flat for tea at 4.30. Meanwhile we had an appointment 3.30 at the Café Royal with the Sitwells. Osbert and Sachie turned up. They are sons of Sir George Sitwell—aristocratic, wealthy, officers in the Guards, Oxford University and what not. But *also* furious socialists, good poets (Sachie very good) and very young (about my own age). They are crammed full of enthusiasm for the future and it is with them that I can imagine myself being associated a good deal in the future. They are wanting to buy *Art and Letters* and Toby will probably let them have it. I remain in it. We talked excitedly for half an hour and then went off to Lewis's flat for tea, having arranged to go to the Sitwells' place Monday evening.

Lewis's flat—lots of stairs to go up, but a view and fresh air at the top and the jolliest suite of rooms: 1 bedroom, 1 sitting-room, 1 bathroom, 1 kitchen sort of place (very small). But all very jolly and dainty. I fancy they cost about £35 a year.

He had a girl there 'to pour out the tea'—I did not catch her name, but she is a young poetess who has not yet published. Quite a nice girl.

We talked till about seven, Lewis growing on me. We must not take *Tarr* too seriously. He loves to hurl indigestible fragments at the public.

His drawings (descriptive of artillery life at the Front) are great. The best war drawings I've seen yet. Full of power and energy, and true.

A nice dinner by ourselves at the Gourmet and then down to Putney for letters and so back here and now.

The details of my future will be fairly settled by the end of this wonderful week.

27.x.18

A more sedate day—as befits the Sabbath. We met Ginner and the Hungarian for lunch, which was very jolly, in one of the foreign places. In the afternoon we went to a concert, where

Moiseiwitch was the chief attraction. After tea we went down to
Brown's at Richmond, where there was an impromptu sort of
concert. Brown is a very nice old fellow and has a nice house full
of good pictures. But rather effusively Bohemian—'Do sit on the
floor.' And it was all rather rococo and last century. Singing rather
bored me and the music was flat after Moiseiwitch, whose wonderful restraint and precision spoil one for emotional orgies. The
greatest thing was meeting Lucien Pissarro, who is our best
landscape painter and a charming character. About fifty with great
black whiskers and two keen eyes peering out of all his bushiness.
He loves the country and gets wonderfully the colour of it in
quite a distinctive way. He might with his knowledge and technique have done more startling things. But he hasn't been ambitious that way. He is a vivid foil to Lewis. In another ten years
people will talk of a Pissarro landscape as they now talk of a
'Turner sunset' or a Whistler nocturne. There is something
amazing in the life-long patience and modesty of this man. It
inspires with some sort of awe, and fills me with a doubt of
organized 'fuss'. It is confoundingly difficult to see a clear path in
my future.

28.x.18

Met Ezra at 11.30. He is really quite a decent sort: his side
whiskers, dainty beard, byronic collar and huge square blue
buttons seem rather absurd. But I believe the man is actually *shy*.
He is certainly a sincere artist and no fool. I broached the future
and found him rather sympathetic.

We went to look up Orage but he was out. But we met Will
Dyson there. Just momentarily, but he too seems a jolly fellow.

In the afternoon I went to a concert given by a certain Helen
Rootham in aid of the Serbian Red Cross. Heard some new
things of Van Dieren who is *the* composer of the future and after
the concert I was introduced to him. Ezra was there (and he, by
the way, is William Atheling of the *New Age*): also the Sitwells,
Nina Hamnett (a painter), Guevara (another), Wolff (another)
and we all went to Helen's for tea.

Dinner with Ginner, the Hungarian (de Merrey is his name)
and Miss Murphy, Ginner's tea-pourer who is very nice.

Afterwards to the Sitwells, who have a wonderful house in
Chelsea, full of all things precious and extreme. Too good to live

in. All the tea party turned up. Ginner went with me. Toby was seedy and stayed at home. Lewis was there and we 'palled on'. I think he rather likes me because I am not of 'the damned pseudo-artistic riff-raff'. And I rather like Lewis. He has brains. That which we do not like in him he excuses quite logically: the stolid stupidity of the Englishman must be shaken and his beastly self-complacency disturbed. He is very bitter about the war: he feels that four years of the most vital period of his career have been torn from his life. He, as everybody of any perception, detests and despises the Northcliffe exhibition of human bestiality.

The Sitwells are rather too comfortable and perhaps there is a lot of pose in their revolt. But they are my generation whereas Lewis's is the generation before and it is with the Sitwells that I must throw in my lot to a large extent. Ezra says we younger men must prepare for a ten-year period of spade work and apprenticeship—relieving his generation of it—and then we shall be entitled to act on our own.

I am meeting Osbert Sitwell on Thursday to discuss the future.

I forgot to describe Van Dieren. He has a wonderful face, like Chopin's, I think, beautifully delicate with dark passionate eyes. His wife, Frieda Kindler, is a brilliant pianist—she played us some Chopin at the Concert.

29.x.18

Now, before I can be intelligible, I must explain how far I have got with the future.

Decided: (1) To chuck the Army.

(2) To take over the working secretaryship of the Allied Artists Association. (The AAA is a kind of artist's Trade Union and at present holds an annual show.) It is rather moribund owing to the war, but before the war could pay its secretary £150 p.a. I will make it do that again pretty soon.

(3) To further develop the AAA by opening a permanent Gallery at which we shall have one-man shows about once a month (lasting the month). We should confine ourselves to the modern people and to the reasonable collector, going especially for things priced £5–£10. We should charge a certain commission on sales and that should pay rent.

(4) If possible to run in conjunction with the Gallery a publishing and book-selling business, starting cautiously and in a small

way, but gradually working up a great independent Authors' Press.

Ezra had advised me to go and see Miss Weaver (Editor of the *Egoist*) re project 4. I went this morning and found her a very charming lady. She is all for combining their publishing business with ours (I mean, she thinks there should be unity of some sort) but Dora Marsden has the controlling voice and she is to talk it over with her. Then she will communicate with me.

Projects 1, 2, and 3 are finally decided on and armed with this decision we sallied forth at lunch time to view some premises we had previously spotted. They turned out fairly satisfactory and the position (Adelphi) is ideal. And rent (rather an important item) is quite reasonable (£70 p.a.). But we want certain alterations doing which will cost the owner something and we may have to rise to £75. But we had previously determined to risk £100. There is a decent front room for the exhibitions, a decent little room at the back for my office and bookshop, and a basement for storing, etc. We await the owner's decision as to alterations. If agreeable we shall 'clinch'.

Meanwhile the war had better hurry off the scene.

30.x.18.

I went to Mrs. Hueffer's to tea. She, of course, is elderly, and again quite 'charming'. Very 'reasonable' sort of body: also very cordial.

Lewis gave us dinner at the Carlton. Besides Toby and me, he had invited Konody, Turnbull and T. S. Eliot. Konody I have explained. Turnbull is a youngish artist at present in the RAF and quite a normal sort of fellow. Eliot was by special request. You may be aware that I have a deal of admiration for his poetry. It is original, true and beautiful. I was very agreeably impressed with him. About 27–29*—a keen intelligent face and good eyes. Not at all flamboyant or Bohemian. He has brains. Of all this crowd I begin to distinguish the poseurs and the real talents. Lewis and Eliot are by far the most *important* figures. They have *strength*: I see that well. Pound is a curious mixture. He makes his undoubted talent less effective by his personal expression of it. He does not allow his brains frank egress.

We rushed off at 9.30 to see the Russian Ballet again—this

* He was 30.

time 'The Good Humoured Ladies'. It was great: Life itself raised to an expression of the highest beauty of colour and motion.

31.x.18

10 a.m. Investiture. Really a boring affair. A long wait: marshalling and a wholesale atmosphere: musical comedy music to accompany (isn't there a Beethoven Eroica that might have been more appropriate in a more cultured land?) But I got the bauble and there is a little satisfaction in that.

I met Sitwell afterwards and had a talk. He is very keen to co-operate in after-the-war plans and we discussed details. We are to issue manifestoes and generally to make ourselves heard in the land.

A little shopping in the afternoon and at 4 p.m. I went to the Ballet once again. This time 'Cleopatra'—music by Borodin, decoration by Delaunay—rather cubist in design. The ballet is much more artificial than 'The Good Humoured Ladies' but all the same is a joy of colour and ecstasy.

The evening at Ginner's—where I was fêted in honour of my DSO. Seven of us and at least five nationalities. Mrs. Bashford, German by birth—a very jolly woman: a Mrs. Sly, Dutch—quite entertaining: the tea-pourer again (Irish) and 'a good sort'. The Hungarian who played again. And three mere Englishmen. We dined off various varieties of polony, etc.—potato salad, cheese, wine and coffee. Quite a gay finale, but I was already beginning to feel rather sad at the approach of the end. It has been a wonderful week: the most *truly* wonderful in my life. I have lived such a lot, learned such a lot and at last I really am on my feet and facing the world.

(undated)   Westbere, Canterbury, Kent

I arrived here this afternoon. An empty house in a desolate village with four colourless officers as housemates—that is the first impression. A general atmosphere of boredom and evidently nothing in the nature of work to do.

I had quite a busy time in London this week making arrangements for our (Osbert Sitwell's and my) first number of *Art and Letters*. I have secured the invaluable co-operation of Lewis and Eliot. I also accidentally met and became very pally with Richard

Aldington. He is a jolly open-faced English type—26 years old—and quite boyish. Altogether a friend to be. He showed me a lot of new poems and I have got some for our first number.

Besides, I have got a short story from Lewis, an article and a poem of my own, an article of Ginner's. Also promised poems by Sassoon, Huxley, Sachie Sitwell, and then Osbert will have something. So you see the first number is already shaping. I hope to get it out about Jan. 14. I want to get the Prospectus out within a fortnight.

I had another long 'jaw' with Ezra Pound. He is really very nice, though his conceit and affectation would alienate you. But his conceit is largely justified and his sincerity excuses his affectation. He withholds his 'concurrence' from *Art and Letters* for two issues and then he will 'see'. He is at present promised to other papers who pay him fairly well, so I can hardly expect him to help us at the sacrifice of bread and butter. But if we get 1,000 subscribers we shall be able to pay pretty decently.

10.xi.18

I had a look round the place yesterday. The Cathedral is rather disappointing. There are some fine perspectives, but the light is not romantic enough—white and glaring. I believe some of the best stained glass has been removed, but there are one or two fine windows left.

Outside the architecture finally convinces me of an opinion I have often played with: that Norman style is infinitely finer than Gothic. The great mass of the building is Gothic, but at the east end are two Norman towers and a chapel. In dignity and repose, which I take as the essential qualities of architecture, they put their overwhelming surroundings in the shade. It is a pity the Norman tradition was interrupted.

But the great thing about the town are the houses—there is greater scope and variety here than in York. They date back right to the 15th century and in the town every style since then is well represented. The 15th-century ones I cannot admire, quaint as they are. They are merely the mud and wattle habitations of a primitive race and I would not live in the lousy dark interiors for a pension. As far as I can see the zenith was reached in Elizabethan days—the 17th century. That was about the time, I think, when they grew tired of building cathedrals, and so devoted their energy and genius to humbler buildings. It was also a period of domestic vitality, as I make out. And so the houses are roomy, enough light, well-built and beautiful. Mud and wattles dispensed with.

I rather think there was a decadence then. At any rate, the only other houses I like are, I think, Queen Anne or shortly after—say 18th century. They sacrifice picturesque effect for more height of room and larger windows. A *solid* period.

The great beastly ugly decadence starts about 1820. The brick-cage ideal. Space begins to cost money, to become a competitive commodity.

Then I think this century (20th) sees a new beginning: the suburban villa is beastly enough, I know, but I think a definite advance on the Victorian brick-cage. The villa shows this improvement. Space (of rooms and of houses) *is* considered: so, in a suburban way, is appearance. Only to make up for the cost of these luxuries (which include w.c. and baths) saving is made on building materials. Beastly red bricks, beastly stucco, cheap windows and doorways.

Today I have written to the War Office cancelling my application for a regular commission. The war, I am glad to say, is over—much to some people's disappointment. I have been fairly disgusted these last few weeks. I do not think the national temper is anything to be proud of. Christian sentiments being out of fashion or obsolete, I thought we might at any rate have exercised the Englishman's renowned sense of fair play—of not hitting a man when he is down, etc. No. That is another damned hypocrisy exposed. We only do that when it pays. At present it will pay most of us to leave Germany incapacitated for foreign trade, etc., for a century. League of Nations? 'Damned idealistic rot. Can't imagine why we let a dreamy bloke like Wilson dictate to us. What I say is: Give 'em a taste of what they gave Little Belgium. Burn their villages, stick their babies, and rape their women. And now for a strong Army & Navy and keep the old flag flying.'

Do you realize that that is the way the average Englishman is talking just now? I'll soon be out of all this, by fair means or foul. At present I am gagged, bound hand and foot, mutely to listen to such rot. If it is not demoralizing, it is enough to drive me mad.

At present I am wondering by what conceivable chain of circumstance, of flattery, promise of ease, blindness to reality, I came seriously to consider staying in the Army.

Two other items of news: Toby has offered to let Sitwell into the running of *Art and Letters*: Sitwell and I to be literary editors and to rejuvenate the thing, perhaps under a new title: Toby to remain art editor. Sitwell and I would run the literary part on very modernist lines and there would be a good chance of making the thing go. There is going to be considerable excitement in the literary and artistic world during the next few years (parallel to the coming social upheavals) and if we could make *Art and Letters* the organ of that excitement things would hum.

14.xi.18

There is this development to report: Sitwell has come into *Art and Letters* as 1/3 (third) shareholder and partner and there is every hope for the future. I expect I shall be meeting him next week and we shall get a 'program' out—and a manifesto.

Everybody went mad the other day.* I felt hopelessly sober. I read Henry James's *Sacred Fount* to the accompaniment of the rejoicings—with a savage zest.

* Armistice Day.

PART THREE

The Falcon and the Dove

I

A Callow Nestling

It will have been seen in the earlier part of this book that there was nothing very exceptional in the circumstances of my childhood: it was the childhood of any farmer's son in the remote English countryside of that time. If it now seems to belong to another world, it is because in the past fifty years two inventions have transformed that kind of life. The farms have lost their isolation, both in the physical and spiritual sense. I imagine that the modern farmer's boy grows up to the tune of a London dance-band, while across his innocent eye flickers the vision of life offered by the television screen. He may not be any the worse for it: he would certainly consider my placid environment a poor substitute for his Babylonian excitements. If I would still prefer my kind of childhood, it is because I am introducing into the comparison an adult sense of values. The seclusion of my first ten years now seems like an age of unearthly bliss, a ring in a rock to which all the strands of my subsequent happiness are tied.

One day in the year 1904, a bewildered and fatherless boy, I was quietly withdrawn from this world and taken a devious train journey across the county. I still retain some memory of the night-marish impression made by the cavernous stations where we changed trains; and I remember our cab rattling along the roughly cobbled streets of the town which was our destination. We climbed up steep hills, past dark satanic mills, and emerged eventually on a high bare moor, at the other side of which rose the largest building I had ever seen. Built of local stone in a style that must, I now realize, have been copied from some monument of the French Renaissance, blackened by the smoke which drifted across the moor from the surrounding factories, this was the orphanage school in which I was to spend the next five years of

149

my life, in an isolation no less absolute than that of my infancy. For six weeks in summer and for a fortnight at Christmas I returned to the countryside, but these were idyllic interludes in what was otherwise a monastic existence. The school, with several acres of ground, was enclosed by high stone walls, and we only passed through these walls, once a week, to march in military formation to a chapel in the town.

I do not intend to write much about this period of my life because I do not think it is of general interest. From the age of ten or eleven to the age of fifteen or sixteen is the least genial period in the life of a boy. He has lost the innocent eye of child-hood and has not yet become an experiencing nature. It is a callow and confused phase, in which the mind is unconsciously acquiring its social armour of habits and inhibitions. It is the stage at which the sensibility of most children is irretrievably destroyed. The sense of sin or guilt is imposed on the innocent impulses, and actions lose their animal playfulness. Relations with other people become conscious instead of instinctive: the child has to begin to plot its way through a maze of regulated paths. How it can come through this intricate process with an undimmed vision or any trace of its original freshness is still unknown: but at least we are now aware that we are involved in an educational dilemma. Any too conscious approach to the problem seems fatal, and the best minds and sensibilities are still apt to be the chance products of a casual upbringing.

There were about two hundred boys in the school; in the same building, but strictly segregated, and only visible at meal-times, were about a hundred girls. The regimen was Spartan: no hot water for washing at any time of the year; meat and vegetables once a day and otherwise only milk and bread, mostly dry bread. The discipline was strict, though not tyrannical, and strongly religious in tone. There were no amenities—no private rooms, not even a reading-room. A boy who wished to read a book outside class-hours had to read it in the shrill pandemonium of the common playroom—an exercise to which I attribute my unusual ease of concentration. There were no luxuries; pocket money was forbidden, and though there was a certain amount of secret trading, it had usually exhausted itself by the end of the second or third week of the term. All the menial duties were done by the boys themselves; we made our own beds and cleaned our own boots. We wore a uniform which consisted of grey trousers and waistcoat, an Eton jacket of blue face-cloth, and a pork-pie cap with a straight flat peak of shiny black leather. In winter we walked out in grey Inverness capes.

This monastic establishment has changed out of all recognition since my time: it has been brought into the general line of secondary schools, thrown open to day-boys, and generally modernized. But when I was there, it still maintained all the features of a much earlier conception of education, such as we can find described in the novels of Dickens; it was not essentially different from the Christ's Hospital described by Leigh Hunt in his *Autobiography*. For the first year I had the company of my younger brother; and our third brother joined us in the second year. But I have never lived under such a cloud of unhappiness as fell upon me once we had taken such a brave farewell of our mother and the guardian uncle who had accompanied us on this first journey. I was by disposition of a quiet nature, but no wild animal from the pampas imprisoned in a cage could have felt so hopelessly thwarted. From fields and hedges and the wide open spaces of the moors; from the natural companionship of animals and all the mutations of farm life, I had passed into a confined world of stone walls, smoky skies, and two hundred unknown and apparently unsympathetic strangers. It is true that among the crowd we soon learned to distinguish a group of a dozen or twenty in the same predicament—the 'new boys' or 'newkers' who had arrived on the same day. And each of us was allotted a 'guardian'—an older boy whose duty was to initiate us into the ways of the school. But nothing could relieve the overwhelming desolation of our life, and this state of anguish continued for at least twelve months.

It is not easy for an adult to recollect the quality of his pre-adolescent emotions. They have been obliterated by thousands of other emotions, which while not necessarily so acute, are more memorable. The emotions of a boy or girl have a baffled intensity which is due to our inability, at that age, to express ourselves. We have found words to describe outward objects, and to express simple sensations, like physical pain. But the vague emotions which are aroused by our environment, by strange experiences, by the unknown—for these we have no ready words. We cannot impart our moods, even to our most intimate friends. Children of this intermediate age suffer like animals, dumbly and vaguely; and the only release is tears. But tears are forbidden by the school-boy's code, so even that outlet is dammed.

The cure, of course, is action, and perhaps that is why sport is forced on the English schoolboy: it is an example of our instinctive social wisdom. Unfortunately sport is competitive, and if you have neither the physique nor the skill to ensure proficiency, it soon becomes hateful. I was neither good nor bad: merely 'middling', as we said, and indifference was my general attitude. I played when it was necessary to play; I avoided play when I could. For I had already discovered the joy of reading—had, indeed, brought it with me to school. This predilection I believe to have been innate. I have already, in 'The Innocent Eye', given evidence of its still earlier manifestations, and I try now, as I tried then, to recollect any influence in my boyhood which might have encouraged this latent tendency. There is none. This taste was self-evident, and I persisted in it against all sorts of obstacles. There was a small miscellaneous library in the school, but it had few volumes to attract a boy of my age. I had no money to buy books: I relied on a small patrimony of my own, and a sporadic system of exchange with other boys. We were, most of us, omnivorous; we read Scott and Ballantyne, Mayne Reid and Henty, but my own imagination was most strongly fired by Rider Haggard, and never have I known such absorption and excitement as gripped me when I first read *King Solomon's Mines* and *Montezuma's Daughter*.

Such an innate taste for reading, which is merely the vicarious exercise of the imagination, is fairly common among boys; what I next discovered in myself, though I did not at that time attach any significance to it, was a taste for writing. I can trace its first appearance back to the age of thirteen, when I was in the Fifth Form; for three or four of us then produced a surreptitious magazine for which I wrote the serial. By that time this faculty was also leading to more practical results, for the essay, which from now onwards became an important subject, became my best subject, and the only one in which I displayed any excep-tional talent. By the time I had reached the Sixth Form, and during the two years I spent there (my fourteenth and fifteenth years) I was taking a very conscious pleasure in this accomplishment. Naturally I was encouraged by some of the masters; I have a

vague recollection of representing the school in a national com-
petition; and to these masters, particularly to the head master,
Mr. Barber, who was a man of noble character and fine discrimination, I owe my first perception of literary form and
structure. But I insist that the impulse to write, the love of words
for their own sake and for the sake of what they could express,
was precedent, and no more to be explained by personal influences
than the colour of my hair or the pitch of my voice.

At the end of our fifteenth year the school cast us, willy-
nilly, out into the world. It is an age at which ambitions are
scarcely formulated, or are merely fanciful. It is not an age at
which a normal boy can make any effective protest against plans
made for him by his elders. By this time my mother had left the
country to take a post in Leeds, and it was in this city that I was
to spend the next five years of my life. I was persuaded to apply
for a clerkship in the local Savings Bank. I succeeded in obtaining
it; my salary was £20 a year.

The Bank was a venerable institution, with a Head Office in
the centre of the city and three branches in outlying working-
class districts. The junior clerks circulated, month by month,
between these four offices. We assembled at the Head Office every
morning, where we met the branch manager and picked up the
cash-bag. At the branch office we opened the doors at ten o'clock
and sat at a desk behind a counter. When a 'depositor' entered, we
took his pass-book and money, handed the money to the manager
to count, and then entered the amount in the pass-book and in the
day-book which we kept on the desk. If the 'depositor' wished to
withdraw a sum, we took his pass-book and checked it against
the ledger. We closed the doors at three, counted the day's deposits
and withdrawals, balanced the day-book, and then made as
quickly as possible for the Head Office, carrying the heavy cash-
bag. We were free by half-past three or four.

This left a considerable part of the day for further activities.
From the beginning I considered the Bank as a stop-gap: it did
not enter at all into my plan of life. I was under a contract to
serve for three years, but this suited me very nicely, for I should
then be eighteen or nineteen, the proper age for entering a university. That, at any rate, was an essential stage in life, whatever
direction my ambitions might afterwards take. My father's only
brother had gone to Cambridge, and my father had always

intended that at least one of his sons should follow this example, even if he then returned to the farm. There must often have been talk about this plan in our family circle, and I cannot explain in any other way my early resolution to continue my education. I was not driven to it by my mother or my guardians—indeed, they urged me to make the most of 'the good opening' I had already found; it was my own sense of the necessary future.

Evening schools and the public library provided me with the means of continuing my education, and my time was divided between the Bank and these useful institutions. In my grey cloak and bowler hat I sped through the sooty streets, timid and intro-spective, and gradually my vague ambitions began to take definite shape. My first idea was to become a doctor. My father's best friend had been a doctor, and perhaps he had become in some degree a father-substitute whom I unconsciously desired to imitate. I began, therefore, to study the sciences, and to collect the prospectuses of various medical schools. But about this time I spent a few weeks recuperating from an illness with this same doctor-friend, and when I confided to him my ambition, he became very distressed, and argued forcibly against my decision. I forget what arguments he used: most likely he was simply con-vinced that I did not possess the right temperament. In any case, he succeeded in unsettling me, and I began to reconsider the possibilities.

Meanwhile another ferment had arisen almost spontaneously in my mind—I had become aware of politics. It was probably difficult to avoid them in those days. The great issues of Free Trade and Protection, Home Rule for Ireland, the Disestablish-ment of the Church, and the Reform of the House of Lords, were being debated with fervour in every newspaper and at every street-corner. Open-air meetings and demonstrations were frequent, and feeling ran high. It became necessary, merely in my daily contacts with my colleagues in the Bank, to declare some kind of attitude. I did not hesitate: I instinctively adopted the attitude which would have been my father's—I became a true-blue Tory. I eagerly acquired the party propaganda; I read Dis-raeli's novels and, carried on by my growing intellectual curiosity, grappled with Canning, Burke and Bolingbroke. I joined the local branch of the Conservative Party and distributed leaflets from house to house. I worshipped my King with a blind emotional devotion, and even managed to make a hero out of Lord Salisbury.

This access of political enthusiasm was not without its influence on the trend of my ambitions. I do not think that I ever formulated the idea of a political career with any precision, but I decided to exchange medicine for law. When I announced this decision, my mother and her advisers were well pleased, and immediately began to devise ways and means of articling me to a solicitor. But this prospect was not altogether agreeable to me. I already realized that the difference between the two branches of the legal profession was the difference between drab realism and romantic potentialities, and I was determined to be a barrister. The difficulties, especially the financial ones, were pointed out to me, and they seemed insurmountable. I weakened to the extent of allowing negotiations with a solicitor to begin; but meanwhile my evening studies had been progressing and I had sat for the matriculation examination. It was in the midst of these negotiations that I passed this Rubicon, and this preliminary success gave me the necessary self-confidence and resolution. I announced my determination to proceed to the University, and to let the question of a career depend on what happened to me there. The problem of financing my studies still remained to be settled, but I had a plan. My grandfather, who had died while I was still at school, had left me a legacy of £300 which was not due to me until I attained the age of twenty-five. I went to an uncle of my father's, a sheep-farmer who was reputed to be rich, and asked him to lend me the necessary money for fees and board on the security of this legacy. He was a dour and silent man, but he had no boys of his own and I think I touched his heart. He consented and the way was open.

This narrative has become much more trivial and personal than I at first intended. There is nothing very unusual in the events I have related, but they do lead to a crisis in my life, and the resolution of that crisis was an act of my own will, carried out in face of general disapproval and even the active opposition of some of my relatives. Such a crisis comes in the lives of most poor but ambitious youths, and it is of some general interest to try and determine the decisive factors. The alignment of forces is always the same: on the one side the caution of parents and guardians, anxious to guide the youth towards some position of economic security and immediate yield; on the other side the youth's self-projection into the future, the fantasy which he has formed of his life, his will to power. If there is no question of immediate or proximate need—if money is no object, as we say—then the crisis is not very intense. It is argued in social terms. To many it will be merely a question of traditional behaviour: the particular public school and the particular college in the University are as predetermined as the cut of the clothes or the accent of speech. The question whether the son of a rich manufacturer should go to Oxford or not (I ignore the finer problem of Oxford or Cambridge) is largely a question of whether the personal contacts he is likely to make there will raise the social status of the family, be good for business, and even lead to a good marriage. To another large class it is a question of a necessary routine: the boy who is destined to be a teacher, a doctor, a technician or a scientist, must go through the mill and acquire the necessary qualifications. Ambition in such cases is specific and narrow, practical rather than romantic. It astonished me to find when I first entered the University of Leeds that the ambitions of ninety out of every hundred of my fellow undergraduates were crude and calculating. They were interested in one thing only—in getting the best possible degree by the shortest possible method. They were anxious to memorize and eager to anticipate the testing questions. Their career was plotted and they were careful not to stray from the thin line which markèd an easy path through the world of knowledge. Perhaps they had been caught young, in a machine which hitherto I had accidentally escaped: they had been selected, in the various centres of popular education from which they came, as 'likely winners'. The scholarships which they had won had already lifted them out of the class into which they had been born—had saved them from the mine or the mill; and they were content with their prescribed destiny. A few of them would, during their three or four years at the university, betray still more exceptional virtues, and this *élite* would be held back for research scholarships and academic honours; for a machine must have its attendants.

Why should the quality of my ambitions have been so relatively vague and indeterminate? It was partly my ignorance of the realities: I simply did not know the ropes of the educational ladder, and had formed a desperate expedient of wings. I would fly to the heights I could not scale pedestrianly, sustained by my active imagination. This faculty, which had grown unchecked in infancy, which had not been through the mould of a normal education, which had had time to expand whilst I wandered like a solitary little alien in the streets of Leeds, now knew no limits. It threw into the cloudy future an infinite ray in which there could always be seen, like a silver knight on a white steed, this unreal figure which was myself, riding to quixotic combats, attaining a blinding and indefinable glory.

2

The Discovery of Poetry

It was not until my seventeenth year that I became conscious of the art of poetry. At school we read and even acted Shakespeare, and there were 'recitations' which must have included some verse. But I never read a volume of poems for choice. It was only later, when I began to read for my matriculation, that I also began to listen more intently to the sound of what I was reading: words and phrases would now linger insistently in my mind. At the evening school I attended there was a teacher who had a genuine enthusiasm for his subject; he read aloud to us with feeling and expressiveness. He communicated his pleasure in poetry to at least one of his pupils. About the same time I made the acquaintance of one who was for many years to be my only confidant and my devoted patron. My brother, eighteen months younger than myself, had left school and found employment with a tailor in the city, who bore our family name —even the same Christian name as my brother—and childless himself, henceforth was to take a great interest in all of us. He belonged to a good Quaker family settled for many generations in the Isle of Axholme. Orphaned at an early age, he had been given into the care of two rich and cultured maiden aunts, who gave him a good education and destined him for a post in the British Museum. But at the age of sixteen or so he had suddenly revolted against the smug religious atmosphere in which he was being brought up, and he had run away. After various adventures he had been compelled to take whatever employment he could get, and this happened to be tailoring, a craft for which he had no liking, but which he was to follow for more than forty years with a quiet stoicism. He was a man of small proportions, gentle manners, and in physiognomy bore a close resemblance to the

158

portraits of William Blake. He had two passions—the reading of poetry and the cultivation of flowers. His reading in every direction was wide, and it was in his house that I first made the acquaintance, not only of innumerable volumes of verse, but of the works of writers like Ibsen, Turgenev, Dostoevsky and Chekhov.

Hitherto my reading had been confined to what could be borrowed from the public library, and what I could buy out of an allowance of one shilling a week which I made to myself out of my meagre earnings as a bank-clerk. But now I not only had an enthusiast's library to draw from, but I rarely visited this friend without coming away with a gift of two or three volumes. It was probably to my advantage then that the blessings thus showered on me were indiscriminate. My friend praised with equal zest W. B. Yeats and Fiona Macleod, Browning and William Cullen Bryant, Francis Thompson and Sir Edwin Arnold. If I failed to share his enthusiasm—as in the case of Emerson—he did not question or complain: he was convinced that I should one day see the light.

I cannot now be certain whether my own first poems preceded this fruitful friendship: I think they did. But I cannot forget the emotion with which my mentor learned for the first time that I was writing verses, and with what eagerness he received my efforts when I offered them for his criticism. His criticism was not very severe, though it did check my absurdities. But for the most part he encouraged me with his praise and was for a long time the only audience I had, but a sufficing one. It is to his memory that I have dedicated my collected poems.

It is difficult to recapture the first access of composition. It descended on me like a frenzy, and a day was not perfect unless it gave birth to a poem. Of one thing I am certain: the breath that first fanned my smouldering tinder was Tennyson's. I soon outgrew Tennyson, and for many years affected to despise him— it was a natural reaction, for we tend to turn on all our adolescent enthusiasms. Now that I have balanced my reactions, and can judge Tennyson with a detached mind, I find that I admire him for qualities which must have appealed, however unconsciously, to my awakening sensibility: for the ease and simplicity of his diction, for a broad if not a very profound intelligence, and for an exact rendering of a special landscape—the watery fens and long dim wolds which were not so remote from my own dales and moors. At times he seems to describe the actual scenes of my own childhood:

> *The seven elms, the poplars four,*
> *That stand beside my father's door,*
> *. . . . . the brook that loves*
> *To purl o'er matted cress and ribbed sand,*
> *Or dimple in the dark of rushy coves,*
> *Drawing into his narrow earthen urn,*
> *In every elbow and turn,*
> *The filter'd tribute of the rough woodland.*

There would be more to say in adequate appreciation of this poet —more to discover, perhaps, of poetic merit than we generally admit; and a very curious personality to analyse. But now I only seek to relate my own sensibility to his, and to explain why he in particular should have been the reagent in the first poems precipitated from my mind. It would have been much more normal if my enthusiasm at this time had been for Shelley: but the very abstractness of Shelley's poetry kept him at a distance. Shelley, I would now say, demands a degree of intellectual development which I had not reached by the age of seventeen or eighteen. Tennyson had a more objective appeal and was therefore more open to my simple sensibility.

Even so, there were limits to my powers of absorption, and neither then, nor since, could I read the *Idylls of the King*. Romantic as I was, and am, this particular brand of archaicism has always been repugnant to me. I hate every kind of literary fustian, every affectation of an earlier style, every exercise or experiment in an old measure. Such a whimsy attitude to the art of writing is impossible to anyone who believes in the immediacy of expression, in the automatism of inspiration, in the creative nature of even poetic evolution: and these are the doctrines of a true romanticism. The rest is dilettantism: not the vital function, but an academic diversion.

The compositions which came to me so easily in these adolescent days were destroyed long ago, and I have no very precise recollection of their nature. They were, I think, mostly short lyrics about flowers, birds, atmospheric moods; the more realistic of them may have attempted to catch something of the poetry of foggy, gas-lit streets, the glow of furnaces by night, the clatter of clogs on the stone pavements. There were no love poems, for my heart was not yet engaged.

It was then that the poetry of William Blake descended on me like an apocalypse. Tennyson had chimed in with my moods, and shown me felicity. Blake shook me to the depths of my awakening mind, scattered the world of my objective vision, and left me floundering in subjective fantasy. I did not, at that time, venture far into the Prophetic Books; but the Songs of Innocence and Experience, and the poems from the Rossetti and Pickering manuscripts, pierced me like gleaming steel, and their meaning was annealed to my mind. Their meaning?—I should rather say their mystery, for many of these poems were not easy to understand, and indeed I did not seek to understand them. From the beginning I was content with the incantation of a poem, and I still maintain that this is the quality essential to poetry.

Blake kept his ascendancy in my mind for many years—indeed, though I have submitted to many influences and have been fired to more than one enthusiasm in the intervening years, there is no poet with whom today I would more readily identify the poetic essence. For me, Blake is absolute. Shakespeare is richer, Milton is more sonorous, Hopkins is more sensuous—one could make many more comparative statements; but Blake has no need of qualifying epithets: he is simply poetic, in imagination and in expression.

A discovery which I then made with some of the same emotional excitement that Blake had aroused was of a contemporary poet. There was published about this time a series of small yellow chapbooks, and in it appeared the first poems of Ralph Hodgson. The poems were in harmony with the archaic style of the production: they seemed to come from a world of gipsies and highwaymen, they were sometimes sentimental, and they had a simple insistent rhythm which haunted the mind:

> *Eve with her basket, was*
> *Deep in the bells and grass,*
> *Wading in bells and grass*
> *Up to her knees,*
> *Picking a dish of sweet*
> *Berries and plums to eat,*
> *Down in the bells and grass*
> *Under the trees.*

Ralph Hodgson was a genuine poet, and I think that in spite of his sentimentality and whimsicality he has a permanent place in our literature. But he was the worst, because the most superficial kind of influence. To be influenced by Shakespeare, Milton or Wordsworth cannot do a young poet any harm: at least, it is only a very poor creature who would be influenced by their idiosyncrasies without at the same time being profitably stirred by their profundities. There is nothing profound in the poetry of Ralph Hodgson, and I am far from implying that all poetry should be profound. But just as one would feel a little silly if one found oneself unconsciously imitating the antics or gestures of another man, and tend to blame the other man for having antics and gestures of an imitable kind, so I feel inclined to criticize Hodgson's verse for its pretty jingle and infectious rhythm. These are qualities to be enjoyed by non-poetic people: the poet must go his own gait.

It is easy to retort that if a poet's genius is strong enough, his diction will be independent enough. But a poet has to undergo a process of birth and growth: he does not discover himself until he has rejected the alternative selves represented by the poetry already existing in the world. Here, perhaps, I am advancing a romantic doctrine. It is possible to conceive of poetry as an established form, and of the poet's duty as merely to add to the general fund. That is the classical conception of the poet. But my conception was, and still is, of poetry as a unique experience: the individual, with his particular moods, emotions, thoughts, trying to express himself integrally, in his own choice of words. It is true that he has to use words which are common to all his countrymen; but there is an infinite number of ways of selecting and combining these words, and from these infinite possibilities one exact, original correspondence of idea and expression must emerge, or the poem will be an affectation and a failure.

To discover what other influences were at work in this early phase of my poetic awakening, I should have to examine the verses themselves, and as I have already related, they no longer exist. But this acquisitive age actually continues until the end of my twentieth year, and for the later stage of it there is the evidence of a small 'brochure' published by Elkin Mathews in 1915 and entitled *Songs of Chaos*. An epigraph from Nietzsche—'One must have chaos within one to give birth to a dancing star'—explains the title, but this sentence which I had printed on the title-page really belongs to a later phase of my development, and the poems in the modest little volume have none of the tremendous implications of such a motto. When, in January, 1915, I joined the Army, I was posted to a battalion stationed in Dorset. I had to travel via London and arrived in that city for the first time in my life. I carried, besides my military baggage, a large bundle of poems, and at King's Cross I told the taxi-driver to go to Waterloo via Cork Street. All I knew about Mr. Mathews was that he had been publishing the kind of poetry I was interested in: I had no introduction to him nor any means of obtaining one. However, he received me very kindly in the back of his shop and undertook to consider the publication of my poems if I would pay a reader's fee, which I willingly did. A few weeks later he sent me the reader's report, which was to the effect that though the poems were too slight and imitative to be published in bulk, a small selection that would pass might be made, and he indicated the ones he thought best. I was not so much dashed by his general criticism as angry at the selection he had made. I insisted on making my own selection, and Mr. Mathews published them at my expense—I do not remember what it cost me, but it was not exorbitant. Six months later twenty-two copies had been sold: but I had already regretted my rash and inexperienced venture, and at my request the remainder of the edition was pulped.

This abortive volume has been out of my mind for many years now, but I still possess a copy and I have unearthed it. It has the musty smell of forgotten books, but as I turn its pages I wonder if I have been too harsh with its simple conceits. I reprinted four of the poems in the 1926 edition of my *Collected Poems*, but in 1935 suppressed even these. The intensity with which I wrote some of these poems is still a vivid memory—it was not an intensity of emotion leading to expression, but an emotion generated by the act of creation. The intensity was due to the discovery that an image could be matched with exact words. The triviality of the image did not seem to matter. Even now, with all my literary and critical experience, I cannot be sure that it matters. I cannot be sure, for example, that a poem which now costs me a qualm to quote is not nevertheless a valid poem and therefore a good poem. It was called 'A Little Girl':

I pluck a daisy here and there—
  O many a daisy do I take!
And I string them together in a ring,
  But it's seldom the ring doesn't break.

O daisies rosy, daisies white!
  If I could string them in a ring
They'd make a bonny daisy chain—
  O why is a daisy a delicate thing?

If, as a very childlike youth, I succeeded in evoking the simplicity of a child's outlook, even a child's insight, then the result is valid. It is only sentimental if as an adult I am trying to exploit childish things.

In looking through this booklet (it ran to no more than thirty-seven pages), the only other influence besides those of Blake and Hodgson which I can now discern is that of Yeats:

When Niordr arose from the burning deep
And bade the waves no longer weep:—
Niordr arose with a golden harp
And touched the strings that never warp,
Bidding the angry waves be still,
And the Vanir gather to obey his will.

Niordr and the Vanir are no longer my familiar spirits, but I am reminded that at this time, at the instigation of the friend to whom I already owed so much, I read many of the Northern myths and sagas, and played with the idea of writing a Viking epic. But other influences, and other ambitions, were to intervene.

At the beginning of the Michaelmas Term, in the year 1912, I enrolled myself as a student at the University of Leeds. I was still not very certain of my intentions: ostensibly I was to become a lawyer of some kind, but secretly (it was half a secret to myself) I was determined on a literary career. I already saw myself as a novelist, a dramatist, or perhaps a journalist—the future would decide which. I was conscious of the scrappiness of my general education, and therefore resolved to spend a year in a way which was not strictly utilitarian: I took the first year course for the B.A. degree. The following year I switched over to my proper studies, which I had decided were Law and Economics, and I was rash enough to attempt to take the two degrees (LL.B. and B.Sc. Econ.) simultaneously. I do not think the prescribed limits of these two curricula would have been too much for me; but I never for a day kept within these limits. I was an anomalous figure among my fellow-undergraduates, whose careers were already determined: they were going to be schoolteachers, or clergymen, or practical scientists and technicians in the local industries. Not a single soul, so far as I ever discovered, was there for the disinterested purpose of acquiring a 'liberal' education. It is true that I too had my purpose; but it was vague and self-selected, and not dependent on a grant or scholarship. I could pick and choose my subjects to suit my own idea of a career; and I did in fact choose my subjects with an abandon which ought undoubtedly to have been restrained. English and French literature, Latin, Logic, Roman Law, Jurisprudence, Common Law, Constitutional Law and History, Political Economy, Social Economics, European History, Geology—the mere list now makes me dizzy. The result was complete mental congestion and over-work. My days were filled with lectures and I read till the small hours every night. But this is not half the toll. I had at the same time been let loose in a library of seemingly infinite dimensions. I used to seat myself at a table in this library in every spare interval between the lectures. By a chance which was almost perverse, the seat to which my instinct first directed me, and which I continued to use whenever I found it free, was sheltered by a high bookcase which contained, like a mountain veined with shining gold, the very names with which my intellectual curiosity was now engaged—Dostoevsky, Ibsen and Nietzsche. I would open my *Gaius* or *Justinian*, Welton's *Logic* or Marshall's *Political Economy*; but soon my eyes would be caught by the tempting titles at my side, and one by one the volumes were drawn out and only the closing bell awakened me from my absorption. With Dostoevsky and Ibsen I was already partly acquainted, but Nietzsche was a new world, and since my discovery of Blake, the most cataclysmic. It was Nietzsche who first introduced me to philosophy—I read far more than I could understand in his pages, but I did not let my ignorance rest. From Nietzsche I passed to Schopenhauer, to Kant, Hegel, Hume, Pascal, Plato—in very much this indiscriminate order. It was as though I had tapped a central exchange of intellectual tendencies; from Nietzsche communications ran in every direction and for at least five years he, and none of my professors or friends, was my real teacher.

These years at the university were thus an orgy of acquisitiveness: what basis of disciplined education had been devised by the university authorities was completely swamped by my own proclivities. It must be remembered that these new universities have no such institution as the tutor—perhaps their greatest failing; and though I could have consulted the lecturers and professors, the very oddness of my position and the indeterminateness of my aims made this, however desirable, not strictly necessary. And this educational machine is so rigid in its workings that any action that is not strictly necessary is almost impossible. I remember that in my second year I did venture to send to the professor of English Literature, F. W. Moorman, two poetic dramas which I had written in North Riding dialect—I ventured to do this because he was a great enthusiast for the dialect, and perhaps the most inspiring teacher in the university. He was completely taken by surprise—though he had, some weeks earlier, been impressed by an essay I had written on Witchcraft and the Elizabethan Drama. It had never occurred to him that one of the hundred odd students who scribbled away taking notes as he lectured should attempt an original composition. He began to take a special interest in me and encouraged me to show him more of my efforts; but then came the war and before I could renew contact with this possible mentor, he had been accidentally drowned whilst bathing.

The experience of these years raises in its acutest form the whole question of disciplined education. Up to the age of fifteen my education had been perhaps more than usually disciplined, but from that age to the present day I have followed my own bent; the order has been of my own devising, and generally the order of my strongest inclinations. This is the kind of education which most authorities find reprehensible. 'I hold very strongly,' wrote Cardinal Newman in the best of all treatises on the subject, 'that the first step in intellectual training is to impress upon a boy's mind the idea of science, method, order, principle, and system; of rule and exception, of richness and harmony. . . . . Let him once gain this habit of method, of starting from fixed points, of making his ground good as he goes, of distinguishing what he knows from what he does not know, and I conceive he will be gradually initiated into the largest and truest philosophical views, and will feel nothing but impatience and disgust at the random theories and imposing sophistries and dashing paradoxes, which carry away half-formed and superficial intellects.' These words, in which I recognize a large measure of truth, are a complete condemnation of the method of education which I pursued, and yet I am not entirely repentant. Admittedly I had some good habits: what I read I tended to read thoroughly; I made notes and to the best of my unaided ability made the ground good as I went on my way. Nietzsche is not a starting-point that Newman would have approved—he would almost certainly have included his works among 'the random theories and imposing sophistries and dashing paradoxes' which he scorns, and my intellect among the half-formed and superficial which are carried away by such theories and sophistries. Nevertheless, Nietzsche *was* a starting-point and all the circumstances considered, not one that I regret. He gave me vistas that were quite outside the range of formal education; he introduced me to the ferment of contemporary ideas. In his company I knew the excitement of an intellectual adventure, that highest exaltation which only comes when truth is conceived as a fleeting quarry in whose pursuit the whole mind must be engaged.

In my subsequent years I was often to come into contact with great men whose intellects had been formed in the gradual and disciplined manner indicated by Newman. Let me admit that I have always felt in their presence a sense of weakness; but it is the weakness of the runner who has returned from the chase and found the imperturbable god of reason still changeless in his niche. I had felt the earth spinning underneath my feet, and the clouds racing me in the sky; beauty had stirred like an animal in the covert and my senses had been assailed from a thousand directions. The flush on my features was a reflexion of the animation in my mind, where the images were as vivid as nature and as restless as the sea. If my ideal had been a static form, then I should have withered like a wreath at the feet of this impassive god; but my ideal was a labile green shoot, an emergent new world, a manifestation of the unknown in the desert of dead facts.

I have found that most people whose minds have responded to a formal university education are like monoliths. They are bodies at rest. They have acquired during their university years a choice armoury of information, and they assume that it will serve them for the rest of their lives. Many of them sell their classics to the second-hand bookseller before they 'come down' from Oxford or Cambridge; or if they keep them, it is for the sake of sentimental associations. They are stored in a glazed book-case behind the 'chesterfield', with a college shield on the wall above and a tobacco-jar on the ledge. In a few years the once proud possessor of a first in Greats will have forgotten all but a few tags of his Greek and Latin, and will be reduced to defending a classical education for its supposed disciplinary virtues. He can boast of having 'done' his Plato or his Aristotle, his Aeschylus or his Euripides; but these are names now, mingled with his senti-mental recollections of professors and dons. They had not become a part of his life, a continuing influence and ever-present inspira-tion. They and the whole galaxy of classical poets and philo-sophers are dead and distant worlds.

There is another side to the argument. Some of these formally educated young men, on leaving the universities, have gone into the Civil Service or business, and have become very efficient administrators. Between their present efficiency and their educa-tion there is a very direct relation: not the relation of a vocational training to the vocation pursued (which is much more the ideal of the modern universities and technical colleges), but a relation sanctioned by the intangible virtues of 'character'—in Newman's words, 'the force, the steadiness, the comprehensiveness and the versatility of intellect, the command over our own powers, the instinctive just estimate of things as they pass before us, which sometimes indeed is a natural gift, but commonly is not gained without much effort and the exercise of years'. These are the virtues which are needed in the upper ranks of any social hierarchy —these virtues rather than specialized knowledge or technical skill—and the Civil Service has quite rightly rejected the notion of a particularized training such as the Army, the Navy and the professions require. Its flexibility, its adaptability, its very humanity depend on this paradox in its recruitment.

The ideals of this kind of education are generally summed up in the word 'character', though latterly the more equi-vocal word 'leadership' has been used. But administration is not the only function of an educated man, nor is leadership a necessity in a community of free individuals. There is an alternative ideal of education, for which I have always attempted to reserve the word 'personality'. Character is the product of a disciplined education: discipline inculcates habits of mind as well as of body, and the result is a firm, dependable set of ideas and reactions upon which a definite type of society can be based. A character is not necessarily conservative: rather it is constructive, and in a time of stress or disintegration might well seem revolutionary. It is moral, though its morality is not necessarily conventional. It cultivates a 'taste', but this taste is rational rather than aesthetic, retrospective and historical rather than experimental and contemporary.

A personality, on the other hand, is distinguished by immediacy and by what I would call lability, or the capacity to change without loss of integrity. Keats, who discerned the quality in himself, gave it the name of Negative Capability; and in Hamlet Shakespeare depicted the type in all its mutability.

Character is only attained by limitation. The senses, which would otherwise be open to the impact of every phenomenal event, must be canalized, protected by a hard cortex or shell, and only allowed to operate when they have been directed by the conscious will; and it can be argued that sensations and their attendant emotions are all the finer for being thus restricted. But the personality will have none of this arbitrary interference with the natural process of selectivity: the senses are open to every impression which falls upon them, and the mind surrenders to its environment. Admittedly, from a moral and social point of view, there is a danger that such a passive attitude will lead to instability and disintegration. But the values of the personality are neither moral nor social: they are religious or aesthetic. Here the word 'religious', put in contrast to 'moral', may cause some surprise; but I would be prepared to maintain that the essentially religious experience described by the great mystics of the East as well as the West, and now generally known in modern theology as the Kierkegaardian 'instant', the Barthian 'crisis' or 'leap', is a surrender of the existential being only possible to a personality, a man of negative capability.

To question the values of the personality, therefore, is to question the values of mysticism and of art. The greatest mistake would be to suppose that a society can be based exclusively on one type of human being. Society needs for vitality, and for effective progress, the contrast and opposition of types, more particularly of these two fundamental types which I have called characters and personalities. The tautness of the social fabric depends on their dialectical counterplay.

It would seem to follow from these considerations that there should be two systems of education, one for character and one for personality. That would obviously be impracticable, and the most we can hope for is an elasticity in the general system which would provide for both types of individual. The present system is directed almost exclusively to the creation of character, and at its best is very successful in this aim. The survival of personality in this system is a matter of chance: sometimes an understanding teacher will give his protection to a boy obviously not made for the mould; but more often the boy revolts and escapes from the system (as Shelley did), or by some chance is never submitted to it—is *privately* educated, as we say. My own case was still more exceptional: I entered the system as a casual and undirected unit, a misfit. I did not consciously reject the system: rather, it rejected me. I played the game, but I did not obey the rules. I did not conform to a regular routine, and before I could be punished for my dilettantism, the war had taken me to another and a more realistic school.

During the whole of this subsequent period I read avidly. Even in the most difficult circumstances—in the most desperate trench warfare—I was never without a book in my pocket. It was necessarily very unsystematic reading, but it included Henry James and Flaubert, Baudelaire and Rimbaud, Plato and Berkeley. But it is not really necessary to isolate this period: I would rather say that the process of self-education was uninterrupted by the war, the only difference being that before and after that event I was better equipped to find or refer to the books of which day by day I became conscious.

I have not lost sight of the original purpose of this chapter, which was to relate my gradual discovery of the world of poetry. But a divagation has been necessary to show what part was played in the process by my education. I think I have shown that it was mainly negative. When I look back on this period of my life, and when I compare my experience with that of other people, my strongest feeling is one of relief. It is so easy to crush a nascent sensibility, or if not to crush it, then to deform it. The poetic sensibility is especially vulnerable, and especially in England. Socially the poet is despised: for the great majority of people he is merely a comic figure, the butt of *Punch* and the music-halls. Poetry as an art has become a secret and shame-faced activity: people are even shy of being seen reading poetry in a train, whereas the public declamation of poetry, as it was practised even in the nineteenth century, and as it is still practised in Russia, is quite unknown. Attempts to reintroduce the art through the very suitable medium of broadcasting have so far been very disappointing.

If this social opposition to poetry is reinforced by what one might call a process of academic sterilization, it is very difficult to retain any trace of free sensibility. Actually the attempt to reconcile art and scholarship is nearly always fatal: poetry cannot be dissected unless it is first killed. I do not imply, however, that poetry—or art in general—should be excluded from the curricula of our schools and universities. On the contrary, I think that the arts should play a greater part in education. But they should be treated as arts and not as 'subjects', still less as sciences. This is not the place to enlarge on the question, but as a general indication of what I mean, I would say that it is necessary to make a clear separation of the historical and the technical aspects of each art. The history of literature or the history of painting (including, of course, the history of their technical development) would be distinct subjects, taught like the history of any other aspect of social evolution. But the technique of literature, like the technique of painting, would be encouraged as a practical activity. Poetry and plays would be written, recited or produced, and the creative artist would be elevated above the academic scholar. It would, of course, revolutionize educational standards if marks were to be awarded, or even a degree granted, on the artistic merits of an original composition; but that, I contend, is the only way in which the arts can be brought into organic relation with a vital system of education.

Otherwise, it is better to let the aesthetic impulse develop unaided, as it did in my own case. Once I had become aware of this creative impulse in myself, I needed no encouragement to educate myself in the subject. I was filled with an insatiable curiosity which extended to all the poetry of the past, to the poetry of other languages, and to the poetry of my contemporaries.

In a few years I had raced through all the poetry in my own language which I thought likely to appeal to me, and was then eager to discover the poetry of France, of Italy and of Germany. I doubt if I should ever have attempted to learn the languages of these countries but for the curiosity engendered by my poetic impulse. Latin poetry had been almost completely destroyed for me by the education I had received in this subject, but a measure of enjoyment was preserved in poets who by chance had never been 'set', such as Catullus and Lucretius. But I must confess that Latin poetry in general has played an insignificant part in my poetic experience. I have excused myself by supposing a lack of sympathy, but this lack may have been due to a deficiency of knowledge. For Greek poetry, however, I have felt much sympathy on the basis of no knowledge at all. I have never had the time, nor perhaps the will, to teach myself Greek, and Greek poetry, in its essential nature, remains unknown to me. I say 'in its essential nature' because it is only in translation that I have read the great classics of Greek poetry; and though this may have given me a certain insight into the Greek spirit, it is futile, as I know from my experience with foreign poetry in general, to pretend that my lips have even touched the rim of the hippocrene fountain.

In this account of my discovery of poetry I have so far not gone beyond Blake and Yeats. I have mentioned Ralph Hodgson, but his influence was short-lived and superficial. The next stage is represented by Donne and Browning among the poets of the past, and by a group of contemporary poets known as the Imagists. Together, these two influences may be said to have completed my poetic education. The years to follow held such surprises as Rimbaud and Apollinaire, Hölderlin and Rilke, but though such poets have deepened my conception of the content of poetry, they have not altered the attitude to the problems of technique which I formed under the influence of the Imagists.

Donne is an influence apart—not in any sense a technical influence, but rather an extension of sensibility, an education in emotional rectitude. The conceits which so disgusted Johnson appealed to me because they were an attempt to bridge the separate worlds of intellect and feeling, and I began to conceive of poetry as an intermediary between these conflicting forces. But it never occurred to me that poets of the twentieth century should use the language and diction of the seventeenth century—they might, with as good reason, dress in the costumes of that period. There was something even in this respect to learn from Donne: he did, after all, refuse to sacrifice his meaning to a conventional ideal of smoothness (which is not the same thing as felicity). Browning's technique I found entirely relevant. He too was occupied by this problem—the expression of intellectual concepts in the language of feeling—though his intelligence was historical and ethical rather than experimental and aesthetic, and his emotions were distorted by the moral conventions of his age. His technique, however, was free: a reaction against the Parnassian polish of Tennyson and Arnold, a return to the rugged exactitude of Donne. Until Hopkins was discovered (in 1918, though odd poems had appeared earlier) Browning was the only English poet of the immediate past who worked as anything like a ferment in the minds of the poets of the decade 1906-15 (the decisive years in the formation of the modern poetic tradition in England). There was also Yeats, but he did not then appear as of the past: he was one of our contemporaries, himself subject to some of the same influences. But even Yeats can to a great extent be discounted—his real influence came later, when his later poems grew realistic and political, and as such appealed to a still later generation. Even before the outbreak of the war, we distrusted Yeats's romanticism. Only the Irish could move freely in the Celtic twilight, though the Americans might assimilate it like any other foreign tradition, and it was the Americans among us, particularly Ezra Pound, who paid most respect to it. For the Anglo-Saxons it might be a fashionable craze, but as a poetic style it was racially foreign to us, only to be adopted as a mannerism and an affectation. The war finally killed it. An epigraph which appeared next to the title-page of the first edition of my war-poems, *Naked Warriors*, was intended as a parody of Yeats, and as a cynical expression of my own disillusionment:

> *War through my soul has driven*
> *its jagged blades;*
> *The riven*
> *dream fades—*
> *So you'd better grieve, heart, in the gathering night,*
> *Grieve, heart, in the loud twilight.*

What I wish to insist on is the importance of Browning in the pre-war years. It is only necessary to turn to the poems published by Ezra Pound—'il miglior fabbro' of us all—particularly the volumes *Personae* and *Exultations*, to see that influence predominant. Even when Pound is writing a poem with a Provençal or Romantic theme, it may be given the manner or diction of Browning. The same influence is not absent from the earlier poems of his friend T. S. Eliot.

Mr. Pound, I know, has many other gods—Fenollosa and Rémy de Gourmont, for example—and he is very jealous on their behalf. But I am not writing about critical influences, which were very various, but of direct mentors of the technique and diction of verse. The modification of Browning's influence came from France—from Rimbaud and Laforgue, and from the early verse of Duhamel, Jules Romains, Jean de Bosschère, André Spire and Apollinaire. There was also T. E. Hulme, but by now his five short poems have begun to assume rather too much prominence in the history of this period. They were certainly good textbook examples of imagist technique, but if Hulme had written fifty or a hundred poems as good, we should not have heard so much about them.

This explanation has been long enough, and I must pick up the residue of my own impressions. If Browning was the last of my historical discoveries, it will now be seen how he came to be fused in my imagination with the activities of a contemporary school which was at that time learning from Browning and applying his technique to the expression of a modern sensibility. I had now reached the vanguard of the art for which I had felt an affinity in my own being. Henceforth my discovery of poetry was to be directed by my passionate participation in its immediate destiny. Hitherto I had read for enjoyment and understanding: I was now to read as if I drew in the substance of life itself, creatively manifested in the minds of living poets.

From this experience, which lasted from the year 1913 to 1917, I quickly evolved what I would have called my philosophy of composition. There was a general feeling then that some new philosophy was necessary, much as it had been necessary when Wordsworth and Coleridge published their *Lyrical Ballads* in 1798, and several attempts to formulate one had been made by the young poets for whom I felt such a strong sympathy. The clearest statement of these years is the Preface to *Some Imagist Poets*, an anthology published in 1915 which included the work of Richard Aldington, H.D., F. S. Flint, and D. H. Lawrence. That preface still remains the locus classicus for the doctrines of the imagist school, and since it is not now generally available, I will quote the six 'common principles'* which it set forth:

1. To use the language of common speech, but to employ always the *exact* word, not the nearly-exact, nor the merely decorative word.

2. To create new rhythms—as the expression of new moods—and not to copy old rhythms, which merely echo old moods. We do not insist upon 'free-verse' as the only method of writing poetry. We fight for it as for a principle of liberty. We believe that the individuality of a poet may often be better expressed in free-verse than in conventional forms. In poetry, a new cadence means a new idea.

3. To allow absolute freedom in the choice of subject. It is not good art to write badly about aeroplanes and automobiles; nor is it necessarily bad art to write about the past. We believe passionately in the artistic value of modern life, but we wish to point out that there is nothing so uninspiring nor so old-fashioned as an aeroplane of the year 1911.

4. To present an image (hence the name: 'Imagist'). We are not a school of painters, but we believe that poetry should render particulars exactly and not deal in vague generalities, however magnificent and sonorous. It is for this reason that we oppose the cosmic poet, who seems to us to shirk the real difficulties of his art.

5. To produce poetry that is hard and clear, never blurred nor indefinite.

6. Finally, most of us believe that concentration is of the very essence of poetry.

Three years later, in the third number of *Art and Letters*, I published my own 'Definitions towards a Modern Theory of Poetry'. I began with the following 'axioms':

1. Form is determined by the emotion which requires expression.

---

* The best *defence* of these principles is F. S. Flint's Preface to *Otherworld*, a volume of 'cadences' published in 1920 (Poetry Bookshop) and dedicated, I am proud to recall, to me. Flint had far more to do with the development of the Imagist school than has generally been acknowledged.

Corollary: Form is not an unchanging mould into which any emotion can be poured.

2. The poem is an artistic whole demanding strict unity.

3. The criterion of the poem is the quality of the vision expressed, granted that the expression is adequate.

Corollary: Rhyme, metre, cadence, alliteration, are various decorative devices to be used as the vision demands, and are not formal quantities pre-ordained.

I was evidently reading Spinoza at the time, and the whole essay is written in a dry analytical style. Terms like 'vision', 'emotion', 'value', 'unity', and 'form' are defined with the aid of a psychological jargon which I should now try to avoid; but the essay, differently worded, would still represent my views on the theory of poetry. What interests me now is to find myself criticizing my friends the Imagists. I admitted that they were the only modern school of poets which showed 'any clarity of creative intention'; but I criticized them because 'in their manifestoes they had renounced the decorative word, but their sea-violets and wild hyacinths tend to become as decorative as the beryls and jades of Oscar Wilde'. I also accused them of lacking 'that aesthetic selection which is the artist's most peculiar duty'— by which I meant, as far as I can now make out, that they thought any passing mood or emotion worthy of poetic expression—they did not apply an aesthetic (or did I mean intellectual?) judgment to the quality of the emotion itself. I concluded: 'Modern England may be "a nest of singing birds", but it is well for us to realize that the poem is still rather a primitive affair, and to make it otherwise there is a call for stern artistic devotion. We must shrink from the exotic and the decadent, and from the sheltered garden of cultivated beauties. Beauty is a discipline, demanding all the intensity of a man's intelligence to present clear and undefiled the infinite quality in things. The artist's vision is the supreme value; the expression of it is the supreme difficulty.'

This essay must have been written early in 1918, that is to say, before the end of the war, though I cannot remember where or in what circumstances I wrote it. I can look back with amusement on its earnest solemnity now, but I think it reflects something of the contradiction that was being forced on us by our daily experience. We were trying to maintain an abstract aesthetic ideal in the midst of terrorful and inhuman events. In my own case I am certain that this devotion to abstract notions and intellectual reveries saved me from a raw reaction to these events. But as the war went on, year after year, and there seemed no escape from its indignity except death, some compromise between dream and reality became necessary. The only worthy compromise, I even then dimly realized, was a synthesis—some higher reality in which the freedom of the mind and the necessity of experience became reconciled. If I had been older that solution might have been a philosophy; but I was not contemplative enough for that, nor wise enough. I therefore sought the solution in art: in a poetry which would represent my aesthetic ideals and yet at the same time deal with the experience that threatened to overwhelm me. The result was a series of war poems, some of which I afterwards destroyed, but most of which I published in a small volume to which I gave the title *Naked Warriors*. (Incidentally, I am sure that I had not at that time seen Pollaiuolo's engraving which so perfectly illustrates the title and the epigraph which I put on the title-page: 'And there were some that went into the battle naked and unarmed, fighting only with the fervour of their spirit, dying and getting many wounds'.) It may seem that this was but a feeble response to such an immense event. In a later chapter I shall discuss my reactions to war in more detail, but on this level of aesthetic response, I would ask the reader to reflect on the millions who were engaged in that conflict and then to examine its poetic aftermath in any of the languages of the nations engaged. It is infinitesimal in quantity and almost negligible in poetic quality. Many years later, in his Introduction to the *Oxford Book of Modern Verse*, Yeats was to offer a reason for this strange disparity—'the same reason that made Arnold withdraw his "Empedocles on Etna" from circulation; passive suffering is not a theme for poetry'; and for the same reason Yeats decided to exclude war poetry from his anthology. It was a judgment that was to arouse a good deal of resentment among the young poets of today, and I am not sure that I myself accept it—at least, not for the reason given. Another sentence in the same paragraph of Yeat's Introduction, though it is metaphorical, seems to me to be nearer the truth of the matter: 'When man has withdrawn into the quicksilver at the back of the mirror no great event becomes luminous in his mind. . . .' In other words, the necessary element is the time-lapse implicit in Wordsworth's phrase, 'recollected in tranquillity',

THE FALCON AND THE DOVE

an element of 'aesthetic distance'. Even passive suffering can be a fit theme for poetry if it is seen objectively enough, against a wide background. The direct expression of suffering is an animal cry; poetry, too, is an animal cry, but of another kind. There is a difference which is the difference between the scream of a slaughtered pig and the song of a nightingale, and this is perhaps the difference between passive suffering and passive joy. But art begins—and I think this was Yeats's meaning—when the joy is purposive, an active sublimation even of suffering and tragedy.

In 1917 and 1918, in the intervals of leave from the Front, I gradually made the acquaintance of the poets whose work I admired—Flint, Aldington, Pound and Eliot—and met other writers with whom I was in sympathy, such as A. R. Orage and P. Wyndham Lewis. Influences that had been literary and indirect now became personal, and the cold communication of the page was exchanged for the intimate give-and-take of conversation. Some of these friendships were to endure without interruption to the present day, some became intermittent, some never developed at all. It is not my intention to discuss my personal relationships in this book, but I cannot avoid a reference to my friendship with Eliot, because it has certainly had a considerable effect on my intellectual development, perhaps just because we are so divergent in origin, education, character and ideals. He has called himself royalist, classicist, and anglo-catholic, whereas I (with qualifications similar to those he made) would call myself anarchist, romanticist and agnostic. A long and uninterrupted friendship has been possible because in spite of these divergences, we have always agreed about things which are perhaps finally more important: the sense of beauty in poetry, the quality of the expression of ideas, and the priority to be given to natural goodness even when the intelligence seems perverse. I think our friendship has a certain general significance, because too much importance, in history and criticism, is given to ideological similarities and not enough to human sympathies. Life, even in its intimate or arcane recesses, is still dialectical.

These friendships no doubt modified my poetic outlook, but I think I may say that by the end of the war I had discovered myself and my style—that is to say, I had made an equation between emotion and image, between feeling and expression. So long as I was true to this equation, I need not be afraid of influences or acquired mannerisms. Poetry was reduced to an instrument of precision. 'Reduced' will imply, of course, a lack of bulk: from that time my output of verse was to be severely restricted. But what I wrote I tended to keep: I no longer destroyed a large part of my writing. Criticism had become innate, composition an instinctive language; and though I am very far from claiming perfection or permanence for the poems I have retained, I do not think it will be necessary for a reader of the future to approach my work with squared shoulders: he can accept or reject me on the instant. By this statement I lay myself open to the charge that there is nothing in my poetry to detain the reader; but that, of course, is not what I mean. One of the essential characteristics of poetry is what Coleridge called 'the power of reducing multitude into unity of effect'. Whatever the nature of poetry, be it lyrical or dramatic, meditative or philosophical, this unity of effect should exist, and be immediately apparent. If that unity is achieved, the poem has that quality which is possessed by all true works of art—the quality of retaining our interest in spite of familiarity.

Here I will break off this account of my discovery of poetry—'break off' because it is an enterprise which still continues. I am not now likely to modify my own technique, and I have reached that becalmed stage of life in which the poetic impulse is often dormant. But I still retain the zest, the insatiable thirst for this pellucid essence of experience. All other sensuous experiences are as nothing to this perception of poetic beauty. A few years ago I took one of my sons, then aged about eleven, to an open-air performance of *A Midsummer Night's Dream*. It was a brilliant sunny day, and everywhere, not least on the green and leafy stage, the atmosphere was gay. But time after time the impact of Shakespeare's words—the words themselves and not their meaning—would send a gush of tears to my eyes, and there was no darkness to hide my paradoxical visage from my neighbours. But they too were absorbed in the play—some in the antics, some in the atmosphere; some few in the cadence of the words that came winged with inexplicable sorrow through the summer air.

3

The Tree of Life

In 'The Innocent Eye' I have already given some idea of the
atmosphere of simple piety which surrounded me in my early
years. My father was not emotional in his religion; he was a
strict Christian and a man of natural, equable goodness. Only
a blizzard would have prevented him from driving the five miles
to church every Sunday. Night and morning we said our prayers
before our parents; there were frequent readings from the Bible,
and as soon as we were old enough we had to learn the Collect
for the day. All this was part of our routine, with no trace of
effort or self-consciousness; and since it was also part of the
routine of the few houses we entered, it never occurred to me to
question it. When, at the age of ten, I went away to school, there
was a very different atmosphere, but no essential change of
practice. The headmaster was again a man of simple natural piety,
and he communicated his spirit to the whole school. There were
daily prayers after breakfast in the dining-room; and every evening each boy knelt down by the side of his bed. The most violent
change was the Sunday service. The school had been founded by
pious Congregationalists, and it was to a Congregational chapel
in the town that we trooped each Sunday—the older boys to the
evening as well as the morning service. It was inevitable that I
should feel a little chilled by the bleaker atmosphere of these
conventicles. The atmosphere I was used to was not luxurious;
but at least it was romantic; and there is no romance in varnished
pine, hygienic distemper, or stencilled friezes. The singing at
Kirkdale had been exiguous and toneless; it was now hearty and
voluminous, but our voices did not chime in. The brief homilies
which even a child could understand had become interminable
moral discourses punctured, more often than not, by a boy's

fainting. Never, during the five years at school, did I or any other boy that I knew of, question the religious discipline which was imposed on us. But the routine was no longer accepted instinctively. We all hated the church parade, the crocodile march, the fight against the fidgets or the giggles. Our real piety, if we possessed any, was reserved for our private prayers before going to bed.

When I left school, at the age of fifteen, a great change took place. For the first time I became consciously religious. I naturally returned to the Church of England, and attended the services regularly. Though the prosperous suburban church to which I went had none of the primitive poetry of Kirkdale, it was romantic in its neo-Gothic way, and worked on my boyish imagination. I was swept away, as boys often are at this age, on a wave of devotional ecstasy. Ecstasy is perhaps a magniloquent word to describe my feelings, but I want to convey the irrational nature of this phase. It preceded the discovery of philosophy to which I have already referred; it was not accompanied by any conscious thought on the problems of religion, nor indeed on any problem, unless it were that of social conduct. It was manifested, firstly in an intensity of prayer; further, in a scrupulous attendance at public worship; and finally in a kind of dazed exaltation during public worship. I did not sing nor even repeat the litany or creed: rather I would fix my gaze on some one point—the face of the preacher, a lamp or a candle-flame—and by concentrating exclude all other sensations. My whole being would hang on this bright point, whilst around me swirled the music of the organ, the voice of the preacher, the soaring Gothic arches. In this way I no doubt felt that I was bringing my consciousness nearer to a perception of the glory of God. But it was a fruitless and insubstantial practice from which I gained only a kind of religiosity, and no strength of mind or grace of virtue. But it is possibly a practice indulged in by other devotees, whose religion lies more in the regions of hypnotic ritualism than of true devotion.

This phase lasted for at the most two years. I passed out of it gradually, and as a result of my own development, without persuasion of any kind. It was a misfortune that the seeds of scepticism began to germinate at the very moment the necessity of confirmation was being pressed on me. This ceremony had been delayed until my brother had left school, and it was my mother's desire that we should be confirmed together. The vicar of the parish in which we then lived was approached and agreed to give us special preparation. He was a venerable old man, of some reputation as a preacher. I am afraid he found us dull and uncomprehending novices. I had now reached a stage of doubt which completely paralysed my mind. I did not dare to confess my thoughts, much less to reveal my scepticism. I did not wish to distress my mother, nor mislead my brother. I went on with the painful farce and reached such a stage of mental confusion that at the end of the preparation I could not even repeat the Creed without error: without conviction, my mind could not memorize the meaningless succession of syllables. But in due course I was confirmed and for some months went to Communion with my mother and brother. Then came the first year at the university, and the open access to the very fount of heresy. I could no longer endure the falsity of my position. First I gave up my prayers and then my attendance at church. My mother was both grieved and baffled, and in vain brought to bear upon me the influence of relatives and friends. But my unbelief was now too positive: I had to persist or resign all faith in myself. I brought much unhappiness upon myself and upon others: my mother was ill and shortly to die. But the dark struggle brought no other issue. And in that state of unbelief I have remained until the present day.

I purposely use this word 'unbelief' (it is the word used by the father of the dumb child in that tragic prayer: 'Lord, I believe; help Thou mine unbelief') because it best describes the purely neutral or agnostic state of my mind. I have never adopted an attitude of active disbelief. It has never occurred to me to prose-lytize on behalf of rationalism or atheism. Indeed, I have always had the greatest respect for genuinely religious people, and many of my best friends, with whom I am in closest mutual sympathy, are devout Christians. This fact, together with my intellectual interest in religion, and at one time my frequent references to scholasticism, has often led to the assumption that I was at least in sympathy with the Catholic Church, and perhaps a neo-Thomist. It is very possible that if I had been born in France rather than England, I should have been drawn into one or other of those Catholic groups which seem to be able to reconcile an intellectual support of the Catholic faith with a complete disregard of, and even contempt for, the Catholic hierarchy. But even that is doubtful. The state of unbelief to which I refer cannot possibly lead to any positive action, least of all to political activity.

Intellectual vanity is most often the charge brought against this state of mind, but I do not think it is really justified. If I had had any clue to the universe to offer as an alternative to theocracy; if I had been a materialist and thought that all the phenomena of our human nature could be explained by means of the various physical sciences; or even if I had consciously deliberated on the different explanations of the universe offered by the religions and philosophies of the world, it would have been a different matter. Then I should have been pitting my individual intelligence against the traditional and relatively universal intelligence of the Church into which I was born. Naturally my state of mind has been influenced and even induced by intellectual considerations, and it is a genuine puzzle to me how anyone with a knowledge of the comparative history of religions can retain an *exclusive* belief in the tenets of his particular sect. But I have generally kept my bewilderment to myself, and since I am willing to admit the inexplicability of the universe and of our human destiny, it is not difficult to accommodate myself to minor mysteries of this sort. I suspect that actually we all construct our private myths, and that even the members of a dogmatic Church, if they have any imagination at all, elaborate a separate phantasy from the symbols and ideas which are communicated to them. An agnostic can acquiesce in such an individual solution, reserving his criticism for the structures of temporal power to which the individual illogically surrenders his intellectual will, his rational and moral science.

The fundamental consideration in our attitude to religion is not intellectual, and cannot therefore be a question of vanity or pride. In most cases it seems to be nothing but the fear, conscious or subconscious, of death. The great majority of men cannot bear to contemplate a universe in which their individual existence is strictly limited, their life a *little* life 'rounded with a sleep'. They cling desperately to the conception of an after-life, and since the decay and disappearance of the physical body is an only too evident fact, they are compelled to postulate a non-material after-life, a spiritual immortality. Once this postulate is made, it is elaborated: the spiritual life after death is given its hierarchy on the analogy of the life on earth, and a being commanding this hierarchy, and logically the whole process of the universe, completes the phantasy. The history of religion in the modern world is the history of the various attempts made by mankind to substantiate this particular phantasy, to give it realistic validity and material evidence. So passionately have men desired to preserve this illusion that they have devoted their best mental energies to its philosophical justification, with the consequence that the world of thought outside the churches cannot compare in depth of feeling or beauty of expression with the art and philosophy inspired by religion. It is true that a great poet like Shakespeare cannot be claimed by any of the churches; but neither can he be convincingly claimed by any brand of heresy or paganism. His sympathetic insight hovers over every manifestation of the human spirit.

My own attitude towards death has never been one of fear—I should say, never one of overt fear, because I cannot be sure of what is going on below the surface of my consciousness. When I first became aware of the brevity of life, my feelings were of anger and resentment. Soon afterwards, when I became a soldier on active service, death was no longer an abstract and relatively distant prospect, but an imminent possibility. But just before I went to the Front, death had robbed me of my mother, and that event had shaken me to the depth of my being. So strong was the psychic shock that when I found myself in a strange country and amidst new surroundings, I began to be haunted by such vivid dreams that for months I existed in a state of uncertainty. Was she really dead? Or had her death occurred only in one of my obsessive nightmares? I did not dare to give expression to this real state of uncertainty, but as the months passed, there came no confirmation of her existence. Meanwhile death was being forced more brutally into my consciousness: men were being killed by my side, before my eyes. The terrible fragility of life was made evident to me; I saw that individuality and intelligence and all the unique make of a man could seep into the ground with a trickle of warm blood. But still I did not fear death, strongly as I wanted to live. The philosophy which was forced on me by this experience was simply fatalistic—it was not resigned enough to be called stoical. It had in it an element of bitterness or resentment which we find in 'the tragic view of life', and fatalism is perhaps the best word to describe my permanent attitude to this problem. My favourite symbol is the Tree of Life. The human race is the

trunk and branches of this tree, and individual men are the leaves
which appear one season, flourish for a summer, and then die. I
am like a leaf of this tree, and one day I shall be torn off by a storm
or simply decay and fall, and become a pinch of compost about
its roots. But meanwhile I am conscious of the tree's flowing
sap and steadfast strength. Deep down in my consciousness is
the consciousness of a collective life, a life of which I am a part
and to which I contribute a minute but unique extension. When
I die and fall, the tree remains, nourished to some small degree by
my brief manifestation of life. Millions of leaves have preceded
me and millions will follow me; the tree itself grows and endures.

Some people can find no consolation in this symbol. They
are the people who fear death—who can only die comfortably
in the illusion that they will continue to live in another world or
on another plane of consciousness. If they can really maintain
such an illusion, they are welcome to it; I have no wish to
deprive them of it, but in my own philosophy I cannot tolerate
any element which might be self-deception.

There is a passage in the Taoist classic, *Chuang Tzu*, which
perfectly expresses the attitude towards death which circumstances forced me to adopt thus early in my life. It has been
beautifully translated into English by Arthur Waley:

'When Chuang Tzu's wife died, the logician Hui Tzu came
to the house to join in the rites of mourning. To his astonishment
he found Chuang Tzu sitting with an inverted bowl on his knees,
drumming upon it and singing a song. "After all," said Hui Tzu,
"she lived with you, brought up your children, grew old along
with you. That you should not mourn for her is bad enough; but
to let your friends find you drumming and singing—that is really
going too far!" "You misjudge me," said Chuang Tzu. "When
she died, I was in despair, as any man well might be. But soon,
pondering on what had happened, I told myself that in death no
strange new fate befalls us. In the beginning we lack not life
only, but form. Not form only, but spirit. We are blent in the
one great featureless, indistinguishable mass. Then a time came
when the mass evolved spirit, spirit evolved form, form evolved
life. And now life in its turn has evolved death. For not nature
only but man's being has its seasons, its sequence of spring and
autumn, summer and winter. If someone is tired and has gone to
lie down, we do not pursue him with shouting and bawling. She

whom I have lost has lain down to sleep for a while in the Great Inner Room. To break in upon her rest with the noise of lamentation would show that I knew nothing of nature's Sovereign Law."*

'This attitude towards death,' Waley remarks, 'is but part of a general attitude towards the universal laws of nature, which is one not merely of resignation nor even of acquiescence, but a lyrical, almost ecstatic acceptance which has inspired some of the most moving passages in Taoist literature. That we should question nature's right to make and unmake, that we should hanker after some rôle that nature did not intend us to play is not merely futile, not merely damaging to that tranquillity of the "spirit" which is the essence of Taoism, but involves, in view of our utter helplessness, a sort of fatuity at once comic and disgraceful.' I like to think that I too possess something of this general attitude towards the universal laws of nature, something of the Taoist tranquillity of the 'spirit'. I had been familiar with a translation of the *Tao Tê Ching* for many years, but it was only later, under the guidance of Arthur Waley's books, that I became acquainted with the main tenets of Taoism, and discovered how closely, and with how many facets, it embodies the truths towards which I have stumbled since I first began to think about the problems of life. It would be absurd to describe myself as a Taoist, because the idiom in which this philosophy of life is expressed is an alien one, coloured by the circumstances and customs of a distant time and land. But Christianity, in its primitive form, is not dissimilar, and embodies not a little of the same tradition. If an Anglo-Saxon of the twentieth century can accept the gospel of a Nazarene whose birth is chosen to mark the beginning of our era, would it be any less strange to find an appropriate philosophy of life in the sayings of a Chinese sage who lived a few centuries earlier? But actually I have not sought out this philosophy, to adopt it. My attitude was inherent in my personality, and was brought to expression by self-examination in the light of experience. An 'influence' is as easily shed as it is acquired. It is not teachers that we should seek, but exemplars who confirm and strengthen the truth we have discovered in ourselves.

* *Chuang Tzu*, XVIII, 2. From *The Way and its Power* (London, 1934), pp. 53–4.

I have confessed that I only discovered the Taoists comparatively recently. I do not think it is likely now that I shall fundamentally modify my philosophy of life, but it may be of some
interest to cast a backward glance over the stages of my development. In doing so, a distinction must be made between intellectual
and philosophical interests—at least, the enthusiasm generated by
various writers falls into two separate categories. My early
enthusiasm for Nietzsche, for example, was purely intellectual:
my life was unaffected—I never became a Nietzschean, either in
thought or deed. Similarly, philosophers like Plato and Spinoza,
both of whom I have read with absorption and sympathy, have
never been a part of my intimate existence. I remember that I once
tried to adopt *The Republic* as a pocket companion, but though I
learned much from it, it was an objective process. Still more
objective was my approach to philosophers like Kant and Leibniz.
The first reading of Kant's *Prologomena* was a revelation. I had
never conceived that the process of abstract thought could be such
a pure pleasure, and I seemed to become conscious for the first
time of the beautiful functioning of the instrument that is the
human brain. Rather different, but still impersonal, is the relationship which I have had with such philosophers as Bergson and
Whitehead. In so far as I have myself indulged in any practical
philosophy—it has been almost exclusively in the field of aesthetics
—I have been strongly influenced by both these writers, but I
have never shared their general outlook. This would apply to
many other modern philosophers of whose thought traces might
be found in my own writings—William James, Benedetto Croce,
Leone Vivante, Max Scheler.

Of philosophers of the other kind, in whom I have found a
sympathy which is emotional rather than intellectual, it occurs
to me to mention only three: Traherne, Kierkegaard and Santayana. It is an odd and apparently disparate trinity, and it would
be difficult to trace any lines of communication between them, or
to give them a place in any orderly scheme of philosophical
development. They just 'happened' to me, and it is a curious and
disconcerting fact that I have remained in stubborn disagreement
with the conclusions of two of them. They have been rather in
the nature of friends whose faults I have seen, whose religious
views I have ignored, but whom I have nevertheless loved and
frequented because from them I derived the greatest pleasure and

profit. Santayana comes first in time. I cannot remember when I first came across one of his books—I may have been led to him by William James, or perhaps it was his Introduction to the volume of Spinoza in the Everyman Library (first published as long ago as 1910) which aroused my curiosity. I also find it difficult to explain the fascination he has exercised on me for many years. I suppose it was partly the fact that here was a modern philosopher with the superficial appeal of a literary style —though the same was true of others, Bergson and Bradley, for example. Santayana's style has limitations, which I have discussed elsewhere; and in spite of his seductive charm, his prose is not easy to read at length. There was undoubtedly some more practical reason, and I can only suggest now that I hoped to find in him a philosophy that would reconcile our knowledge of the physical universe with some recognition of spiritual values. I never had much use for idealistic philosophy; I was a materialist, but for my materialism I wanted a philosophical, though not necessarily a metaphysical, sanction. 'Now in natural philosophy,' Santayana has said, 'I am a decided materialist—apparently the only one living; I am well aware that idealists are fond of calling material-ism, too, metaphysics, in rather an angry tone, so as to cast dis-credit upon it by assimilating it to their own systems. But my materialism, for all that, is not metaphysical. . . . I wait for the men of science to tell me what matter is, in so far as they can discover it, and am not at all surprised or troubled at the abstract-ness and vagueness of their ultimate conceptions: how should our notion of things so remote from the scale and scope of our senses be anything but schematic?'* This has been my own attitude—a materialism which is not so much a part of my philosophy, as an external limitation, marking its boundaries. Though I still read metaphysics when it comes my way or suits my mood, I have been prevented from becoming a metaphysician by a strong feeling that anything not evident to our senses, or to the extension of our senses provided by scientific instruments, is not of great importance to our lives. Even scientific speculations cease to interest me when they can only be handled by means of mathe-matical symbols. If I cling to a realm of supermaterial values, which Santayana calls the realm of essence, it is because the exist-ence of such values is as evident to my senses as sticks or stones.

* *Scepticism and Animal Faith*, London, 1923, pp. vii-viii.

For a knowledge of the reality of these values I do not need to go further than the realm of aesthetics. The poetic essence, for example, cannot be measured by any scientific instruments: it is available to intuition alone, and the poetic data which are given by intuition belong to a world as real as that from which scientific observation draws its data. Whether poetic data belong to the same order of existence as physical data—whether, that is to say, there is any relationship between the world of matter and the world of values—this is the kind of problem that Santayana discusses with such acuity; and it is because he discusses such problems in relation to human life rather than to a logical system that I have always been drawn to his writings. 'The hierarchy of goods, the architecture of values, is the subject that concerns man most. Wisdom is the first philosophy, both in time and authority; and to collect facts and chop logic would be idle and would add no dignity to the mind, unless that mind possessed a clear humanity and could discern what facts and logic are good for and what not.'* In renouncing metaphysics it was under Santayana's guidance that I became what must, I suppose, be called a moralist.

My attraction to Traherne is still more difficult to explain. *Centuries of Meditations* is in purpose a manual of devotion, far removed from my practices and beliefs. It is not as such that it has attracted me. 'There are invisible ways of conveyance by which some great thing doth touch our souls, and by which we tend to it,' says Traherne himself. It is some such invisible communication that runs between this book and me. There is, of course, the purely external and visible quality of the prose style to which full justice has not even yet been done. Of his period, only Jeremy Taylor and Milton come into comparison, and though Traherne lacks the sustained eloquence of the one and the grandeur of the other, he has his own incomparable felicity. His lyrical spirituality, though it has a parallel in the contemporary poetry of Vaughan and Crashaw, is quite unique in English prose. But nevertheless it is not for its style alone that I have returned again and again to this book. It is for its content. 'An empty book,' Traherne begins, 'is like an Infant's Soul, in which anything may be written. It is capable of all things, but containeth nothing. I have a mind to fill this with profitable wonders. And since Love made you put it into my hands, I will fill it with those

* *Reason in Science*, p. 217.

truths you love without knowing them: and with those things which, if it be possible, shall show my Love; to you, in communicating most enriching Truths: to Truth, in exalting her beauties in such a Soul.' It is an intimate induction, intended for the eyes of a friend, and it immediately puts the reader in the place of that friend. It gives us the key to the understanding of the book which follows. That there are Truths we love without knowing them must be the experience of everyone who finds that his actions are guided by a principle which finds no expression in his declared philosophy of life. This principle the Christian mystics have identified with Love—a universal love analogous to human love. And it is this love, in all its aspects, that Traherne describes. 'Love is deeper than at first it can be thought. It never ceaseth but in endless things.' It is an expansive love which gradually illuminates the whole universe and everything in it. 'Till your spirit filleth the whole world, and the stars are your jewels; till you are as familiar with the ways of God in all Ages as with your walk and table: till you are intimately acquainted with that shady nothing out of which the world was made: till you love men so as to desire their happiness, with a thirst equal to the zeal of your own; till you delight in God for being good to all: you never enjoy the world.' Traherne's religion is positive and joyful, far removed from the gloomy doctrines of predestination and original sin which had triumphed in his own life-time (he died in 1674). His mysticism is an affirmation of sensuous enjoyment— 'by the very right of your senses you enjoy the world. . . . It is of the nobility of man's soul that he is insatiable.' The senses are God's instruments, and we minister to his power and goodness with these divine engines. We thus acquire a sense of the glory which is immanent in the world, and which we live to exploit, like veins of gold in the dull ore of experience. It is a pantheistic doctrine, since it holds that we only attain true happiness when we actively participate in the processes of nature.

Traherne more than any other writer—more than the Golden Legend or the chronicles of the Middle Ages, more than Plutarch or Vauvenargues, William Blake or Henry James—all recognizable tributaries—confirmed me in that sense of glory which from my early youth I have identified with the source of all virtuous and unselfish actions. I have given this title, *The Sense of Glory*, to a collection of essays which help to define, however obliquely, what I mean by the phrase. But the truest and deepest meaning, of which my meaning is only a dim reflection, will be found in Traherne's *Centuries*. 'I will not by the noise of bloody wars and the dethroning of kings advance you to glory: but by the gentle ways of peace and love.' But the gentle ways are the ways of ecstasy: and ecstasy that comes from perceiving bright perfection in natural things, felicity in natural feelings, and celestial joy on your own threshold:

> *But little did the infant dream*
> *That all the treasures of the World were by,*
> *And that himself was so the cream*
> *And crown of all which around about did lie.*
> *Yes thus it was! The gem,*
> *The diadem,*
> *The ring enclosing all*
> *That stood upon this earthly ball;*
> *The heav'nly eye,*
> *Much wider than the sky,*
> *Wherein they all included were,*
> *The glorious soul that was the king*
> *Made to possess them, did appear*
> *A small and little thing!*

Between Traherne and Kierkegaard there are, again, no visible communications. But when I read such a sentence of Traherne's as: 'To think well is to serve God in the interior court', then I am reminded of Kierkegaard. Kierkegaard is much the latest of these three influences. From time to time I had noticed his name in connection with German philosophy, and more rarely he was referred to by French writers. But it was not until about 1930 that I began to search for his own works, in German or French translation, (it was only later that English translations began to appear). The revival of interest in Kierkegaard has been due largely to theologians, both Catholic and Protestant, and it is not possible to separate Kierkegaard's theological ideas from the rest of his work. Nevertheless, it is for his psychological and aesthetic implications that I have read him. He is the very incarnation of the principle of Negative Capability: the mythical Hamlet become flesh, in Hamlet's own haunt. His long search for a principle of true inwardness, for 'something which grows together with the deepest roots of my life, through which I am, so to speak, grafted upon the divine'—in this I found a new justification for my doctrine of the personality as opposed to the character. 'It is with joy,' writes Kierkegaard in his *Journals*, 'and inwardly strengthened, that I contemplate those great men who have thus found the precious stone, for the sake of which they sell all, even their lives, whether I see them intervene forcefully in life, and without faltering go forward on the path marked out for them, or discover them remote from the highway, absorbed in themselves and in working for their noble aim. And I look with reverence even upon the errors which lie so near by. It is this divine side of man, his inward action which means everything, not a mass of information; for that will certainly follow and then all that knowledge will not be a chance assemblage, or a succession of details, without system and without a focusing point. I too have certainly looked for such a centre.'* Kierkegaard was essentially a poet, a child of the Romantic Movement; and he analyses every aspect of life with profundity, with irony, and often with lyrical feeling. His *Journals* have been compared with the *Confessions* of St. Augustine, the *Pensées* of Pascal, and the *Apologia* of Newman; they have something of the quality of all these great books, but they have something more—something nearer to Nietzsche than to anything suggested by these other names. In Kierkegaard, in fact, I was picking up the Nietzschean threads which I had let fall some ten years earlier. Kierkegaard belongs to an earlier age, and there is no evidence that Nietzsche was influenced by him. But many critics have been struck by the resemblance between these two great thinkers—a resemblance which has nothing to do with the content of their thought, but is rather due to the identical nature of their spiritual unrest—that unrest 'which goads the thinking spirit of man to go forth, beyond everything known, and to seek after the peace for which, without doubt, he longs'.†

We might say that there was the possibility of Nietzsche in Kierkegaard, but that it was a possibility he deliberately rejected. Kierkegaard realized that the thinking spirit could only find peace in some firm anchorage. 'In order to sew one must knot the thread' was the metaphor he used; and he argued that there were

* *Journals*, translated by Alexander Dru. (Oxford, 1938), pp. 16–17.
† *Soren Kierkegaard*, by Theodor Haecker. Translated by Alexander Dru. (Oxford, 1937.)

three—and only three—such knots to tie in the otherwise unending process of dialectical reasoning. One is materialism—the world of observed and measured facts; a world of thought limited by our perceptions, but nevertheless a possible world to rest in. The second knot is aesthetics, which Kierkegaard, like Plato, recognized as the world of pure form—'form seeking and symbolizing the austere peace of eternity' (Haecker). The third knot is revelation, 'where dogma for both thought and thinker is the embodiment of the spirit, will, and word of God' (Haecker). Kierkegaard himself chose this third knot: he found that only a belief in the Christian myth could save him from despair; the aesthetic life in particular, he held, led to despair. One of his greatest books, *Enten/Eller* (Either/Or), is devoted to this dilemma: either the aesthetic life—or the ethical. That the aesthetic was for him, not merely a philosophical category, but a deep and real experience, is proved by his enthusiasm for the music of Mozart—not merely by the enthusiasm as such, but by the fact that the enthusiasm was precisely for Mozart, one of the most absolute artists that ever lived. 'Immortal Mozart! Thou to whom I owe all, to whom I owe it *that I lost my reason*, that my soul was in amaze, that I was dismayed in my inmost being. Thou to whom I owe it that I did not go through life without anything occurring that was capable of perturbing me deeply. Thou to whom I give thanks that I did not die without having loved, even though my love was an unhappy one.' That is the tribute of a man who has experienced the aesthetic act, not as reflection but as immediacy. The erotic immediacy which he found in the music of Mozart, and whose potentiality existed in himself as a poet, was something far too actual to be dismissed, in the manner of the philistine philosophers, as insignificant. It was, properly understood, a principle of life itself—a principle which Kierkegaard rejected, but which I, in all humility, have accepted. I am not confident enough to assert that in my case it can never entail the despair which Kierkegaard thought inevitable; but I do suggest that the principle was insufficient for Kierkegaard, and productive of despair, for personal reasons. 'Doubt is despair of thought, despair is doubt of the personality.' Darkening the whole of Kierkegaard's life is a sense of doom and retribution, an acceptance of death as a happy release from fear. The aesthetic principle is, however, an affirmation of life—of life as a sensuous end-in-itself, with spirituality satisfied in the contemplation of pure form. But this eudemonism has its mysticism: the immediacy of the aesthetic act, the sheer leap of genius into the freedom of creativity—that event which many great artists have described. Eudemonism is not a limited or shallow ethic; as Kierkegaard realized, it is a complete alternative to the religious ethic, and the only question is its subjective adequacy. But there is insolence in the very attempt to formulate absolute values, for an individual can only contemplate his particular aspect of the universe. If he is wise he will not insist on the exclusiveness of any aspect; for just as he cannot stand in two places at one and the same time, so he cannot see the universe from more than one aspect: *either* one *or* the other. Standing at the aesthetic point, Kierkegaard saw before him an abyss of despair. For myself, I can only say that standing at this same point, I feel secure and happy.

It would take me too far from my immediate purpose to expound the aesthetic philosophy of life in any detail. Like religious philosophy, it has a rational justification: a philosophy of pure form derived, ultimately, from the physical laws of the universe, the laws which determine, not only the movement of planets and stars and the coherence of the structure of matter, but also the growth of organic life. But like religious philosophy, it cannot be included within such a rational framework: there is a limit to rationality, an 'instant' in which the spirit leaps out of the logical framework of thought, and is creative. What we call classical art is satisfied with the laws of universal beauty: harmony, balance and proportion. But what we call romantic art passes beyond these laws and proclaims its freedom, its novelty, its uniqueness. This act of freedom cannot be justified logically, any more than can an act of faith. It is an intuition, not merely of form and its plastic expression, but also of the paradox of a particular individual, a particular personality.

I shall be accused of reading my own views into the philosophy of Kierkegaard, but in justification I would like to quote a paragraph which Kierkegaard inserts into his eulogy of Mozart (in *Either/Or*). The paragraph is obscure if it is simply detached; what I give, therefore, is a paraphrase.* I have taken only one liberty: the obscurity of the paragraph is partly due, especially in

* Based on the translation given by Dr. Walter Lowrie in his *Kierkegaard* (Oxford, 1938).

an English translation, to the use of impersonal pronouns; what the pronouns stand for is obvious from the context—on the one hand they denote the 'erotic immediacy' of the aesthetic experience; on the other hand, Kierkegaard himself, or the poet who renounces the aesthetic experience. I have therefore ventured to actualize the passage: it is simple to use the personal pronoun for the poet, but to personify the forces latent in the aesthetic experience I have taken the 'angelic host' of Rilke's *Duinese Elegies*. This may seem a bold and unauthorized procedure, but I am convinced that what Kierkegaard and Rilke are writing about is an identical experience. Kierkegaard's paragraph would then read:

> *The angelic host I have loved,*
> *   with whom I have lived fervently*
> *   all my youthful years,*
> *the voices that have whispered to me secretly—*
>
> *Shyly I approach them*
> *my feelings mingled and confused*
> *because of the questioning purpose in my mind.*
>
> *Little by little I have learned to speak their tongue,*
> *   gathering their accents as a bird gathers wisps of straw,*
> *   more joyful over each scrap and fragment*
> *   than over all the rest of the world.*
> *My loving ear has listened to them in solitude,*
> *   alone in the great crowd,*
> *   unnoticed in my secret hiding-place.*
> *My greedy insatiable ear has sucked in their music,*
> *my avaricious ear has jealously treasured their songs,*
> *   never feeling secure;*
> *my sleepless ear, ever attentive, has caught their softest resonance.*
>
> *Theirs are the voices I have lived with by day,*
> *theirs the voices I have heard in the night,*
> *voices that have banished sleep and made me restless,*
> *voices that have haunted my dreams,*
> *voices I have wakened to, only to dream of again awake,*
> *voices that have made me spring up in the night*
> *   lest I should forget their message.*

Such is the angelic host that appeared before me in my ecstasy.
They have followed me in the bright moonlit nights
   and to the solitary forests by the sea;
they have walked by my side in the dark streets
   at midnight and at break of day;
they have raced by my side on horseback,

they have accompanied me in my carriage,
they have filled my house with their presence,
they have penetrated into my own room.
Their voices have sounded in my ear
   and resounded in my soul:
the tissue of my soul is spun from their delicate strains.

—And now, like fabulous creatures from the sea
that rise with the seaweed clinging to their limbs,
these angels invade my reasoning mind
rise up out of the sea of recollection
   clothed with memories.

My soul is full of sorrow
   and my heart is tender,
for now I must say farewell to the angelic host.
We are parting
   never to meet again in time or eternity.

I am full of fear
as though I had broken a most solemn vow.
I am no longer the same,
   no longer young,
   no longer like a child.
I am afraid because I have lost the angelic voices
   that made me happy and joyful;
I am afraid lest the voices themselves should falter and hesitate
   unable to answer
the questions which throng to my mind.

Alas, alas! all is lost.
The angels vanish
   nevermore to answer my call.

Kierkegaard realized—was perhaps the first philosopher to
realize—that there exists between reason and inspiration exactly

the same unbridgeable chasm as between reason and faith. Art, like dialectics, can proceed a certain distance with the aid of measurable quantities—the quantities of rhythm and harmony, for example; but there comes a point at which the creative spirit must leap into the unknown. It is at this point that romantic art begins. I do not imply that there is any relationship between romantic art and religion; indeed, what I have implied is that they are totally distinct aspects of the universe. But the relationship of the creative artist to his art is analogous to that between the believer and his faith.

Art is not in any sense a substitute for religion: the choice is between aesthetics and ethics. But just as ethics tends to seek the sanction of religious ritual and dogma, so aesthetics becomes existential and self-sufficient in the work of art. The aesthetic view of life is not, however, confined to those who can create or appreciate works of art. It exists wherever natural senses play freely on the manifold phenomena of our world, and where life as a consequence is found to be full of felicity. The problem is to preserve the naturalness of the senses—to avoid their distortion by the strains introduced into society by economic scarcity; to avoid their dissolution in systems of abstract thought; to avoid their defamation by the gloomy myths of those who fear death and turn against the bright manifestations of our earthly existence. In the past the equilibrium of society has been dependent on chance factors of climate and military power; but there is a prospect that in some not very distant future an equilibrium may be established by the reason and skill of a fully-conscious humanity. If that day comes, then the sense of glory which has only made intermittent appearances in our history will pervade the whole realm of existence. This does not mean that we shall escape the tragic sense of life which comes when we accept death as inevitable, arbitrary, and final. Only those who have experienced the anguish and sorrow at the base of human existence are brave enough to seek to transfigure its brief span.

4

The Earthly Paradise

English farmers are a conservative class. Whether they are yeoman farmers owning their own land or tenant farmers renting it from a landlord, they tend to identify their interests with the land-owning aristocracy. They never seem to question the right of the landlord to a tax which often amounts to several hundred pounds annually and which must be paid not for the enjoyment of a property, but for the right to cultivate it. Such cultivation, without which the land would go to waste, is due to the skill of the farmer and the physical energy of the farm-labourer—the hardest worker in the country and the worst paid. The farmer is, in fact, the buffer between the landlord and the labourer. In many cases he is little more than an agent or bailiff, farming the land for the benefit of the landlord, and dependent on that landlord for the upkeep of his capital goods—his barns and stables, his roads and fences. Corresponding to this economic bond is a social bond: the farmer subscribes to the local hunt, hunts with the gentry as a social equal, and at such functions as the annual hunt-ball associates even more intimately with them. The local Conservative Party is merely an extension of this social chain: it would be a queer sort of farmer that identified himself with the local Labour Party, and therefore with the political outlook of his labourers. In my father's time there was no Labour Party, but the Liberal Party was in this respect little better. If it did not openly solicit the labourer's vote, it leaned to that side of the social scale. More fundamentally, by its policy of free trade it was the party of those commercial and industrial interests that were willing to sacrifice England's agriculture for the sake of a general expansion of trade.

By tradition and almost by instinct, therefore, I at first adopted the politics of the Conservative Party. From the age of fifteen I began to take a serious interest in the subject, and as I have already related, I absorbed, not only the propaganda of the party, but even its historical and philosophical background. I remember that I almost learnt by heart a small book on *Conservatism* which Lord Hugh Cecil wrote at this time. My appreciation of Burke and Bolingbroke must have been superficial; but Disraeli was another question. He was the first author that I read systematically—I read his novels one by one until I had exhausted them, and I studied all the published material about his life. This infatuation was, of course, significant. Disraeli is a romantic figure, and his writings are romances in the strict meaning of that word. But he wrote no romance half so entrancing as his own life. That this obscure Jewish boy should rise, by virtue of his talents alone, to become the leader of the British aristocracy, the Prime Minister and favourite confidant of the Queen, and, more fantastic still, the statesman who first made the British Empire a conscious unity on the Roman model—this is one of the strangest stories in history. It is strange to the point of being grotesque, and its very possibility is perhaps a crystallization of the paradox which lies at the heart of an empire like ours. For empires are not planned: they are the gradual actualization of a myth: as splendid, as formless and as impermanent as the clouds that gather in an April sky.

I think it is conceivable that Disraeli, with his two nations of the rich and the poor, planted the first seeds of doubt in my conservative mind. But in Toryism—which word, in spite of Peel's intention, represents something more fundamental and philosophical than Conservatism—there is an ethical strain which easily gives birth to a social conscience. It has often been remarked that many of the greatest social reforms have been carried out by the Tory party. To some extent this is a reaping of the harvest which other parties have sown; but it is also due to a sense of responsibility, last remnant of the feudal tradition, and to that rare form of patriotism which puts the welfare of the nation before the interests of the commercial classes. The distinction between Town and Country, the City and the Land, upon which the old two-party system was really based, has been largely obliterated; but one still finds conservatives who are not to be identified with Capital and who have a far wider and more generous outlook than many who profess to represent the poor and oppressed.

The fundamental contrasts between town and country, industry and agriculture, wealth and poverty, were forced upon me by my daily experiences in Leeds. Up to the age of fifteen I had no knowledge of town life; for the next six years I was to see little else. For three years, with only one week's break in the year, I walked these streets—I could not afford a tram fare. From my home on the outskirts to the Bank in the middle of the city; from the head-office of the Bank to the branches at Armley, Beeston and Chapeltown, I passed through areas in which factories were only relieved by slums, slums by factories—a wilderness of stone and brick, with soot falling like black snow. Drab and stunted wage-slaves drifted through the stink and clatter; tramcars moaned and screeched along their glistening rails, spluttering blue electric sparks. These same wage-slaves brought their savings to the Bank—we accepted deposits of three-pence and upwards—greasy coins which blackened the fingers that counted them, and were then entered into pass-books permeated by grime and sweat. For a year or two my way home passed through the City Square, where a political agitator sometimes drew a crowd round him; and sometimes I would stop and listen. In one way or another, this environment gradually penetrated the armour of my inherited prejudices. Ugliness and poverty, dirt and drabness, were too universal to be ignored. The questioning intelligence which was slowly awakening in me began to question the material things before my eyes. I found that other people had questioned them: not only Disraeli, but Carlyle, Ruskin and Morris; and that they were being questioned by people round about me.

Plato has written about the windows that open into the mind, and it is a very true image. The mind of youth is a room without an escape: there is perhaps a dim inner light, and an endless succession of pictures flicker on the walls. Then suddenly, on one side, the shutters are drawn and through an open space the youth looks out on to the light and landscape of the real world. Some time after, another window is opened, and the world is seen from another aspect. The process should continue until there are windows open on every side of the mind, and the whole universe is visible to the inquiring eye.

This sudden awakening to the nature of my social environment was indeed like a new window opening on to the world: a window through which I not only saw the social realities, but by whose light I also read what had been written about them. Again I read eagerly and indiscriminately—chiefly Carlyle, Ruskin and Morris, but also a mass of propagandist literature, periodicals like Blatchford's *Clarion*, Fabian tracts, obscure pamphlets of all kinds. Later, in my second year at the University, and until I left for the Army, I was to study these questions more systematically: I read the classical economists under D. H. Macgregor and Henry Clay, social economics and economic history under Arthur Greenwood. Indeed, economics is the one subject in which I have possibly had what pedagogues would call a 'thorough grounding'. It is a subject of which I have made least use in life.

This 'thorough grounding' did not, of course, include anything so unorthodox as Karl Marx and Bakunin; but all the same I was inevitably drawn to these two opposed forces in the socialist movement. I still possess the copy of the Sonnenschein edition of *Capital* which I bought at this time, and its well-scored pages indicate with what care I studied the whole volume. On the other side I was much influenced by Kropotkin's *Fields, Factories and Workshops*, and by his pamphlets on *Anarchist Morality* and *Anarchist Communism* (published by the Freedom Press in 1912 and 1913). A pamphlet by Edward Carpenter on *Non-Governmental Society* (1911) was even more decisive, and I find tucked into the copy which, like my Marx, has survived all these years, the following 'statement' of my own views:

'As I believe that the society outlined in this pamphlet is an ideal not immediately realizable, I should like to sketch out the path along which I think society will evolve.

'There are two distinct types of modern socialism: Collectivism, which looks at things solely from the consumer's point of view; and Syndicalism, which looks at things solely from the producer's point of view. Both are fundamentally wrong: society must be regarded as an entity—a co-ordination of consumer and producer. But these two forces, acting in opposite directions, will produce, as though by a parallelogram of forces, a resultant force which will be the true Socialism, combining the good of both Collectivism and Syndicalism. For the present, both Collectivism and Syndicalism have their respective duties. The rôle of

Collectivism is the expropriation of Capital. This is to be brought about by the nationalization of industry. But Collectivists are wrong in regarding nationalization as an end in itself: it is only a means. For whilst the Collectivist state is evolving, Syndicalism will be playing its rôle—i.e. it will be developing the economic, industrial and educational functions of the Trade Unions. Trade Unions are, I am convinced, the units upon which the future society will be built. They must be organized and extended so as to be powerful enough to demand, and fit enough to undertake, the control of industry when it has been nationalized by the state. When we have travelled so far, society will be capable of evolving into the ideal state suggested by this pamphlet. By a devolution of power, a decentralization of control, and, above all, by a development in the social conscience of the nation, the ideals of today will become the realities of tomorrow.

'And morality, which has always evolved parallel to the economic evolution of society, will change with these changes. The perfect morality is only possible in the perfect society.

'The true social faith is, I think, to work for the immediate practical objects of socialism, but at the same time to keep before us always some ultimate ideal—some goal to which we may aim.'

This cannot have been written later than the summer of 1914, and it might be as much as a year earlier. In the many years that have since elapsed, my political opinions have varied considerably (though always within the broad basic principles of socialism). What surprises me now is to find that the views I expressed at the age of twenty are substantially the views I still hold. I should not now express them so naïvely; and the evolution of the Trade Unions since 1914 has brought them to a condition of bureaucratic conservatism hardly compatible with the rôle ascribed to them in my statement. It must also be confessed that syndicalism, both as a name and as a movement, has not in this country become the established force that seemed imminent in 1914. But whether we call it syndicalism or not, a movement that will look forward to the organization of the Trade Unions as units of production is essential equally to the collectivist and the anarchist form of socialism. The fundamental difference between anarchism and collectivism does not concern the economic function of the Trade Unions, but rather their relation

THE EARTHLY PARADISE

to the·state, and generally the distribution of power or authority between the centre and the periphery of the economic sphere.

Anarchism was to suffer an almost complete eclipse in this country after the war. Kropotkin returned to Russia and died there in 1921, disillusioned and rejected. The intellectuals who in this country might have given their support to the movement were drawn away to the alternative of Guild Socialism, then being advocated with great fervour by A. R. Orage in the *New Age*. I myself became a sympathetic supporter of this new policy, and contributed at least two articles to the official organ of the group, the *Guildsman*, then edited by G. D. H. Cole. But meanwhile another influence intervened—Georges Sorel. His *Reflections on Violence* was published in a translation by T. E. Hulme in 1916, when I immediately acquired it. Few books have impressed me so deeply and so permanently. It worked on me in a surer way than Nietzsche had done. It appealed to something more fundamental than my intellect—namely, to my temperament and instincts— and again opened up endless new perspectives. It was from Sorel, if I remember rightly, that I passed to Bergson, and certainly to Proudhon. But his main function, in my case, was to supply to socialism the imaginative qualities which I found lacking in Marx. It is true that there were implications in Sorel which I did not then grasp, and which in the years to come were to lead in the direction of fascism rather than of socialism; and I only swallowed his doctrine of classicism because it seemed to me to be more romantic than romanticism itself—rather like Goethe's classicism. To expect a return of the classical spirit through the struggle of the classes; to maintain that only under the influence of the classical ideal could the working-class movement succeed in regenerating society —that, indeed, was more romantic than, say, Marx's General Law of Capitalist Accumulation.*

The proselytizing fervour with which I adopted Sorel's views is shown by a letter which I wrote to the *Yorkshire Post* on the

*It is significant that those critics who have been most influenced by Sorel's classicism and anti-humanism have tended to discard his revolutionary syndicalism, whilst those whose tendency has been to retain the syndicalism have discarded the classicism. Sorel's inconsistency is thus proved by the subsequent history of his ideas. If it is argued that a more perceptive intelligence would have been attracted to the superior consistency of Marx's theory of history, the reply would be that consistency in this case has proved no less fallible, and has been far more disastrous in its practical consequences.

appearance of a review of *Reflections on Violence*, and which they printed under my initials.

M. SOREL AND SYNDICALISM

To the Editor of the *Yorkshire Post*

Sir,—Your reviewer of Sorel's *Reflections on Violence* fails to present your readers with the true import of that book. His interpretation of the rôle of proletarian violence is completely misleading, simply because he does not recognize that Sorel's theories are complementary and not complete. Sorel perfects a social philosophy; he does not posit one. His theory is nothing more than an amplification of Marx's hypothesis of a fatalistic revolution.

You will remember, Sir, how Marx conceives a capitalist class progressing and concentrating; a proletariat, organizing; and a social revolution as a *coup d'état*.* Now it is vital to this hypothesis that the capitalist class should progress, distinct and powerful. If once it becomes intermingled with the proletariat; if once it surrenders a part of its power—then Marx's hypothesis is defeated. A successful revolution becomes impossible. Hence the syndicalist opposition to schemes of co-operation and social amelioration. Hence Sorel's concern for the vigour of the middle classes. Not, as your reviewer has it, because he wishes to preserve them as directors of the social organism, but because their progress is vital to revolution—because, when the revolution does come, he wishes the revolutionaries to inherit an economically vigorous society and not a slough of economic decadence. He sees the capitalist and the proletariat as the participants in a world tragedy —a tragedy having as its dénouement not the reformed society of the 'worthy progressive', but a new society with new cultural values. But listen to Sorel himself:

'The dangers which threaten the future of the world may be avoided if the proletariat hold on with obstinacy to revolutionary ideas, so as to realize as much as possible Marx's conception. Everything may be saved if the proletariat, by their use of violence, manage to re-establish the division into classes, and so restore to the middle class something of its former energy; that

* As the editor of the *Yorkshire Post* pointed out in his reply, a *coup d'état* was not at all characteristic of Marx's conception of revolution.

is the great aim towards which the whole thought of men—who are not hypnotized by the event of the day, but think of the conditions of tomorrow—must be directed. Proletarian violence, carried on as a pure and simple manifestation of the class war, appears thus as a very fine and very heroic thing; it is at the service of the immemorial interests of civilization; it is perhaps not the most appropriate method of obtaining immediate material advantages, but it may save the world from barbarism.'

Now, perhaps, your reviewer will understand why Sorel regarded a great European war as an alternative to proletarian violence. It is because such a war tends to accentuate, in its after-effects, class differences. The resultant quickening of commercial interests will give to the middle classes new life and independence. The aftermath of poverty and disorganization of labour will inspire the proletariat with heroic and revolutionary spirit. Once more we shall have the social protagonists implacably opposed. And the premises of Marx's fatalistic hypothesis will be present and the conclusion duly fulfilled.

It is hopeless for anyone to attempt to understand or accept this new social doctrine unless he rid himself of every post-Renaissance humanistic prejudice in his thought. Syndicalism is not the babblings of a lot of ignorant workmen. It is the political equivalent of anti-Romanticism in literature. It is the social manifestation of anti-humanistic revolt—of a return to a classical and a pessimistic conception of the universe.—Yours, etc.

The last paragraph of this letter is a paraphrase of Hulme's Introduction to the translation of *Reflections on Violence*. I think now that there is more in it of Hulme than of Sorel, and certainly more of Hulme and Sorel than of my own views. I have no doubt that at the time I did genuinely profess anti-humanistic and anti-romantic opinions, but they were based on the historical ambiguity of these words. The confusion is due to Hulme rather than to Sorel; Hulme's own ideas were in a state of flux at the time, as his collected papers (*Speculations*) which I was to edit after the war, sufficiently prove. Looking through Sorel's book now, I find nothing classical, in the normal sense of the word, in his conception of violence and revolution. His tragic conception of life, and his belief in absolute values, do indeed spring from his admiration of Greek drama. But the mistake is to assume that

Greek drama is necessarily anti-humanistic or even anti-romantic. Neither a tragic conception of life nor absolute values are inconsistent with romantic art, as represented, for example, by Homer, Shakespeare or Blake. In the following passage from Sorel's book, which I marked with emphatic approval in 1916, there is latent the whole of my subsequent elaboration of a doctrine of romantic art:

'Like industry, art has never adapted itself to the demands of theorists; it always upsets their plans of social harmony, and humanity has found the freedom of art far too satisfactory ever to think of allowing it to be controlled by the creators of dull systems of sociology. The Marxists are accustomed to seeing the ideologists look at things the wrong way round, and so, in contrast to their enemies, they should look upon art as a reality which begets ideas and not as an application of ideas.'

It is precisely the academicians, the natural supporters of classicism, who attempt to make of art an instrument for the application of ideas (of *their* ideas, of course). Sorel was certainly not an academician; nor, in this sense, was he a classicist.

My political education continued actively during the war, and I occasionally gave expression to my opinions in the *New Age* and elsewhere. But when, after the war, I entered the Civil Service, I found myself under a much stricter censorship, and though I never 'dropped' politics, I ceased to write about them. When in 1931 I left the Civil Service and was once more at liberty to take part in the public discussion of political issues, some people assumed that I had 'just discovered' Marx, that the turn of political events had forced me from the seclusion of an ivory tower, that I had adopted anarchism as a logical counterpart to my views on art. Actually there was an unfailing continuity in my political interests and political opinions. I would not like to claim that they show an unfailing consistency, but the general principles which I found congenial as a young man are the basic principles of the only political philosophy I still find congenial.

In calling these principles Anarchism I have forfeited any claim to be taken seriously as a politician, and have cut myself off from the main current of socialist activity in England. But I have often found sympathy and agreement in unexpected places, and there are many intellectuals who are fundamentally anarchist in their political outlook, but who do not dare to invite ridicule by confessing it. The word is, of course, nearly as ambiguous as 'classicism' and 'romanticism'; and like these words it indicates a general outlook, a Weltanschauung, rather than a practical programme. Most people are content with practical issues: they think that if they plan the economy of the state for the immediate future by reconciling all conflicting interests, or by subordinating these interests to the general good, they have done all that is necessary, or humanly possible. Their ethos, if they have one, is vaguely religious, and complacently traditional. They forget that you cannot move one step without moving in a specific direction; and that if you do not keep looking at a fixed point on the horizon, you walk in circles. Anarchism is a point on the horizon: it has no plan to be put into being tomorrow or the next day. It does not believe in plans, which are rational constructions that always leave out the imponderable and elusive factors of human feeling and human instinct. When Confucius complained to Lao Tzu that though he had tried to get seventy-two rulers to adopt his plans for the government of the state—his six scriptures—not one of them had any use for them, Lao Tzu replied: 'It is a lucky thing that you did not meet with a prince anxious to reform the world. Those six scriptures are the dim footprints of ancient kings. They tell us nothing of the force that guided their steps. All your lectures are concerned with things that are no better than footprints in the dust. Footprints are made by shoes; but they are far from being shoes.'*

Confucius was a conservative planner; but Lao Tzu would have said the same to a socialist planner. There is only one necessary plan—the plan of nature. We must live according to natural laws, and by virtue of the power which comes from concentrating upon their manifestation in the individual mind. Anarchism asserts—it is its only assertion—that life must be so ordered that the individual can live a natural life, 'attending to what is within'. But once you begin to work out the implications of this principle, you do not end until you have abolished the state. For if people began to live by natural law, there would be no need for man-made laws, nor for a government to enforce such laws.

We agree, many people will say but what about our immediate

*From *Three Ways of Thought in Ancient China*, by Arthur Waley (London 1939).

problems? What about poverty and unemployment; slums and malnutrition; aggression and war? These problems, I readily admit, must be solved. Let us solve them in the manner suggested by democratic socialism—that seems the fairest and most practical method, but only if we keep the anarchist principle in mind at every stage and in every act. Then we shall avoid the fatal mistakes that have been made in Russia. We shall avoid creating an independent bureaucracy, for that is another form of tyranny, and the individual has no chance of living according to natural laws under such a tyranny. We shall avoid the creation of industrial towns which separate men from the fields and from the calming influences of nature. We shall control the machine, so that it serves our natural needs without endangering our natural powers. Thus in a thousand ways the principle of anarchism will determine our practical policies, leading the human race gradually away from the state and its instruments of oppression towards an epoch of wisdom and joy.

5

The Impact of War

At the outbreak of war in 1914 I was already in a military camp. This was not the outcome of any immediate patriotic zeal on my part, but was to some extent a consequence of my patriotic past. A year or two before I became an undergraduate, and while still contemplating the possibility of a medical career, I had joined the local territorial unit of the Royal Army Medical Corps in the vain hope that I should acquire some practical experience. By the time I reached the University, this had become a meaningless and arduous engagement, to which I was nevertheless bound for a period of years. But at the University there was an Officers' Training Corps, and I eagerly seized the opportunity to transfer my military bond to this more agreeable branch of the service. It is true that as time went on and my political ideas developed in the manner just related, I had certain qualms of conscience. But very few of those who joined the O.T.C. in those days had any serious motive. War was considered as a very remote contingency, and meanwhile here was an open-air club, with possibilities of friendship and youthful enterprise, and an annual camp which was in effect a free holiday for many who could not otherwise afford one. I was not interested in sport of any kind, and the O.T.C. provided me with my one physical diversion. I enjoyed the game very much.

There, happily at play, I was caught by the war. In the years that followed I was often to ask myself what I would have done if I had been a free agent. Politically I was a pacifist, and regarded the war as a conflict between rival imperial powers which would bring destruction to the peoples engaged. I hoped that the war would be stopped by international working-class action, and the failure of the responsible leaders to bring about a stoppage was my first lesson in political disillusionment. But fundamentally—that is to say, ethically—I could not claim to be a pacifist. It must be remembered that in 1914 our conception of war was completely unreal. We had vague childish memories of the Boer War, and from these and from a general diffusion of Kiplingesque sentiments, we managed to infuse into war a decided element of adventurous romance. War still appealed to the imagination. To this romantic illusion must be added, in my own case, a state of uncertainty about my future. Though I was ambitious and full of determination, I had no precise career marked out: I was to be a free-lance of some sort, and a free-lance finds a very appropriate place in an army. The war meant a decision: a crystallization of vague projects: an immediate acceptance of the challenge of life. I did not hesitate.

I received a commission within six months and was posted to a battalion of the Green Howards, my local North Riding regiment, then training in Dorset. This battalion had, like most of the newly-formed units, a nucleus of regular officers drawn from one of the first-line battalions, together with a few reservists, but the bulk of the officers were recruits from the O.T.C. It happened that a considerable group in my particular battalion came from Eton (including two masters, Young and Slater); and practically all the others were from public schools. I had, therefore, stumbled into a very select and at first very uncongenial coterie. It must be remembered that I had not hitherto been outside my provincial fastness; but it was not so much my rawness (concealed as it was by my natural diffidence) as my incredible naïveté which was at fault. I will give two examples. I had become a regular reader of the *New Age*, at that time the most independent and lively periodical being published. The officers' mess occupied a building ordinarily used by the local masonic lodge, and there we had an ante-room where all the usual magazines and newspapers were available. They were displayed on a green-baize table, and there, when I had read it, I left my copy of the *New Age*. I was seated deep in an armchair one afternoon when the senior subaltern, traditionally responsible for the social conduct of the junior subalterns, came up to the table and casually picked up the *New Age*. He looked at it for a minute or two and slowly the colour deepened in his rather florid face. He turned suddenly to address the room, and holding the paper up between his finger and thumb as though it was unclean, he shouted in a loud voice: 'Who brought this bloody rag into the mess?' I wish I could say that I sprang to my feet to defend my intellectual interests; but alas, I was not so naïve as that. I shrank still deeper into my chair and watched the angry senior subaltern stalk out in disgust, throwing the offensive periodical into the waste-paper basket as he passed. I had learned my lesson, and in the future read the *New Age* in the privacy of my tent or cubicle.

The other incident was similar and occurred shortly afterwards. The mess was actually the only place where, that bitter winter, one could read in comfort—I was still under canvas. One Sunday afternoon I took down with me a book I had just bought—Butler's *Erewhon Revisited*—and was soon absorbed in it. The mess was, as I had anticipated, nearly empty, but presently Captain Slater, the Eton master already mentioned, came in and, passing behind my chair, observed the title of my book. 'O God! O Montreal!' he cried, 'that I should find someone reading Sam Butler in the British Army.' He was genuinely amused and interested, and though we were too disparate in age and temperament ever to become close friends, a sympathetic bond did henceforth exist between us.

But that, too, was a lesson. So long as we remained in England I confined my mess reading to the *Tatler* and the *Bystander* and other periodicals of the kind which were the only literary recreations of the majority of His Majesty's officers. When we reached the Front the situation changed, in this as in many other respects.

Meanwhile I was reacting to a new and unexpected mode of life. For the first time I was compelled to be continuously active in the open air, and though the strain was great, there was exhilaration in meeting it. For the first time, again, I was thrown against all sorts and conditions of men: on the one side I had to adapt myself to the manners and habits of my fellow-officers, most of whom came from an entirely different and wealthier social world; and on the other side I became personally responsible for a platoon of soldiers, the majority of them toughened in the mines and factories of Durham and North Yorkshire. I found the officers more difficult than the men. The colonel was comprehensible: he was an English gentleman of a type I had been familiar with in my childhood, a good soldier in wartime and a good squire in peacetime; and there were two or three other regulars who were at any rate efficient and experienced. But the majority—young subalterns fresh from Sandhurst and the public-school boys already mentioned, struck me as snobbish and intolerant, and as trying to import into the Army the prefectorial spirit which they had acquired at school. Luckily I was not alone outside this predominant group, and some half a dozen of us managed to make our own society.

This sense of disunity lasted during the training period in England. In France the pressure of events, particularly the test of danger, quickly changed the atmosphere. Social values yielded to realistic values. In England we had unconsciously accepted the habit of command and the air of superiority which environment and education had conferred on the sons of the *élite*. Now we discovered that something else mattered more: that irreducible element of personality which is the raw material of education and the principle of growth persisting through every environment. It is my conviction that education and environment cannot change this innate spirit of an individual. Education can adapt the individual to his environment: it can explain life and reality to him and thus enable him to face them more skilfully with the gifts with which he is naturally endowed. It can also make him more conscious of the scope or limitation of these gifts. In the same way war, which is so often made the melodramatic agent of changes in character, does not affect the inherent quality of the person. As the months went by, I was to see all the proud pretensions which men had acquired from a conventional environment sink into insignificance before the basic facts of body and spirit. In my own case I was to discover, with a sense of self-confidence wholly new to me, that I could endure the experience of war, even at its worst. This is far from claiming that I was fearless: the first days in the trenches, the first bombardment or attack, was a draining sickness of the spirit. But I presently recovered, as from a plunge into a cold sea. What I found most difficult to accustom myself to, even after months at the Front, was the sight of human blood, and the stiff horror of a human corpse. That one does eventually get used to such things does not necessarily mean a deadening of the sensibility; but when an experience is repeated often enough, one has to rationalize it—in other words, make one's philosophy fit the facts.

I do not intend to give a detailed account of the four and a half years I spent in the Army: it is the totality of the experience which has significance for my present purpose. But there are two incidents which I have related with some attempt at an analysis of my accompanying feelings while they were still fresh in my mind—a raid which took place in the early summer of 1917 and the retreat of the Fifth Army from St. Quentin in March, 1918. The first of these narratives was published in 1930 in a small collection of prose pieces which I called *Ambush*; the second was written in 1919, but first published by Leonard and Virginia Woolf at the Hogarth Press six years later.

These short narratives are reproduced as separate chapters in the following pages. To the best of my ability 'The Raid', which will not be found to deviate in any essential point from the briefer account given in the War Diary (pages 99–102), adequately represents for me the subjective experience of war. The raid itself was, of course, a comparatively intense moment in the general course of that experience, and there were long stretches of boredom and inaction which should no doubt be reckoned as part of the total impact. But in so far as fear is the core of that experience, and the phenomenon about which those who have not experienced war betray the most curiosity, the analysis given in this narrative is the only evidence I have to offer. Whether we reach the reality by analysis, which is a subjective instrument, is another question; but in so far as the events can speak for themselves, they do so in 'In Retreat', which I have tried to make an objective record.

If I had entered the war in a certain spirit of adventurous acceptance, as it was prolonged year after year it began to conflict with the impatient spirit of youth. One week in the trenches was sufficient to strip war of its lingering traces of romance: there was nothing, in the Ypres Salient where I first went into the line, but primitive filth, lice, boredom and death. Even the novelty of the experience, in such circumstances, is no palliative. But after weeks, and then months, and finally years of such a life, with no moral sanction to support the spirit, no fervour or enthusiasm, no hatred of the enemy, the whole business became fantastically unreal, a monstrous nightmare from which one could not awake. It should be remembered that a modern army is largely made up of young civilians without political experience, and the propaganda which is designed to inspire them (and perhaps does inspire them for a time) soon wears thin against the crude realities of war. If only,

I used to think, we poor bloody soldiers could walk out, walk home, and leave the politicians to make the best of a quarrel which we did not understand and which had no interest for us! But though these were the sentiments of nine men out of ten, there was no possibility of proceeding to action. A soldier is part of a machine: once the machine is in movement, he functions as part of that machine, or simply gets killed. There is very little scope for individual initiative, for non-co-operation. It is true that one need not—and I did not—industriously strive to kill. During the whole war I never deliberately or consciously killed an individual man, with the possible exception of the one who was accompanying the German officer in the raid I am going to describe. I fired in self-defence, at advancing masses of men; but I never in cold blood selected my mark, with the intention of bringing to an end a human life. In April, 1918, when on a daylight 'contact' patrol with two of my men, we suddenly confronted, round some mound or excavation, a German patrol of the same strength. We were perhaps twenty yards from each other, fully visible. I waved a weary hand, as if to say: What is the use of killing each other? The German officer seemed to understand, and both parties turned and made their way back to their own trenches. Reprehensible conduct, no doubt, but in April, 1918, the war-weariness of the infantry was stronger than its pugnacity, on both sides of the line.

The impact of war on my sensibility is best revealed in the change which came to my writing during the period. As I have already said, it was a change of content rather than of technique. In 1915 I was already writing in the imagist manner, and from the Front I sent to the *Gryphon*, the student's magazine at Leeds, various contributions of which the earliest must have been written within a few weeks of my war experience. They are, as imagist poems should be, coldly objective. The following is an impression of Ypres:

> *With a chill and hazy light*
> *the sun of a winter noon*
> *swills*
> *thy ruins.*
>
> *Thy ruins etched*
> *in silver silhouettes*
> *against a turquoise sky.*

Lank poles leap to the infinite,
 their broken wires
  tossed like the rat-locks of Maenades.

And Desolation broods over all,
 gathering to her lap
  her leprous children.

The sparrows whimper
 amid the broken arches.

Besides these poems, some short prose sketches in a 'Zara-thustran' style called 'Fables from Flanders', were published during 1916. They are still very idealistic, but a realistic note is creeping in, and towards the end of 1916 I find two poems which I called 'Truth for a Change—an Epilogue to the Fables'. In 1919 I apparently thought they were too sentimental to be included in *Naked Warriors*, but I reproduce one of them now as a contrast to the poem already quoted:

Such a lad as Harry was
Isn't met with every day.
He walked the land like a god,
Exulting in energy,
Care-free,
His eyes a blue smile
Beneath his yellow curling locks;
And you'd wonder where a common labourer got
Those deep Rossetti lips
And finely carven nose. . . .
I saw him stretch his arms
Languid as a dozing panther,
His face full to the clean sky—
When a blasted sniper laid him low:
He fell limp on the muddy boards
And left us all blaspheming.

I do not suggest that from a literary point of view such relatively crude and sentimental realism is an improvement on the earlier idealism: indeed, if there is any difference of merit, I am inclined to think that the Ypres poem is better than 'Truth for a Change'. But I should not have thought so in 1916—much less so in 1917 or 1918. My experience, that is to say, was modifying my literary values, and not altogether for the good. It is still a common assumption—Mr. Desmond MacCarthy makes it as I write this chapter—that generous feelings and humane sentiments are more important in poetry than what he calls 'tessellating together unexpected words'. It depends on what Mr. MacCarthy means by his derogatory phrase; but in fact poetry is made with words and cannot be made without a fine sense of the right words. Can Mr. MacCarthy discover much 'thought and feeling' in 'Kubla Khan'? Poetry, it would seem from this supreme example, can get along with a minimum of sentiment, provided it has a sufficiency of sensibility. But this is not to deny that good poetry can be made out of emotional situations, and in so far as the war induced me to write about emotional situations, it meant an enlargement of my literary experience. But it does not need a war to effect that change in a poet: I should have been brought to it by the impact of life itself.

The war did, of course, broaden in an altogether unexpected fashion my human contacts—far more than any school or university could have done. As the war developed, I found in my fellow-officers a rough equivalent of the society of a university, but more diverse, and deepened and concentrated by the common sharing of dangerous purposes. I had such friends then as I had never had before and have never had since—friends with whom one lived in a complete communal bond of thoughts as well as goods. When peace came, and the bond was destroyed, we drifted apart, back to the alien ways of our different social levels, our different environments and careers. Perhaps most significantly, we lost our masculine exclusiveness.

The most broadening of contacts was, however, that with the rank and file. I can only speak for the infantry, and I only speak of the infantry at war, away from the barracks and parade ground. Then between the company officer and his men there is every opportunity for the development of a relationship that abolishes all class distinctions and that can have a depth of understanding and sympathy for which I know no parallel in civilian life. Unfortunately the word 'leader' now belongs to the ideology of fascism, and in its blustering, commanding sense it was never applicable to a boyish officer in his early twenties, in charge of sixty or more men, many of whom would be much older and more experienced (now it may be different for there is more uniformity of age in a conscript army). The relationship was much more like that of a priest to his parish: for the company officer was the medium of communication with higher authority, one who interpreted the orders and strategy laid down by that authority, one who was therefore the ear and the voice of his group. Within the group he was responsible for the material welfare and comfort of his men—their food and billets, their health, their correspondence, and he it was who communicated with their relatives in case of death. In the trenches a platoon officer would often be isolated for many days with his men, and away from the rest of the officers; his closest companions were at all times his sergeant, his batman and his runner. It was only the social misfit, the public-school snob or the worse snob who came from the fringes of the working-classes, who could not develop a relationship of trust and even of intimacy with his men.

During the war I used to feel that this comradeship which had developed among us would lead to some new social order when peace came. I used to imagine an international party of ex-combatants, united by their common suffering, who would turn against the politicians and the profiteers in every country, and create a society based on respect for the individual human being. But no such party came into existence. The war ended in despair in Germany, in silly jubilation in England, and in an ineffective spirit of retribution in France. The societies of ex-combatants that were formed in England devoted themselves either to jingo heartiness or to the organization of charitable benefits. We left the war as we entered it: dazed, indifferent, incapable of any creative action. We had acquired only one new quality: exhaustion.

I shall relate in a later chapter the stages by which I re-adapted myself to civilian life. Here I only wish to describe the immediate reaction and disillusionment. My political ideas had continued to develop during the war. I published articles on syndicalism and guild socialism in 1917 and 1918. But the political situation of 1919 offered no basis for allegiance or enthusiasm. The political parties were all in the hands of non-combatants, especially on the left; and deep within me was a feeling that I could not speak the language of such people, much less co-operate with them. It was not that I despised them: I even envied them. But between us was a dark screen of horror and violation:

the knowledge of the reality of war. Across that screen I could not communicate. Nor could any of my friends who had had the same experience. We could only stand on one side, like exiles in a strange country. Twenty-six years have passed and we have experienced another war. My feelings have not changed. I have seen the men of another generation engaged in a similar enter-prise. Perhaps they have been less confident than we were, less liable to be deceived; but we do not know—they were conscripts and as such their motives were enigmatic. And since it was not the same kind of war, its debris is heaped in a different shape.

In the last days of our war its tragedy was to strike me with a sudden personal violence. My youngest brother, who had fol-lowed me into the Green Howards and had served on the Italian Front, was killed in France by a stray bullet. I knew his battalion had been transferred to the French Front, but I had had no particular anxiety for him: he was so young and vivid that the mind could not entertain his image and death's together. I was back in England at the time, stationed at Middlesbrough among strangers; but perhaps I was grateful for this isolation. My grief was too violent to tolerate sympathy or consolation. I walked about blinded by tears. I remember that I fled from the Garrison Headquarters and sought the seclusion of a park in the town. For the first and the only time I sought to expel my emotions by actualizing them in verse. It was a bleak October day, with the emblems of death and grief around me. The lines of an elegy came spontaneously to my mind:

> The autumn leaves were an augury
> And seemed to intend
> As they yellowly drooped in the languid air
> That life was a fragile mood and death
> A tremendous despair.

> The yellow leaves fell
> Like slow tears of gold on the face of the day:
> They fell to the earth with a faint, sad sigh.
> They sighed
> As the feet of the passers-by
> Crushed them into the moist, black soil.
> They sighed when the gentle wind
> Lifted them along the way.

THE IMPACT OF WAR

In the Park
Old men swept the dead things in a heap to burn:
Their last fragrance
Floated about the naked trees.
I thought as the women walked in the moist, still day
Wearing yellow chrysanthemums in their coats,
A chrysanthemum was
A pale, dishevelled emblem of death.

The sun
Was a silver pervasion across the sky:
From the sky
The dead leaves fell.

There was a good deal more of the poem, angry and resentful, and vainly consolatory; but too raw for publication even at this distance of time. When the Armistice came, a month later, I had no feelings, except possibly of self-congratulation. By then I had been sent to dreary barracks on the outskirts of Canterbury. There were misty fields around us, and perhaps a pealing bell to celebrate our victory. But my heart was numb and my mind dismayed: I turned to the fields and walked away from all human contacts.

6

The Raid

It was early summer and the warm sun seemed to reanimate the desolate land. Before one of a group of huts a young subaltern was seated at a table. He was bareheaded and the sun played on the bright yellow strands of his hair. He played nervously with a match-stalk, splintering it with his finger-nails, scraping it aimlessly about the table. The sun played on the white bleached wood of the twirling match-stalk and on the dark blistered polish of the table. Nervous fingers rolled the hard stalk between soft plastic flesh. At times everything was very still. The dreamer wandered. The shreds of match-stalk seemed far away, brittle legs of birds, pattering on the hard brown table. The sun was buoyed in some kind of space, hard to conceive; where, too, the mind swayed in utter helplessness.

Why had all the horror suddenly become potent? Lieutenant P—— had been in France four months now, and all the time, in some degree, his life had been threatened. He had been sick, sick all the time—but the hunted life had each day sunk into renewing sleep; and day had succeeded day, and somehow the faith had been born that the days would pass in such a succession until the long terror was ended. But the present eventuality had made a difference. He had been selected to lead a raid, along with me, and a volunteer party of about thirty men. This sudden actualization of the diffused terror of our existence had made a difference to my friend. I could divine it as he sat there in his restless abstraction.

I was lying within the hut, beneath the corrugated vault of iron. My body was listless, my mind content. I saw P——, crumpled in his chair—his boots drawn under, his untidy puttees, his rounded shoulders and over-big flaxen head. I saw men

220

walking about the grassy plot in front of us, and in the sky, an easier reach for my recumbent eyes, a lark, a dot, a lark that was always singing in this region at the time of our stay there. The lark, and the men walking very near on a horizon, were more real to me than the vague wonder about my fate in the raid. I was afraid, but more interested in P——'s fear. I decided that he must in some way be imprisoned in his flesh—despite that mind, floating vacantly in the ether. He was an undersized but thickset man of about twenty-three. He had a pale fleshy face and china-blue eyes, a coarse voice and a tendency to blush. He had been a teacher. He had a mother and a sweetheart, and he spent a lot of time writing letters. He never got free from his home thoughts; he was still bound in some sort of personal dependence to these ties. His mind, at any rate, was not free to lead its own existence, or to create the conditions of its existence. I think that is why he was a coward.

For he was a coward, in the only concise sense that can be given to that word. A coward is not merely a man who feels fear. We all experience fear; it is a physical reaction to the unknown extent of danger. But it is only cowardice when it becomes a mental reaction—when the mind, reacting to the flesh, submits to the instincts of the flesh.

As the time appointed for the raid grew nearer, P——'s manner began to change. We had always been thrown together a good deal: we were the only officers in the Company with tastes in common. But we were scarcely friends; there was something in his physical nature that repelled me. But now he began to make up to me more insistently. Presently the remainder of the battalion went into the trenches and we were left to rest and train for our enterprise. P—— then grew more confidential and spoke often of his home affairs. He seemed afraid to be out of my presence. He began to confess to me; to bemoan his fate; to picture the odds against us—the utter unlikelihood that we should ever come out of this business alive.

I asked him if he was afraid. He blushed and said: 'Yes, damnably.' He was obviously in an agony of mind, and then I began to have my own fear: that he would bitch the show and bring disgrace on us all. I put this to him. We had left camp and were on a visit to battalion headquarters, a mile or two behind the line. There was some sort of gun emplacement or old trench line into which we had climbed to look out over the sun-soaked plain: the larks were singing as always in the still clear sky. But P——'s face looked aqueous and blotchy. His eyes were uneasy, reflecting all his anguish. After a while I asked him to make a clean breast of it all to the Colonel. But I saw that he would never do that. He just hung his head and looked stupid.

When we reached the battalion I left P—— outside and went into the Colonel's shanty or dugout. I told him about P——; deliberately. He was immediately taken off the raid and S——, an elderly subaltern who had already taken part in a previous raid, was asked to take his place. This he did with a bad grace.

P—— was killed in a bombardment some months later. A night of confused darkness and sudden riot.

We greased our hands and faces and then blackened them with burnt cork so that they would not shine out in the dark night. We muffled our rifle slings and accoutrements so that no little noise should betray us. Then we made our way into the trenches to the point selected for our sally. A terrace such as is often found in French fields ran across no-man's-land, at right-angles to the trenches. It led to an elbow in the enemy's line, and the concerted plan was that at midnight exactly the artillery and trench mortars should isolate this elbow with a barrage of fire, whilst we penetrated into the trenches and secured some of the enemy, dead or alive. We raiders were to creep along the guiding line of the bank in Indian file until within thirty yards or so of the enemy's position, then to creep round into a compact line facing the trench: this movement to be achieved by midnight. Then, immediately the barrage fell, we were to rush forward and do our best.

It was agreed that I should head the Indian file, and that S—— should bring up the rear. He was to prevent straggling and to see that the line swung round into position when I sent back the signal. The last thing we did before going out was to give each man a stiff dose of rum: then there were a few whispered farewells and a handshake or two. The night was moonless, but fair, and not quite pitch dark. You could distinguish a silhouette against the skyline. As soon as we passed our own wire entanglements we got down on our bellies and began to crawl. I had already explored the ground in two or three special night patrols, and had no difficulty in finding the bank and getting the right direction. I advanced a step at a time, the sergeant close behind me.

I felt that I ought not to neglect a single aspect of that slow advance to the enemy's lines, for in those few minutes I experienced a prolonged state of consciousness during which I hung over a pit of fear, weighted down by a long and vivid anticipation of its nature, and now brought to the last tension by this silent agony of deliberate approach. Fear is more powerful in silence and loneliness, for then the mind is more open to the electric uprush of the animal. There is safety in action and unanimity in all the noisy riot of strife—until even that safety is beaten down by the pitiless continuance of physical shock; then there is safety only in the mind again, if it rise like a holy ghost out of the raw stumps of the body.

I remember for a time feeling my heart unrulily beating in my breast, and a tight constriction at the throat. That was perhaps only excitement, or tense expectation of activity. It was not the shuddering grovelling impulse, the sudden jet of pus into the thrilling blood stream, that would sometimes, on the sudden near detonation of a shell, poison one's humanity. That, as I have said, is the only real kind of fear—the purely physical reaction. From that state a few men can recover because they have minds that can surmount a physical state: an imaginative sense of equilibrium. *Imaginative*—it was the men of imagination that were, if any, the men of courage. The men of mere brute strength, the footballers and school captains, found no way out of the inevitable physical reaction. Their bodies broke in fear because the wild energy of the instinct was impingeing on a brittle red wall of physical being. That was the feel of it, that was the reality. And P——? P—— was in another state of being. Because he had imagination he could visualize and thus anticipate this physical nature of fear. He could immerse himself in the imaginative embodiment of that impulse, and because he had no animal faith he had to succumb to that imaginative condition. Faith was the deepest reality we tested as we crawled for a few minutes along that bank—a few minutes that actually seemed an age. Faith is of many kinds but our faith was simply a level condition of the mind. It might be Christian— sometimes was, I observed. But more often it was just fatalistic, and by fatalism I mean a resolve to live in peace of mind, in possession of mind, despite any physical environment. Such was the faith, or philosophy, that belonged to a great body of men, and was held in very different degrees of intellectuality and passion. In some—they were the majority—it was a reversion to a primitive state of belief. Every bullet has its billet. What's the use of worryin'? But in others it was a subtler state of consciousness. The war seemed to annihilate all sense of individuality. The mass of it was so immense that oneself as a separate unit could not rationally exist. But there is a sense in which the death of individuality means the birth of personality. This truth is the basis of all sacrifice and martyrdom. A saint may die for his faith, but only because that faith is an expression of his personality. And so in the presence of danger, and in the immediate expectation of death, one can forget the body and its fears and exist wholly as a mind.

We had gone perhaps three parts of our way, when we heard the sound of men working. Muffled coughs, thuds, indefinite clinks. I was nonplussed. The explanation did not immediately occur to me. It hadn't time. I had a sudden sick fear that we must return, empty-handed shameful fools. I think this thought and image lasted the brief interval I had for reflection. For immediately the sergeant tugged my leg and crept close to my ear. He indicated somehow the right. I turned my head. Two figures loomed indistinctly in the dark. Approaching us. 'We must rush them,' I whispered. The sergeant said: 'Right; you give the tip.' The two figures blundered nearer. I could see them hesitate on the other side of the rim of a shell-hole. My heart had suddenly become calm. I was filled with a great exaltation. My body didn't exist, save as a wonderfully unconscious mechanism. I gave a great inhuman cry and dashed forward, barking with my Colt at the shadowy figures not ten yards away. One gave a wild bestial shriek and fell into the darkness. The other fired. We duelled, there in the dark. But I ran on, impelled by an unknown energy, the sergeant by my side. Just then the concerted moment arrived. A dark rainbow of shells hissed through the sky. The flash and detonation of heavy shells. The pale wavering rockets of the star-shells, they curved round us, fell among us. In that incessant theatrical light I saw my enemy dash into the shell-hole at his feet and fall down crying for mercy. I had my foot on the squirming body, sergeant his bayonet. It was an officer. I perceived that quickly, clearly. It was enough. I gave the order: 'Back to the lines.' We turned. The barrage was over now. Only a blind hiss of bullets from the German line. We walked back to the trenches. My men came chattering round, peering with black faces at the prisoner. Prodding him with their bayonets. Crying happily. Lusting to kill him. I tried to keep them off. The prisoner was talking to me, wildly excited. At last he found his French. I understood. He was so pleased! Explained that he was married and had children. He wanted to live. I tried to calm him. He was a professor of philology and lived at Spandau. I took away his revolver; the sergeant took his bright dagger. And thus we reached our own line. As the German hesitated on the parapet someone kicked him violently on the backside, so that he fell down. I cursed the fellow, but didn't stop to identify him. S——was there, waiting for me, very much mystified by the turn of events, but jubilant at the sight of a prisoner. We made our way to the headquarters' dugout and descended with our charge.

We blinked in the brilliant light of several candles. It was a square dugout with a fixed table served by benches from the walls. To get to the benches we had to crawl under the table. Our Colonel was a Welshman, temporarily attached from another regiment. When away from the trenches he was pleasant enough, thought at bottom a weak and emotional nature. We did not trust him, for he was known to be 'a white-livered funk'. A bottle of whisky was by him on the table, as he sat facing the stairway. He had drunk a great deal, for he was highly nervous about the result of the raid, which would reflect on his reputation. He welcomed us effusively. I don't remember all the chatter and confusion in that confined space, but eventually some kind of order did emerge. D——, our signalling officer, who knew German, began to question the prisoner. The poor fellow was docile enough. He gave up his letters, papers and maps, but asked to keep a photograph of his wife, which we allowed. But a more disgusting scene followed. He had on his finger a signet-ring, perhaps rather a pretty one. The Colonel insisted on having it, and because it would not pass the knuckle, urged us to cut it off. The man was in a delirium and of course we disregarded him. But he made efforts to reach the prisoner himself and in the effort fell drunkenly over and rolled under the table. He lay stupidly there and fell asleep. I watched the prisoner. He was terribly excited, but self-possessed. He was standing against the dark entrance, speaking forcefully and at length. D—— explained to us at intervals. He was passionately defending the German cause, arguing persuasively that we, the English, had been faithless to our common Teutonic stock. The future of Europe was with the German nations; they alone had the energy, the fresh spirit, the nascent culture, for the creation of a new world.

S—— left at about two o'clock to report particulars to the Brigade Headquarters, and at dawn I set out with the prisoner and the happy raiders. We had lost only one man, and there were no serious wounds. We filed-down the communication trenches, leisurely enough, for we were tired. Our faces were still black with the charred cork. The sun rose up to greet us, and when finally we got out into the open country the day was warm and beneficent. The larks were singing again, as on my journey up with P——. But now the sky was pulsing with their shrill notes. On the way I talked to the prisoner, and once we rested for a while, sitting side by side on a fallen tree. He explained that when we first surprised them (he was a company officer with his orderly, visiting parties out at work on the battered wire entanglements) they had taken us for Senegalese troops, and his orderly's terror was perhaps largely due to this mistake. But we talked mostly of other things. I was eager to learn anything about their side—their state of mind, their public opinion, the possibility of revolution and an end of all this meaningless strife. Nietzsche was at that time still fresh in my awakening mind, and I stammered in broken enthusiasm about his books, but got no response. He was now too aware of his liberty, his safety, his bodily emancipation to think of such things. He was happy to be safe at last, but perhaps he was also a little chagrined. He was amazed at my youth and perhaps a little ashamed of being captured by what looked like a boyish prank. We strolled on again. I only recall his features with difficulty. He was fair and rather short. But I should not know him if I met him again.

When we reached the Brigade Headquarters I handed him over and stayed to watch him questioned. He stood at attention before a table in the open. And when this was done, he was given into the charge of a guard to be taken down to the Divisional Camp. I last saw him standing at a distance from me, waiting to move.

I gazed at him eagerly, tenderly, for I had conceived some sort of vicarious affection for this man. I had done my best to kill him a few hours before. I waved my hand as he left, but he only answered with a vague smile.

I then made for my battalion reserve and found a hut and a bed. I slept for more than twelve hours and in my sleep, perhaps from weariness, or because of some relaxation in my nerves, my heart seemed to stop and my blood to sweep round in a dark red whirlpool. In my dream I wondered if this was death. But when I awoke I was fresh and content. I was alive. There was light streaming in through the windows, and friendly voices.

7

In Retreat

A JOURNAL OF THE RETREAT OF THE
FIFTH ARMY FROM ST. QUENTIN,
MARCH, 1918*

I

We received the warning order just before dinner, and for a while talked excitedly round the mess fire, some scoffing at the idea of an imminent battle, others gravely saying that this time at any rate the warning was justified. Two deserters, with tales of massing guns and the night-movements of innumerable troops, had reached our lines the previous day. Of course, deserters usually had some such tale designed to tempt a captor's leniency, but this time it was likely to be the truth. What else could the enemy's long silence mean? To that question we had no answer. We went early to bed, expecting an early awakening. The harnessed horses stood in lowered shafts.

* (A) The scheme, common to the Fifth Army, was a defence by distribution in depth. The original front line was reduced to a line of observation posts, from 100 to 500 yards apart, each consisting of a section of men. These men were not intended to resist: they were to observe and give warning to the main line of defence about 200 to 500 yards behind them. This main line was well dug and well wired. But the battalion fronts were extremely long—as long as 2,000 yards—and three companies, perhaps each 100 to 120 strong, became very attenuated along this distance, especially when the men on the observation posts had been deducted. But the line was exceedingly well sited, and, under ordinary circumstances, the machine and Lewis guns, helped by what rifle-fire there was, would have been adequate to cope with any attacking force.

(B) Behind the main line of resistance came the battalion redoubt. This was a circular defensive system, perhaps 800 yards in diameter, manned by the company in battalion reserve, battalion headquarters, and a Machine-Gun

228

There was scarcely a wall standing in Fluquières: everywhere demolition and bombardment had reduced the village to irregular cairns of brick and plaster. Winding among these cairns were the cleared roadways. Men and horses rested in patched sheds and an occasional cellar. S—— and I were in a small repaired stable, each with a bed-frame in a manger. I had livened the cleanly white-washed walls of the place with illustrations from a coloured magazine. That evening all save our trench-kit had been sent to the transport-wagons, and we were lying on the bare netting with only our trench coats thrown over us.

Corps unit. The construction of these redoubts was not yet completed, especially in the matter of wiring, and I remember how the colonel used to go round raging about the folly of the man who left his back door undefended.

There was one of these redoubts to each battalion, so that between each redoubt there was a gap of some 1,000 yards. These gaps were covered by machine-guns, and elaborate barrages were worked out by the artillery to cover the approaches to them.

(C) At varying distances behind the front-line system came a second line of redoubts occupied by the brigade in support. These were carefully sited and more or less echeloned with the redoubts 1,000 to 3,000 yards in front. It was one of these redoubts that we occupied at Roupy, and a detailed description of the defence is given in paragraph (F).

(D) Behind this system of redoubts, resting in near villages and camps, came the brigade in reserve. They could be utilized to reinforce or counter-attack any part of the division's frontage.

(E) A line of continuous trenches was in preparation behind the redoubt system, but on our frontage, on the 21st of March, this had only been outlined by removing the sods, and by the construction of one or two machine-gun emplacements. We had only a vague idea of what troops were in Army Reserve, and subsequent experience proved these to be negligible.

(F) The defences we occupied on the morning of the 21st were distributed as follows: the headquarters were in Stanley Redoubt: round this core was the wired ring of the redoubt, occupied on its eastern side by one company. Towards the enemy in front of the redoubt a short line was occupied by another company detailed to counter-attack should the line in front be broken. This front line was a crescent-shaped irregular line about 1,000 yards long, occupied by two companies. The headquarters of each of these companies was about 200 yards behind the front line in a small keep, wired and defended by a small company-reserve. Communication trenches connected the front-line companies with the counter-attack company, and the counter-attack company with the redoubt. The front-line companies were not well connected with the corresponding companies of the battalion on their flanks. There were gaps which could only be covered by visiting patrols.

The system was, according to British standard, fairly well wired, and the redoubt was well stored with ammunition and reserve water and rations.

For some time I was too excited to sleep, and none too warm. But weariness did at length triumph, and when, a short while afterwards, I was roughly awakened, I had become unconscious enough to forget the continuity of things.

II

Yes: suddenly I was awake. A match was being applied to the candle stuck on the bed-frame above my head. With his excited face illumined in the near candle-light, an orderly bent over me and shook my shoulders. I heard confused shoutings, and the rumble of gunfire. I had hardly need to read the message-form held out to me: 'Man Battle Stations'—the code words I knew only too well, and all that they implied. I was shivering violently with the cold, but in the shaking candle-light I scribbled messages repeating the code to the company commanders, the transport officer, and to others. S—— was moving on the other side of the wall that divided the mangers.

'We're in for it, my lad,' he yelled, above the increasing din.

Just then there was the sudden shrieking rush of a descending shell and its riotous detonation very near. Our candles jumped out, and we were in darkness, with bricks and earth falling like a hail on the roof. My servant came in, and hastily helped me to gather my equipment together. He handled the two or three books I always carried with me, asking me if I would take one in my pocket. I took Thoreau's *Walden*, because I had not yet read it, and anticipated two or three weary days of passive defence. For even if now we realized the actuality of the enemy's attack, so confident were we of our defensive system that we contemplated nothing more than a short successful resistance. When in the front line, we had ceaselessly reconnoitred all approaches, and so fine were the sweeping fields of fire that stretched away towards St. Quentin, so skilfully placed were our machine-guns, that always we pitied the folly of the enemy should he assail a defence so deadly. We reckoned with one factor unseen.

I fixed my revolver and ammunition securely, and set out to the orderly room, some five hundred yards away. It was now about five o'clock and still dark. I picked my way along a path which led across the great heaps of rubble. Shells were falling in the village. I still shivered with cold. My electric torch was nearly exhausted, so that I kept falling as I went. When I reached the orderly room, which was in a restored cottage, I found everything in a great hubbub, orderlies coming and going, the sergeant-major shouting orders. Inside, the doctor was bandaging a wounded man.

S——, who had been assembling the headquarter staff, came to say that something terrible had happened to the Lewis team (at that time a Lewis-gun team was attached to each battalion headquarters): would I come round with my torch.

They had been sleeping, some six men, beneath tarpaulin sheets, stretched across a half-demolished out-house. A shell had fallen in the middle of them. In the weak glare of my torch, we saw a mangled mass of red brick-dust and of red glistening blood. Here and there we distinguished a tousled head of hair. One man, pinned beneath beams and brickwork, was still groaning. We quickly began to extricate him, but he died whilst we worked.

I then joined the colonel, and with one or two orderlies and the sergeant-major we followed the companies along the back lane that led from Fluquières to Roupy, a distance of about a mile and a half. The morning was cold and a heavy dew lay on the ground. As we walked the light of dawn began to reveal a thick wet mist.

III

At 6.50 I sent a message to the brigade, informing them that the battalion was in position. We had been shelled all along the way, and when we neared Roupy, the cross-roads seemed to be under a continuous barrage. Nevertheless, we got into position with very few casualties. Safe in the bowels of the headquarter dugout, we thought the worst was over, and began casually to eat the tongue sandwiches and drink the tea provided by the mess-corporal.

The dugout was new and spacious, and odorous of the fresh chalky earth. It was about thirty feet deep, and partitioned into three sections, of which the middle one was occupied by the headquarter officers. Because it was new it was unfurnished, and we had to squat on the bare floor, grouped round a few candles.

For me that cavern is a telephonic nightmare. The instrument, a 'D III converted', was placed on the floor in a corner of the dugout. Two signallers sat with their legs straddling round it. At first the companies, then the neighbouring battalions, and, finally, the brigade, kept me there crouching on the floor, yelling till I was hoarse into the execrable instrument. When I was not speaking, the signallers were receiving or sending Morse messages.

Above the ground the situation was disquieting. The thick mist of the early dawn persisted: a man ten yards away could not be distinguished. The gunfire, tremendous in its intensity, continued hour after hour to pound into the invisible foreground. The earth vibrated almost hysterically. An occasional shell crashed near us, but after the first three hours (at 7.30) the enemy's fire seemed to be concentrated on our front-line defences. No messages, telephonic or written, came to relieve our anxiety.

The gradual accumulation of our anxiety should be realized. Every minute seemed to add to its intensity. By ten o'clock or so, our hearts were like taut drum skins beaten reverberantly by every little incident.

Then the skin smashed. Bodily action flickered like flame, the sense of duration was consumed away.

Shortly after eleven o'clock, a gun team galloped madly down the main road. Then two stragglers belonging to the Machine-Gun Corps were brought to headquarters. They informed us that the front line had been penetrated. Later, an officer from the front line battalion, with five or six men, came to us out of the mist. Most of the party were wounded, and as the officer's leg was being bandaged in the dugout, he told us his tale. He was haggard and incoherent, but the sequence was awfully clear to us. The enemy had attacked in great strength at 7.30. They had apparently reached the observation line unobserved, and overpowered the few men there before a warning could be given or an escape made. Advancing under cover of a creeping barrage, they had approached the main line of defence. No fire met them there, or only fire directed vaguely into the fog. The fight at the main line had been short and bloody. Our men, dazed and quivering after three hours' hellish bombardment (I could see them cowering on the cold mist-wet earth), had been brave to the limits of heroism; but pitifully powerless. The ghastly job had been completed by 8.30. About nine o'clock fresh enemy battalions passed through their fellows and advanced towards the front-line redoubt (L'Épine de Dallon). Our artillery fire must have been useless by then, still falling on the old enemy front line. At any rate, the enemy quickly surrounded the redoubt, and then penetrated it. This officer himself had been captured, and later had made his escape in the mist. He thought it possible that the headquarters of his battalion were still holding out.

We were still questioning our informant when an excited voice yelled down the dugout shaft: 'Boches on the top of the dugout.' Our hearts thumped. There was no reason why the enemy shouldn't be on us. They might have been anywhere in that damned mist. We drew our revolvers and rushed to the shaft. We did not mean to be caught like rats in a hole.

I remember my emotion distinctly: a quiet despair. I *knew* I went up those stairs either to be shot or bayoneted as I emerged, or, perhaps, to be made prisoner and so plunge into a strange unknown existence.

Half-way up the stairs, and a voice cried down: 'It's all right: they're our fellows.' Some artillerymen in overcoats, straggling across the open, had looked sinister in the mist.

We turned to the dugout, the released tension leaving us exhausted.

Patrols from our front companies had been feeling outward all morning, at first without result. At 12.30 B—— (commanding the left front company) reported: 'Machine-gun and rifle-fire on left and right can be heard. Shelling very hard. Can see nothing. Patrols are being sent out.' At 1 p.m. he reported: 'Boche are in quarry just in front of me. We are firing Lewis guns and rifles at him. He seems to be firing from our right flank too, with machine-guns.'

These and other messages all came by runner. The telephonic communications to the companies had broken down before noon, though I think we remained in touch with the brigade until late in the afternoon.

About midday the mist began to clear a little. At one o'clock the enemy, having massed in the valley five hundred yards immediately in front of us, attacked in mass strength. The fusillade that met them must have been terrific. They came on in good order, extending and manœuvring with precision. At 1.20 B—— reported: 'No. 5 Platoon report enemy on wire in front. Artillery assistance is asked for. We are firing rifle grenades into them.' And again at 1.30: 'Boche attacking in strength with sections in front. Front troops are in valley in front. They are also heading to my left flank.' Between 1.30 and 1.40 the attack reached its greatest intensity. By 1.45 it had withered completely before the hail of our fire.

At 1.45 B—— reported: 'Boche running back like hell near Savy. They seem to be running from artillery as much as anything.' (Savy was one and a half miles to our left front: it was on the slope that rose away from the valley in front of us where the enemy had massed his forces before his attack.)

For a moment we became elated. There was cause enough. The mist had lifted, and a pale sun shone. We had defeated a strong attack. We received a message from the Inniskillings on our right to say they still held their positions intact. And wider afield the co-ordination of the enemy's advance seemed to have broken down.

We have made haste to distribute our reserve ammunition, to clear the dressing-station, and generally to make ourselves ready for the next happenings.

In reply to my inquiries B—— sent this message, timed 2.15 p.m.: 'It is very difficult to tell numbers of enemy. I can see the ground north to Savy, and saw them scattered. The line advancing had about 30 men to every 100 yards. We do not require S.A.A. yet. Can you instruct Rose* to fire up Soup Valley, please? We will want Very lights for the night. Will a supply be forthcoming? Can see no movement now. Boche is putting up white lights all along valley.'

IV

The lull was not of long duration. Either we had been deceived by the movements near Savy, or the enemy had made a miraculously swift recovery. At 2.45 I received another message from B——: 'Enemy movement at F. 12 at 4.0. They appear to be carrying in wounded. Enemy also advancing across valley on left on F. 5, in small parties. Estimated total strength seen, 50 men. Boche aeroplanes are flying about 300 feet above our lines, and have been for a short while past. There is still some machine-gun fire in front. Is a redoubt holding out?'

The aeroplanes were evidently making a preliminary recon-

* Code name for a company.

naissance, and I guessed the movement to be significant of a new attack.

On the mists clearing, the aeroplanes were able to sight position, and soon the artillery on both sides became active. Our own artillery, alas, fired short, smashing our already weakened defences. The Germans brought up their light field guns with great skill and rapidity. Several batteries were observed coming over the ridge at L'Épine de Dallon—only a few hours ago the headquarters of the battalion we were supporting. We now realized our position in earnest, and I sent a detailed account of the situation to the brigade.

Towards four o'clock, the enemy shelling increased in intensity. The second attack was now imminent. B—— sent the following message, timed 4.30 p.m. 'Boche is attacking on right about 400 strong, and is massing in the valley right in front of Roupy. We want some more S.A.A. During the Boche retreat the rifle-men and Lewis guns did good work, killing many. Shelling very heavy.'

The heavy shelling continued, and under cover of its intensity the enemy again massed in the valley in front of us. The men held on grimly. Thus B——, timed 5.10 p.m.: 'Line holding still with some casualties. Reports not in. Line heavily shelled. S.A.A. received correct. Situation still the same. Touch is being kept with battalion on our right, and patrols go constantly. Our chloride of lime is missing and cannot be found. Machine-guns very active.' And again at 5.40 p.m.: 'The Boche is 50 yards or less from our line, and is also passing down the valley for another attack.'

Then suddenly those massed men leapt from cover, and came on in their grey, regular formations. At headquarters we were only aware of the angry surge of rifle and machine-gun fire, deadening even the detonations of shells. All this time I was spending tiring, exasperating hours at the telephone, striving to get in communication with brigade and artillery headquarters. Again and again the wire was broken, and again and again the linesmen went out into the mist to mend it. Then it got disconnected irreparably. We were isolated in that chaos.

About 6.30 B—— sent the following momentous message: 'Boche got inside our wire on right and left. No. 5 Platoon are all either wiped out or prisoners. No. 7 Platoon took up position on left of keep, but Boche were in it when I left. They also were in trench on right of road left by C. Company, and we killed several on road near camouflage. I am now in redoubt with 25 men.'

The climax had come. We had still one card to play—the counter-attack company. On receipt of B——'s message, the colonel decided to order C—— to attack in accordance with the pre-conceived plan.

We only heard of this counter-attack from the mouths of a few survivors. It was one of the most heroic episodes in the retreat. The company gathered together in the shell-battered trench that they had occupied all day, and then took the open. No artillery covered their advance. It was hopeless, insane, suicidal. They had perhaps one hundred and fifty yards to cover. They advanced at a jog-trot, lumbering on the uneven ground. One by one they fell before the fusillade that met them. C—— had reached the enemy with about a dozen men. These leapt in among the Boches, and a hand-to-hand struggle ensued for a few minutes. C—— was last seen cursing, pinned to the trench wall by a little mob of Germans, in one hand his empty smoking revolver.

V

It was now dusk, and with dusk came peace and silence. And at dusk this was our position—The front rim of the redoubt was in the enemy's possession. The counter-attack company had disappeared. The company-keeps still held out with a few men in each. The inner ring of the redoubt was held by one company, and the remnants of three. B—— had survived with one of his officers. But several officers in the three front companies had been either killed, wounded, or captured. There were probably two hundred men still surviving in the battalion.

In the darkness the colonel and I walked up to the line. As we went along the road, the stillness was abruptly broken by the sound of three or four shots, screams and curses. We flung ourselves on the roadside, our revolvers ready. We shouted: 'Who goes there?' English voices answered, and the sergeant-major went to investigate. Two German privates had walked into a sentry on the road, *coming from behind us*. No one could understand what they said, and they were sent back to brigade headquarters. And I don't remember that any one of us was perturbed by the incident, eerie though it was.

Just after one o'clock in the morning, we received long-awaited instructions from the brigade. The battalion in reserve was to deliver a counter-attack. The line of deployment was given, and the direction of attack. The battalion was to leave its position at 12.45, and the guns were to start a creeping barrage at 1.33 a.m.

The whole thing was a ghastly failure. The night was black, and the battalion attacking was unfamiliar with the ground it had to cover. We waited hours for a sign of their approach. About two o'clock a stray officer came to us, having lost his company. Eventually, about four o'clock, one company did appear. It went forward in the darkness, but got dispersed and uncontrollable in the effort to deploy into attack formation. Dawn found us as dusk had found us, with the sole difference that some two hundred men of the counter-attack battalion had found refuge in our redoubt, and in the keeps in front.

I think by then we were past hope or despair. We regarded all events with an indifference of weariness, knowing that with the dawn would come another attack. We distributed ammunition, reorganized our Lewis guns, and waited dully, without apprehension.

Again the morning was thickly misty. Our own artillery fire was desultory and useless. Under cover of the mist, the enemy massed in battle formation, and the third attack began about 7 am. We only heard a babel in the mist. Now our artillery was firing short among our men in the redoubt. About ten o'clock the enemy penetrated our left flank, presumably in the gap between us and the battalion on our left, which was still in position. Machine-gun fire began to harass us from that direction, somewhere in the ruins of the village. We never heard from the battalion on our right, and a runner I sent there did not return. I think they must have withdrawn about ten o'clock.

This new attack petered out. I fancy it was only half-hearted on the part of the enemy—probably only a demonstration to see if we intended to make a determined resistance, or to fight only a rearguard action. Finding the resistance determined enough, they evidently retired to prepare the real thing.

This fourth attack was delivered about midday. The mist still persisted thinly. One could perhaps see objects fifty yards away.

THE FALCON AND THE DOVE

I don't know what resistance the platoon-keeps offered. They were in a hopeless position, and would easily have been swamped in a massed attack.

Shortly after midday, the enemy came in direct contact with the inner ring of the redoubt.

We fired like maniacs. Every round of ammunition had been distributed. The Lewis guns jammed; rifle bolts grew stiff and unworkable with the expansion of heat.

In the lull before noon, the colonel and I had left the dugout, in which we were beginning to feel like rats in a trap, and had found an old gun-pit about two hundred and fifty yards farther back, and here we established our headquarters. An extraordinary thing happened. The gun-pit was dug out of the bank on the roadside. About two o'clock one of our guns, evidently assuming that Roupy had been evacuated, began to pound the road between Roupy and Fluquières. One of these shells landed clean on the road edge of our pit. We were all hurled to the ground by the explosion, but, on recovering ourselves, found only one casualty: the colonel had received a nasty gash in the forearm. We then went two hundred to three hundred yards across the open, away from the road, and found a smaller over-grown pit. The colonel refused to regard his wound as serious; but he soon began to feel dizzy, and was compelled to go back to the dressing-station. I was then left in charge of the battalion.

It was now about 2.30. The attack still persisted in a guerrilla fashion. But the enemy was massing troops in the trenches already taken. At 4 p.m. the intensity of the attack deepened suddenly. A new intention had come into the enemy's mind: he was directing his attack on the flanks of our position in an effort to close round us like pincers. On the left he made use of cover offered by the ruined village, and eventually brought machine-guns to bear against us from our left rear. On the right he made use of the trenches evacuated by the Inniskillings.

In the height of this attack, while my heart was heavy with anxiety, I received a message from the brigade. Surely reinforcements were coming to our aid! Or was I at length given permission to withdraw? Neither: it was a rhetorical appeal to hold on to the last man. I rather bitterly resolved to obey the command.

Another hour passed. The enemy pressed on relentlessly with a determined, insidious energy, reckless of cost. Our position was now appallingly precarious. I therefore resolved to act independently, and do as perhaps I should have done hours earlier. I ordered B—— to organize a withdrawal. This message dispatched I lay on my belly in the grass and watched through my field-glasses every minute trickling of the enemy's progress. Gradually they made their way round the rim of the redoubt, bombing along the traverses. And now we only held it as lips might touch the rim of a saucer. I could see the heads of my men, very dense and in a little space. And on either side, incredibly active, gathered the grey helmets of the Germans. It was like a long bowstring along the horizon, and our diminished forces the arrow to be shot into a void. A great many hostile machine-guns had now been brought up, and the plain was sprayed with hissing bullets. They impinged and spluttered about the little pit in which I crouched.

I waited anxiously for B—— to take the open. I saw men crawl out of the trenches, and lie flat on the parados, still firing at the enemy. Then, after a little while, the arrow was launched. I saw a piteous band of men rise from the ground, and run rapidly towards me. A great shout went up from the Germans: a cry of mingled triumph and horror. 'Halt Eenglisch!' they cried, and for a moment were too amazed to fire; as though aghast at the folly of men who could plunge into such a storm of death. But the first silent gasp of horror expended, then broke the crackling storm. I don't remember in the whole war an intenser taste of hell. My men came along spreading rapidly to a line of some two hundred yards length, but bunched here and there. On the left, by the main road, the enemy rushed out to cut them off. Bayonets clashed there. Along the line men were falling swiftly as the bullets hit them. Each second they fell, now one crumpling up, now two or three at once. I saw men stop to pick up their wounded mates, and as they carried them along, themselves get hit and fall with their inert burdens. Now they were near me, so I rushed out of my pit and ran with them to the line of trenches some three hundred yards behind.

It seemed to take a long time to race across those few hundred yards. My heart beat nervously, and I felt infinitely weary. The bullets hissed about me, and I thought: then this is the moment of death. But I had no emotions. I remembered having read how in battle men are hit, and never feel the hurt till later, and I wondered if I had yet been hit. Then I reached the line. I stood petrified, enormously aghast. *The trench had not been dug, and no reinforcements occupied it.* It was as we had passed it on the morning of the 21st, the sods dug off the surface, leaving an immaculately patterned 'mock' trench. A hundred yards on the right a machine-gun corps had taken up a position, and was already covering our retreat. I looked about me wildly, running along the line and signalling to the men to drop as they reached the slender parapet of sods. But the whole basis of my previous tactics had been destroyed. I should never have ordered my men to cross that plain of death, but for the expectation that we were falling back to reinforce a new line. We found an empty mockery, and I was in despair. But I must steady the line. On the actual plain the men obeyed my signals, and crouched in the shallow trench. But even as they crouched, the bullets struck them. On the road, the straight white road leading to the western safety, there was something like a stampede. S—— and the sergeant-major went and held it with pointed revolvers. But it was all useless—hopeless. On the right, I saw the enemy creeping round. They would soon enfilade us, and then our shallow defence would be a death-trap. I accordingly gave the signal to withdraw, bidding the two Lewis guns to cover us as long as possible. Once more we rose and scattered in retreat. It would be about seven hundred yards to the next trenches—the village line round Fluquières—and this we covered fairly well, sections occasionally halting to give covering fire. The enemy had not yet ventured from the redoubt, and our distance apart was now great enough to make his fire of little effect. And I think as we moved up the slope towards the village we must have been in 'dead' ground, so far as the enemy advancing on the right was concerned.

We reached Fluquières, which lay on the top of the slope, and found there some deep trenches on each side of the road at the entrance of the village. Further to the left, I found certain London troops commanded by a major. One of my Lewis guns still remained intact, and this I placed to fire down the straight road to Roupy. The enemy had now left the redoubt and were advancing in line formation.

We were at Fluquières about an hour. The enemy evidently did not intend to rest content with his capture of the redoubt. It was just beginning to get dusk. Earlier we had noticed sporadic contact lights go up. But now they shot into the sky from all along the plain. Low-flying aeroplanes hovered over the advancing line, and their wireless messages soon put the German guns on to us. Big black high-explosive shells began to fall on our position, making our tired flesh shudder. I now began to be amazed at the advancing contact lights. They did not merely stretch in a line in front of us: *they encircled us like a horse-shoe, the points of which seemed* (and actually were) *miles behind us.* On the right the enemy was enfilading us with machine-gun fire.

I searched for the major commanding the troops on my left, but could not find him. By this time I was determined to act, and therefore gave the order to withdraw. The men filed through the village, gathering fresh ammunition from a dump at the crossroads. From the village the road went up a slope leading to Aubigny. The enemy's fire soon followed us, and we proceeded along the ditches on each side of the road.

Three-quarters of the way up the slope I observed a trench running at right-angles to the road on each side of it. I ordered the London men to go to the left, my own to the right, there to reorganize into companies. The twilight was now fairly deep, and I thought that with evening the enemy's advance would stay. The major I had seen in Fluquières now appeared again, and cursed me for giving the order to retire. I was too tired to argue, and even then a gust of machine-gun fire swept above our heads. They were going to attack again. We could hear them moving in the semi-darkness. Something else we could hear too—the throb of a motor cycle behind us It was a dispatch rider, and when he drew level to us, he stopped his machine and came towards me with a message. I opened it. It ordered all troops east of the Aubigny defences to retire through Ham.

I was glad. I believe I thought then that it was the end of our share in the battle. I went to the men, and assembled them in companies, and in close artillery formation we retired across country due west. We came to the Aubigny defences, manned by fresh troops, about a mile further on, and then we gathered on the road again and marched wearily along. I remember coming to a water-tank, where we all drank our fill—our mouths were swollen with thirst. When we reached Ham, an officer met us and ordered us to proceed to Muille Villette, about two miles further on, and there billet for the night. Ham, as we walked through its cobbled streets, seemed very hollow and deserted. The last time we had seen it, it had been a busy market-town, full of civilians. Now only a few sinister looters went about the empty houses with candles. We saw one fellow come out of a door with a lady's reticule and other things over his arm. We should have been justified in shooting him, but we were far too tired. We just noticed him stupidly.

The road seemed long, and our pace was slow, but at last we reached the village of Muille Villette. We found it full of artillerymen, and a few infantry. Every available shelter seemed to be occupied, but at length we got the men into a school. Our transport had been warned of our station for the night, and turned up with bully-beef and biscuits. These we served out.

I had four officers left with me. We could not find a billet for ourselves, but finally begged for shelter in a barn occupied by artillerymen. They looked on us unsympathetically, not knowing our experiences. On a stove one of them was cooking a stew of potatoes and meat, and its savour made us lusting beasts. But the artillery men ate the slop unconcernedly, while we lay down too utterly weary to sleep, languidly chewing bully-beef.

VI

It was after midnight when we came to Muille Villette; I suppose about 2 a.m. we fell into an uneasy sleep. At 4 a.m. we were awakened by the stirrings and shoutings of the artillerymen. I drew my long boots on my aching feet, and went out into the cold darkness. I found an officer of some kind. The enemy were reported to have attacked and penetrated the Aubigny defences, and to be now advancing on Ham. All the troops stationed in Muille Villette had received orders to withdraw.

We assembled the men, stupid with sleep. I knew that brigade headquarters were stationed at Golancourt, a mile and a half along the road. I resolved to proceed there and ask for orders. We marched away while the dawn was breaking.

I found the brigade established in a deserted house. T——, the brigade-major, was seated on a bed lacing his boots. No orders for the brigade had yet been received, so T—— advised me to find billets for the men, where they could rest and get food. The companies then sought billets independently, and, what was more blessed than anything, we managed to get them hot tea. I went and had breakfast with the brigade staff. The tea revived me, and

I remember how voracious I felt, and that I tried to hide this fact. The brigadier came into the room and seemed very pleased to see me: apparently he was very satisfied with our conduct, and especially with the frequent reports I had sent back. Till then I had only felt weariness and bafflement—even shame. But now I began to see that we were implicated in something immense—something beyond personal feelings and efforts.

The brigadier told me as much as he knew of the general situation. It was not much. The communications had apparently broken down. But it was enough to make me realize that more than a local attack was in progress: the whole of the Fifth Army was involved: but there were no limits to what *might* be happening.

I also learnt that Drury—where the divisional headquarters had been stationed—a village some five or six miles south-*west* of Roupy, had been captured about two o'clock on the afternoon of the 22nd, several hours before we had evacuated the redoubt. Only a miracle of chance had saved us from being cut off.

The brigade seemed to have difficulty in getting into touch with the division, or, at any rate, in obtaining orders from them. But at 10 a.m. I was told to march to Freniches and await orders there. We assembled in the village street and marched on again. The road was busy with retreating artillery and a few infantrymen. From behind us came the sounds of firing: the enemy were attacking Ham. We trudged on, passing villages whose inhabitants were only just taking steps to flee. They piled beds, chairs, and innumerable bolsters on little carts, some hand-pulled, some yoked to bony horses. They tied cows behind. There were old men, many old women, a few young women, but no young men. They and their like proceeded with us along the western road.

We had gone perhaps five miles when an orderly on horseback overtook us with orders. We were to report to the —th Division at Freniches.

This we eventually did, and a fat staff colonel studied a map, and then told me to take my battalion to Esmery-Hallon, a village four miles due north, and there take up a defensive position. This was more than I expected. I explained that my men had been fighting continuously for forty-eight hours, and were beaten and spiritless. But I received no comfort: the situation demanded that every available man should be used to the bitter end. I hardly dared to face my men: but I think they were too tired to mind where they went. We turned off at a right-angle, and slowly marched on. The road led through a beautiful patch of country, steeped in a calm, liquid sunshine. We tilted our bodies forward, and forced our weary muscles to act.

About two miles south of Esmery-Hallon, an officer (a lieutenant) appeared on a motor cycle. He was in command of a scrap lot—transport men, cobblers, returned leave men, etc. He seemed to have the impression that the enemy were upon us, and wanted me to deploy and take up a position facing east. I explained that we were much too tired to do any such thing. He expostulated. Did I realize this, that, and the other? I explained that I had cause to realize such things better than he did. He raved. I told him finally that I didn't care a damn, but that I had orders to defend Esmery-Hallon, and thither I must go. He went off in a rage, seeming incredibly silly and fussy to us all.

Esmery-Hallon is a small village perched on a detached conical hill, overlooking the plain on all sides. The defence was simply arranged. Two companies of engineers were entrenched in front of the village. I sent a look-out on to the top of the church tower, and extended my men astraddle the hill on each side of the village, north and south. The men on the south found a ditch, which made an admirable trench. The men on the north extended over the ploughed land, and dug shallow pits for shelter. We had no machine-guns or Lewis guns, but every man had a rifle and a decent amount of ammunition. I established my headquarters on the north side by a quarry, where I had a wide view of the plain.

The day was very still, and the distant rattle of machine-gun fire carried to us. A few enemy shells fell ineffectively about the landscape. I got into touch with a major of the Inniskillings in command of one hundred and fifty men on my right, and we co-ordinated defences on that wing. My left wing was in the air, so to speak—not a soul visible for miles.

When our dispositions were finally made, I returned to the quarry edge. My servant T—— had already been away to search the village and now came laden with samples of red wine and cider which he had found in a cellar. So I sent him back to the village with other men, telling them to search for food also. They soon returned with bottles of red wine and a large tin of army biscuits. Evidently there was any amount of wine, but I was afraid to distribute it among the men for fear lest on fasting stomachs it should make them drunk. So S—— and I each took a wine glass, and starting at different points, we began to go a round of the men. Each man lay curled up in his shallow pit, resting. To each we gave a glass of wine and a few biscuits. They took it thankfully. There was a lull in the distant fighting: I don't remember any noise of fire during that hour. The sun was warm and seemed to cast a golden peace on the scene. A feeling of unity with the men about me suddenly suffused my mind.

VII

It was nearly two o'clock when we got settled. About this time I interrupted a message which gave me the useful information that the enemy had been seen in Ham at 10 a.m. I guessed that the silence meant they were now consolidating along the Somme Canal. Later in the afternoon a cavalry patrol trotted up to our position. Officer, men, and horses all looked very debonair and well fed. The officer was very condescending towards me, but made a message of the information I gave him, thought it would not be worth while venturing further on to the plain, so rode away back, harness jingling, the sun shining on well-polished accoutrements.

About five o'clock, I judged that we were to be left alone for the night, and made my plans accordingly. I sent the following message to B——, who was in charge of the men on the right of the village: 'We hold on to our present positions unless otherwise ordered. When it is getting dark close your men in a little to form about 7 or 8 pickets. From these pickets send standing patrols out about 150 yards, or to any good observation point within warning distance. Any show of resistance should drive off any enemy patrols. But as far as I can make out the Boche is still east of the canal. Should you be attacked by overwhelming numbers, withdraw fighting in a due westerly direction under your own arrangements. I should do the same in case of need. I suggest you come up to have a look at our position before dark.'

But just after dark, I received orders to relieve the Royal Engineers in front of the village. I regretted this order, but had to obey it. We now found ourselves in freshly dug trenches on the flat of the plain, our view to the left and right obstructed by woods.

Included in the orders mentioned was a message to the effect that advance parties of the French would probably arrive that night, and the positions would be shown to them. This message filled us with wild hope; we became almost jaunty.

But the night was very cold, and heavily wet with dew. We improved the trenches, and stamped about, flapping our arms in an effort to keep warm. I sat with L——, bravest and brightest of my runners, on a waterproof sheet beneath a tree in the centre of our position. We waited for the dawn: it was weird, phantasmagorical. Again the fateful mist. As it cleared a little, the woods near us hung faintly in the whiteness.

At 8 a.m. we began to observe troops retreating in front of us. They came in little groups down the road, or straggled singly over the landscape. The mist gradually lifted. We heard machine-gun fire fairly near, somewhere on the right. The stragglers informed us that the enemy had crossed the canal in the early dawn, and was advancing in considerable force. We waited patiently. At 9 a.m. the enemy came into touch with our fellows on the left, and here we rebutted him successfully. At 9.30 the troops on our right were reported to be withdrawing. About ten o'clock, there happened one of those sudden episodes, which would be almost comic with their ludicrous *bouleversement* were they not so tragic in their results. Seemingly straight from the misty sky itself, but in reality from our own guns, descended round after round of shrapnel bursting terrifically just above our heads, and spraying leaden showers upon us. Simultaneously, from the woods on our right, there burst a fierce volley of machine-gun fire, hissing and spluttering among us. We just turned and fled into the shelter of the village buildings. I shouted to my men to make for the position of the quarry. We scuttled through gardens and over walls. By the time we reached the quarry we had recovered our nerve. We extended and faced the enemy, who were advancing skilfully over the plain on our left. We on our part were a scrap lot composed of various units. We hastily reorganized into sections. Retreat was inevitable. Then followed a magnificent effort of discipline. A major took charge of the situation, and we began to retire with covering fire, section by section, in perfect alternation.

We were now on a wide expanse of plain, sloping gently westward. We stretched over this—a thin line of men, perhaps a thousand yards long. We were approaching the Nesle-Noyon Canal. When within a few hundred yards of the canal, we closed inwards to cross a bridge (Ramecourt). At the other end of the bridge stood a staff officer, separating the men like sheep as they crossed, first a few to the left, then a few to the right. Here I got separated from the majority of my men, finding myself with only fifteen. We were told to proceed along the bank of the canal until we found an unoccupied space, and there dig in.

As we crossed the bridge, we saw for the first time the sky-blue helmets of French troops peeping above a parapet. I think our eyes glistened with expectation of relief.

We went perhaps half a mile along the bank of the canal, and there I halted my attenuated company. The sun was now blazing hotly above our heads. We dropped to the ground, utterly exhausted. Presently some of the men began spontaneously to dig. R——, the only officer left with me, also took a pick and joined the men. I began to feel ashamed just then, for I would willingly have died. I took a spade (there was a dump of such things just by us) and began to shovel the earth loosened by R——. I seemed to be lifting utterly impossible burdens. My flesh seemed to move uneasily through iron bands; my leaden lids drooped smartingly upon my eyes.

We dug about three feet, and then ceased, incapable of more. At the foot of the bank there was a small pool of water. The enemy was not now in sight, so we plunged our hot faces and hands into its weedy freshness, and took off our boots and socks, and bathed our aching feet.

In the evening, about 5 p.m., a few skirmishing patrols appeared on the horizon. But our artillery was now active and fairly accurate, and machine-guns swept the plain. The patrols retired, without having advanced any distance. A large German aeroplane, with a red belly, floated persistently above our line. We fired hundreds of shots at it, but without effect. T——, my batman, nearly blew my head off in his efforts.

We had gathered a lot of sun-scorched hemlock and bedded the bottom of our trenches; and when night came on we posted sentries, and huddled down to the bedding. The night was clear, and I gazed unblinkingly at the fierce stars above me, my aching flesh forbidding sleep. Later, I must have dozed in a wakeful stupor.

VIII

The next daybreak, that of the 25th, was less misty. Bread and bully-beef had come up during the night, and we fed to get warmth into our bodies. But the sun was soon up, and we began to feel almost cheerful once again. There was no immediate sign of the enemy, and I walked along to the bridge we had crossed the previous day to glean some information of our intentions; but the only plan seemed to be the obvious one of holding on to our positions. I noticed some engineers were there ready to blow up the bridge if need be.

About 8 a.m. we saw little groups of enemy cavalry appear on the horizon. Through my glasses I could see them consulting maps, pointing, trotting fussily about. Our artillery was planting some kind of scattered barrage on the plain, and an occasional near shot made the horsemen scamper. We watched them rather amusedly till ten o'clock and then we saw signs of infantrymen. They came from the direction of Esmery-Hallon, and at first seemed in fairly dense formation. But they extended as they cut the sky line, and we soon perceived them advancing in open order. As they got nearer, they began to organize short rushes, a section at a time.

We were now well stocked with ammunition—there were piles of it lying about—and as soon as the advancing troops were within anything like range, we began to 'pot' them. In fact, the whole thing became like a rifle-gallery entertainment at a fair. But still they came on. Now we could see them quite plainly—could see their legs working like dancing bears, and their great square packs bobbing up and down as they ran. Occasionally one dropped.

Immediately in front of our trench, about eight hundred yards away, there was a little copse of perhaps fifty trees. This they reached about eleven o'clock and halted there. If only our flanks held out, I guessed they would never get farther, for between the copse and our rifles and Lewis guns there was not a shred of cover; and we were well entrenched, with a wide canal in front of us.

Of course, the artillery was busy all the while: not methodically, but thickly enough to give the day the appearance of a conventional battle. But then the unexpected (really we had no cause

248

longer to regard it as unexpected), the fatal thing happened. A
battery of ours shortened its range, and got our position exactly
'taped'. The shells fell thick and fast, right into our backs. We
were, remember, dug in on the top of a bank, perhaps fifteen feet
high. All along this bank the shells plunged. Immediately on our
right, not fifty yards away, a shell landed cleanly into a trench,
and when the smoke cleared there remained nothing, absolutely
nothing distinguishable, where a moment ago had been five or six
men. We grovelled like frightened, cowed animals. Still the shells
fell: and there was no means of stopping them. I glanced dis-
tractedly round; men on the right were running under cover of
the bank away to the right. Other men on the left were retreating
to the left. I resolved to get out of it. Immediately behind us, fifty
yards away, was a large crescent-shaped mound, very steep, like a
railway embankment, and perhaps sixty feet high. It occurred to
me that from there we should command, and command as
effectively as ever, the plain in front of us. I made my intention
known, and at a given signal we leapt down the bank, and across
the intervening fifty yards. We were evidently in sight, for a hail
of machine-gun bullets made dusty splutters all round us as we
ran. But we reached the mound without a casualty, and climbed
safely on to it. There I found a few men already in occupation,
commanded by a colonel, under whose orders I then placed
myself.

The enemy's artillery fire now increased in volume. I saw a cow
hit in a field behind us, and fall funnily with four rigid legs
poking up at the sky.

At 3.30 we saw the French retiring on the right, about a
thousand yards away. They were not running, but did not seem
to be performing any methodic withdrawal. We then fell into one
of those awful states of doubt and indecision. What was happening? What should we do? There was angry, ominous rifle-fire on
our immediate left. About 4 p.m. there was a burst of machine-
gun fire on our immediate right. I noticed that the stray bullets
were coming over our heads. This meant that the enemy were
advancing from the right.

I then saw English troops withdrawing about six hundred yards
away on the right—evidently the troops that had been defending
the bridge. I did not hear any explosion, and so far as I know the
bridge remained intact.

At 4.15 I saw the colonel with his men suddenly leave his position on my immediate left. Although I was within sight—within calling distance—he did not give me an order. I was now alone on the mound with my fifteen men.

I did not wait long. I resolved to act on my own initiative once more. We had now moved off the maps I possessed and might as well be in an unknown wilderness. I resolved to proceed due west, taking the sun as a guide. We moved down the back slope of the mound. At the foot we found a stream or off-flow from the canal, about ten feet wide and apparently very deep. As we hesitated, looking for a convenient crossing, a machine-gun a few hundred yards away opened fire on us. There were a good few trees about which must have obstructed the firer's view: the cut twigs, newly budded, fell into the water. We hesitated no longer: we plunged into the stream. The men had to toss their rifles across, many of which landed short and were lost. The sight of these frightened men plunging into the water effected one of those curious stirrings of the memory that call up some vivid scene of childhood: I saw distinctly the water-rats plunging at dusk into the mill-dam at Thornton-le-Dale, where I had lived as a boy of ten.

The water sucked at my clothes as I met it, and filled my field-boots. They seemed weighted with lead now as I walked, and oozed for hours afterwards.

We came out facing a wide plain, climbing gently westward. Machine-gun and rifle-fire still played about us. We could see a church steeple on the horizon due west, and I told the men to scatter and make for that steeple. Shrapnel was bursting in the sky, too high to be effective. We ran a little way, but soon got too tired. A——, a faithful orderly, had stayed with me, and soon we walked over the fields as friends might walk in England. We came across French machine-gunners, who looked at us curiously, asked for news of the situation, but did not seem very perturbed.

We eventually came to the village on the horizon (probably Solente). An officer of the engineers stood by the side of his horse at the cross-roads, smoking a cigarette. He asked me why I was retreating. The question seemed silly: 'We shall have to fight every inch of the way back again,' he said. 'These Frenchmen will never hold them.' I went on, too tired to answer.

Here I saw for the first time a new post stuck on the roadside. It had on it an arrow and 'Stragglers Post' in bold letters. So I was a straggler. I felt very bitter and full of despair.

I followed the road indicated by the arrow. It was dotted with small parties of men, all dejected and weary. We trudged along till we came to the village of Carrepuits. Military police met us at the entrance, and told us to report to the Traffic Control in a house a few hundred yards away. It was now getting dusk. I went into the cottage indicated, and here found an officer, very harassed and bored. Men were collected, and separated into the divisions they belonged to, and then given orders to report to such and such a place. I found a party of about fifty men of my division, and was instructed to take them and report to a divisional headquarters situated in a certain street in Roye.

I've forgotten that walk: it was only about two miles, but our utter dejection induced a kind of unconsciousness in us. It would be between ten and eleven o'clock when we got to Roye. I reported to a staff officer, who sent me off to the town major to get billets. The town major I found distracted, unable to say where I should find a billet. Apparently the town was packed with stragglers. We peered into two great gloomy marquees, floored densely with recumbent men. Meanwhile two other officers joined me with their men, and together we went off to search on our own. We found a magnificent house, quite empty, and here we lodged the men. Some kind of rations had been found. They soon had blazing wood fires going, and seemed happy in a way.

The town major had indicated a hut, where we officers might get rest, and perhaps some food. We went round, tired and aching though we were; we lifted the latch and found ourselves in a glowing room. A stove roared in one corner—and my teeth were chattering with cold, my clothes still being sodden—and a lamp hung from the roof. A large pan of coffee simmered on the stove, and the table was laden with bread, tinned-foods, butter; food, food, food. I hadn't had a bite since early morning, and then not much.

I forget, if I ever knew, who or what the two occupants were, but they were not stragglers. Roye had been their station for some time. One of them was fat, very fat, with a tight, glossy skin. I don't remember the other. We explained that we would like a billet for the night—anything would do so long as it was warmth. They were sorry: they had no room. Could they spare us some rations? They were sorry: this was all they had got till tomorrow noon. We stood very dejected, sick at our reception. 'Come away!' I said. 'Before I go away,' cried one of my companions, 'I would just like to tell these blighters what I think of them.' He cursed them, and then we walked away, back to the men's billet. I looked in at my fellows; most of them were naked, drying their clothes at the fire. Some slept on the floor.

We went upstairs into an empty room. Two of us agreed to make a fire, while the other, the one who had given vent to his feelings, volunteered to go off in search of food. We split up wood we found in the house, and lit a fire. I took off my clothes to dry them, and sat on a bench in my shirt. If I had been asked then what I most desired, besides sleep, I think I would have said: French bread, butter, honey, and hot milky coffee.

The forager soon turned up. God only knows where he got that food from: we did not ask him. But it was French bread, butter, honey, and hot milky coffee in a champagne bottle! We cried out with wonder: we almost wept. We shared the precious stuff out, eating and drinking with inexpressible zest.

As we supped we related our experiences. I forget their names; I don't think I ever knew them. Were they of the Border Regiment? I'm not sure; but they were Northerners. They had been trapped in a sunken road, with a Boche machine-gun at either end, and Boche calling on them to surrender. I don't think either of them was more than twenty years old: they were fresh and boyish, and had been faced with this dilemma. They put it to the vote: there, with death literally staring them in the face, they solemnly called on the men to show hands as to whether they would surrender, or make a run for it. They had voted unanimously for the run. Half of them perished in the attempt. But here, a few hours afterwards, were the survivors, chatting over a blazing wood fire, passing a bottle of coffee round, very unperturbed, not in any way self-conscious. We stacked the fire high and stretched ourselves on the floor in front of it, and slept for a few hours.

IX

We were up at six the next morning, the 26th of March, and reporting to the Assistant Provost-Marshal, who was reorganizing stragglers. We congregated in the Town Square, and I was amazed at the numbers there. The streets were thickly congested with infantrymen from several divisions, with French armoured cars, cavalry, and staff officers. We fell in by divisions, and presently marched off, a column a mile or two in length. Cavalry protected our flanks and rear from surprise.

At Villers-les-Roye I found B——, the man who had been separated from me at Ramecourt Bridge. We were glad to be united again, and from there proceeded together. B—— had had orders to go to a place called La Neuville, where the first-line transport awaited us. We were now passing through the battle-fields of 1916, and everywhere was desolate and ruined. We marched on as far as Hangest-en-Santerre, where we met our battalion cookers loaded with a welcome meal. Just as we had devoured this, and were starting on our way again, we were met by a staff colonel, who, after inquiring who we were, ordered us to turn back and proceed to Folies, where our brigade was reorganizing.

We could but mutely obey, but with dull despair and an aching bitterness. We had never thought since leaving Roye but that we were finally out of the mêlée. To turn back meant, we knew, that we might still be very much in it. We crossed country to Folies, about two miles away, in a blazing sun. There we found the details of the brigade, consisting mostly of returned leave men, already holding a line of trenches. We were told to reinforce them.

Here the second-in-command rejoined the battalion and assumed command. My endurance was broken, and I was ordered down to the transport lines. I pointed out that the men were as weary as I, and should on no account be ordered into action again. It was useless: no man could be spared. But there was not much more for them to bear. Good hot food came up to them again at dusk. The night was warm and restful.

On the morning of the 27th, the enemy had possession of Bouchoir, a village about one mile to the south-east. He began to advance during the morning, and a skirmishing fight went on during that day and the next; and during this time the battalion was withdrawn from the line without suffering any serious casualties.

X

But I had gone back with the transport officer on the 26th. I mounted the transport-sergeant's horse, and in a dazed sort of way galloped westward in the dusk. I arrived half-dead at La Neuville, and slept there for twelve hours or more. The next day we went to Braches, and thence on foot to Rouvrel. About here, the country was yet unscathed by war, and very beautiful. On a bank by the roadside, I took *Walden* out of my pocket, where it had been forgotten since the morning of the 21st, and there began to read it. At Rouvrel the rest of the battalion rejoined us the next day. On the 29th I set off on horseback with the transport to trek down the valley of the Somme.

When evening came and the hills of Moreuil were faint in the twilight, we were still travelling along the western road. No guns nor any clamour of war could be heard: a·great silence filled the cup of misty hills. My weary horse drooped her head as she ambled along, and I, too, was sorrowful. To our north-east lay the squat towers of Amiens, a city in whose defence we had endured hardships until flesh had been defeated, and the brave heart broken. My mind held a vague wonder for her fate—a wonder devoid of hope. I could not believe in the avail of any effort. Then I listened to the rumbling cart, and the quiet voices of the men about me. The first stars were out when we reached Guignemicourt, and there we billeted for the night. In this manner we marched by easy stages down the valley of the Somme, halting finally at Salenelle, a village near Valery, and there we rested four days.

8

The Artist's Dilemma

There is no book in English literature that I read more often than Coleridge's *Biographia Literaria*. It is not only the source-book and quasi-sacred scripture of that school of literary criticism to which I belong: it is also the intimate confession of one of the most instructive geniuses that ever lived—instructive because so potentially great, so tragically unsuccessful. There is one chapter in this book, the eleventh, to which I have turned again and again, in moments of doubt and when filled with that sense of frustration which affects so many writers today. It is entitled 'An affectionate exhortation to those who in early life feel themselves disposed to become authors', and there are certain passages in this chapter that have had a quite decisive influence on my life. The following passage in particular haunted me for years:

'With the exception of one extraordinary man, I have never known an individual of genius healthy or happy without a *profession*, that is, some *regular* employment, which does not depend on the will of the moment, and which can be carried on so far *mechanically* that an average *quantum* only of health, spirits, and intellectual exertion are requisite to its faithful discharge. Three hours of leisure, unannoyed by any alien anxiety, and looked forward to with delight as a change and recreation, will suffice to realize in literature a larger product of what is truly genial, than weeks of compulsion. Money, and immediate reputation form only an arbitrary and accidental end of literary labour. The hope of increasing them by any given exertion will often prove a stimulant to industry; but the necessity of acquiring them will in all works of genius convert the stimulant into a narcotic'.

When I left the Army at the end of January, 1919, I was still uncertain what to do. I had even, for some weeks, considered the possibility of taking a regular commission. My ultimate aim was clear enough: to become an author; and even the Army might be a means to this end. We looked forward then to a long period of peace, and an officer's life in peace-time, I argued, would provide the three hours of leisure which, according to Coleridge, was all I needed. But the more I considered the prospect, the less I liked it. The conditions which had made us 'comrades in arms' would be exchanged for conditions bringing back that world of parade, discipline and snobbery whose fringes I had touched at the beginning of the war, and such a world I could never have tolerated. I soon renounced this possibility, and when I reached London in February of that year, a free man again and a civilian, two careers seemed immediately open to me: politics or the Civil Service.

I did not take long to decide between these alternatives. It is true that I had, in the pre-war period, sometimes thought of a political career, and had become an active speaker in the University Debating Society. But by 1919 my purely literary ambitions were predominant, and I saw no possibility of combining poetry and politics. I therefore decided to enter the Civil Service.

In the Army, as an adjutant, I had already found administrative work to my taste, and even now I take a disinterested pleasure in it. The business of co-ordinating details, presenting summaries, writing minutes and memoranda, though I never saw it as an end in life, never seemed irksome or difficult for me: it was simply part of one's literary aptitude. I was not therefore temperamentally unsuited for the career which opened out to me. Nevertheless, I was profoundly unhappy. I quickly discovered that the Civil Service, and especially a clerkship in the Treasury, was no sinecure. I became a private secretary and from that moment anything like leisure disappeared. It is true that we did not begin work until ten o'clock in the morning, and the lunch hour was often extended to two. But I rarely left the Treasury before half-past six or seven, and by the time I had reached home, for a late dinner, I was tired and exhausted.

The more I contemplated the course ahead of me, the less I liked it. My colleagues around me were for the most part absorbed in their departmental work: it was their main interest, to which they willingly devoted all their energies. But my main interest was outside the service, in the field of literature. I was already associating with the poets and painters whose ideals I shared, and I was actively concerned with the editing of a literary review, *Art and Letters*, which Frank Rutter and I had founded in 1917.* The strain between these two loyalties became intolerable.

Again and again I turned to Coleridge's 'affectionate exhortation', but presently I could only read it with ironical bitterness. In one passage he addresses his sensible young author in these terms: 'My dear young friend, suppose yourself established in any

* The idea of a monthly review had been first conceived at Leeds before the war. It had originated with Frank Rutter, then director of the City Art Gallery, my friend and mentor in those days. The project was postponed on account of the war, but during 1916 and 1917, in the course of our correspondence, Rutter and I gradually came back to our plan, though in the modified form of a quarterly review. As an officer in the Army I was not able to take any open part in the project, but I was in effect a joint editor, and I contributed to the original cost. Rutter discussed the project with his friends in London and began to gather contributions, which he sent to France for my consideration. The first number was published at the end of June, 1917, in a quarto format of thirty-two pages.

In a prefatory note we made a statement which was unexpectedly topical again twenty-five years later: 'The production of a new Review at the present time seems to call for a word of explanation, though not for apology. . . . Objections on the score of scarcity of paper and shortage of labour may surely be overruled when we remember the reams of paper wasted weekly and the hundreds of compositors daily misemployed on periodicals which give vulgar and illiterate expression to the most vile and debasing sentiments. Friends serving at the Front—some of whom contribute to this first issue—remind us that there are educated men in the Army who would gladly welcome an addition to the small number of publications which appeal to them. Engaged, as their duty bids, on harrowing work of destruction, they exhort their elders at home never to lose sight of the supreme importance of creative art.' The contents which followed were perhaps but a slight substantiation of this aim, but they included drawings by Sickert, Lucien Pissarro, Gilman, Ginner and McKnight Kauffer. The most important article was a survey of the position of painting by Ginner. My own contributions were two poems and a review of James Joyce's *Portrait of the Artist as a Young Man*. Altogether, it was a modest beginning, 'agreeably free', as the *Times Literary Supplement* noted with relief, 'from extravagance and affectation'. *Art and Letters*, with various changes of editorship, survived until the spring of 1920. Its contributors included Richard Aldington, Aldous Huxley, Siegfried Sassoon, T. S. Eliot, the three Sitwells, Wyndham Lewis, Ezra Pound, Ronald Firbank, Ivor Richards and Katharine Mansfield.

honourable occupation. From the manufactory or counting-house, from the law-court, or from having visited your last patient, you return at evening,

Dear tranquil time, when the sweet sense of home
Is sweetest—

to your family, prepared for its social enjoyments, with the very countenances of your wife and children brightened, and their voice of welcome made doubly welcome, by the knowledge that, as far as *they* are concerned, you have satisfied the demands of the day by the labour of the day. Then, when you retire into your study, in the books on your shelves you revisit so many venerable friends with whom you can converse. Your own spirit scarcely less free from personal anxieties than the great minds, that in those books are still living for you! Even your writing desk with its blank paper and all its other implements will appear as a chain of flowers, capable of linking your feelings as well as your thoughts to events and characters past or to come; not as a chain of iron, which binds you down to think of the future and the remote past by recalling the claims and feelings of the per-emptory present.'

Dear Coleridge! It is only too plain that from the anxieties of his peremptory present he was looking towards an ideal that existed only in his imagination. For the picture he paints is at best half true. It is true that one returns from the counting-house free from the personal anxieties that beset the professional author; and the sweet sense of home is all the sweeter after a routine day in another atmosphere. But that writing desk with its blank paper and its bright implements (a fountain-pen and a portable typewriter), inviting as it undoubtedly was, more often than not could only serve as a support for a tired head and an exhausted brain. Nevertheless, to that desk I would tie myself, from ten o'clock to midnight, night after night, year after year, for all the years I remained in the Civil Service. As the products of this self-imposed discipline began to appear in the press and in book-form, people would remark on my industry, even those who did not realize that by far the greater part of my day was spent in another occupation. I do not say this in pride: the ex-perience is only significant because it gives rather a different interpretation to Coleridge's observations. A routine occupation imposes a rhythm on life, if only the repetition of regular hours, regular meals and constant movement. With such a rhythm it is comparatively easy to add, like an additional gear to a machine, a subordinate activity of two hours' daily application to a writing-desk. In short, such a life favours productivity of some sort; but it is more than doubtful whether such productivity is more 'truly genial' than the irregular spurts of inspiration upon which a comparatively idle writer will depend. An eye on the clock is already a leakage in the forces of concentration. Neither continuous logical thought nor long imaginative flights are possible under such conditions. If to one's routine duties one adds a normal measure of sociability, more than twenty-four hours will often intervene between the periods given over to composition. I have known days, and sometimes weeks, lie between the beginning and the completion of a sentence!

The first few years, my years at the Treasury, were the most painful in this respect. My mind was full of projects—projects for novels, plays and long poems which needed seclusion and ample leisure for their execution. As month after month went by with nothing accomplished, I worked myself into a desperate state of dissatisfaction and revolt, until I came near to resigning my post in the Civil Service in order to retire to some cottage in the country where I could write uninterruptedly. But before doing this I took the precaution to consult two or three of my literary friends who had already committed themselves in this way and were, in defiance of Coleridge's advice, pursuing literature as a trade. By far the most experienced of these was Ford Madox Ford, whom I had first met in 1918—I had discovered his name, much to my surprise and delight, in the list of officers attached to the Tees Garrison, whose staff I had joined in August or September of that year. Ford was busy trying to forget that he was a writer, but he welcomed the intrusion of a young and enthusiastic disciple, and for a few years we were very good friends. Those few years were the years during which I still clung to the ambition of being a novelist, and Ford was not unwilling to adopt the rôle of mentor—had he not nursed Conrad himself from obscurity to fame! What confidences I made to Ford I cannot remember; but I still have a few letters of his, inviting me to come down to Hurston or Bedham, to talk over whatever work was in progress. He preferred to talk, and he was a magnificent talker; but sometimes

he would write, and then he was a good letter-writer. The
generality of his advice was always the same, and I found it
entirely reasonable and sympathetic:

'Education Sentimentale is Stonehenge; but What Maisie Knew
is certainly Stratford on Avon (though God forbid that the Old
Man should hear me say so!). Le Rouge et le Noir is the perfect
thing upon which to model one's style, if one does not model it
on Coeur Simple—which is worth a wilderness of apes, monkeys,
Times Literary Supplement Reviewers and almost every other
thing in the world. . . . But the Real Thing is nearly as good.
Only Henry was just a *little* provincial-pharisaic, whereas Flaubert
was so large, untidy, generous—and such a worker! Still, as
someone or other said, L'un et L'autre se disent, and if you aren't
in the mood for Stonehenge the Birthplace is a very good substitute—and Henry Beyle, perhaps, a better still.'   (11:6:20)

If the style of Stendhal was modelled on the Code Napoléon,
then mine might have proved not incompatible with the writing
of Treasury minutes. It was not the question of style, however,
that was worrying me, but the broader problems of composition
and execution. 'Broader' problems—I should rather say 'physical'
problems. To model myself on Flaubert and Henry James at the
fag-end of a busy day in Whitehall—on that physically impossible
strain I finally broke.

The dilemma that was forced on me can be stated simply
enough: there was only one kind of fiction I had the conscience
to write, and there was no chance of writing it so long as I stayed
in the Civil Service. The fact that I decided to stay in the Service
depended to a considerable degree on the critical attitude I had
adopted to this particular art. This attitude I owed entirely to
Henry James, to whose work I had first been introduced by Frank
Rutter in 1913 or 1914. Previously I had been, so far as fiction
was concerned, almost completely under the spell of Turgenev and
Dostoevsky, though Meredith, whom I had read in his entirety,
perhaps prepared me for Henry James. In those days I fancy we
regarded Meredith as the immediately preceding stage in the
evolution of the novel—a misunderstanding of essential values
which would have horrified James, whose direct ancestry was
undoubtedly French. It was from James that I myself worked
back to Maupassant and Flaubert. Between 1914 and 1920 I read
practically the whole of James's work, the greater part of it while

I was still in the Army. I became a fanatical admirer of his art—more particularly of his formal conception of the novel, though at that time I was equally eager to defend his style and the significance of his subject-matter. The style was the idiosyncrasy of the man, and I never had the least temptation to imitate it; and the subject-matter was, superficially, a social world of which I had no knowledge. But this social world concealed, beneath its polished surface, all the moral issues which are the particular concern of the novelist. For me one of James's greatest virtues was that he perceived that the contemporary scene held all the challenges upon which the dramatic structure of art is built. He did not seek to create a fictitious world with its faked tragedies and easy feelings. Everything in these novels was real and authentic, and yet out of this genuine material, without the slightest violence or distortion, James made his faultless works of art with their formal relations and figures—elements upon which the profoundest aesthetic emotions depend. It is, as I still believe, an art carried to the pitch of perfection; and the desolating sense that such an art could never be surpassed—could never, without a devotion as long and as severe as his, be equalled—this sense had not a little to do with the decision I took at this time of inner crisis.

Ford, with a persuasive charm that was difficult to resist, threw all his forces on the side of the novel. I still have a long letter which he wrote to me in the September of that fateful year, and I feel no compunction in quoting most of it:

'. . . I don't know that I am the most sympathetic person to come to for one inclined to desert the practice of novel writing for the indulgence of metaphysics. For, firstly, I never knew what metaphysics were and, secondly, I have for years and years and years held that the only occupation to which a serious man could seriously put himself was the writing of novels—if only because, in all the varied domains to which the very limited human intelligence applies itself this is the only one that is practically unexplored—the only one in which it is possible to find a New Form. And it is only the finding of a New Form that is a worthy occupation.

'So at least I see it—and the immense advantage that the Novel has over the frivolous apparition called the Serious Book—is that, if you are really serious enough you can say what you like. . . .

THE FALCON AND THE DOVE

I mean that you can ram all the metaphysics in the world into it and it can still be a fine work of art. . . . Or all the Strategy, Biology, Bibliography and Philately that count.

'I don't see what Yorkshire* has to do with it—except that all Yorkshire people, as I have known them, are singularly lazy and singularly self-sufficient (Present Company, of course, always excepted!) My friend Marwood, as you say, was a case in point: he had the clear intelligence of a poet but, rather than trespass on his own shyness and shamefacedness he would spend days making corrections out of his head on the Margins of the *Encyclopaedia Britannica*. He just—peace to his ashes—wanted to bolster up his self-conceit to himself (he didn't boast of the achievement to any other soul), and, of course, to remain très grand seigneur, Marwood of Busby, and so on. . . . That is at the bottom of most Yorkshire dislike of the Arts—a sort of shyness and love of ease! Your country folk see a Poet performing coram populo! They say to themselves: We dare not appear in public: they say aloud: That is a contemptible fellow! And gradually their public utterance becomes themselves and they end as sidesmen in the local Bethel! And conceal the Venus of Milo, as she used to be concealed in the Leeds Art Gallery, behind aspidistras!

'Don't let yourself undergo that hardening process; it is a very stupid one; and try to forget that you come from the Sheeres at all. . . . Whitechapel is really a better lieu de naissance. . . .

'Of course I see you aiming at becoming another Henri Beyle: But it is a miserable ambition. . . . Learn of Stendhal all you can—and there is, if you do not happen to be Middleton Murry, an immense deal to learn in an artistic sense. . . . But don't model yourself on him. . . . I can imagine no more terrible being to himself, than a Yorkshireman, true to type, and modelling himself on Mr. Beyle! . . . The end would be the most horribly costive neurasthenic you can imagine, with incredible sex obsessions sedulously concealed, swaddled up to the ears in red flannel for fear of draughts, and with more hypochondrias and phobias than are to be found in all Freud, Jung and the late Marie Bashkirtseff put together. . . . And with a yellow, furred tongue, and a morgue britannique beyond belief. . . .

'No, try not to become that. . . . You may not like novel

*I fancy it was part of my plan to retreat to Yorkshire and become a regional novelist.

writing but it would be a good thing to stick to it so as to avoid turning your soul into a squirrel in a revolving cage. . . . Still, it is not for me to interfere with the destiny of others and, if you will you will.'

Ford treats the problem as one of arbitrary choice: he had an old-fashioned idea of the Civil Service, as an elegant profession for a gentleman, and had no conception at all of the rationalized bureaucratic machine which it had become, within a short time and under the direction of that very department of the Treasury in which I served. As for his warnings about the desiccating effect of metaphysics and psychology, these sprang, not so much from Ford's consideration for me as from his antipathy to any kind of logical thought—even the logic of ordinary consistency in conversation and reminiscence. In this same letter, for example, he writes:

'You are unjust, rather, to Conrad. . . . He is a Pole, and, being a Pole is Elizabethan. He has done an immense deal for the Nuvvle in England—not so much as I, no doubt, but then that was not his job, and he is of the generation before mine. I learned all I know of Literature from Conrad—and England has learned all it knows of Literature from me. . . . I do not mean to say that Conrad did not learn a great deal from me when we got going; I dare say he learned more actual stuff of me than I of him. . . . But, but for him, I should have been a continuation of DANTE GABRIEL ROSSETTI—and think of the loss that would have been to you young things. . . . And think what English Literature would be without Conrad and James. . . . There would be nothing!'

(19:9:20)

This might be read as humorous bluffing, but not by anyone who knew Ford. He did actually believe that he had been an essential link in the evolution of modern English literature, finding his place somewhere between Conrad and James, but extending past Conrad to 'you young things'. That Conrad owed a lot to Ford, no one who knows the facts can deny; but Conrad owed still more to James himself; and as for James, he had something like pity for the efforts of the 'monstrous Master Mariner', as he called Conrad; and I suspect that he looked on Ford as one of the young things, and in no sense a coeval.

This falsity in Ford's claim, too obvious to be hidden from even friendly eyes, affected my reception of his advice. I was never actually in any danger of undergoing the hardening process, or of taking Henri Beyle as a model. I did not, that is to say, accept the view that an interest in metaphysics or 'the Serious Book' necessarily meant a loss of humaneness, or even of humour. Ford had such an exclusive feeling for the novel that he was willing to 'ram' anything into it: the form could be inflated until it absorbed the man. My view was rather that the man, the person, came first; and that it was immaterial in what particular form he expressed himself—poem, novel, essay, metaphysics or criticism—so long as he remained true to himself and to his aesthetic principles. The choice of form had to be determined by his circumstances.

Such, at any rate, was my decision. I remained in the Civil Service and my novels remained unfinished or unwritten. I did not dismiss the possibility of returning to the form if at any time I should become free; but I still wonder in what direction the novel can evolve. After Henry James came James Joyce—a stylistic liberation of some significance, but a monument to this same sense of frustration. Is there anything else that comes within comparable range of James? There is an immense amount of clever and condign writing, but compared with the tradition of Flaubert and Henry James, it is either primitive or derivative. Nowhere does the novel exist as a vital art form—as anything but entertainment or reportage (including in this latter term the reportage of the novelist's own ideas and sentiments). It comes nearest to the real thing in certain 'romans policiers'—Simenon in France, Edward Anderson in America, Peter Cheney here, but what a gulf, nevertheless, between *The Golden Bowl* and *Dames Don't Care!*

The decision I had taken meant that such time as I could reserve was to be devoted to the poem and the critical essay. The poem, according to my belief and practice, would come when it would: its generation being a mystery of the unconscious, no precautions that I could take would increase my product by one line. I do not dismiss the possibility of inducing poetic metaphors and images by assiduous exercise: the very act of writing and rhyming is a call-boy to the unconscious. But for such leisurely means I equally had no time. The critical essay is different. One can accumulate notes and ideas over three or four weeks, in trains and buses no less than in the blessed evening hours; and

then, when the moment is ripe, a week-end will suffice for the
first draft—did suffice for me. Most of my books were built up
in this manner, essay by essay. An exception, like *The Green Child*,
owes its existence to an unexpected break in the routine; this
book I am writing now, to another.

Luckily I have the ability to write without fuss or hesitation,
rapidly and enjoyably. I concentrate quickly and in almost any
surroundings. Without this faculty, I could not have accomplished
half my writings. Indeed, any difficulty in composition would
probably have been fatal, for the creative impulse dies if not given
a quick chance to materialize, and a continuous sense of frustration
is finally too much for the spirit. A sense of frustration was not to
be avoided, even in my case; my path is strewn with abandoned
projects, with poems damned by not one, but a procession of
persons on business from Porlock, with plays which never got
beyond the first act and 'ideas for a book' which faded in some
attic of the mind. But I have never faltered and never idled, and
within certain limits I have written what I wanted to write—not
as much as I would like to have written and not necessarily what I
would have written for my own pleasure.

The main cause of my frustration was after three years suddenly alleviated. One day, in the normal course of my duties, a
letter came up for the signature of the Controller of Establish-
ments which stated that My Lords of the Treasury were pleased
to sanction two additional assistant-keeperships in the Victoria
and Albert Museum. In a flash I saw a way of escape. If I could
be transferred from the Treasury to one of these new posts, then
I should be doing work which was not only congenial, but which
would surely allow me, far more easily than my duties at the
Treasury, to pursue my literary career. I took the letter in for the
signature of my chief. As his pen hovered over the sheet of paper,
I blurted out my request. The scene that followed was friendly but
embarrassing, but my request was granted. With the blessing of
the Treasury I went to interview the Director of the Museum,
and within a very short time I was appointed to one of the
vacancies.

From a worldly point of view my action was irresponsible.
I not only sacrificed a considerable part of my income (£150 out
of £400), but I threw away one of the most coveted positions in
the whole Civil Service. But I have never regretted my action.

It is impossible to say what would have happened to me if I had stayed in the Treasury. I might have risen gradually in the hierarchy of that office, or I might have been transferred to some less onerous post in a subordinate department. In any case, the work would not have been congenial, whereas at the Museum I spent ten years full of interest and enlightenment.

I was posted to the Department of Ceramics, a subject about which I then knew nothing. The museums in this country do not normally require any previous expert knowledge as a qualification for a junior post, and though this sometimes shocks our foreign colleagues, who enter their museums armed with doctorates in the history of art, my experience convinces me that the English system is right. A theoretical knowledge is almost entirely irrelevant to the practical work of a museum, and efficiency in theory, which is based on the faculties of memory and reasoning, may give a quite erroneous value to an individual who, in his practical work, must rely on his sensibility and his organizing skill. Sensibility is innate, and it is entirely reasonable that some evidence of possessing this quality should be given by the candidate; it is possible that administrative ability might also be tested in some way. But the real school is the museum itself, and training can only begin with the handling of the actual works of art.

These works, in my case, might not seem to possess much significance in the history of art, and it is, of course, true that the masterpieces of the potter or the glass-blower cannot be compared with those of the painter or sculptor. But I soon discovered that the humblest and least conscious work of art may be more representative of its period than the grandiose masterpiece, which is so often encumbered with irrelevant ideological motives. It depends to a considerable extent on the period. There is practically no aesthetic difference between a Sung vase and a Sung painting; the difference between a maiolica plate and a painting by Piero della Francesca is immense. But even in this Italian example, there is a mutual relationship, and I should suspect a sensibility that made an absolute distinction between them. Certainly no such distinction was made during the Renaissance, and the tradition that Raphael and other masters did not disdain to paint maiolica is only consonant with the whole spirit of the age. In any case, I found the close and systematic study of one branch of art an ideal approach to an understanding of art in general; and ceramics has this unrivalled advantage—its material has rarely suffered by the passage of time: it does not decay or fade, and one has the knowledge that the object presents to its present-day beholder exactly the same basis of sensation that it had for the artist who made it.

Ideal as my new occupation was from the general point of view of interest and congeniality, it had an unsuspected disadvantage from the point of view of an author: it was *too* interesting. It was not a mechanical activity which absorbed only my physical energy and left my mind free. It was in itself a branch of critical activity, and it was quite impossible to make any clear distinction between the work done in official hours and the work done outside. The history and the criticism of art, in which I was involved as part of my duties, merged naturally into the history and criticism of literature, and both took their place in any general conception of culture. It was because I could not make any distinction between these two activities that I inevitably became a critic of art; and since the criticism of art has been relatively neglected in this country since the time of Ruskin, I found plenty to occupy my attention.

The less applied forms of literary activity were bound to suffer, and I was again continually under the necessity of abandoning projects that had no vocational or economic urgency. I still cling to the belief that I was nevertheless expressing myself, and that even art criticism is a literary form. But modern art criticism, which has to abjure the impressionistic graces of a Ruskin or a Pater, which has the historical task of incorporating in art criticism the revolutionary discoveries of anthropology and psychology, must cope with intractable material. Precision and efficiency necessarily take the place, in a modern prose style, of euphony and symphonic rhythm. These new qualities are aesthetic too; but as in modern architecture, the public is slow to recognize them.

I shall describe later the aesthetic philosophy which I gradually evolved as a result of my study of art. That philosophy is an existential one: it is the expression of all my faculties, of the whole consciousness of a living organism; but it was immensely strengthened by this practical application to the material of art. For ten years I was in daily communication with the symbols in which, throughout the centuries, this philosophy has been embodied.

I ended, therefore, by following Coleridge's advice; but Coleridge never followed his own advice and he did not realize the measure of renunciation it entailed. It is perfect advice if a writer is content to express himself in minuscule; but it would not have suited Coleridge's friend Wordsworth—that 'one extraordinary man' he himself excepted—not Milton, nor Shakespeare; for their major effects the whole stage of life had to be cleared of impedimenta, even impedimenta domestica.

This last phrase suggests that I have avoided one of the issues. Coleridge, with Christian largess, assumes that the writer has a family. It is true that the crisis which I faced, and which every writer without independent means has to face, is considerably reduced in acuteness if marriage and its consequences are renounced. The artist, if he is to devote himself entirely to his art, should be celibate; not only celibate, but monastic. The lives of most artists who have married end in tragedy or bitterness; but the lives of the unmarried artists are not noticeably happier. If we take the two extremes of Tolstoy and Baudelaire—one almost patriarchal and the other Ishmaelish—they will be found to produce, by different means, the same miseries. Indeed, the problem of celibacy or marriage, of life with women or life without them, is probably quite subordinate, or at most contributory, to the fundamental problem. There is in the artist a psychological condition that is favourable to the functioning of the creative imagination: it is a certain condition of dialectical stress or tension. Such a condition is not likely to arise from a life of placid contentment. The greatest enemy of art is, alas, happiness. I do not know enough about the lives of great composers; but I can think of no great poet or painter whose life can be described as predominantly happy. If they achieve happiness at some stage, it will be found that the works of art they then produce could not have existed without a precedent period of stress; that actually their best work is a direct product of such periods. Naturally, by stress I do not necessarily mean a condition of open distress: the tension, that is to say, may be hidden in the unconscious.

From a vague awareness of this truth, a wrong conclusion is sometimes reached about the relations of the artist to society. It is pointed out that some of the most artistically productive periods in history—the Renaissance in Italy, the Elizabethan period in England—have been periods of war, tyranny or social unrest. It is true that such social conditions may affect the life and happiness of the individual artist; but it is false logic to assume that they are the only or a necessary cause of cultural activity. The relation of the artist to society, and of culture to civilization, is extremely complicated. It is probably much more a question of mental reactions to moral and psychological pressures and releases than of any external conflict. The artist himself prefers peace: peace which allows him to concentrate his powers and hold his audience. There are enough wars within his own mind to occupy his attention; and the dialectical contradiction between this inner stress and an outward calm is probably the condition most favourable to the creative impulses. A study of English literature between 1815 and 1915 would support this view.

To return to my subject: the marriage of a poet cannot be judged by the plus or minus of happiness which it brings, because happiness is inessential. What is far more important is that the poet should experience certain depths of feeling in the natural man which can only come from marriage and parentage. However vicarious the imagination, in its external visitations, it can never recover the elemental emotions which are those of the husband and wife, the father and mother. And what have these elemental emotions to do with the nature of art? Only this: before there can be art there must, as Rilke said, be memories, and before there can be memories there must be experiences. It is not so much on the variety of experience that the poet depends, but on certain essential experiences which have depths: the innocent eye of childhood, the blurred ecstasies of adolescence, the intense joy of love, the shock of death; and to these I would add the experience of marriage.

Each artist must find an individual solution of the dilemma which is implicit in his acceptance of society. To a few who are favoured by tradition and wealth the solution may come easily; they have probably nothing to fear but the uneasy conscience of the rentier and the envy of their colleagues. But for most artists some form of sacrifice or renunciation is involved: they must surrender their isolation; they must subordinate their artistic ideals to the baser demands of entertainment. Or they may prefer to keep their ideals and curtail their ambitions. But this alternative is apt to bring with it an occasional bitterness of the spirit. One willingly throws ballast overboard so long as it consists of replaceable things; but when we come to the children of our imagination, then the hand is reluctant.

9

Profitable Wonders

This story of the awakening of my mind has reached a point at which I can conveniently break it off; the story is not finished, nor, I hope, will it ever be finished so long as I retain the faculties of perception and reasoning. But before I bring the narrative to an end there are certain influences which ought to be acknowledged. They had not been mentioned before, either because they are the kind of influences which any educated man may be assumed to have undergone, or because they are influences which have been so completely absorbed that, like mother's milk, they have been forgotten. There may be still others which one would like to forget because they have been outgrown and discarded. These, too, should be recorded.

Among the influences which are not only assumed, but absorbed to the point of being no longer conscious, are the English Bible and Shakespeare. I am glad that I was born soon enough to be brought up as a matter of course on the Bible. It was given to us as scripture, but we absorbed it, unconsciously, as art; and it stands in almost the same relation to English prose as Shakespeare does to our poetry. I say 'almost' because, in the first place, 'the voice that roars along the bed of Jewish song' is not a prosaic voice, even in our translation. This is not the place for observations on the nature of English prose style—I have made them elsewhere; but from the Bible there derives one special kind of exalted prose—the prose of Taylor, Browne and Ruskin—which is far removed from the functional prose of Swift and Maine. But this exaltation, Oriental or Hebraic in its source, is crystallized in the primitive grandeur of the Authorized Version, and thence infuses the imaginative genius of our race. An exotic element, it is not the less evident, for those who have ears to hear, than the visible traces of Syrian and Byzantine art that lie scattered across our country, even as far as the wastes of Northumbria and the Hebrides.

I do not wish to imply that the English Bible should be treated only as a literary document; nor that its influence on me was entirely, or even predominantly, artistic. Nevertheless, the effect of the Bible in itself is not in any profound sense religious: it is an epic story and not a manual of devotion. But as an epic, a religious epic, it is what we call in our poor critical jargon 'a human document'. Such episodes as the legend of Joseph, the afflictions of Job, and scores of others, not to mention the Passion of Jesus, work upon the primary emotions and make us acquainted with the full pathos and tragic significance of our human destiny. When all religions have passed, or become transformed, or merged, this book will still remain as the Bible of Mankind.

I cannot claim, like some people, to have lived continuously with Shakespeare's works. He is, for me, the greatest of the romantic poets, and the justification for all time of the romantic theory of art. For that reason alone he occupies an essential place in my intellectual world. But perhaps just because he is so completely romantic, he is so didactically negative. Not even the German critics have been able to reconstruct Shakespeare's 'Weltanschauung'. We can find in Shakespeare half a dozen separate philosophies of life, according to the mood and predilection with which we read him. It is true that there is what has been called an 'essential' Shakespeare, but there is no clue to it except what another poet can provide by his sympathy and intuition. Shakespeare was everyman—that is an acceptable commonplace. But the capacity to be everyman—that is only given to the poet, and it is only in so far as one has felt the poetic ecstasy in one's self that one has penetrated to any idea of the essential Shakespeare.

Shakespeare has been for me, therefore, the essential poet, 'self-school'd, self-scann'd, self-honour'd, self-secure'. I have turned to him whenever I wished to renew my sense of what was primordial in the nature of the poet. He would not, of course, have held this peculiar position in my regard, and in the regard of all romantics, if he had not been the supreme English poet—supreme, I mean, in the actual texture of his verse. It is possible to argue about

Shakespeare's philosophy, or his dramatic structure, or even about his identity; but the verbal beauty of his language is unquestionably supreme. The only question is whether this supremacy, this 'loftiest hill' which

> *Spares but the cloudy border of his base*
> *To the foil'd searching of mortality,*

has not so dominated English poetry that it has acted as an inhibition. The seventeenth century, which was too near to him, and the eighteenth which ignored him, escaped the dilemma; but from the time of the Romantic revival every poet has had to contend with Shakespeare's stylistic influence, and submit to it or flee from it. The trouble is that Shakespeare's poetic diction is such a quintessence of the English language, that the poet can only escape from it into artificialities—the artificiality of Milton's latinity, of Wordsworth's 'common speech', of Browning's elliptic harshness. On the whole, it is better to acknowledge and accept his supremacy, as Keats and Shelley and Tennyson did: in that way there are variations to be won. The only honest alternative is one which has been attempted by several poets of our own generation: to sacrifice the music for the sake of the poem's immediacy or intensity.

Others have written so fully on Shakespeare and the Bible that there is nothing new to say at this late day. The best tribute to the Bible is Ruskin's, who was himself obsessed by this influence; and it is to Ruskin that I would now like to pay my tribute. When I first began to read Ruskin, about 1909 or 1910, his tradition was still alive. There were still many people who had known him personally, who were in effect his disciples, and who regarded him as a seer and a prophet. This Ruskin fellowship had inevitably created a reaction, and a slump in his reputation set in. The second-hand bookshops were flooded with his works, and one could pick up excellent editions at sixpence or a shilling a volume. There is still, I believe, a Ruskin Society, but though some faithful followers survive among our septua- and octogenarians, his readers must now be few, and his influence practically extinct. It is, I am convinced, a temporary eclipse. He presents two aspects for our continued consideration: his thought and his style; and it is of his style that I am most confident. It has a wide range, from exact objective description to the emotive evocation of beauty and pathos, and it is always superb. It was another great prose artist, in another language, who was to pay this style the highest tribute—the tribute of transplantation. Marcel Proust applies the style to a very different material, but though it then strikes such an individual note in French literature, it is very familiar to anyone accustomed to the rhythms of Ruskin's style. What is surprising about this style is not its simplicity, which one might have expected from a man so obsessed with the English Bible, but its variety and complexity, its intellectual control of the sensuous verbal elements. A sentence like the following, necessarily long, has the elaborate phrasing of a musical cadenza:

'Every blade of grass burned like the golden floor of heaven, opening in sudden gleams as the foliage broke and closed above it, as sheet-lightning opens in a cloud at sunset; the motionless masses of dark rock—dark though flushed with scarlet lichen, casting their quiet shadows across its restless radiance, the fountain underneath them filling its marble hollow with blue mist and fitful sound; and over all the multitudinous bars of amber and rose, the sacred clouds that have no darkness, and only exist to illumine, were seen in fathomless intervals between the solemn and orbed repose of the stone pines, passing to lose themselves in the last, white, blinding lustre of the measureless line where the Campagna melted into the blaze of the sea.'

An age devoted to functional values cannot appreciate such prose; but there is more than one kind of prose, and not to respond to Ruskin betrays a sensibility as limited as that of the modern dilettante who cannot enjoy the paintings of Poussin or Claude—or those of Turner, to give a more exact parallel. But to appreciate the range of Ruskin's style, a passage of the kind I have quoted should be compared with the invective of *Fors Clavigera* or the simple 'talk' of *Praeterita*. It may be that Ruskin himself despised his artistic genius ('I don't care whether you have enjoyed them [his books] or not. Have they done you any good?') and at one time he was cynical enough to use his evocative powers as so much stylistic gilding for the ethical pill: he deliberately went over some of his books and worked in purple passages to make them more attractive to the public. But Ruskin is not the first nor the last artist to despise (or fear) his artistic powers; the main thing is that he used them, and that by the exercise of a little patience we can still read with enjoyment what he wrote with inspiration.

The patience is necessary, not merely because Ruskin is an irregular and rambling writer, but also because his ideas are a mass of contradictions, perversities, irrelevancies and truths. I shall not refer to his ethical nor (what almost comes to the same thing) his economic ideas, though these are by no means out of date or visionary; for by the time I had reached Ruskin I had also reached Morris and Marx, Kropotkin and Carpenter, and their political writings made more impression upon me because they were more rational and more realistic. But Ruskin's writings on art were a different matter. Before I could read German (which I learned between 1922 and 1925), Ruskin, with the exception of Baudelaire, was the only critic of art that I could at once read and respect. People still do not realize how primitive the criticism of art is in this country—not merely as a science, which it can never, strictly speaking, become, but as a logical activity. Art as a mode of knowledge with its own epistemology; art as a language with its own linguistics; the psychology of art which must precede any philosophy of art—all these are aspects of the subject which were unknown, unthought of, at the time of Ruskin's death. But when Ruskin himself first approached the subject, the situation was infinitely worse: art criticism was nothing but descriptive impressionism; and impressionism is too flattering a word for what was little more than an account of the sentimental associations aroused by a work of art. There had been a certain amount of philosophical generalization about art—the best of it, represented by Reynolds, being tempered by practical common sense; but Ruskin was the first critic to insist on a definition, not merely of philosophical terms like 'truth' and 'beauty', but of psychological concepts like 'colour', 'space', 'imagination', and 'expression'; and he made some attempt to relate the aesthetic activity to life as a whole. Ruskin did not evolve any comprehensive or coherent theory of art; and he is usually treated with contempt by modern aestheticians. But if one is not a system-maker; if one seeks for truth of perception rather than logical coherence, then there is more to be learned from Ruskin than from any previous writer on the subject, with the possible exception of Hegel; and it is not until we come to Nietzsche, Croce and Bergson that we once again pick up the threads of vital thought. Croce would rather trace his affinities to Vico, Hegel and De Sanctis; but for all his contempt of Ruskin, it is Ruskin's theory of expression, his theory of art as language, that come nearer to Croce's aesthetic than any preceding treatment of the subject.

If we turn from theory to historical interpretation, the greatness of Ruskin is all the more apparent. The Gothic Revival was almost a spent force when Ruskin began to publish *The Stones of Venice* in 1851 (it was unfortunately to continue as an ecclesiastical habit); but that Revival had been largely an artificial taste, a sophisticated reaction to an equally artificial classicism. It was Ruskin who first got under the stones and revealed the spirit of Gothic, who first interpreted the social economy of the Middle Ages in the terms of this spirit, and who analysed the characteristics of the art which expressed this spirit. His famous chapter on 'The Nature of Gothic' still remains a masterpiece of generalization based on the exact knowledge of particulars—the greatest essay in art criticism in our language. Nearly a hundred years have elapsed since Ruskin studied this subject, and we now have a much greater fund of historical and archaeological facts; but in all these years we have not advanced on Ruskin's love and understanding of the art which, for two or three brief centuries, was the supreme expression of the transcendental values of the northern races. If we ever recover our sense of these values—and we must recover them if we are to produce another great art style—we shall return to Ruskin for inspiration and guidance.

William Morris, whose name I have mentioned and would like to mention again, came as an appendix to Ruskin. A disciple of Ruskin's, he had qualities which made him in many ways a more sympathetic figure; but these were qualities of his personality rather than of his writing: his robustness, directness, and practical energy. Though in my youth I read *News from Nowhere* and *The Dream of John Ball* with enthusiasm, and though I have always felt that Morris is a valuable connecting link between art and socialism, his predominant ideas have been a hindrance rather than a help. He can confess on one and the same page his hatred of modern civilization and his inability to read economics. His 'practical' socialism was only possible as an ideal because he ignored the major problems of the age: the problems created by the growth of populations and the development of mass production; the disequilibrium due to the uneven distribution of natural resources; and many other related factors. His ideals were retrospective: he had tried to read Marx, but he did not realize that the process of history is always dialectical—a synthetic leap forward from existing contradictions—and that we must not scrap our machinery, but perfect and control it; we must not assume that art and machinery are mutually exclusive, but experiment until we discover a machine art. Always we must go forward with the instruments which evolution or invention has placed in our hands, and if only we had intelligence enough to establish our principles and sensibility enough to express them, then a new art might develop in a new world. We have now lived long enough to be aware of the first signs of such an art.

The theoretical interest in art first aroused in me by Ruskin and Morris eventually led by devious paths to Croce's *Aesthetic*, and from that book, aided by its historical survey of the subject, I branched off into an exploration of a whole province of human thought—a province remarkable for its wastes and scrub rather than for any fertile ground. Croce's book was an essential stage in my development, but I never became a Crocean—some innate empiricism left me indifferent or uncomprehending before his idealism. The more I tended to accept his intuitional theory of art, the more baffled I became by his critical judgments, which seemed to proceed from a narrow classicism and even from a moral priggishness; until I concluded that he had always been a victim of his own environment. But Bergson, to whom I inevitably came, was much more to my taste, and his *Creative Evolution* is certainly one of the books that have had a decisive influence, not merely on the direction of my intellectual growth, but also on its quality. Like most people, I was to outgrow Bergson (though never to become entirely faithless), but when I read him at the age of twenty-five, it was with a passionate absorption which I was never to recover, never to devote to any other philosopher. The explanation is probably simple. The loss of religious faith, which I have described in an earlier chapter, had left me with little more than a mechanistic interpretation of the universe—a bleak rationalism which was not consistent with my romantic temperament. Bergson, keeping within the world of scientific fact—indeed, drawing all his evidence from that world—offered an interpretation of the universe that was neither mechanistic nor finalist—that provided a way out of the closed system of predestined fact. He showed that the system contains a principle of change: that simply to exist is to change: that to change is to mature, and that to mature is to create ever new elements in the universe. He gave validity to such terms as consciousness and intuition—terms upon which, I already then perceived, any philosophy of art must rely. (I should perhaps say any philosophy of romanticism, but that is a distinction which, as I shall presently suggest, makes no difference.) 'Art lives on creation and implies a latent belief in the spontaneity of nature.' Sentences like this showed that Bergson himself was aware that art had some evidence to offer for his theory; and when he comes to define intuition, by which he means 'instinct that has become disinterested, self-conscious, capable of reflecting upon its object and of enlarging it indefinitely', he uses the aesthetic faculty as a proof that such a process is possible. 'Our eye perceives the features of the living being, merely as assembled, not as mutually organized. The intention of life, the simple movement that runs through the lines, that binds them together and gives them significance, escapes it. This intention is just what the artist tries to regain, in placing himself back within the object by a kind of sympathy, in breaking down, by an effort of intuition, the barrier that space puts up between him and his model.'*

Passages like this in *Creative Evolution* and in other works of Bergson's made me wish that he would one day give us his own Aesthetic, but though he continued to throw intermittent lights on the subject, especially in his *Deux sources de la morale et de la religion*, that desired work remained unwritten. Perhaps it would not have been adequate: the material upon which any satisfactory aesthetic should be based has, with recent advances in anthropology and psychology, become extremely complex, and it will need a youthful energy to cope with it. Not that Bergson's mind was clouded in his later years. The book which I have just mentioned, which was published in 1932, is still as clear and as profound as the great works that made his reputation. The tide of fashion has receded from this figure; but whatever new idols have been found seem to me to owe something to Bergson.

I fancy that the rise of Freud's influence had a good deal to do with the decline of Bergson's. Not that they are at all comparable—one is a metaphysician using scientific material, the

* Translated by Arthur Mitchell, Ph.D. (London: Macmillan, 1914).

other a scientist who occasionally trespasses, not always success-fully, into metaphysics. But Freud's hypothesis of the unconscious, a hypothesis which he has established by scientific method and demonstrated by therapeutic practice, is so revolutionary in its implications that it makes a revision of our philosophical and moral concepts a first necessity, and that revision affects the very terms, such as consciousness and instinct, upon which Bergson's metaphysical structure depends. I began to read Freud as soon as the translations of his works appeared in this country, and it at once became evident to me that my own particular sphere of aesthetic criticism would henceforth have to revolve on a new axis. The extent to which I was alarmed may be judged from an article on 'Psycho-analysis and the Critic' which appeared in the *Criterion* in January, 1925; and my *Collected Essays* show, for anyone who has the interest to trace their chronological develop-ment, the increasing influence of Freud's psychology upon my critical method. Even before I read Freud, I tended to probe beneath the surface of the work of art, my conviction being that the work of art is either an objective phenomenon which we accept integrally and sensuously and therefore without intellectual understanding; or that alternatively it demands for its under-standing, not merely a measured view of its external aspects, but also a complete analysis of the circumstances in which it came into existence. This latter type of criticism I have called genetic, and it may, if so desired, be separated from aesthetic criticism. But an adequate criticism must include both methods, for we must understand, not only form, rhythm, harmony, composition, tex-ture, handling, etc., but also imagery, allegory, analogy, motiva-tion, social significance, and many other aspects of the work of art to which psychology alone can offer the right approach.

I shall not say anything more about Freud's influence, because it is still active, and psycho-analysis itself is by no means a subject that can yet be clearly focused. I have used Freud's name too exclusively: I prefer his method and his general outlook, but I am not an uncritical disciple. I believe that Roland Dalbiez has given a fair and objective estimate of his position in *La méthode psychoanalytique et la doctrine freudienne*; and I believe that some of Freud's errant disciples, particularly Jung and Trigant Burrow, are nearer than their master to certain aspects of the truth.

I began these random notes with the English Bible and have ended with Freud. Influences should by nature be solemn and impressive; it is only when we come to speak of preferences that we can bring forward minor figures. Many of my preferences should by now be obvious. Books that have influenced us, even decisively, may now gather dust on our shelves, as Croce's and Bergson's do on mine. But our preferences are in continual use, a bright part of our equipment. I confess that there are very few books which come into this category in my case. I have already spoken of some of my favourite poets: I return to Donne, Blake, Coleridge and Hopkins most frequently, and never tire of them. Shelley and Whitman I read at longer intervals, but then fairly intensively; and Shakespeare himself comes into this division. I have refrained from speaking of Wordsworth, partly because I have written a separate book about him, partly because he is a little too near to me. We both spring from the same yeoman stock of the Yorkshire dales, and I think I have a certain 'empathetic' understanding of his personality which gives a sense of betrayal to anything I write about him. If I do not write more fully about him now, it is not because I forget how much his poetry has meant to me.

It would be vain and superfluous to pass in review all the poets whose work has, at some time or other, stirred my imagination, or even to trace the mutations of their appeal. But there is one type of book which is perhaps exceptional. It is not easy to classify, but somewhere within its shifting outlines it includes the prose-form I most admire and would like to emulate. It is represented by Sterne's *Sentimental Journey* and De Vigny's *Servitude et Grandeur militaires*; Meérimée's *Carmen* and De la Motte-Fouqué's *Undine*; Mörike's *Mozart auf der Reise nach Prag* and Jacobsen's *Niels Lynne*. Usually it has an historical incident or episode as its basis, but it may be a pure phantasy, like Alain-Fournier's *Le grand Meaulnes*. It is short, it is deliberate; at once realistic and imaginative, objective and reflective. It avoids the psychological approach of the novel and is more than a short story. When it has a moral or satirical motive, like Voltaire's *Candide*, it is sometimes called the *conte philosophique*. The philosophy, however, is best left to the inference of the reader.

Such writings are not constructive art forms: they have neither the organization of the novel nor the simple unity of the short story. They are rather projections of an idea, of an incident, of a phantasy; intellectually conceived, but exhibiting the fresh texture of a personal style and the brightness of a concrete imagination. It is impossible to justify my preference for this genre on any theoretical grounds: I fancy that it is determined simply by the material conditions which make it the form most easily within my grasp, both as a reader and as a writer. Certainly it is not that the informality of such writings is in itself a romantic preference: romanticism is not essentially a formal question, but something much more profound. Among my strongest personal preferences are poets like Arnold and Hopkins, novelists like Flaubert and Henry James, and painters like Poussin and Seurat, in all of whom formality is almost an obsession. The constructive movement in modern architecture, sculpture and painting is again of a formal purity not excelled in any classical period; and yet it is an essentially romantic art, or I would not have spent so much of my energy in its defence. Le Corbusier, Brancusi, and Ben Nicholson are romantic artists; but I would make the same claim for Luciano di Laurana, Bernini, and Piero della Francesca. Romanticism and classicism are defined, neither by a period nor by a style, but by a psychological attitude to the process of artistic creation—on the one side inspiration, daring and originality; on the other, derivation, conformity and timidity.

PART FOUR

A Dearth of Wild Flowers

I

Under the Hill

More than forty years passed before I could return to the scenes of my childhood. I then found a house—Sterne would have called it a 'philosophical cottage', but it is about twice the size of Shandy Hall—situated two and a half miles to the south-east of the Farm, on the other side of that long ridge from which the windows of Stamper's Farm had once sent out their flashing signals. This ridge, known as Cauklass Bank, lies like a great green caterpillar in the basin of the Vale, and along its top runs a wide track, some three miles long. The caterpillar eats its way towards Gilling Gap and Coxwold in the west, as if trying to escape from the basin, its tail still trailing in Ness, a hamlet where as a child I had bought my 'goodies'. But, alas, the sweet shop has gone, with much else from memory's bright inventory.

To reach Stonegrave from the Farm you must pass through the village of Nunnington, where I received my first schooling, and then ascend an ancient avenue of limes and sycamores, nearly half a mile in length. On reaching the top of the bank (as hills are called here), you will suddenly seem to be at the still centre of the world. Cauklass (the name being a corruption of caulk leys, or chalk lands), is a hill 'celebrated both for the salubrity of its air, and the beautiful views which it commands'. So wrote the Reverend Thomas Alexander Browne, curate of Nunnington, in 1824, and his further description of this place, to become my familiar haunt, must be quoted:

'The surface, before the inclosure took place, was covered with a strong bent, a kind of short, coarse, elastic grass, similar to that on the training ground, Hambleton, and being a mile or more in extent was formerly used, occasionally, for a similar purpose; and at some distant period, as appears from the old map and plan, was a race-course; at the western extremity of which, near Stonegrave, was erected a stand. This course has run parallel to, if not in the very line of, the present avenue of aged firs, which crowns the summit of the hill, and forms so conspicuous an object, in whatever direction it is approached.'*

Browne continues his enthusiastic description of Cauklass, which, he says, being situated between two lovely vales and commanding one of the most beautiful and extensive prospects in the neighbourhood, need not shrink from a comparison with the artificial beauties of the grounds at Castle Howard, Gilling and Duncombe Park. 'From hence,' he boasts, 'on a clear day, may be seen distinctly no less than twenty-two towns, villages, and hamlets, and sixteen churches . . . These views are noticed in the third Canto of Mrs. Dunlop's poem, entitled Edmund of Ryedale. . . .'

Stonegrave, to which I came in September 1949, is situated on the steeper southern slope of Cauklass—a small but neat village, says Browne, 'so completely hid in approaching it from the north, that the traveller stands on the very precipice that immediately overlooks it, before he is aware of its presence. Here, sheltered from the northern blast, and, as it were nestling, and seeking protection under its friendly bank, may each inhabitant feelingly acknowledge the truth and beauty of those celebrated lines of Goldsmith:

> *Dear is that home to which his soul conforms,*
> *And dear that hill which shields him from the storms,*
> *And as a child, when scaring sounds molest,*
> *Clings close and closer to his mother's breast,*
> *So the loud tempest, and the whirlwind's roar,*
> *But bind him to his native mountain more.'*

* *Historia Rievallensis: containing the history of Kirkby Moorside, and an account of the most important places in its vicinity; together with brief notices of the more remote or less important ones. To which is prefixed a dissertation on the animal remains and other curious phenomena, in the recently discovered cave at Kirkdale.* By the Rev. W. Eastmead, author of *Observations on Human Life*, and Honorary Member of the Yorkshire, Hull, and Whitby, Literary and Philosophical Societies. London and York, 1824.

The Rev. Thomas Alexander Browne contributed to this volume the articles on Nunnington, Stonegrave, Oswaldkirk, Gilling, and Slingsby.

In Domesday Stonegrave is spelt *Stanegrif*, or *Steingrif*, and there are several other variations in ancient documents, all of which show that the termination (like those of other places such as Mulgrave and Walsgrave) comes from the Saxon word *griff*, which Young, in his *History of Whitby*, defines as 'a dingle, or narrow valley, with a rocky fissure-like chasm at the bottom'. This is rather too extreme as a description of the site of Stonegrave, but the road that passes through the village is steep, and on its northern side is a vertical cliff, against which some of the cottages are built.

Apart from the church and the rectory, the village now consists of three farmsteads and fourteen cottages, with a total of about sixty inhabitants. A hundred years ago it was considerably larger —some houses have disappeared and those that remain are not so densely populated as they must have been in 1824—Browne relates the 'singular and amazing fact, that the late rector of Stonegrave, and his parish clerk, had the unusual number of fifteen children each; a singular and remarkable coincidence, which can scarcely be paralleled in the annals of any other parish in the kingdom'. In our own time no family has exceeded a third of that number, and one or two of the cottages are occupied by single people. The parish records show that in 1743 there were about 40 families in the parish; in 1764 33 families. In 1831 the population was 189; by 1881 it had sunk to 140, and in 1900 to 127 (26 houses). In 1931 the parish boundaries were redrawn, which probably accounts for the further drastic reduction in the number of inhabitants.

The shrinking population, apart from any decline in the Christian faith, led to a uniting of the benefices of Stonegrave and Nunnington in 1946. But the Stonegrave rectory had been abandoned as a rectory some fourteen years earlier and sold (with protests from the indignant ghosts of former rectors) to a Roman Catholic family, who had the tithe-barn, which had also served sometimes as a school, consecrated as a chapel. They repaired the house, but after a few years left it, and it was the second of its secular owners who sold it to me in 1949.

I must have been there as a child—I vaguely remember a tea-party on the lawn—and since the school at Nunnington served also this village, I must have known boys from Stonegrave. The house is about thirty-eight paces in length, with two shorter wings projecting to the north. This northern aspect is regular and even severe, but as soon as one emerges on the southern side it presents a very different face, long and even in elevation, but broken by twenty windows irregular in design and spacing. It is built of honey-coloured stone and roofed with the warm crimson pantiles characteristic of all the old houses in Ryedale.

We know almost exactly when it was built, or rebuilt, for it was a rector called James Worsley, appointed to the living in 1747, who had this done, presumably soon after his induction. That a rectory existed on the site before this is certain—parts of the present structure are earlier than 1747 and indeed there is ghostly evidence of two or three houses: the 'two wings towards the Town street', as they are called in a terrier of 1786, had then been recently added. But in the main the building is 'Queen Anne' in style, though 'Georgian' by date. It was erected of local stone by local masons, and differs little (save in size) from the nearby farm-houses of the same period. As the word indicates, as a 'rectory' it had since the Reformation been in the King's books, and in 1824 its value for taxation was £23 6s. 8d.

These details are perhaps of no great interest to the common reader, and my own concern is not with history or topography, but with personal and spiritual associations. It is sufficient to say that once I had seen (or revisited) the place, which was in the summer of 1948, my heart was set on possessing it; and though the negotiations were more prolonged than might have been anticipated, I did finally secure possession, and made such arrangements of my work and social obligations that I was able to live for at least half the days of the year in a house some 215 miles from London.

The village is small—but for the church it would be called a hamlet. It once had an inn, which to my delight I discovered was called 'The Wings of Liberty'. Small as the village is, its church has a recorded history that goes back to the eighth century. In 757 it is mentioned in a letter from Pope Paul I to Eadbert, King of Northumbria, in which the king is ordered, as he values his salvation, to restore the monasteries at Stonegrave, Coxwold and Jarrow to their rightful owners. Such a monastery was probably an outlying missionary post from Whitby where an abbey for monks and nuns had been founded by Oswy, king of Northumbria, in 658, in celebration of his victory over Penda, king of

Mercia. Saint Hilda was its first abbess, and the poet Caedmon, the earliest English Christian poet 'who sang the beginning of created things', became a monk there in Hilda's time. The Saxon cross now in the church is all that survives from the period before the Norman Conquest, and it may be a remnant of this first monastery.

This church dedicated to the Holy Trinity once had a wall-painting of 'Sta Maria Salome', and a chapel dedicated to Saint Lawrence. The twelfth-century arches are noble, and on the north side have alternate courses of light and dark stones, as in Durham Cathedral. There are two small but fine corbels, carved with stylized animal heads in the Hiberno-Saxon style, and round one of the scalloped capitals is a band of ornamental medallions in the Byzantine style; one of them depicts a mermaid upside down. The carver must have been interrupted in his work, for the series breaks off with an uncompleted design. There is much fine woodwork in the church, including a screen dated 1637, but all this and much else was displaced and reconstituted in the necessary but disastrous restoration of the church, which took place in 1862. Scraped and dressed, re-roofed and redeemed, it stands like the village church everywhere, a monument to an age of faith and a melancholy reminder of crafts now defunct.

The sense of the past invests the whole village, the church, and the house in which I now live. To succumb to this sense is sentimental, and can be destructive of a proper sense of the present, of reality. I, who cannot be accused of having no sense of the present —or indeed, of the future: have I not been identified with 'the Demon of Progress'?—indulge the sense of the past only by instinct, by some unconscious craving for equanimity, for compensation. In other countries—in Sweden, in Brazil, in British Columbia—I have found houses that are the perfection of modern taste, visual expressions of the abstract harmony and grace that I admire in the art of the present. I have tried to imagine life in such crystal cabinets, but I have not had the desire or the will to achieve it. The art of living is in this respect like any other art—it must be spontaneous if it is to be deeply enjoyed. Only organic processes are spontaneous, and what the intellect plans, logically and coherently, is never organic. The dweller in a crystal cabinet must from time to time flee to the primeval forests of Africa or to the Cyclades to fill his sensibility with a wild contrast. But between these extremes lies the vast conglomeration of our industrial civilization—a wilderness so arid and offensive that no organic life is possible within its limits. This civilization will either destroy itself or transform itself—at present it seems bent on self-destruction. Meanwhile either we are imprisoned (by economic necessity, it will be said, but also by our psychological obsessions) or we escape—into artificial wildernesses. A house in the country is not the only artificial wilderness: there are, if we can afford them, yachts and caravans, or, if we have a vocation, monasteries and colleges. Country houses are miniature monasteries, not perhaps much larger than Whitby in Saint Hilda's time; completely anachronistic, hated by the bureaucratic taxmen, resented even by the industrialized farmer, islands of green comfort in a land that slowly but inevitably lies fallow to the tractor and the bull-dozer. In the last ten years I have seen more than one beautiful country house razed to the ground, every stone and beam vanish, to be replaced by a timber-yard or a bacon-factory. There are still a sufficient number of quixotic Englishmen who will deny themselves all other pleasures so that they may for a few years live in these green oasic mansions; but it is not for long. The past has vanished and we are the last outposts of a civilization in retreat.

2

Kin to the Stone

This was a phrase used by one of the last of the moorland masons, to explain his addiction to a craft in which his sons would not follow him: he could not change because he and his like were 'kin to the stone'. Stone differs from brick and other building materials in that it is used in its natural state, quarried from the earth itself and 'dressed' by hand. Only wood can compete in naturalness, but it perishes too quickly if exposed, and easily catches fire. I have seen beautiful wooden houses in Western Canada and in Scandinavia, but they feel too impermanent, cabins for a brief stay on this earth. Wooden architecture has no visible history. As for bricks: the Egyptians and Assyrians made them because stones were so rare that they had to be reserved for the construction of temples and the carving of sacred images. Brick, in stone country like Yorkshire, Cumberland or the Cotswolds, is a shoddy intrusion.

I am stating a prejudice, for I must admit that when compelled to make the best of this material, as in Amsterdam and some of the cities of northern Germany, brick can be gracious and colourful: a pinchbeck substitute for golden stone, but still a matter of art. But it gives me no pleasure as a sheltering substance, as a shell within which to live and have my being. Always at home in stone country, I am vaguely ill at ease within a cold oven of baked bricks.

The landscape round Stonegrave is pocked with small quarries from which people have taken the stone to build their houses and churches. The modern quarry with its machinery is often an ugly scar on the hillside, but the old quarries were soon covered with undergrowth; bramble and hazel, and sometimes conifers find sufficient substance for root-hold. Most of the wild life that survives has found a refuge in these oases of the deserts made by the tractor.

The love of landscape must feed on intimacy as well as on magnitude: there must be a continual counterplay between the inscape of nature and its 'waking empire, wide as dreams'. Gerard Manley Hopkins, who invented the necessary word 'inscape', understood this perfectly, as perhaps only Traherne before him. In his Journal (May 9, 1871) there is a passage about bluebells which expresses this sense in utmost acuity: 'In the little wood opposite the light they stood in blackish spreads or sheddings like the spots on a snake. The heads are then like throngs and solemn in grain and grape-colour . . . The bluebells in your hand baffle you with their inscape, made to every sense: if you draw your fingers through them, they are lodged and struggle with the shock of wet heads; the long stalks rub and click and flatten to a fan on one another like [sic] your fingers themselves would when you passed the palms hard across one another, making a brittle rub and jostle like the noise of a hurdle strained by leaning against; then there is the faint honey smell and in the mouth the sweet gum when you bite them. But this is easy, it is the eye they baffle . . .'* There follows a minute description of the form of the bluebell, but my point has been made: the eye, in its near infinite range, must travel from the inscape of a flower, of a bird's feather, the rime on twigs or the skeleton of a leaf to the roll and rise, the imbricated nabs and scars of the distant moorland reaches. Mountains I have no love for; they are the accidents of nature, masses thrown up in volcanic agony. But moors and fells are moulded by gentle forces, by rain water and wind, and are human in their contours and proportions,† inducing affection rather than awe.

Nevertheless, the moors have sublimity, the sublimity Emily Brontë so beautifully celebrated. I shall speak about it in a later chapter, but here I am concerned with milder feelings. They begin

* *The Note-Books and Papers of Gerard Manley Hopkins.* Edited by Humphry House. Oxford, 1937, pages 145-6.

† Compare Wordsworth, *Topographical Description of the Country of the Lakes* (1820), conclusion:

'. . . a happy proportion of component parts is generally noticeable among the landscapes of the North of England; and, in this characteristic essential to a perfect picture, they surpass the scenes of Scotland, and, in a still greater degree, those of Switzerland.'

with the stone flags of the kitchen floor and passages of my house, each a pattern as beautiful as a painting by my friend Antonio Tapies; they extend to the external walls, abraded by rain and frost, sun-soaked and annealed to the hill behind the house. Each step in the garden, and beyond the macadamized scar of the public road, is like the shift of a slide in some magic lantern, revealing a new pattern of stones or grasses, of bark or leaves, bushes and gateposts, cart-tracks and hedges, till finally the eye lifts to the explosive splendour of the oaks and ashes, the beeches and elms. One immense poplar near my house, a cotton-wood if I am not mistaken, has all the calligraphic passion of a brush drawing by Sesshu. It is a Zen shrine to which I pay habitual homage, but already one large branch has fallen and it is a question whether the shrine will outlast its solitary worshipper.

I never exhaust the beauty of trees and woods. Careless of their species, I observe them as patterns against the sky, perhaps most beautiful when leafless. But though leafless they are never lifeless. The leaves are scarcely fallen when new buds begin shyly to press through the tender bark, like dark blebs of blood. There are three hundred and sixty-five days in a year and a tree has the same number of faces, or rather facets, for it is a composite picture of many minute changes.

Woods in this region are of every conceivable size and composition, short of the forest. Forests we had, like the famous Galtres Forest that stretched from the Howardian Hills to the walls of York, which was one of the haunts of Robin Hood—a conical hill at the northern extremity, at the foot of Whitestone Cliff, is still known as Robin Hood's Outlook. But now the only forests are those planted by the Forestry Commission. Sentimental naturalists despise these mustered ranks of conifers, but I confess I love to wander along their geometrical glades. I love the dark needle-soft aisles, where only fungi grow, and a fox spreads his pungent trail.

Perhaps only once or twice a year there is a chance to wander in these woods when sunlight has succeeded hoar frost or a light fall of snow, and the whole scene scintillates in electric brilliance. Very rarely such an event takes place in April, when the first pale green leaves have already unfolded, and the undergrowth is starred with primroses and violets. I am then reminded of something very unnatural but still poetic, those crystallized fruits we sometimes eat at Christmas; but these are clumsy compared with a frosted veil of snowflakes on a bed of violets.

One of the special joys in springtime is to wander along the banks of the Dove in Farndale. It is too far away to walk there from Stonegrave, so I leave the car in Low Mills some week-day (for alas, the sight is now so famous that thousands of people descend at week-ends from far and wide, so that we natives must turn 'wardens'). Here for miles along the banks of the beck blooms 'a crowd, a host, of golden daffodils'. Wordsworth's poem, and Dorothy's Journal,★ are so familiar that it is impossible to feel the same ecstasy that William and his sister experienced when they were first surprised by the sight of wild daffodils growing in a long belt along the shore of Grasmere. I have no wish to claim some superior virtue for the daffodils of Farndale, but there is a difference. Dorothy's daffodils 'grew among the mossy stones about and about them; some rested their heads upon these stones as on a pillow for weariness; and the rest tossed and reeled and danced, and seemed as if they verily laughed with the wind, that blew upon them over the lake; they looked so gay, ever glancing, ever changing'. William heightened these effects in his poem though I feel that some of the words he used (he added them in 1815, eight years after the poem was first composed) words like 'twinkle', 'sprightly', 'jocund', take away from the perfect natural-ness of Dorothy's description. The daffodils in Farndale are not jocund, nor sprightly, for they are not agitated by a wind blowing directly over a lake. The Dove flows through the loveliest of all these dales, and meanders through the meadows, now cutting steeply into its banks, now darting into a little grove of willows. The daffodils bloom on the sandy peninsulas made by the meandering beck. They may sometimes rest their heads on a stone, but more often shelter against the mossy stump of a willow, or bunch in the gnarled veins of exposed tree-roots. They are shy and small, their compact heads steady on rather sturdy stalks, and though in the sunshine they seem from a distance like a golden overflow from the beck, they are perfectly indigenous, one with the willows and the primroses, part of an Eden that should remain forever undesecrated.

From a distance these green and flowery dales are invisible in

★ *Journals of Dorothy Wordsworth.* Edited by E. de Selincourt. 2 vols. London, 1941. The Grasmere Journal (1802), 15th April.

the humped grandeur of the moors. The moors are one's natural love, the body to which trees and flowers, running becks and wooded dales, are but incidental, green wrinkles on an immense and ageless visage. The detail of a moor is as fascinating as any I know, but I admit its beauty is not easily transmitted. Apart from a few flowering grasses, some worts and celandines, the ground is densely thatched with heather, ling and bracken. Where a gill cuts into the slope, one may find rarer and more delicate ferns, but the overwhelming texture is rough and springy. The stems of a heather plant are metallic in their bronze or black glossiness, and with age aggregate into a dense network, against which the grouse shelter. The grass that grows in irregular patches between the clumps of heather is equally wiry, but the horned and black-faced moor-sheep find sustenance in it. These sheep are part of the landscape, self-subsisting in flocks that may number two or three hundred. They are rounded up and branded after lambing-time, but their numbers, and even their ownership, remain indefinite.

On the riggs or ridges of the moors are many howes, the barrows or burial mounds of the Celtic people who first inhabited this region in neolithic times. All of them have long since been excavated, mostly by amateurs about a hundred years ago. Canon Atkinson, in *Forty Years in a Moorland Parish*,★ which was first published in 1891, confesses to the examination of between eighty and one hundred of them, and though most of the mounds had been tampered with before his time, 'a blank day was a thing we hardly knew'. On one occasion he carried home 'no less than eight sepulchral vessels of one kind or another; and one of them was found on examination to contain, over and above the usual complement of bones, a very beautiful and finely polished axe-hammer of fine-grained granite'. Atkinson considered himself a scientific antiquarian, and was indeed a very cultured clergyman, but he relates how on one occasion his spade 'suddenly passed through no less than four thicknesses of "Ancient British" pottery', whereas his 'energetic friend with his trenchant shovel shore off at one stroke one third part of a rather large cinerary vase'. This particular howe had been disturbed before Atkinson began his digging, but he was lucky enough to find 'in the very middle of this medley of burnt human bone and sherds . . . a small

★ *Forty Years in a Moorland Parish.* By Rev. J. C. Atkinson, D.C.L. London (Macmillan), 1892.

delicately moulded and decorated vase of the type usually known as "incense cups" with its own proper deposit of incinerated remains and accompanying flints'. He then quotes the detailed description of it that he published in the *Gentleman's Magazine*: 'One inch in height and under one inch and a half in greatest diameter, of red ware, and scored with lines crossing one another diagonally, but so as to leave a space of three-eights of an inch all round, nearest to the bottom, untouched. It was placed mouth upwards, in the centre between four flints laid east, north, south, west, and comprising a very flat leaf-shaped arrow-point, another of the same description, but thicker, a thumb-flint or scraper, and some other implement; but all of them coarsely or rudely fashioned and chipped,—that is, as compared with many others found by the writer.'

The careful construction of the howes and the burial vessels associated with them are the only evidences of a civilization that prevailed for some centuries before it was destroyed by the invading Danes and Norwegians with their invincible bronze weapons. There seems to have been no mingling of the races such as took place between the Danes and the Normans (themselves a mixed race). The only trace of the 'Ancient British' are these desecrated howes, and that word was given to their graves by their conquerors (Danish: *hoj*).

Canon Atkinson, like his contemporary on the Wolds, Canon Greenwell, has had some hard words said about him for his un-systematic rifling of the howes, but I cannot leave him in bad odour. *Forty Years in a Moorland Parish* is a delightful book, and the personality of the man who walked more than 70,000 miles 'in the prosecution of his clerical work only' is very endearing. And his book lives as literature, and there are many pages in it that come near to the stylistic vividness of Hudson or Aksakoff. I will quote one of them:

'I was coming through the upper part of our Crag Wood one evening several years ago, after a day's shooting in Fryup, when, seeing a wild pigeon flying over my head and rather high up I fired, in the belief that it was within range. It fell to the shot, evidently killed on the instant. Falling from a considerable height, which was added to by the fact that it fell some little way below me on the very steep hill-side I was standing on, it dropped with great velocity, and the force with which it struck the ground—for the wood-pigeon is a weighty bird—was very considerable. I have written "struck the ground"; but in reality it struck a bare rock-fragment, and to my surprise I saw a sort of spring jet of brilliant scarlet objects sparkling upwards from the place of its fall. It lasted but a moment, of course; but it was striking enough for that moment. On going to pick the bird up, I found more than half a pint of holly-berries strewed all round it. The fact was, it had been getting its evening meal from among the many and large holly-trees which abound in the wood in question, and having filled its crop to repletion—you may see these birds' crops actually protrude from fulness as they fly past or over you on their way to their night's roosting-place—naturally it burst when the bird fell with such force against the hard rock.'

3

The Scarlet Chamber

Shortly after coming to Stonegrave the Rector handed me for safe keeping a small manuscript volume bound in leather. The binding, I afterwards ascertained, was probably Cambridge work of the seventeenth century, and it was, in fact, the commonplace book of a seventeenth-century Rector, Thomas Comber.* It had been presented to the church in 1936 by his great, great, great, great grandson, a clergyman in Cheshire. It is filled with minute but graceful writing easily legible, and the first forty-two and the last sixty pages are extracts in Latin, Greek, Hebrew and English from various theological writers. The intermediate pages are autobiographical: *The History of my Life: Collected Anno Domini: 1695 & 96*, followed, in Latin, by a *Brevis Narratio Vitae Meae*, and a *Theatrum Divinae Benevolentiae*.

The opening words of the English *Life* immediately engaged my sympathies: 'Being fixt by Providence in a remote country, 200 miles and above from the place of my nativity; I see fitt to give some account of myself, as well that I may not seem ungratefull for God's mercys: as that others may not be ignorant of my obligations to his providence.'

Thomas Comber was born at Westerham in Kent at the end of the year 1644 and he records the significant detail that he was the last child that was christened in the font at Westerham Church by the Common Prayer form 'which the Rebels then put down'. The Rebels were the Presbyterians under Cromwell, who defeated the King that same year at Naseby. The Comber family remained

---

* The commonplace book of Comber has been printed with other documents and memorials in the Publications of the Surtees Society, Vol. 156–7. Durham (Andrews & Co.), 1946–47. *The Autobiography of Mrs. Alice Thornton* is Vol. LXII (1875) in the same publications.

loyal to the King, and 'the rebellion growing hot', Comber's father was forced to fly into Flanders for four years, leaving the sickly infant in the care of a 'most dear, and indulgent mother'. Indeed, the infant Thomas was so weak that he was four years old before he could walk. But as soon as he could walk he went to an English school. Two years later he removed to a Latin master, a reverend and learned old gentleman named Mr. Thomas Walter, who had then a flourishing school at Westerham. This master 'grounded' Thomas in the Latin tongue, 'and having composed a Greek grammar, but being disabled by the palsy to transcribe it himself fair, he taught me to write, and read Greek, before I was ten years old'.

There followed brief intervals at a school in London, and at the great free school at Sevenoaks. After the inevitable disturbances of measles and smallpox, the boy, still only thirteen years old, was judged fit for the university, but on account of his being so very young, he remained with the minister at Westerham for another year, reading in 'choice Greek and Latin authors'. But then, at the age of fourteen, he was admitted to Sidney Sussex College, Cambridge, where he had a Reverend Edmund Mathews for his tutor, 'who lent him all sorts of books', and taught him privately 'all kinds of sciences and ingenious Arts; viz. experimentall Philosophy, Geometry & Astronomy, Painting, Musick, Dialling, and other parts of Mathematicks; and besides made me understand all the Orientall Tongues, and put me into an excellent method to reduce all that I should read in Philology and Divinity into Common places, of which I have found incredible benefit in all my studys'.

Comber made such good progress with his studies that after three years he took his Bachelor of Arts degree 'after a strict and public Examination . . . being not then eighteen years old'. He then spent some months studying at home, serving as a deacon to his old master the rector of Westerham (who had meanwhile removed to Staining), reading in Sion College library, until, in September of 1663, he was invited (by way of a friend of the Rector's) to come to Stonegrave as a curate.

He set out for Yorkshire on September 28, broke his journey at Cambridge (where he discovered, to his chagrin, that he had been passed over for a fellowship) and at Southwell (where Gilbert Bennet, the Rector of Stonegrave, was then incumbent), and finally reached Stonegrave on October 17. He was still only nineteen years old and had preached but twice before; but he mounted the pulpit with confidence and 'finding that I needed not write notes any more than the heads: I ventured to trust my memory for the matter, & my invention for the expressions, which as it gave great content to the people, so it gave me a great deal of time to study, which I did so employ, that I filled my Common Place Book in a few years time'.

The young curate who came to Stonegrave must have been singularly attractive in appearance and manners. A portrait of him is now in the church, given to the parish quite recently by a descendant of the family. It is probably the one which he describes as 'finished this day but will not be dry for a fortnight or so' in a letter he wrote from London on June 29, 1678—that is to say, in his thirty-fifth year. It depicts him with blue eyes and a fresh rosy complexion, the hair being long and wavy. The expression is candid, the brow smooth, and one would say that it represented a metaphysical poet rather than a divine.

The letter I have just mentioned was written to Madam Alice Thornton, the châtelaine of what was then the largest manor in the parish of Stonegrave, and whom by that time he could address as 'my dearest Mother'. When he arrived at Stonegrave the rectory was presumably still occupied by Mr. Bennet's family, so Comber found lodgings, at first in the village and later in the neighbouring hamlet of Ness (at that time within the parish). But Ness was two miles from the church and whether for this reason, or because the Thorntons were already prepossessed by his personal charm, they invited him, in March 1665, to take up his residence at East Newton (at not much less distance from the church). And there the young Comber found, not only 'for many years great opportunity of improving both in piety and all sorts of learning; it being a fine retirement, and yet affording me very choice company', but also, in the daughter of William and Alice Thornton, a wife.

Of this family we have an intimate account in the Autobiography of Alice Thornton which was for the first and only time published by the Surtees Society in 1875. It is a fascinating document which deserves to be better known, both as a family history of that time, and as a pious confession that reveals far more than it relates. Alice had been born at Kirklington on February 13,

1626–7, the daughter of Christopher Wandesford, a cousin of the Earl of Stafford, whom he accompanied on his mission to Ireland, and there became Lord Deputy. But he died in December, 1640, at the early age of 48. His widow maintained for a time the great household he had in Dublin, but in October of the next year 'that horrid rebellion and massacre of the poor English protestants began to break out in the country'. It is said that above forty thousand Protestants were butchered with almost every conceivable circumstance of cruelty; and in the immediate alarm Mrs. Wandesford took refuge with her children in Dublin castle. 'From thence we were forced into the cittie, continuing for fourteen days and nights in great fears, frights, and hideous distractions and disturbances from the alarms and outcries given in Dublin each night by the rebells, and with these frights, fastings, and pains about packing the goods and wanting sleep, times of eating, or refreshment, wrought so much upon my young body, that I fell into a desperate flux, called the Irish desease, being nigh unto death, while I stayed in Dublin, as also in the ship coming for England.' But thanks to the care and determination of her mother, Alice's young body survived all these endurances and the whole family disembarked at a beerhouse near Neston, in Cheshire, and stayed there several weeks.

As soon as Alice was well enough, the family moved from this beerhouse to Chester, and there they were beleaguered by the parliamentarians. But the siege was raised by a strange accident. Three 'grenadoes' were shot into the city. The first landed into the 'sconce' of the defenders, whereupon two men, 'having an oxe's hide ready, clapt it thereon, and it smothering away in shells did not spread, but went out'. The second landed short of the city, 'in a ditch within a pasture amongst a company of women milking, but was quenched without doing them harm. . . .' The last fell amongst their own horse, again short of the town, slaying many of them, and by that means the siege was raised. During the siege there had occurred one of those miraculous interventions of Providence for which Alice in her autobiography is always offering up devout thanks, 'Standing in a tirritt in my mother's house, having been at prayer in the first morning, we were beset in the town; and not hearing of it before, as I looked out at a window towards St. Mary's church, a cannon bullet flew so nigh the place where I stood that the window suddenly shut with such a force the whole tirritt shook; and it pleased God I escaped without more harm, save that the waft took my breath from me for that present, and caused a great fear and trembling, not knowing from whence it came.'

After several more 'passages and deliverances', for which the Lord is duly thanked, Mrs. Wandesford and her children set off with two trunks of wearing linen towards Yorkshire, passing through Warrington and Wigan (which they found 'sorely demolished, all the windows broken') and after some rough handling at the border, arrived at Snape, near Bedale, where Alice's sister Catherine, married to Sir Thomas Danby, was sheltering from the troubles. Mrs. Wandesford had the intention of living in York, where the two boys might be well educated; but the clash of arms had just reached that city and they were warned not to proceed. They found lodgings at Kirklington, not far from Hipswell, the dowager house of the family, which they went to as soon as it could be put in good repair. There they were troubled with the Scots one while, and the parliament forces another while, and for eighteen to twenty months were compelled to quarter the troops and endure their 'domineering & insulting voluptuousness'. Alice, who was now seventeen, was importuned by a Scots captain named Innes quartered on them, 'soe vild a bloody looked man, that I trembled all the time he was in the house', who plotted to kidnap her; and about the same time she had 'a great deliverance from the violence of a rape' from Jerimy Smithson, the son of a local baronet. She narrowly escaped drowning as she was crossing the Swale on horseback, a fate which befell her brother George in the same river seven years later.

King Charles I was beheaded on January 30, 1649, an event which Alice bemoans in eloquent and melancholy prose. The country began to settle down under Cromwell's stern rule, and Mrs. Wandesford, 'a desolate widow in times of desertion and troubles', now wished to see her daughter married. Her only remaining son Christopher was married to Sir John Lowther's daughter in September, 1651, and in the same year William Thornton presented himself as a suitor. Alice had no desire to give up her 'happy and free condition', but she was an obedient child and after much discussion of revenues and religion (Thornton's past being tainted with Presbyterianism), she submitted and was

married on December 15 of that same year. But at two o'clock
on that very day she 'fell suddenly so ill and sick after two o'clock
in the afternoon, that I thought, and all that saw me did believe,
it would have been my last night, being surprised with a violent
pain in my head and stomach, causing a great vomiting and
sickness at my heart, which lasted eight hours before I had any
intermition'. Her mother attributed the fit to the fact that in
preparation for the wedding she had been so incautious as to
wash her feet at that time of the year.

The business of what Alice herself calls 'breeding' began at
once and she was delivered of her first child on August 27 of the
next year. The child, alas, did not live. A second child, a daughter
named Alice, was born on January 3, 1654, and survived. A third
born on February 14, 1655, died eighteen months later. A fourth
child followed in June 1656, and a fifth, the first son, in December 1657. A second son was born in April, 1660, but died
being scarce fourteen days old.

All these children were born at Hipswell, but meanwhile
Thornton was rebuilding the family mansion at East Newton,
which took six years and cost above £1,500, a large sum in those
days. They moved in mid-June, 1662, and Alice describes how
'being great with child', she 'walked from Oswaldkirk with our
company, having a great deal of strength and health given me
from God'. The seventh child was born in September, and an
eighth three years later, on September 23, 1665. By then the new
curate was there to officiate at the thanksgiving; he had been in
the house since March of that year, 'improving himself in his
studies in this retired course of life'. Her husband, she says, 'took
great delight in his facetious company and exercise of his religion,
and ingenuity, and severall times would say to me and others that
Mr. Comber, being a man that took such delight in his studies
and learning so young, he was confident, being a man of such
learning and parts, would come to great preferment in the church,
if not to be a bishop'.

The new house must have been very beautiful. Two wings still
survive, one serving as an unusually large farmhouse, the other as
a barn. The middle range of the house has gone, and there are
only some stone mullions to the windows of the fragmentary
wings, and some panelled rooms within, to remind one of a
former stateliness. But at the entrance to what is now the drive-in

to the house there still stands a small square tower which was Comber's hermitage, and here he wrote the *Companion to the Temple* and other works of piety. From this tower he could look eastward up the dale, and it is only a few hundred yards across the meadows to the Rye, which here flows through deep banks with the sinuous and silvery vitality of a snake. The blue moors are in the distance, and here I love to wander with the ghost of Comber.

But if the Thorntons and the ingenious Comber found in this idyllic spot a refuge from civil wars and rebellions, their peace was soon to be disturbed by internal malice. Many pages of the *Autobiography* are taken up with an account of the affair, at once fulsome and confused. But the following is a reasonable reconstruction of the episode. Alice's elder sister Catherine, as already related, had married Sir Thomas Danby of Thorp Perrow and Masham. He had a second son Christopher, who in Virginia, without his father's consent, had married Anne Colepepper, niece of John, Lord Colepepper, Master of the Rolls. Anne was therefore Mrs. Thornton's niece by marriage, and being left a widow at some time before this, and being out of favour with her father-in-law, had received much kindness from her aunt. We first hear of her as godmother to Mrs. Thornton's ninth child, baptized at Newton on November 11, 1667 (the child died three weeks later). She was presumably staying at Newton at this time, and then met Thomas Comber. At any rate, as Alice Thornton admits, two years later Anne was then 'his great friend (pretended so, however), whose advice he was ever inclined to observe, as from a wise and prudent friend'. But the advice she tended Comber did not suit Alice Thornton. For whatever reason, Mrs. Danby was determined to detach Comber from the Thorntons, and marry him to a woman of her own choice, a Mrs. Mary Batt whom she brought to Newton with that intention. Madame Thornton had countered with a proposal that Comber should marry her own daughter Alice, who at that time was only fourteen years old. Events reached a climax one day in a panelled room called the Scarlet Chamber at Newton, where Mrs. Danby and her servant were staying. Mrs. Danby accused her aunt of wishing to marry Comber to her child to cover her own illicit relations with him. 'By these lyes I was ruined and brought to a public scorn, as poor Susanna was before the judges who was wronged by the false

witness of two wicked Elders. Even so was I and my poor child
accused and condemned before her in her chamber by her servant
in a most notorious manner, and all my chaste life and conversation most wickedly traduced, so that she railed on me and scolded
at me and my poor innocent child, before our faces, with the most
vile expressions could be imagined . . . I was so extremely tor-
mented with these slanders that I mourned and wept so extremely,
with her loud clamours against us, that my dear husband, being
then walking in the hall, heard the sad tragedy and abuse was put
on me, and in a great anger he came to the door of the scarlet
chamber and broke it open, and hearing my complaint, and seeing
my condition, did kick that wench down stairs, and turn her out
in a great rage for so wickedly doing against us; and had certainly
kicked out Mrs. Danby too, but that I begged he would not,
because she had no house or harbour to go to, and I trusted God
would revenge my cause.'

The exact date of this scene is not given, but it was probably
in the summer of 1668. Both Alice Thornton and her husband
were physically upset by the calumnies. Alice says that by September she 'had fallen into a very great and dangerous condition
of sickness, weakness of body, and afflicted mind, with excess of
grief thereon'. But the condition of her husband must have been
worse for he died suddenly of a palsy while on a visit to Malton,
on September 17. Exactly two months later, on November 17,
Comber was secretly married to the daughter Alice in 'that very
chamber in which Mrs. Danby had been hatching and contriving
all her malice against us three'. 'This business was transacted with
great gravity and piety, after which my daughter and myself went
to prayer, to beg a blessing and a mercy upon our great undertaking . . . the bridegroom, as in those cases, laid down a wedding-
ring and several pieces of gold, as a token of his faithful and
conjugal love to his dear bride, over whom he expressed abundance
of joy and inward satisfaction to have obtained so virtuous and
chaste a wife of God. . . .'

Why was such a great undertaking kept secret for a time? Mrs.
Thornton tells us that an 'abominable beast, Mr. Tankred, who
envied anyone's chastity . . . had laid a wager with my dear Lady
Yorke of £100, that if my husband were dead I would be married
within a month to Mr. Comber'. Tankred's malice, she explains,
was due to her having disappointed him on the foreclosure of a

mortgage he held on Leysthorpe, land adjoining East Newton—
she had cleared the mortgage in time. All the more reason, one
might conclude, that Tankred should be openly thwarted in
the matter of the wager. 'By reason of our adversaries' malice,'
is the illogical reason for secrecy given by Mrs. Thornton; but
she also explains that the publication of the event would have been
'too near the time of my sorrow and great mourning for my dear
husband, it was by consent thought fit that the solemnity of the
getting the bride to bed should be deferred till it was convenient
to invite all Mr. Thornton's relations to the publication of their
marriage'. This event took place six months later, on May 19,
1669, when many friends and neighbours were invited to 'as
handsome an entertainment as I could be able to procure, considering my own weakness and ill habit of health'. 'At night they
had also a good supper, and those usual solemnities of marriage,
of getting the bride to bed, with a great deal of decency and
modesty of all parties was this solemnity performed.' Comber
himself was moved to write the following poem:

> Have you not seen the glorious sun,
> After the darksome night was gone,
> Nimbly climb up the azure sky,
> Scattring his beams of majesty;
> Rejoicing mortals every where,
> Who long had wish'd he would appear?
> O! What a smile doth seem to sit
> On ev'ry brow to welcome it;
> And glowing Phaebus whips amain
> His weary steeds to mount the plain;
> Disbanding all the mists of night,
> Filling the world with joy and light.
> Just such a welcome waits upon
> Th'appearance of my lovely one.
> Make haste, dear love, oh! do not stay,
> Nor in adorning spend this day!
> Your beauteous form was dress'd before
> With virtue, piety, and store
> Of all attractive charming graces;
> And these are more to me than laces,
> Pendents or jewels, knots or rings;

Let those who from these trifling things
Do borrow all their worth, take care
Of these: thou need'st them not my fair!

Comber's bride was born on January 5, [n.s. 1654]. She was therefore still only fourteen years old at the time of her marriage, and there may have been some scruple against publishing the marriage of a child of this age. Comber himself, in the *History* of his life, says that 'to prevent my moving back to the South, Madame Thornton had given consent that I should have her daughter Mrs. Alice; and as I had been a means to secure her fortune and her sister's during her Father's life: so she finding me likely to be more serviceable to the family after his death (the heir being but 7 years old, and the daughters being both very young) resolved to grant my request, and gave me leave by licence from York, *privately* to marry my now dear wife, her eldest daughter Mrs. Alice: the marriage being made at Newton, November 17 in this year by Mr. Charles Man, but was not made public *for some reasons* till May 17th in the next year'. The reasons remain unstated: I can only conclude that Madame Thornton was determined to retain Comber, that Comber was not unwilling to be retained, and that the means Madame Thornton used were such that they could not be immediately made public without aggravating the scandal that prevailed.

The marriage was a happy one. It was not until five years later that a first son was born and then 'the infant expired as soon as it was born and could not be baptized'. Meanwhile Comber in his turret had completed his first book, *A Companion to the Temple,* and his mother had visited him in Newton, 'had read and heard many divers sheets before her death to her abundant comfort'. She died at Newton and was buried on the right hand of the altar at Stonegrave; a brass plate that Comber had made to record her virtues is still in place.

William Thornton seems to have been thriftless and incompetent in affairs. Alice was left with a large house and little money, and most of the remaining pages of her autobiography are taken up with an account of her afflictions. Her brother, Sir Charles Wandesford, turned against her and compelled her to strip herself of all the arrears due to her; there is much talk of rent-charges and mortgages, of great taxes, sessments and public charges, and of

what should be sold to pay her husband's debts. Even the great
bed in the scarlet chamber, 'being a very rich flowered silk
damask bed, with all answerable to it of the same, and a large
one . . . a noble down bed, with bolsters, pillows, blankets and all
suitable', even this prized possession was impounded.

But Madame Thornton bore it all with Christian fortitude and
with many prayers to God's almighty power to bring her out of
it all. 'My poor ability,' she says, 'was in teaching my dear and
only son to read, and hear him his catechism, prayers and psalms,
getting proverbs by heart, and many such like duties. But one day,
above all the rest, being as I remember, on my own birthday, in
the afternoon, having kept the other part separate in fasting and
prayer, February 13, 1668–9—as I was sitting on the long settle
in my chamber, and hearing read in the gospel of St. Matthew,
my heart was full of sorrow and bitterness of spirit, being overwhelmed with all sorts of afflictions that lay upon me, considering
my poor condition, either to pay debts, to maintain this poor
young child, or to give him the education which I would, and
designed, by God's blessing, to bring him up a clergyman, and a
true minister of the gospel . . . Such was my sad condition at this
time, that passion and a flood of tears overcame my reason and
my religion, and made me to leave my dear child when I was
teaching him to read, and could not contain my great and infinite
sorrows, but scarce got to my bedside for falling down, when I
then cast myself across the bed, fell in bitter weeping and extreme
passion for offending God, or provoking his wrath against me, to
leave and forsake me thus forlorn. But while I was in this desperate
condition, and full of despair in myself, behold the miraculous
goodness of God, even the God who I apprehended had forsaken
me and cast me off for ever, in that very instant of time did bring
me an unexpected both relief and comfort, tho' a mixture of His
gentle reproof for my too great passion and impatience under His
hand and correction. My dear son Robert, seeing me fallen down
on the bed in such a sad condition and bitter weeping, comes to
me to the bedside, and being deeply concerned to see me in such
extremity, crept on the bed with his poor hands and knees, and
cast himself on my breast, and imbracing me in his arms, and laid
his cheek to mine with abundance of tears, cried out to me in these
words: "Oh! my dear, sweet mother; what is the reason that you
do weep and lament and mourn so much, and ready to break

your heart? Is it for my father that you do mourn so much?" To which I answered: "Oh! my dear child, it is for the loss of thy dear father. Have I not cause? for I am this day a desolate widow left, and thou art a poor young orphant without help or any relief." To which my dear infant answered, "Do you not, my dear mother, believe that my father is gone to heaven?" To which I replied again, "Yes, I do believe and hope through Christ's merits and sufferings for us that thy dear father is gone to heaven." Upon which he said to me again, "And would you have my father to come out of heaven, where he enjoys God, and all joy and happiness, to come down out of heaven and indure all those sickness and sorrows he did, to comfort you here? Who is the father of the fatherless, and husband to the widow? Is not God? Will He not provide for you? Oh! my dear mother, do not weep and lament thus very sore, for if I live I will take care for you and comfort you, but if you weep thus, and mourn, you will break my heart, and then all is gone; therefore, my dear mother, be comforted in God, and He will preserve you." All which words, uttered with so great a compassion, affection, and filial dearness and tenderness, can never be forgot by me. But this excellent counsel came from God, and not from man; for none but the Spirit of God could put such words into the mouth of a child but six years old and four months.'

There is one other incident which completes the self portrait of this good woman, which must again be told in her own words. About March 25, 1669, she had begun to recover her strength and was writing the First Book of her Life, as she calls it. 'There was a poor little creature, harmless in itself, and without any gall or malice to do hurt, a little young chicken not above fourteen days old, which had been exposed, and picked out of the hen's nest that hatched it, and by her was turned out from amongst the flock she had newly hatched, being about nine in number. All which she brooked, and made much of, but this poor chick she had turned out of the nest in a morning when the maid came to see if she was hatched; and finding this poor chicken cast out of the nest on the ground and for dead and cold; but the maid took it up and put it under the hen, to have recruited it by warmth. But the hen was so wild and mad at it, that she would not let it be with her or come near her, but picked it, and bit it, and scratched it out with her feet twice or thrice when the maid put it in, so that she saw no hopes of the hen to nurse it up as the rest, so she took it up and put it in her breast to recover it. And so she brought this poor creature to me, and told me all this story with great indignation against the unnaturalness of its mother. But I, pitying this forlorn creature in that case, could not withhold my care, to see if I could any way save the life of it, and carried it to the fire, wrapped it in wool, and got some cordial waters and opened its bill and put a drop by little and little, and then it gasped and came to life within an hour, giving it warm milk, till it was recovered and became a fine pert chicken.

'Thus I saved it and recovered it again, making much of it, and was very fond of it, having recovered it to life, and kept it in a basket with wool in the nights, and in my pocket in the days, till it came to be a very pretty coloured and a strong bird, about fourteen or sixteen days old, and sometimes put it into my bosom to nourish and bring it up, hoping it had been a hen chick, and then I fancied it might have brought me eggs in time, and so get a breed of it. This was my innocent diversion in my melancholy hours; till one day, about Candlemas, 1669, having begun a book wherein I had entered very many and great remarks of my course of life . . . I took out this poor chicken out of my pocket to feed it with bread, and set it on the table besides me. It picking about the bread, innocently did peep up at my left eye. Whether it thought the white of my eye had been some bread, while I was intent on my book, in writing held my head and eye down, not suspecting any hurt, or fearing any evil accident, this poor little bird picked one pick at the white of my left eye, as I looked downward, which did so extremely smart and ache that I could not look up, or see of either of my eyes. And the pain and the blood-shot of it grew up into a little knot or lump, with the hurt and bruise in that tender part, that I was sore swelled and blood-shot, that it took away the sight of it for a long time, and had a skin and pearl of it, and with pain and sickness brought me to my bed, and I could not see almost anything of it, and endangered the sight of both . . .'

Instead of bemoaning her lot, Madame Alice thanks God for his great mercy in preserving her right eye, and after six weeks or more of suffering, in restoring the sight of her left eye. And then comes the end of the story, which is so revealing of this woman's goodness of heart. 'Nor could I suffer this poor creature to be killed, as I was put upon for this, for it did it in its innocency. There was some who jested with me, and said, they had heard of an old saying of "bringing up a chicken to pick out their eye". But now they saw I had made good that old saying, both in this bird, and what harm I had suffered from Mrs. Danby, of whom I had been so careful, and preserved her and hers from starving. But I told you that her crime was more impardonable, for what was done by her was out of malice, and unmerited from me; and what I did for hers and her was out of my Christian charity, and God's cause; and only of pity I saved that dying chicken.'

Madame Thornton's autobiography ends with this year 1669, and almost with this incident; but she lived on, always at East Newton. Comber settled down to an assiduous career in the Church. He had many preferments, became first a prebend and then precentor at York, Chaplain-in-ordinary to Queen Anne and afterwards to William and Mary, and finally (1691) Dean of Durham. He wrote many polemical works against the Papists and the Quakers, *A Discourse on Duels* and *A Historical Vindication of the Divine Right of Tithes*. A bibliography of his published writings amounts to forty-two items. But throughout this career he remained Rector of Stonegrave, and a faithful friend and protector of Madame Thornton. He died at East Newton on November 25, 1699, at the early age of fifty-five, and against a forfeiture was 'buried in linen' (instead of wool, as prescribed by an Act of 1666 intended for the encouragement of the woollen trade) in the choir of Stonegrave Church, where a large black marble slab still marks his resting-place, and is engraved with a long and eloquent tribute to this *Vir Pietate, Eruditione, Ingenio, Judicio, Caeterisque Animi Dotibus Clarus*. 'I am come to lay my bones near you and my other mother,' he announced to Madame Thornton.

Madame Thornton survived, not only Comber, but Robert, her only surviving son, who had died in 1692; and even her grandson, Comber's son William, who died in 1703. As the years passed she seems to have been stripped of everything but her noble and now empty house. Her will, which she made in 1705, contains a long list of her gifts to Stonegrave church, mostly perishable textiles. Her 'harpsicall virginalls' she left to her dear daughter Comber for her life with her wedding ring and a gold seal. She left the sum of twenty pounds for the rebuilding of the chapel at East

Newton, 'which was long since demolished', and 'unto the chapel to be rebuilded, my great brass pot of bell metal to be cast into a bell, and there to remain for ever'.

But the chapel was never to be rebuilt nor the metal cast into a bell. Alice Thornton's own grave in Stonegrave Church is a plain slab of stone with no record of her many virtues and charities, but her name only and the date: ALICE THORNTON 1706. Comber's son Thomas continued to live at East Newton until he died in 1765; and his son, also Thomas, born in 1722, who was a Doctor of Laws of Jesus College, Cambridge, and Rector of Buckworth and Morbourne, was buried at Stonegrave in 1778. It was this grandson of Comber's who found among the medieval manuscripts that had lain in East Newton since the dissolution of the Cistercian Monastery of Rievaulx, a volume which aroused his curiosity and which he eventually sold (perhaps with the estate?) to the Earl of Feversham at Duncombe Park. This was the *Centum Sententiae* of Walter Daniel, monk of Rievaulx, which contains the life of his master, the Abbot Ailred, a document of great interest and charm with which I shall be concerned in the next chapter.

East Newton must have been abandoned as a gentleman's residence about this time and allowed to fall into ruin; from which ruins the present farmhouse was redeemed; and by some chance, though in bad state, Comber's turret.

4

Saint Ailred

A little more than ten miles from each end, Stonegrave lies half-way on a straight line drawn from Rievaulx Abbey to the palace built by Sir John Vanbrugh for the Earl of Carlisle at Castle Howard. Castle Howard has no place in my childhood memories, and I cannot remember when I first visited it. But these two edifices gradually began to assume a symbolic significance for me, perhaps sharpened some years later by a reading of Henry Adams's *Mont-St.-Michel and Chartres*. This book was published in 1913, and I must have read it during, or shortly after, the First World War. It was the first intimation I had of the mediatory function of architecture. When Adams wrote of Chartres that it expressed an emotion—'the deepest man ever felt—the struggle of his own littleness to grasp the infinite', I knew at once, from my early experiences at Rievaulx, what he meant. I now think that Adams was addicted to the pathetic fallacy. He combined to a dangerous degree two qualities that usually destroy each other—sentiment and intellect (to be clearly distinguished from sensibility and intelligence). *Mont-St.-Michel and Chartres* is a Sentimental Journey by a man with a scientific mind (and one might say the same of his masterpiece, *The Education of Henry Adams*). This queasy American had come to the conclusion that 'the twelfth and thirteenth centuries, studied in the pure light of political economy, are insane', and the reason he found, oddly enough, in their effeminacy. It was an epoch dominated by Queens, and above all by the Queen of Heaven, the Virgin. 'The scientific mind is atrophied' in such a female world—'suffers under inherited cerebral weakness, when it comes in contact with the enternal woman Astarte, Isis, Demeter, Aphrodite, and the last and greatest deity of all, the Virgin . . . the study of Our Lady, as shown by the art of Chartres, leads directly back to Eve, and lays bare the whole subject of sex.'

It certainly laid bare, however unwittingly, the whole subject of Henry Adams, but I shall not pursue it here. Perhaps Adams did little more than elaborate certain of Ruskin's insights about the place of woman in the development of civilization and about the conflict of technology and humanism. Adams found his symbol for technology in the dynamo, and he thought that the cathedrals had been in some ways more industrial than religious. 'The mere masonry and structure made a vast market for labour; the fixed metal-work and woodwork were another; but the decoration was by far the greatest. The wood-carving, the glass-windows, the sculpture, inside and out, were done mostly in workshops on the spot, but besides these fixed objects, precious works of the highest perfection filled the church treasuries.' And all this manufacture was in aid of the Virgin, a vast world's fair of votive offerings.

Adams made a precise distinction between expression and construction, and in Chartres the construction had been subordinated to expression—to a celebration of the personal presence of the Virgin. If you would argue that Light, too, had symbolic value, as the visible emanation of Godhead, and that Suger, in interpreting St. Augustine and the Pseudo-Dionysus, was making the construction serve this more abstract conception, Adams would have maintained that the same light was nevertheless required to illuminate the Virgin as she travelled into darker latitudes. Paris or Laon might be ambiguous, but the church at Chartres belonged 'not to the people, not to the priesthood, and not even to Rome; it belonged to the Virgin . . . the Chartres apse shows the same genius that is shown in the Chartres rose; the same large mind that overrules—the same strong will that defies difficulties. The Chartres apse is as entertaining as all other Gothic apses together, because it overrides the architect. You may, if you really have no imagination whatever, reject the idea that the Virgin herself made the plan; the feebleness of our fancy is now congenital, organic, beyond stimulant or strychnine, and we shrink like sensitive-plants from the touch of a vision or spirit; but at least one can still sometimes feel a woman's taste, and in the apse of Chartres one feels nothing else'. But another and more recent commentator, Otto von Simson, finds in that same nave 'that virile, somewhat coarse-grained genius which characterizes the work of the master of Chartres throughout'. And adds: 'Obviously, both the master and his stone were natives of the same soil.'*

All this may only prove that symbols are multivalent, but I take it as a warning against giving any general validity to my own subjective associations with Rievaulx. That these are sentimental cannot be denied. The setting of the abbey is sufficient in itself to induce a mood of quiet devotion. When Dorothy Wordsworth and William visited it on the way to Brompton where the poet was married to Mary Hutchinson in 1802, 'thrushes were singing, cattle were feeding among green-grown hillocks about the ruins. These hillocks were scattered over with *grovelets* of wild roses and other shrubs, and covered with wild flowers. I could have stayed in this solemn quiet spot till evening, without a thought of moving, but William was waiting for me . . .' The abbey stands in what Dorothy called 'a larger valley among a brotherhood of valleys', and its precise geometry seems like some crystalline symbol of the natural beauty around it. I believe the beauty of the construction is demonstrably rhythmical or harmonical—mathematical, in fact. The abbey, like Chartres or any other church of the period, was no doubt 'designed and experienced as a representation of an ultimate reality', but it is the representation that is experienced, not the ultimate reality. All our symbols are intermediaries, bridges thrown across a great chasm, and they do not move the divided mountains. It is the structure of the bridge that becomes the reality, announcing a connection between the known and the unknown.

Though Daniel's *Sentences*, which I am about to mention, were at East Newton in Comber's time, probably with other manuscripts from the despoiled abbey, he does not anywhere mention Rievaulx. He probably associated if with the sect against which he directed so much of his polemical zeal, and thought of it as well out of the way. But if he had read the *Sentences*, and had been able to abate his prejudice, he would have found in the personality of Ailred, as lovingly depicted by Walter Daniel, a kindred spirit.

Daniel's *Vita Ailredi* was acquired by the Rylands Library in 1914, and only in 1950, the year after I came to Stonegrave, was it published in the original text with an English translation by

* *The Gothic Cathedral: Origins of Gothic Architecture and the Medieval Concept of Order*. By Otto von Simson. New York (Bollingen Series) and London (Routledge & Kegan Paul), 1956.

Professor Powicke.* I have never felt so grateful to a scholar or to
a publisher, for this volume not only reconstitutes the abbey in all
its early and pure enthusiasm, but also brings us into the living
presence of a saint. How much I am indebted to Professor Powicke
will be obvious in the following pages.

Ailred was a Northumbrian, a son of Eilaf of Hexham, a
married priest with land and good connections. He was born in
1110, his father being a friend and ally of King David of Scotland.
David's son Henry was his childhood companion. 'I lived with
him from the cradle; we grew up together in boyhood; we knew
each other in our adolescence,' Ailred was afterwards to relate.
Walter Daniel tells us that the King was so fond of Ailred that he
made him great in his house and glorious in his palace. He was
made 'echonomus' or steward in the royal household and
'nothing, inside or out, was done without him'. He stood in the
presence of the King at dinner, but often, when 'serving the dishes
and dividing the food in turn to the eaters, his thoughts would
be in the other world, and oblivious to outward things, as one
caught up in an ecstasy to the heavenly heights, he would forget
the affairs of the belly in a pleasant excess of contemplation on the
apostolic words: "Meats for the belly, and belly for meats: but
God shall destroy both it and them." For he practised from his
boyhood spareness of living'. Daniel tells us much more of the
modesty and decency of the young Ailred: such as, that he
'avoided elaborate confections, as the wear of the proud and
effeminate; his dress consisted of an ordinary toga and a cloak,
each as simply and sparely cut as was consistent with decency'.

In 1134 Ailred came to the neighbourhood of York, on an
official visit to the archbishop. In the neighbourhood was Waldef,
King David's stepson and a companion of his youth, who by this
time had become prior of Kirkham Abbey. It was probably from
this close friend that he learned how certain monks, some two
years before, had come to England from across the sea and established a monastery in the valley of the Rye—'white monks by
name and white also in vesture—for . . . as the angels might be,

---

* *The Life of Ailred of Rievaulx*, by Walter Daniel. Translated from the Latin.
with Introduction and Notes by F. M. Powicke, F.B.A. London (Nelson) 1950.
I would like to pay my tribute, not only to the scholarship of Sir Maurice
Powicke, for which he is justly esteemed, but also to the beauty of his prose
style.

they were clothed in undyed wool spun and woven from the pure fleece of the sheep. So named and garbed and gathered together like flocks of sea-gulls,* they shine as they walk with the whiteness of snow'.

These monks from Citeaux in Normandy had come to Yorkshire at the invitation of Walter Espec, one of Henry the First's leading barons, a gigantic man who lived in the castle at Helmsley (which is the market town on the Rye between Stonegrave and Rievaulx). Espec had turned pious in his old age, and was eventually to end his days as a monk in the abbey he had founded. The monks 'set up their huts' on a site skilfully chosen for its beauty and convenience. Daniel is as eloquent as Dorothy Wordsworth about it: 'High hills surround the valley, encircling it like a crown. These are clothed by trees of various sorts and maintain in pleasant retreats the privacy of the vale, providing for the monks a kind of second paradise of wooded delights. From the loftiest rocks the waters wind and tumble down to the valley below, and as they make their hasty way through the lesser passages and narrower beds and spread themselves in wider rills, they give out a gentle murmur of soft sound and join together in the sweet notes of a delicious melody.'

According to Daniel, Ailred was so excited by the story of these monks that he rushed back to his lodging, mounted his horse and with the hastiest of farewells to his hosts, galloped off to Helmsley castle (twenty-four miles from York) which he reached before nightfall. Lord Walter welcomed him, told him more about the monks, and the next day he was taken to Rievaulx to visit them. Ailred was moved to tears by all he saw and heard, but returned that day to Helmsley castle and spent another night there. The next morning he set off with his servants on horseback to rejoin the court of the King in Scotland. But the road north from Helmsley leads past the place where a very steep path descends to Rievaulx, and there Ailred paused, and asked one of his servants whether he would like to go down to the abbey again and learn something more than he had seen the day before. The servant said, 'I am for going down,' so down they went and Ailred never came up again as a layman. 'He divided all his goods, he abandoned everything that he had. He kept beside him only the

* Flocks of sea-gulls are still a common sight in Ryedale—they fly in from the coast thirty miles to the east.

one man of his company who was willing to stay. As he owned to me afterwards, the four days of waiting where he was were like a thousand years, so great was his longing and haste to be taken to the novice's cell. He had no eyes for the light of day; all that time he saw only the horror of night.'

So began a warfare, as Daniel calls it, 'adorned with the three marks of the monastic life, holy contemplation, sincere prayer and honest toil'. Or, in more picturesque language, 'like a busy bee flitting about the meadows of virtue, he filled the store-room of his heart with three sorts of things, honey, oil and butter; the honey of the contemplation by which he drank in the pleasures of heaven, the oil of piety which made him shine, the butter of compassion for his neighbour, for whose sins he poured out his prayers to God'.

Ailred rose rapidly in the esteem of the abbot, William, so rapidly that nine years later, in 1143, he was sent to Rome to plead before the Pope the case of the Cistercians in the North of England, who had raised objections to the appointment of a new Archbishop of York, accusing the candidate and the responsible canons of simony (this archbishop was later to be canonized as Saint William of York). On his return, Ailred was made master of novices, and in this same year was sent into Lincolnshire to establish a monastery at Revesby. He returned to Rievaulx in 1147 and began to write that work which Walter Daniel considered the best of all his works, the *Speculum Caritatis*. It was at this time 'he had built a small chamber of brick under the novice-house, like a little tank, into which water flowed from hidden rills. Its opening was shut by a very broad stone in such a way that nobody would notice it. Ailred would enter this contrivance, when he was alone and undisturbed, and immerse his whole body in the icy cold water, and so quench the heat in himself of every vice'.

William, the first abbot of Rievaulx, who had been St. Bernard's secretary at Clairvaux, died in 1145. His place was taken by a monk called Maurice, but he retired two years later, and then Ailred was chosen for the office. He was now thirty-seven years old, but already afflicted by stone in the bladder, from which he was to suffer abominably for the remaining twenty years of his life. Of Ailred's many good works Daniel gives good account. Under his rule Rievaulx doubled in size and in activity—'indeed, he trebled the intensity of the monastic life and its charity. On feast days you might see the church crowded with the brethren like bees in a hive, unable to move forward because of the multitude, clustered together, rather, and compacted into one angelical body'. When he died in 1167 the community consisted of 140 monks and 500 *conversi* (lay brothers proper) and laymen (hired servants).

Daniel gives vivid descriptions of Ailred's sufferings in the last ten years of his life, by which time arthritis had been added to his old distress. 'So dreadfully afflicted was he that I have seen him suspended in mid-air in a linen sheet, held by a man at each of its four corners, being carried to relieve himself or from one bed to another. A mere touch affected him like a piercing wound, and his cries revealed the measure of his pains.' He had a cot constructed from which he could interview his brethren or dictate his letters and sermons. In that abode of his, says Daniel, he wrote many memorable works. He also performed miraculous cures, the titles of which are eloquent enough—the monk with a stomachic disease who became dumb, the shepherd who was dumb for three days, the young monk with heart failure who lost the use of his faculties, the young man who swallowed a frog while drinking some water to quench his thirst ('and which had grown in his belly and eaten away his entrails day by day, gathering thence by what it lived')—all these he restored immediately to perfect health.

In his last years Ailred grew very emaciated—'hardly any flesh clung to his bones; his lips alone remained, a frame to his teeth'. He spent his time in prayer and vigils, and in reading the Confessions of Augustine, 'for it was these that had been his guide when he was converted from the world'. The light of angelic visitation would shine upon his head, and 'he talked with heavenly spirits just as he was wont to talk with men; and when he was alone there many voices used to be heard there, and that place became very dreadful'. A racking cough was next added to his afflictions, and he found difficulty in breathing. But he still occasionally preached to the brethren, and Daniel mentions in particular one sermon 'crowned with a proem of deep humility, delivered from the heart to the heart, and with much fatigue of body'. On his death bed he ordered to be brought to him his glossed psalter, the Confessions of Augustine, and the text of John's gospel, the relics of certain saints and a little cross that had belonged to Henry Murdac, Archbishop of York. He lived for ten days without food, but with senses unimpaired. The monks stood about him, now twelve, now twenty, now forty, now even a hundred—'so vehemently was this lover of us all loved by us'. Hasten, hasten, he cried to the angels that were waiting to receive his soul; 'and often he drove the word home by calling on the name of Christ in English, a word of one syllable in this tongue and easier to utter, and in some ways sweeter to hear'. And then Daniel interrupts his Latin text to give these words in English: 'Festinate, for crist luve.' *Luve* is how this word is still pronounced in Rievaulx.

'He died about the fourth watch of the night before the Ides of January, in the year of the Incarnation one thousand one hundred and sixty-six, which was the fifty-seventh year of his life. When his body was laid naked before us to be washed, we saw how the glory to come had been revealed in the father. His flesh was clearer than glass, whiter than snow, as though his members were those of a boy of five years old, without a trace of stain, but altogether sweet, and composed and pleasant. There was no loss of hair to make him bald, his long illness had caused no distortion, fasting no pallor, tears had not bleared his eyes. Perfect in every part of his body, the dead father shone like a carbuncle, was fragrant as incense, pure and immaculate in the radiance of his flesh as a child.'

Ailred's bones still lie under the grass in the ruined choir. No doubt many good and holy monks and abbots lived after his time in Rievaulx, but it is only Ailred's presence that is still palpable— Why? He was against the spirit of romance and I do not wish to idealize him in a romantic spirit. Professor Powicke allows himself one interesting speculation. A casual reference in the *Speculum Caritatis* suggests that Ailred was familiar with the Arthurian legend. A novice had confessed to him that he had often shed tears over the story of a certain Arthur. It is also recorded that Walter Espec in Helmsley once borrowed Geoffrey Monmouth's *Historia Regum* for Dame Cunstance, wife of Ralf fit Gilbert, Lord of Scampton, who was helping Gaimar to collect materials for his *Lestorie des Engles*. We know that wandering *conteurs* were about in the North Riding, for the counts of Brittany had long ruled in Richmond. Ailred could not foresee, suggests Professor Powicke, that 'the Arthurian legend would give the sanction of

beauty to most of those earthly joys which he (Ailred) was training his novices to forget. The spirit of romance, a mightier influence than St. Bernard's, was abroad. In the course of time it has
submitted even monks and cloisters to its fancies. Today it reigns
in the place where Ailred taught, and waves its magic wand over
the ruins of Rievaulx'.

It was the same magic wand that waved over the boy of 'The
Innocent Eye'. But now I see in Ailred something more substantial, something he would not have disowned, something not
at all to the Virgin's taste, as interpreted by Henry Adams. Two
of Ailred's principal writings, the *Speculum Caritatis* (1142–3)
and the *De Spirituali amicitia* (*c.* 1160) are largely concerned with
friendship, and there can be no doubt that friendship was an
emotional as well as a spiritual necessity for him. Throughout the
Speculum, Professor Powicke tells us, 'he seems to have been
sustained by the sweet and solemn sense of obligation to two close
friendships: one—the greatest friendship of his life—for a monk
called Simon, who had recently died, and to whom he devotes in
his book a moving chapter; the other to the prior Hugh, who had
left Rievaulx'. Simon, a 'model young man, well born, beautiful
and holy, may possibly have been the Simon de Sigillo, whose
psalter was preserved in the following century in the library. . . .'
There was a later and younger friend, whose name is not known
but who may have been Geoffrey of Dinant, who became Ailred's
confidant and finally sub-prior, who also died before the dialogue
on friendship was written.

Spiritual friendship is not to be confused with physical attraction, but as Plato first so beautifully demonstrated, such friendship
is a great daemon that holds an intermediate place between what
is divine and what is mortal, and that is how Ailred experienced it.
His ideal was masculine, brotherly, communal, and that is why I
find it difficult to think of the Virgin as the dictator of his taste.

It is true that Rievaulx was dedicated to St. Mary the Virgin,
and this presumably from the time of its foundation. But Ailred
was a Northumbrian, and his favourite saint was St. Cuthbert—
while he journeyed to the general chapter at Citeaux or visited
the daughter-houses of Rievaulx in Scotland, Ailred, Professor
Powicke tells us, put himself under the protection of St. Cuthbert.
St. Cuthbert's Cathedral at Durham is the most masculine building
in Christendom.

Among the many tributes to love in the *Speculum Caritatis* is one which clearly illustrates its meaning for Ailred: 'The other day when I was going round the cloister garth of the monastery, the brethren were seated together like a crown that is most dear to me; it was as though I were amid the liveliness of Paradise and I kept admiring the flowers and leaves and fruits of each of the trees, and I found no one in that multitude whom I did not love and by whom I was not confident that I was loved. I was suffused with a joy so great that it surpassed all the delights of the world. For I felt my spirit transfused into all and that the affection of all had passed over into me, so that I said with the prophet: "Behold how good and how pleasant it is for brethren to dwell together in unity." '*

The building of the church at Rievaulx was begun in 1145, twelve years before Ailred died. The original transepts remain nearly to their full height on the west, and have plain round-headed windows in a style still Romanesque, but the eastern arm of the church was built in the new and more graceful style during the second quarter of the thirteenth century, fifty years after Ailred's death. Chartres, which must have been familiar to the architect of Rievaulx, was built between 1194 and 1220 under strong Platonist influence—a Neoplatonic tradition had been established there as early as the eleventh century by Bishop Fulbert. John of Salisbury, 'the most famous of all the bishops of Chartres', was not only a Platonist who believed in the ethical value of music, but he was also in sympathy with the Cistercian movement. At Chartres the laws of musical harmony were deliberately applied to architecture. At Rievaulx too.

At the Suppression there were three chapels in the presbytery, dedicated to Our Lady, St. John the Baptist and St. John the Evangelist, each containing a gilded image. But that was nearly four centuries later: there were no such chapels in Ailred's time, and certainly no gilded images. In *Speculum Caritatis* Ailred denounces all such extravagances. But long before the Suppression Ailred's spirit was dead, the spirit of Plato was dead, the spirit of Saint Augustine was dead. The stones might still vibrate with silent music but there were no ears to hear them, and they might therefore be left to perish. But for those whose minds have been

* Trans. by T. Edmund Harvey, *Saint Aelred of Rievaulx*. London, 1932, pp. 91–2.

attuned to the divine philosophy, even in this late day there are a few melancholy notes to be heard in the bare ruined choir—in the early morning, before the coaches arrive, or in the twilight, long after they have departed.

Alas, Poor Yorick!

Four miles to the south of Rievaulx, divided by steep wooded scars and a high bare moor, are the ruins of a second Cistercian abbey, Byland. Less complete than Rievaulx, and not so cunningly sited, these ruins are nevertheless all that is left of a monastery that was once the equal of Rievaulx, and, indeed, one of the most elaborate ecclesiastical buildings in England. The abbey church had the same length as Beverley Minster and it may have been the largest of all the Cistercian churches in England. It is possible to get some idea of its area from the detached archway still standing on the road that leads to Oldstead.

An abbey was founded on this site only after much tribulation. The story is told by Philip, the third abbot, and is printed in Dugdale's *Monasticon* (v. 349). In 1134 twelve monks under their abbot, Gerald, were driven out of Furness Abbey by Scottish plunderers and fled towards York in a wagon drawn by eight oxen. There are two versions of what then happened, but somewhere in the neighbourhood of Thirsk they encountered the steward of Gundreda, the mother of Roger de Mowbray, who was still an infant. Gundreda sent the little band to interview her uncle (or nephew), Robert de Alnetto, who had been a monk at Whitby but was now living as a hermit at Hode. The hermit seems to have recommended Gerald to break with Furness, but for this purpose it was necessary to journey to Savigny in France to obtain permission from a chapter of the order. Gerald set off on this mission, but on his way back died at York. Meanwhile the monks had made the most of 'the cow pasture of Cambe' and other land in the neighbourhood of Hode, but their numbers had increased and they appealed to Gundreda and Mowbray to give

them a site for a new monastery. The church and village of Byland
were assigned to them—not the present Byland, but a village now
called Old Byland which is only two miles up the dale from
Rievaulx. (The Reverend W. Eastmead states that the name was
originally La Bellalanda, or pleasant land; and why not if a hermit
in the region could have a name like de Alnetto? Roger's name,
too, was originally de Albini.) Here in 1143 they erected their
first monastery, but alas, the sound of the bells of Rievaulx went
up the dale and the sound of the bells of Byland went down the
dale and the monks of both monasteries were distracted beyond
endurance—'quod non dicebat nec diu potuit aliqualiter sustineri.'
So four years later the newcomers reduced their holding to a
grange and went over the hill to Oldstead (then called Stocking)
and here they cleared a large tract of woodland and drained a
marsh, and on the eve of All Saints, in the year 1177, they dedicated
a new abbey to the Blessed Virgin, 'having a noble cathedral, and
monastery, which continued in a flourishing condition till the
general dissolution'.

Here, indeed, the Virgin may have presided over the building.
The lancets that remain are slender, and there is a suggestion of
grace and fantasy in the trefoil-headed doorways. It is significant,
perhaps, that Laurence Sterne, who is the main subject of this
chapter, associated the place with nuns. 'When I am at Coxwold
in the summer,' he wrote to Eliza, his 'Brahmine' and last brief
love, 'what a sweet companion will thy idea be unto me; and
what new pleasures will it afford me when I go to visit my nuns!
—I give this title to an afternoon pilgrimage I frequently make to
the ruins of a Benedictine Monastery, about a mile and a half from
my cottage.

'These remains are situated on the banks of a clear gliding
stream; on the opposite side whereof rises a bold ridge of hills,
thick with wood—and finely varied by jutting rocks and broken
precipices; and these are so very abrupt, that they now not only
by their magnitude, but by the shade they cast, increase the
solemnity of the place.—Many parts of the ruin are still entire;
the refectory is almost perfect, and a great part of the chapel has
hitherto defied the power of time.—A few bunches of alders grow
fantastically among the broken columns and contrast, with their
verdure, the dark green ivy which clings to the walls.—But it is
not all solitude and silence!—A few cottages are scattered here

and there in the suburbs of this venerable pile, which has, I suppose, furnished the materials for erecting them.

'To this place, after my coffee, unless prevented by inclement skies, I guide my daily steps. The pathway leads, by a gentle descent, thro' many beautiful enclosures and embowering thickets, —which gradually prepare the mind for the deep impressions which this solemn place never fails to make on mine.—There I rest against a pillar till some affecting sentiment bring tears upon my cheek:—sometimes I sit me down upon a stone, and pluck up the weeds that grow about it,—then, perhaps, I lean over a neighbouring gate, and watch the gliding brook before me, and listen to its gentle murmurs; they are oftentimes in unison with my feelings. Here it is I catch those *sombre* tints of sentiment which I sometimes give to the world—to humanize and rob it of its spleen.'★

It is a self-indulgent picture, but essentially true to Sterne's character, and I would not need any other justification for my great devotion to his name and memory. The clear gliding stream he speaks of is probably the one now called the Long Beck; but the Holbeck, which glides at the end of my own field in Stonegrave, rises at the foot of that same bold ridge of hills; and I would only have to walk to the source of my beck to meet the gentle ghost of Yorick.

Such physical proximity would perhaps in any case have aroused my interest in Sterne's character and work, but I soon discovered some deeper spring of sympathy. I have already published two or three essays on Sterne, and do not wish on this occasion either to defend the character or praise the work: but I can perhaps explain the sympathy.

Even I would not maintain that Sterne was a typical Yorkshireman, but Sterne's father was the son of a county family which for several generations had had a small estate at Elvington six

★ *Laurence Sterne, Second Journal to Eliza.* Hitherto known as *Letters Supposed to have been written by Yorick and Eliza* but now shown to be a later version of the *Journal to Eliza.* Transcribed from the copy in the British Museum and presented with an Introduction by Margaret R. B. Shaw. London (Bell), 1929.

Other quotations in this chapter are from the Shakespeare Head Edition of the Writings of Laurence Sterne, Oxford (Basil Blackwell), 1927. Cf. also *A Sentimental Journey.* By Laurence Sterne. Edited with an Introduction by Herbert Read. London (Scholartis Press), 1929.

miles east of York, and his great-grandfather, Richard Sterne, was Archbishop of York from 1664 to 1683, that is to say, in Thomas Comber's lifetime. Comber knew the Archbishop well, called him 'a pious, learned and grave man; a lover of scholars, prudent, and well skilled in the laws'. He died at the age of eighty-seven, still in office, and Comber was among those who carried him to his grave.

Sterne is something unique in English literature—a free spirit. It may be that the wandering existence he led as a child ensured that his heart, as he once expressed it, was not encompassed with adamant. His father, as a younger son, had decided on a military career, and as an ensign of the 34th Foot (a crack regiment) had gone to the wars in Flanders and there married the daughter-in-law of 'a noted sutler'. ('N.B. He was in debt to him.') The marriage was an unfortunate one and Sterne never knew a mother's affection. His father, whom he described as 'a little smart man—active to the last degree, in all exercises—most patient of fatigue and disappointments, of which it pleased God to give him full measure—he was in his temper somewhat rapid, and hasty—but of a kindly, sweet disposition, void of all design; and so innocent in his own intentions, that he suspected no one; so that you might have cheated him ten times a day, if nine had not been sufficient for your purpose'.

In the short 'memoirs' which he wrote for his daughter Lydia, from which I have taken the above description, Sterne gives us a dizzying list of the places to which his mother, as an officer's wife, was transported: Clonmel in Ireland (where Sterne was born in 1713), Elvington, Exeter, Dublin, the Isle of Wight, Wicklow, Dublin, Mullengar, Carrickfergus—all in ten years. Other children were born and (all but one) died. But from Carrickfergus at the age of ten, Laurence was sent to a school near Halifax.

It so happened that I, too, at the age of ten, and a hundred and eighty years later, was sent to a school near Halifax. It is a little uncertain whether Sterne's school was the Heath or the Hipperholme grammar school—possibly he divided his time between masters at both. My school did not exist then, but it lies between Heath and Hipperholme, and I was familiar with them both. This, however, is a trivial coincidence. My real links with Sterne are the villages and becks in which, unless prevented by inclement skies I too guide my daily steps. When I first read *Tristram*

Shandy I met the people that still, in my innocent days, lived about me.

That a regional novel should also be so universal is one of those natural paradoxes which I have attempted to explain elsewhere (though Coleridge had explained it before me). There is no philosophical problem, for humanity does not change from Ithaca to Yorkshire, from one millennium to another. The difficulty is to be human in literature, for literature is a convention and language itself a dark screen between our first impressions and our present memories. The miracle of Chaucer, Shakespeare and Sterne—and I put them on the same level in this respect—is that language with them is transparent—or, if that implies a lack of attention, which would be misleading, let me say translucent. Memory and meaning shine through the words without distortion, and this metaphor would serve for the sentiment, which is transmitted without loss of warmth.

I believe George Eliot once said that the people we most admire, whether in life or in literature, are not necessarily those most like ourselves. But equally we must not assume that an author is like his writing, and that Sterne therefore spent his life in unconstrained frivolity. He often describes himself as grave or serious, and Nollekens in his beautiful bust carved him thus. 'When I was a poor curate,' he told Eliza, 'and a poorer Vicar in Yorkshire, and confined by necessity to my cottage,—I cultivated, as far as the chill hand of poverty would let me, a little knowledge of painting and music; and was, really, a very tolerable proficient in both, considering my situation, and how unfavourable it was to such elegant attainments.' He was punctilious in the performance of his duties to his parishioners, delivered better sermons than most vicars, and until fame came to him, lived modestly in his 'philosophical cottage'. Between his ministrations he would dig and root in his garden, fish for a trout, pick a dish of strawberries, and sit in the evening under his bower of honeysuckle. Occasionally—perhaps frequently in the season—he would ride into York to spend an evening in a coffee-house or at the Assembly Rooms; and sometimes he would go to Scarborough for his health. For complete relaxation he visited his Cambridge friend John Hall-Stevenson at Skelton Castle, near Saltburn, within a day's drive. At Crazy Castle, as Hall-Stevenson had renamed his seat, there was good fare and a well-kept cellar, and above all a finer library than Sterne could ever hope to possess. There were also, on occasion, the Demoniacs, a club of convivial spirits whom Hall-Stevenson entertained every October—'a jollier set never met, either before or since the flood'. Sterne, who was called the Black-bird on account of his clerical dress, entertained them with his fiddle, which he played reasonably well.

Sterne discovered his talent for writing late in his short life—the first volumes of *Tristram Shandy* were published on January 1, 1760, and he died eight years later (on March 18, 1768), a month after the publication of *A Sentimental Journey*. He burnt himself out in these last few years, and his character may have suffered under the ordeal. It was a sudden glory, and he would have been the last to complain. But this is not the Sterne I think of, as I rest against a pillar at Byland or pass through Coxwold or Sutton. I think of the first forty-seven years of his life, before the world outside Yorkshire united to destroy the man who called himself Yorick.

Yorick is a sentimental name for a sentimental man, but it was well chosen, as was Shandy for his house—a Yorkshire dialect word meaning crazy. Shakespeare's Yorick, was 'a fellow of infinite jest, of most excellent fancy', but his name, to Hamlet, was a *memento mori*, 'and now how abhorred in my imagination it is!' This sinister undertone may not be present in *Tristram Shandy*, but the figure he depicts in *Tristram Shandy* has its shadow:

'. . . instead of that cold phlegm and exact regularity of sense and humours, you would have look'd for, in one so extracted;— he was, on the contrary, as mercurial and sublimated a com-position,—as heteroclite a creature in all his declensions;—with as much life and whim, and *gaité de coeur* about him, as the kindliest climate could have engendered and put together. With all this sail, poor *Yorick* carried not one ounce of ballast; he was utterly unpractised in the world; and, at the age of twenty-six, knew just about as well how to steer his course in it, as a romping, unsuspicious girl of thirteen: So that upon his first setting out, the brisk gale of his spirits, as you will imagine, ran him foul ten times in a day of some body's tackling; and as the grave and more slow-paced were oftenest in his way,—you may likewise imagine, 'twas with such he had generally the ill-luck to get most entangled. For aught I know, there might be some mixture of unlucky wit at the bottom of such *Fracas*:—For, to speak the truth, *Yorick* had an invincible dislike and opposition of his nature to gravity;—not to gravity as such;—for where gravity was wanted, he would be the most grave or serious of mortal men for days and weeks together;—but he was an enemy to the affectation of it, and declared open war against it, only as it appeared a cloak for ignorance, or for folly; and then, whenever it fell in his way, however sheltered and protected, he seldom gave it much quarter.'

And then, after declaring that the very essence of gravity is design, and consequently deceit, there follows Sterne's rendering of Rochefoucauld's definition of it: *A mysterious carriage of the body to cover the defects of the mind.*

We know that Keats was familiar with *Tristram Shandy*, and it may be that his notion of *Negative Capability* ('which Shakespeare possessed so enormously') owes something to Sterne's character of Yorick—in any case, Sterne was certainly also 'a man . . . capable of being in uncertainties, Mysteries, doubts, without any irritable reaching after fact and reason'. It is usual to call his philosophy Shandeism, but there is nothing crazy about it and perhaps Yorickism would be a better word. Bagehot, in his essay on Sterne, asserts bluntly, 'Sterne was a pagan'—which does not alarm me. Bagehot does not tell us what a pagan is, save that he leads an easy life, but he tells us that Sterne was a great author because of his wonderful sympathy with, and wonderful power of, representing simple human nature. 'He excels, perhaps, all other writers in mere simple description of common sensitive human action. He places before you in their simplest form the elemental facts of human life; he does not view them through the intellect, he scarcely views them through the imagination; he does but reflect the unimpaired impression which the facts of life, which does not change from age to age, make on the deep basis of human feeling, which changes as little though years go on . . . His mind was like a pure lake of delicate water: it reflects the ordinary landscape, the rugged hills, the loose pebbles, the knotted and the distorted firs perfectly and as they are, yet with a charm and fascination that they have not in themselves.'*

This is well said, and yet I do not feel it is the whole truth, and it would seem to contradict one of Bagehot's criticisms of

* Walter Bagehot's essay on 'Sterne and Thackeray' was written in 1864 and reprinted in *Literary Studies*, 1879.

Sterne—that he was *provincial*—'redolent of an inferior society'. I don't know what superior society Bagehot was thinking of— perhaps that of Lombard Street. For how can the elemental facts of human life, which do not change from age to age, and are impressed on the deep basis of human feeling, be at the same time barbarous, inferior, provincial? Sterne admittedly has not the myriad mind of Shakespeare, but his Uncle Toby is of the same stuff and stature as Falstaff, and Yorick himself is a Hamlet of the Enlightenment. We must not make the mistake of giving Sterne a mysterious carriage of the body, but he himself once confessed (to Jean Baptiste Suard) that he owed everything (beyond his natural endowments and the daily reading of the Old and New Testaments) to a prolonged study of Locke 'which he had begun in youth and continued through life'; and it is quite true, as he then said, that anyone acquainted with Locke might discover his hand 'in all his pages, in all his lines, in all his expressions . . . (Locke's philosophy) is a philosophy which never attempts to explain the miracle of sensation; but reverently leaving the miracle in the hands of God, it unfolds all the secrets of the mind; and shunning the errors to which other theories of knowledge are exposed, it arrives at all truths accessible to the understanding'.

'The miracle of sensation'—there again is a phrase that binds Sterne to Keats ('O for a life of Sensations rather than of Thoughts') and points to the nature of his pagan philosophy and the pellucid quality of his art. In this respect Sterne is central to the whole of the English Romantic tradition, as I have traced it in *The True Voice of Feeling*, and this more than anything else probably explains the attraction he has for me as a writer. But it was not my intention to discuss the writer, but rather the man and his associations with my native background.

In spite of the sudden glory of the last years of his life, Sterne died a poor man, and the auction of all the household goods and furniture from Shandy Hall was a pathetic occasion. The lots included a cow, 'a parcel of hay, a handsome post-chaise with a pair of exceeding good horses, and a compleat set of coloured table-china'. His books went for £80, and his personal effects altogether realized £400, but his debts amounted to £1,100. A scramble for his literary remains took place in the ensuing years; they were submitted to a process of vamping by his widow and an unscrupulous hack called William Combe (of Dr. Syntax fame) with the result that what is genuine among them has now to be detected by a stylistic divining rod.

I have said nothing of Sterne's domestic life, which was un- happy; nor of the solace he received from several romantic friend- ships with young ladies. There is no evidence to suggest that he was vicious, though he was undoubtedly, even unconcernedly, unwise. I like to think of his life at Coxwold as he described it to Eliza, the last of his loves:

'O tis a delicious retreat! both from its beauty & air of Solitude, & so sweetly does everything about it invite your mind to rest from its labours and be at peace with itself & the world—That tis the only place Eliza I could live in at this juncture—I hope one day you will like it as much as your Bramin—It shall be decorated & made worthy of you by the time Fate encourages me to look for you—I have made you a sweet sitting-room (as I told you) already—& am projecting a good bed-chamber adjoining it, with a pretty Dressing-room for You which connects them together— & when they are finished will be as sweet a set of romantic apart- ments, as you ever beheld—the sleeping room will be very large— the dressing room thro which you pass into your Temple will be little—but big enough to hold a Dressing Table, a couple of chairs, with room for your Nymph to stand at her ease both behind and on either side of you—with spare room to hang a dozen petti- coats, gowns, etc.—& shelves for as many Bandboxes—Your little Temple I have described—& what will it hold—but if it ever holds You and I, my Eliza—the room will not be too little for us—but we shall be *too big* for the Room.—'

And three days later: '*I wish I was in Arno's Vale!*—But I am in the Vale of Coxwold & wish you saw how princely a manner I live in it—tis a land of Plenty—I sit down alone to Venison, fish or wild foul, or a couple of fowls—with curds & strawberries & cream and all the simple clean plenty which a rich valley can produce—with a Bottle of wine at my right hand (as in Bond Street) to drink your health—I have a hundred hens & chickens about my yard—& not a parishioner catches a hare a rabbit or a trout but he brings it as an offering—In short tis a golden valley— and will be the golden age when you govern the rural feast my Bramine, & are the Mistress of my table, & spread it with elegancy and that natural grace & bounty with which heaven has dis- tinguished You ... Time goes on slowly—every thing stands still

—hours seem days & days seem years whilst you lengthen the distance between us—from Madras to Bombay—I shall think it shortening—and then desire & expectation will be upon the rack again—Come—Come—'

But the Bramine never came. Sterne had met her first in January 1767; she was the wife of a merchant in India and she left for that country in April of the same year. Within a year, having meanwhile written the Journal to Eliza and *A Sentimental Journey*, Sterne died alone in his Bond Street lodgings in London. He was buried in the burial-ground belonging to St. George's Church, Hanover Square, which was along the Bayswater Road. A legend was subsequently spread that the resurrection men stole his body to sell for dissection, and that his bones finally came to rest in the Anatomical Museum at Cambridge. Sterne would not have cared greatly: he may often have meditated on the bones of Cromwell, whose body had been snatched by a trick from the executioner when it was ordered to be exposed at Tyburn, and secretly interred by his daughter in Newburgh Priory, half a mile from Shandy Hall. Yorick was his chosen name, and he knew to what base uses our bodies return. 'Alexander died, Alexander was buried, Alexander returned to dust, the dust is earth, of earth we make loam, and why of that loam whereto he was converted might they not stop a beer-barrel?'

Shandy Hall is now a private farm-house and I should be doing its worthy tenants a bad service if inadvertently I encouraged anyone to visit it. But it is much as it was in Sterne's days, and still retains the ingenious system by means of which an air duct at the side of the large open fireplace in his study conveyed the warm air to his bed-chamber above. It is not a large house—a 'philosophical cottage'—but an immortal 'fragment of life' was conceived here, and since there is no plain marble slab to mark a grave in the near-by churchyard, 'tis here that the passenger going by should stop to cast a look upon the only material memorial to Sterne's ghost that exists—sighing, as he walks on,

Alas! Poor YORICK!

6

The Mill at the World's End

As soon as I was once more established among the scenes of my childhood, I decided to revisit Bransdale, that oasis on the Moors which I have described in 'The Innocent Eye'. It is no longer inaccessible: the road from Kirbymoorside has been metalled and fettled and carries one over the shoulder of Rudland Rigg to the head of the dale, which is strangely called Cockayne. One can even continue past the shooting lodge and then diagonally up the dale side and over Pockley Moor and the head of Riccal Dale to Helmsley, the whole circuit from Stonegrave amounting to little more than thirty miles.

But that is not the way I prefer to visit Bransdale. It is now even more difficult than in my childhood to make one's way on foot through Kirkdale Woods, and along Hodge Beck. The slopes of the river bank are sometimes precipitous, and one must cross and re-cross the rocky bed of the stream many times. There are two or three oases in the dale, the first after Kirkdale being Hold Cauldron, a mill formerly kept by one of my grandfather's brothers; but these small isolated mills were gradually put out of business by improvements in machinery and transport, and I think my great-uncle must have been the last of the millers—he went to America: the millhouse is now a small farm, and chickens roost among the rusty wheels.

At the head of Bransdale, now difficult to discover because the track to it is overgrown, is another deserted mill, and this too once belonged to an ancestor of mine, but on my mother's side of the family—his name, like that of my grandfather, was William Strickland. An inscription on the face of the mill tells us that W.S. rebuilt it in 1812. There are other inscriptions on the walls of the house, still precise after more than a century. Over the lintel of a door William carved the admonition REMEMBER THY END and the date A.D. 1817, and beyond the immediate precincts of the mill, at the edge of the moor, he erected a sun-dial and on this carved the mottoes *Quod hora est vide* and *Time and Life move swiftly*. The date on the sun-dial is 1819, but William added the year from the creation of the world, A.D. 5824.

On the western wall of the house William's son Emmanuel (also the name of one of my grandfather's sons) carved Hebrew and Greek texts, and beneath them recorded in Latin that this was done 'per me E¹ Strickland, B.A. Coll. Reg. Cantab. et Sacerdotem Vicarium, Ingleby Greenhow, Cleveland, 1837'. Ingleby Greenhow lies on the northern edge of the moors, about six miles across the bleak hump of Cockayne Rigg. The sources of Hodge Beck, which turned the miller's wheel in Bransdale, are but a few hundred yards from the sources of the beck that runs past the vicarage in Ingleby Greenhow.

The records at Ingleby show that Emmanuel served as a curate there in 1835 and again in 1837, but a certain John Dixon was vicar in these years, which suggests that the son went on living at the mill after the father's death. These vain inscriptions are the only memorials of a family that has vanished from the scene. The stone was well cut and the lettering is still clear, but no one now visits this forlorn ruin. In winter the sheep and shaggy moorland cattle shelter against the sturdy walls, but the windows are all broken and the loosened tiles slither one by one into the beck. Time and life stand still.

I have often thought of seeking permission to rebuild the house so that I might retire to this idyllic spot, but such intentions always seem to conflict with inescapable duties, and there is one sufficient deterrent. It is said that some years ago a cloudburst at the head of the dale caused a sudden downpour, which rushing down the steep slopes, overwhelmed the mill-dam and flooded the little oasis. Elaborate precautions would have to be taken to safeguard against a similar disaster.

If I have not moved bodily to Bransdale, I have often been there in spirit—it is my spiritual hermitage, the 'bright jewel' to which I often retire in moods of despair. But who was Bran, and what do the place names in this little oasis signify—Clegret, Groat, Yoad, Smout, Breck, Wath, Urra and Hagg? I am no philologist, but they sound to me like Norse names, and all Norse names are an archetypal music to my ears:

beck, dale and gill
garth, force and fell
holm, lund and keld
ness, scar and tarn
scale, thorpe and toft
thwaite, with and wath

The Vikings came to England in the eighth century, sacked Lindisfarne in 793 (which it is hard to forgive them), devastated Jarrow in 794, and no doubt moved inland from these beach-heads. They went further—to Western Scotland and Ireland, to the Orkneys and Man, to Normandy, Russia, Iceland. They took prisoners in Morocco (they called them 'Blue-men') and raided Provence. They sailed to Italy and captured Pisa and threatened Rome. In some places they stayed, or left settlements, and this north-east corner of Yorkshire seems to have been one of them. Why they should have left a settlement in this moorland oasis of Bransdale is more than I can say—perhaps they were driven into it as a redoubt by subsequent invaders—by the Normans who ravaged Yorkshire in 1068. But for ten centuries, in which peace has been more devastating than war, they have retained, not only their place-names, but a sense of belonging to their homesteads. There has been more weakening of that sense in the past fifty years than during the preceding millennium: what William the Conqueror could not obliterate has crumbled under the relentless pressure of economic laws. Those silent and deserted farmsteads are there to bear witness. I wrote *Moon's Farm* as an elegy for this waste land.

These moorland dales—the upper reaches of Ryedale, Bilsdale, Bransdale, Farndale and Rosedale—are still to me the most romantic and least desecrated landscapes in England, but not for long. All this region is now a National Park, which means that it will swiftly become a parking lot for caravans and coaches. Their season may be short, and the rarest beauty of the dales is in early spring or late autumn—even in winter they have the wistful beauty of sleeping children. That is a pathetic fallacy, no doubt, but there is a valid association of landscape and body-images as certain sculptors have realized (above all, the Yorkshireman

Henry Moore), and these particular moors and dales are not black and rugged, like Emily Brontë's moors in the West Riding, but sinuous and pearly, their contours as smooth as youthful limbs, their languour never drooping into slackness or dullness, but always infinitely still.

> A distant, dreamy, dim blue chain
>   Of mountains circling every side;
> A heaven so clear, an earth so calm,
>   So sweet, so soft, so hushed an air;
> And deepening still the dream-like charm,
>   Wild moor-sheep feeding everywhere.

That, in its gentleness, will serve for the Cleveland moors, but there enters into Emily's verses notes of wildness that are too violent:

> Awaken, o'er all my dear moorland,
>   West-wind, in thy glory and pride!
> Oh! call me from valley and lowland,
>   To walk by the hill-torrent's side!
>
> It is swelled with the first snowy weather;
>   The rocks they are icy and hoar,
> And sullenly waves the long heather,
>   And the fern-leaves are sunny no more.
>
> There are no yellow stars on the mountains;
>   The bluebells have long died away
> From the brink of the moss-bedded fountain—
>   From the side of the wintry brae.
>
> But lovelier than cornfields all waving
>   In emerald, and vermeil, and gold,
> Are the heights where the north-wind is raving,
>   And the crags where I wandered of old.

There are no crags on my moors, and no wuthering winds, but the spirit of the moors that pervades Emily's poetry has always been in my own blood, and I am never wholly myself unless they are a background to my thoughts. As I return from York and reach the ridge of the Howardian Hills above Hovingham, and see the misty-blue circuit around me as far as the eye can reach, I cry with Emily:

x

For the moors! For the moors, where the short grass
Like velvet beneath us should lie!
For the moors! For the moors, where each high pass
Rose sunny against the clear sky!

For the moors, where the linnet was trilling
Its song on the old granite stone;
Where the lark: the wild skylark: was filling
Every breast with delight like its own!

But what, asks Emily in another, perhaps her greatest poem, have these lonely 'mountains' worth revealing? And she answers:

More glory and more grief than I can tell:
The earth that wakes one human heart to feeling
Can centre both the worlds of Heaven and Hell.

A pantheistic notion, no doubt; but a landscape in which we are born and to which we must always return for the release of the tensions born in exile, has this mysterious power of reconciliation, of absolution. That is one of the truths neglected by the modern world, and in any case there are now too many alienated souls to make a universal centring of Heaven and Hell possible. But the need for roots exists: the need which unappeased drives the human heart to paralysis and self-destruction.

7

A Dearth of Wild Flowers

David Thoreau held that it requires a direct dispensation from Heaven to become a walker, and I believe him: *ambulator nascitur, non fit*. I walk as naturally as I breathe, or perform any other bodily function: to exist is to walk, to assert freedom of bodily movement. And this freedom is basic to all other freedoms—there is no progress in my thoughts unless they are geared to a slowly changing landscape. Some of the Greek philosophers rightly associated thought with walking, and were for that reason called peripatetic. But walking in our time, like philosophy in our time, has declined to a state of paralysis. I live in the deep country, yet apart from an occasional game-keeper or a gipsy poaching, I do not remember in the past ten years meeting another walker. The paths across the fields have long since been ploughed away; even bridle-paths which in my childhood were busy with human traffic have completely dis-appeared.

Two causes have contributed to this rapid obliteration of path-ways: the internal combustion engine and the decline in church-going. Many of the old footpaths radiated from the church, and one of the pleasantest scenes of the age of faith was to see the little groups of people in their Sunday clothes, carrying prayer books and parasols, converging on the village church from distant farms and cottages. Nowadays, if they ever come to church, they may walk along the village street for a few yards, but from any dis-tance more than half a mile they will come in a car or a bus. In some parishes elaborate schemes for picking up the faithful exist: faith now moves on wheels.

And so does labour. The farm-hand has become a tractor-driver, and keeps to the roads. He will take a tractor half a mile to pick up an empty sack or a discarded coat. He travels to his work or from his work in a bus or on a motor cycle. Walking he regards as a waste of time and energy, and since his work is arduous, one cannot blame him. He has more excuse than the townsman who sits in an office all day and in a car all the week-end.

The obliteration of footpaths has forcibly restricted the range of the walker, but luckily there still exist deserted woodland paths, and the dales and the moors. Even in such places the solitary walker is not encouraged: he is suspected of breaking down fences or of disturbing the pheasants. He has lost the footpaths that were his legal ground, and must now be suspected as a poacher. But if he uses his discretion, and knows when to keep his dog to heel, he may still be tolerated. There is a legal provision, which I have never had to exercise, to the effect that an immediate offer of a shilling to pay for any damage you may be accused of causing, protects you from eviction and wilful prosecution. It is better to be on friendly terms with the farmers and landlords: to be accepted as a familiar figure in the local landscape.

In what consists the pleasure of walking? Partly, of course, the gentle well-being induced by such an exercise of limbs and body. Essentially, however, the experience is a stimulus to one's thoughts, a calming of one's nerves. The stimulus comes from external things—the texture of the ground, the weather in the sky, the contours of the hills, the infinite patterns of the trees. Calm follows from the gentle rhythmic movement of the body.

I may go the same walk a hundred times in a year, but it is never the same experience. The weather is never the same, the light and temperature change, the birds have a different behaviour, the cattle have moved into a different field and assumed a different grouping. But most of all the textures have changed—the textures of the grasses and the hedges, of the trees and the stones. What infinite variety there is in the colour of bark from day to day, from hour to hour, even in one tree: and how the grass changes its texture beneath the plodding feet! More rarely one may experience the exquisite sensation of walking over the crisp surface of frozen stubble. Ditches are an endless delight: their ruddy beds where crystal-clear water trickles slowly, the ferns and flowers that spring from their spongy banks. Hedges of fantastic intricacy: some tortured by man into tidiness, others agonized by the raving winds. There are thorns of great antiquity, their boles and branches twisted like Laocoon's family, with hollows full of the berries the wild birds have hoarded.

But rich as these delights may be, they are not so various as they were fifty years ago. The animals are scarcer—myxomatosis has cleared the land of the rabbit, a pest well lost, however much he may have added to the interest of a walk. He may have had some part to play in the economy of nature—he certainly helped to keep the man-made footpaths cropped—but I will not attempt to make out a case in his defence. The hare is immune, and may have increased in numbers. Occasionally I surprise a young family at play. More rarely I see a fox or a stoat, but I am not abroad long enough nor range far enough to make such chances frequent. In general, in a landscape in which even the horse is now a rarity, the animal life of the countryside is much poorer than it used to be.

I have never mastered the migration of birds, and at any time of the year hardly know what to expect. A few herons nest above Gilling and I know a marsh along the banks of the Rye where I can occasionally surprise them. More rarely still a buzzard flaps heavily away from my path. Partridges and pheasants abound, and one can never sufficiently wonder at the Oriental splendour of the cock pheasant, a legendary bird brought to England by the Romans. The Romans said the Argonauts brought it into Europe, but the ornithologists believe it to have been indigenous.

There is more than one variety of pheasant: the *P. Colchicus*, the common pheasant, which is said to have come from the River Phasis in Colchis; the Chinese or ring-necked pheasant; the Japanese or green pheasant—but all these species interbreed and perhaps the commonest of them all is a hybrid. I have seen a white pheasant but whether it was an albino or the rare snow-pheasant (if that is white) I do not know. I heard a raucous squawking in the field below my house and approaching saw half a dozen pheasants fluttering in and out of the branches of the trees and occasionally swooping down to the ground. I then noticed a movement low in the grass and coming nearer saw a white bird ducking as if to hide itself. It rose as I got nearer and I then saw that it was a white cock pheasant: it flew off pursued by the others. I can only suppose that its oddity made it an object of suspicion to the conventional pheasant: an instinctive reaction not unknown to the human species.

The greatest deprivation suffered by the solitary walker is among the flora rather than the fauna of the countryside. The memory-images from childhood are too precise to be deceptive. The common cornfields were bright with red poppies and blue cornflowers; speedwell and pimpernel carpeted the arable land and the pastures in spring would be ablaze with buttercups. All these have vanished, victims to the selective weed-killers that science has perfected. Some weeds seem to be indestructible, but they are the dull ones—thistles and dandelions. Grasses, too, seem to have been 'standardized'; that extraordinary sense of 'bounteous' or 'pied' meadows that one finds in Spenser and Milton, indeed, in all English lyrical poetry, is no longer there. Grovelets of wild roses still flourish, and there is the annual miracle of the hawthorn hedges which lace all England with delight; but everywhere else there is a dearth of wild flowers.

All modern developments—weed-killers, motor-cars, tractors, mechanization, tourism, the radio, the cinema, urbanization (words as ugly as the things they signify)—have combined to destroy the countryside that was evident to my innocent eye. There are improvements—in housing, in health services, in education—but the price that has been paid for them is not only the destruction of a society that may have been insufferably patriarchal, but the end of a way of life out of which whatever poetry and intelligence we possess arose as naturally as poppies and cornflowers from the undisciplined earth. It has often been remarked how much of the genius of England is associated with the country house, particularly the parsonage. It is no less evident how much delinquency and crime are associated with the modern city. It may not be the city as such that breeds such a contrast: it is more likely to be the alienation of sensibility that is the inevitable consequence of mechanization. It is as simple as that: we have lost touch with *things*, lost the physical experience that comes from a direct contact with the organic processes of nature. The man who followed the plough felt a tremor conducted from the shining thrust of the coulter in the earth along his arms and into his heart. To dig, to harrow, to sow; to weed, to prune, to scythe; to walk, to ride, to swim; to watch the birth and death of animals; to be conscious of defecation and slow decay, bloom and rot; to participate with all one's senses in the magical rhythm of the seasons—all these are such elementally human experiences that to be deprived of them is to become something less than human. There has never been and never can be a civilization that is not rooted in such organic processes. We know it—instinctively we know it—and walk like blind animals into a darker age than history has ever known.

8

The Adamantine Sickle

And having received also from Hermes an adamantine
sickle he flew to the ocean and caught the Gorgons asleep.
APOLLODORUS, II, iv. 2.

I

The reader who has followed my narrative thus far will perhaps have been left with the impression that I have taken him to three or four halting-places and given no hint of a final destination. More than once I have emphasized the fact that I do not consider even the ordinary process of education at an end; my intellectual curiosity remains insatiable. But the mere acquisition of knowledge has never been my aim—otherwise I could so easily have become an academic scholar or an archaeologist. I am only interested in facts that feed an interest which is total, directed to the universe and to life as an existing whole; and it is my intuition of the nature of that wholeness, my desire to hold it within my mind as a coherent conception, which drives me on to the discovery of facts and their reconciliation in a philosophy of life. In a sense I am a solipsist: that is to say, I believe that the world I discover, as well as the philosophical interpretation I give to it, is contained within myself, and inevitably conditioned by my temperament. Nietzsche's command: Become what thou art, seems to me to be an improvement even on the Delphic oracle. Thus, so long as I remain true to that command, I find myself continually returning to certain fundamental beliefs or attitudes which have their unity or reconciliation in my personality. In this final chapter I shall try to describe them.

344

If I begin with aesthetics, it is because I have accumulated most evidence of this kind, and found it a sufficient basis for a general philosophy. I do my ideas too much honour by calling them a philosophy, and it seems doubtful if I shall ever have the time or leisure to elaborate them even into the outline of a philosophical system. But such as they are, these ideas are universal in their implications, and referable to other lives than mine.

My profoundest experience has been, not religious, nor moral, but aesthetic: certain moments of creative activity and, less intense but more frequent, certain moments of sensibility in the presence of works of art. The very vividness of this kind of experience led me to wonder about its nature and to inquire into its place in the universal scheme of things. It gradually became clear to me that the aesthetic experience was not a superficial phenomenon, an expression of surplus energy, a secondary feature of any kind, but rather something related to the very structure of the universe. The more we analyse a work of art, whether it be architecture, painting, poetry or music, the more evident it becomes that it has an underlying structure; and when reduced to abstract terms, the laws of such a structure are the same whatever the kind of art— so that terms such as 'rhythm', 'balance' and 'proportion' can be used interchangeably in all the arts.

It was a short and obvious step to recognize at least an analogy and possibly some more direct relation, between such a morphology of art and the morphology of nature. I began to seek for more exact correspondences, first by making myself familiar with the conclusions reached by modern physicists about the structure of matter, and then by exploring the quite extensive literature on the morphology of art. Certain correspondences are easily established—the prevalence, for example, in art and in both organic and inorganic matter of the proportion known as the Golden Section. In the course of my research I naturally came across D'Arcy Thompson's *Growth and Form*, and this book, by showing that certain fundamental physical laws determine even the apparently irregular forms assumed by organic growth, enormously extended the analogy between art and nature. All this was a question of exact measurements and demonstrable equations, and merely gave a contemporary scientific sanction to the intuitions of Pythagoras and Plato, who centuries ago had found in *number* the clue to both the nature of the universe and the definition of beauty. Modern physicists, I found, might express themselves much more obscurely, but their implications were the same. In 1922 I found every confirmation I needed in Whitehead's *Principles of Natural Knowledge*, and I noted with zeal passages such as the following: 'Life is complex in its expression, involving more than percipience, namely desire, emotion, will, and feeling. It exhibits variations of grade, higher and lower, such that the higher grade presupposes the lower for its very existence. *This suggests a close identification of rhythm as the causal counterpart of life; namely, that wherever there is some rhythm there is some life, only perceptible to us when the analogies are sufficiently close.* The rhythm is then the life, in the sense in which it can be said to be included within nature.' There are other passages in this book which might, without any violence, be transposed from a work on physics to one on aesthetics. Here is one more example: 'A rhythm involves a pattern and to that extent is always self-identical. But no rhythm can be a mere pattern; for the rhythmic quality depends equally upon the differences involved in each exhibition of the pattern. The essence of rhythm is the fusion of sameness and novelty; so that the whole never loses the essential unity of the pattern, while the parts exhibit the contrast arising from the novelty of their detail. A mere recurrence kills rhythm as surely as does a mere confusion of differences. A crystal lacks rhythm from excess of pattern, while a fog is unrhythmic in that it exhibits a patternless confusion of detail.'

The analogy, particularly with the qualification implied in this second passage quoted from Whitehead, would account for the formal appeal of a large part of the world's art. But the more I thought of it, the more I became convinced that it would not include everything; and the part that was excluded was the part in which I was especially interested—romantic art. At one time I was tempted to find the distinction between classic and romantic art precisely in this difference: that the one observed the formal laws inherent in the structure of nature, whilst the other ignored them for the sake of some other values. But I think it has now been convincingly demonstrated (at least, in such test cases as the Parthenon) that even in its most pure and formal manifestations, classic art intuitively avoids an *exact* observation of the laws of natural morphology. It comes very near to them, and then, as if to assert the freedom of the artist's will, narrowly avoids them.

In romantic art, however, there is no such flirtation. Certain laws, of proportion and rhythm, are observed in all but the most anarchic types of expressionism; but having gone so far on the basis of such laws, the work of art then seems to take a leap into the unknown. The laws themselves are contradicted, or are entirely disregarded; and a new reality is created, requiring a sudden passage from perception to intuition, and carrying with it a heightened mode of consciousness.

The analogy for this transition was ready waiting in the new quantum theory. But to pursue this analogy, even granted that the quantum theory itself had been definitely established, would have been too delicate and difficult a task. I was content with the fact that physics had apparently provided an escape from a situation that threatened to be wholly mechanistic. If all art could be referred to natural laws, to a system of numerical proportions, then evidently we were within reach of tests and measurements— in short, of academic rules which meant an end to all creative originality (in the Bergsonian sense) and therefore to all artistic evolution. But though physics might still have its problems to solve, and though the universe was far from being mapped out in its entirety, my analogical excursions had convinced me that a profound relation exists between the reality of art and the reality of nature—a conviction which Whitehead, approaching from the opposite direction, had also reached.

In short, the aesthetic view of life, which Kierkegaard had perceived as a possibility, had become much more realistic and practical, and I began to consider how far it would carry one in the conduct of life.

In the sphere of morals there did not seem to be any difficulty. Having rejected any code of morality dependent on a super- natural sanction, the only alternatives seemed to be, either an egoism as extreme as Max Stirner's, or a social code determined by the needs and guaranteed by the laws of the community of which one was a member. This latter solution was too relative and too pragmatic for my taste; and fundamentally I had no belief in social sanctions of any kind—they are only an excuse for tyranny. I therefore fell back upon some form of egoism, but though I recognized the logicality of the extremist position, and its freedom (Stirner took his motto from Goethe: 'Ich hab' mein' Sach' auf Nichts gestellt'), I was not prepared for its consequences, which seemed to me to involve hedonism (a life of unrestricted sensuousness, which always ends in despair) rather than a desirable eudemonism (a life of ordered goodness). But it gradually occurred to me that the principles I was working out in the aesthetic sphere could, as Plato had already suggested, be carried over into the ethical sphere, and that a valid analogy exists between the order of the universe, the order of art and the order of conduct. Goodness is living beauty—life ordered on the same principles of rhythm and harmony that are implicit in a work of art. Vulgarity is the only sin, in life as in art. The only danger of such a code was that it might lead to a priggish conformity or preciousness; but here again the analogy of the quantum theory came to my aid. At certain moments the individual is carried beyond his rational self, on to another ethical plane, where his actions are judged by new standards. The impulse which moves him to irrational action I have called the sense of glory, a phrase which is sometimes misunderstood, but which I find too appropriate to abandon. Related to this concept of glory is the concept of honour, which is the personal aspect of the sense of glory and a modest restraint on its expression—'L'honneur, c'est la pudeur virile', wrote De Vigny. No considerations of utility or expediency can explain the actions of men who at the inspired moment will throw away life itself to achieve their glory or to safeguard their honour; but without these concepts, life is reduced to a routine and cautious existence only worthy of meaner animals.

Admittedly such a morality has its dangers, and may be used in self-justification by any lunatic with a lust for power. But lunatics are a product of a diseased society, and I do not accept the gloomy doctrine that society is necessarily diseased. The impulse to depart from normal standards of the good and the beautiful usually arises from the felt need of new and higher standards. If it is asked who is to be judge of this need, then the answer is: the artist—the artist in that broad but special sense which includes all men who are capable of acts of creative originality, of instants of intuitive understanding of the nature of reality. An artist in relation to morals is more commonly known as a mystic, and it is sometimes very difficult to say where the poet ends and the mystic begins (I have already mentioned St. Theresa and St. John of the Cross, and Blake is the best English example).

To what extent these doctrines are supported by modern

psychology is perhaps a matter of opinion: to some extent it will depend on the interpretation we give to the findings of that science. But the moment of creative inspiration, whether it takes place on the plane of ethics or of art, is dynamic: it is caused by the sudden release of some kind of energy, and the only energy in question is psychic energy. I have put forward my own hypothesis in *Art and Society* (Chapter V), and it fits in with Freud's anatomy of the mental personality. It is only necessary to say here that this hypothesis accounts, not merely for the source of the energy underlying the phenomenon of inspiration, but also for the formal unity and ideological significance given to the verbal or plastic expression of such inspiration.

It was on the basis of this philosophy of art that I gave my support to that movement in contemporary art known as Surrealism. Some of my friends and critics, recognizing the reasonableness of my general attitude, have accused me of inconsistency —of 'flirting with the disreputable muse of Surrealism'. Whether what I mean by Surrealism corresponds to what that word means to its foremost French exponents is perhaps not certain: my interpretation is probably much wider. I have always regarded Surrealism as a first step towards a revindication and re-integration of the romantic tradition. Surrealism has developed various experimental methods: automatic writing, psychopathic simulation, 'paranoiac criticism'; but the means must not be confused with the end, which is nothing less than the application of the dialectical method to the problems of art, leading to a new synthesis of reality and unreality, of reason and unreason, of reflection and impulse. The laws which govern material reality, and which are the conscious or unconscious basis of a rational art, only carry us to the threshold of another order of reality, to which the dream is our main clue. 'It is only at the approach of the fantastic,' André Breton has said, 'at a point where human reason loses its control, that the most profound emotion of the individual has the fullest opportunity to express itself.' More than two thousand years ago Plato made much the same observation, in that immortal passage in *Ion* which concludes: 'For the poet is a light and winged and holy thing, and there is no invention in him until he has been inspired and is out of his senses, and the mind is no longer in him: when he has not attained to this state, he is powerless and is unable to utter his oracles.'

II

A unity of the aesthetic and the moral should logically include the practical, for this philosophy of mine though general is not abstract or idealistic, but in the proper sense of the word, existential. It is made actual in deeds: in the deed which is the work of art, in the deed which is an inspired moral act. In this sphere again I have been led by logic and by history to the adoption of what is commonly regarded as an irrational doctrine: anarchism. I have written a separate book on this subject (*Anarchy and Order*) and here I intend to do no more than show the relation of this political doctrine to the general philosophy of life which I am now attempting to outline.

Anarchism, by its more philosophical exponents, has always been advocated as the *natural* order of society. But this ideal may be interpreted in more ways than one. An anarchist like Thoreau interprets it in a regressive sense. Mankind is one of the species that have to live on the products of the earth, and as a consequence we are intimately bound to that earth. We break the bond at our peril. Modern industrial civilization has broken the bond and we are therefore miserable and unhealthy. We must abandon such an artificial mode of life and return to the fields and the woods to live in direct contact with the soil from which we derive our spiritual no less than our bodily sustenance.

This doctrine is a literal interpretation of natural laws and might be best called 'naturism'. I do not dismiss it entirely: it expresses a fundamental law, one which we must take into account. But man, by virtue of his consciousness and intellect, has raised himself on to a plane higher than that of animal existence. He has elaborated his life in many directions; and these elaborations, which include his aesthetic perceptions and enjoyments, demand a mode of life which is correspondingly complicated. The highest achievements of humanity—a Greek tragedy, a Beethoven symphony, a novel by Flaubert or Henry James—are an expression of this complication and can only be appreciated fully in a highly civilized environment.

It is the quality of this civilization that we must control. The fact that we have not controlled it, by any universal standard, has led to the present chaos. Complication without order or principle is the very definition of chaos. There is now a general realization of this fact, and we only differ as to the nature of the order or principle that should be introduced. Those people who hide their lack of principle under the word realism can only conceive of a rational order of society invented by a minority (sometimes a minority of one) and imposed on the majority by force. Another party can only conceive of a moral order guaranteed by a supernatural sanction, and accepted not so much by reason as by goodness of heart. Such a moral order is the idea of a Christian society, and it is an idea that can still attract the mind as well as the heart. Its weakness is that it demands a voluntary emotional surrender, or alternatively an intuitional recognition of absolute values: it cannot appeal to any external objective standard. The way which I consider the true way of thought is based on natural laws, but instead of giving them a literal interpretation, thereby reducing mankind to the level of animal life, it allows an analogical interpretation—exactly the same kind of relationship that we have discovered between nature and art.

The laws of nature are physical laws: they can be grouped under such general terms as rhythm, proportion, balance, precision, economy, etc. These laws, which we derive from the observation of the process of the physical universe, must be applied to our social universe. To discover these laws and to live in accordance with them is a matter of individual discipline and conduct. It is possible to discover the laws by observation and measurement—the method of science. It is also possible to discover them by self-observation and meditation—the method recommended by Lao Tzu. To live in harmony with natural law—that should be our one sufficient aim. To create a society that enables the individual to pursue this aim is our political duty.

Such a society, itself reflecting the organic rhythms and balanced processes of nature, would give the individual the greatest degree of liberty consistent with a group organization. A group organization is itself a necessity only in order to guarantee this liberty. It will be a society that reduces the machinery of government to a minimum. It will safeguard itself against the rise of tyrants and will automatically destroy any form of authority which threatens the balance of its social metabolism. It will live and act as a communal unit whose only object is the provision of the material means of security and happiness. It will be governed by a final realization that happiness is only to be secured by the individual who is free to retire within himself and discover within himself that which the Taoists call the Way: the natural Truth. Such a society is anarchist.

It was noted that in aesthetics and morals, the physical analogy provided an escape from the prison of a closed system: a quantitative leap on to a new plane of consciousness or experience. But it is doubtful if the analogy can be pursued to this extreme on the social plane, which is the plane of the practical. Here we are limited by our economic and bodily needs, and the only escape from these is death, or that stasis of bodily functions practised by Buddhist monks as a preparation for death. The final leap can only be into Nirvana, into the Heaven of the Christians, or into that more ideal and less individual immortality for which I have used the symbol of the Tree of Life. This ideal immortality, which is the only kind of which I myself can entertain an expectation, does not offer any consolation to those who, because they have not found the Way, identify their existence with their idiosyncrasies. But consolation is not necessary to the man who has shed his idiosyncrasies and accepted the laws implicit in the visible and material universe. Of such a man Santayana has said: 'The eternal has absorbed him while he lived, and when he is dead his influence brings others to the same absorption, making them, through that ideal identity with the best in him, reincarnations and perennial seats of all in him which he could rationally hope to rescue from destruction. He can say, without any subterfuge or desire to delude himself, that he shall not wholly die; for he will have a better notion than the vulgar of what constitutes his being. By becoming the spectator and confessor of his own death and of universal mutation, he will have identified himself with what is spiritual in all spirits and masterful in all apprehension; and so conceiving himself, he may truly feel and know that he is eternal.'*

III

Through all the mutations of these years I have relied on a weapon which I found in my hand as soon as I was compelled to abandon my innocent vision and fight against the despairs of

* *Reason in Religion* (1905), pp. 272-3.

experience. This weapon is adamantine and invincible, like the sickle which at the beginning of legendary time Earth gave to Cronus and with which he mutilated the divine father. The Furies were born from the drops of blood which fell in that fray. An adamantine sickle was also the weapon with which Hermes armed Perseus, and with which the head of Medusa was shorn off; and it was from that raw wound that the winged Pegasus sprang to life. Such a weapon is reason, which alone can slay despair, and cut the fetters of doubt and superstition which bind us to an Ethiopian rock. But as we wield this weapon, we find that it deals not only death, but life; and that new beings, the furies and the muses of our inspiration, gather round the carnage.

I called my first book of essays *Reason and Romanticism*, and the title was at once descriptive and prophetic. In this story of the growth of my mind, every advance has been due to the exercise of the faculty of reason; but that advance is not uniform, unimpeded. It abounds in deviations and contradictions: the opposed terms of a dialectical progression. The very bases of reason, the perceptions of an unclouded intellect, are continually being contradicted by the creative fictions of the imagination, by a world of illusion no less real than the reality of our quick awareness. It is the function of art to reconcile the contradictions inherent in our experience; but obviously an art that keeps to the canons of reason cannot make the necessary synthesis. Only an art that rises above conscious reality, only a transcendent or super-real art, is adequate. In this fact lies the final and inescapable justification of romantic art, and it is to the elucidation and illustration of this truth that I have devoted my intellectual energy in the years that are now spent.

ENVOY

I

You cry as the gull cries
dipping low where the tide has ebbed
over the vapid reaches: your impulse
died in the second summer of the war.

The years dip their boughs
brokenly over the uncovered springs.
Hands wasted for love and poetry
finger the hostile gunmetal.

Called to meaningless action
you hesitate
meditating faith to a conscience
more patently noble.

II

But even as you wait
like Arjuna in his chariot
the ancient wisdom whispers:
Live in action.

I do not forget the oath
taken one frosty dawn
when the shadows stretched
from horizon to horizon:

Not to repeat the false act
not to inflict pain:
To suffer, to hope, to build
to analyse the indulgent heart.

ENVOY

Wounds dried like sealing-wax
upon the bond
but time has broken
the proud mind.

No resolve can defeat suffering
no desire establish joy
beyond joy and suffering
is the equable heart

not indifferent to glory
if it lead to death
seeking death
if it lead to the only life.

III

Lybia, Egypt, Hellas
the same tide ebbing, the same gull crying
desolate shores and rocky deserts
hunger thirst death

the storm threatening and the air still
but other wings
librating in the ominous hush
and the ethereal voice

thrilling and clear.

Buffeted against the storm's sullen breath
the lark rises
over the dried grasses
rises and sings.